Principles of
Speech Communication

Seventh Brief Edition

Principles of
Speech Communication

Seventh Brief Edition

Bruce E. Gronbeck,

The University of Iowa, contributed extensively to the
revision of the outlines and other illustrative
materials of the manuscript, to the teaching
apparatus at the ends of chapters, to the writing of
the headnotes and running commentary for the
Speeches for Study and Analysis, and to the
editing of the Public Discussion Tapescript.

Principles of Speech Communication

Seventh Brief Edition

Alan H. Monroe
Purdue University

Douglas Ehninger
The University of Iowa

Scott, Foresman and Company
Glenview, Illinois   Brighton, England

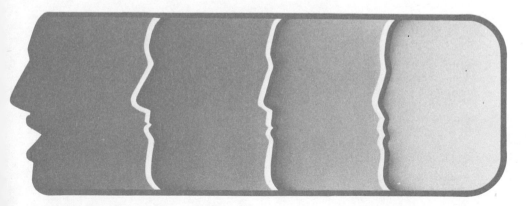

ISBN: 0-673-07965-1
Library of Congress Catalog Card Number: 74-79848

List of Illustrations, Pictures, and Credits

Illustrations, Pictures, and Credits (continued)

Cover design, chapter-opening illustrations, and internal artwork by Dick Brooks.

Preface

Principles of speech communication, Seventh Brief Edition, has been significantly restructured, and much new material reflecting current trends and emphases in the field of speech communication has been introduced throughout the text.

"Communication and Change," an introductory paradigm preceding Chapter 1, provides a realistic and practical illustration of the role that oral communication in its various forms plays in mobilizing action to effect social change. An entirely new chapter, "Factors in the Speech Communication Process," describes the common principles underlying interpersonal, group, and public speech transactions and supplies an easily understood model which emphasizes the importance of physical setting and social context in shaping speaker behavior and listener response.

Chapter 2, "Listening: Speaker-Audience Interaction," a subject treated but briefly in previous editions, is now given full-fledged development. It has been accorded this prominent position near the beginning of the book because it emphasizes the unique role that listening plays in the total speech transaction and also stresses the concept of *interactive responsibility* by both listener and speaker as a foundation for effective communication of any kind. Another new inclusion, Chapter 13, "Communicating with Another Person," provides an in-depth consideration of the person-to-person interchange and applies its principles operationally to the information-gathering and job-seeking interviews.

In significantly reorganized form, the process of speech preparation—now treated separately as Chapter 3, "Planning and Preparing the Speech"—has been appreciably expanded to include a more detailed treatment of audience analysis and is supported with fresh, lively illustrative examples and passages. Additional evidence of the extensive reworking which the text has undergone may be found throughout the chapters having to do with speechmaking materials, speech structuring, and speech formats—all noticeably strengthened by pertinent citations of recent research studies, numerous new illustrative passages, and many new sample outlines. New to this edition also are most of the model Speeches for Study and Analysis, together with a full transcript of a model Job-Seeking Interview and the complete prize-winning Kent State University tapescript from the Fourth Annual College and University Public Discussion Contest, transcribed and edited so as to retain its original oral flavor.

At the end of each of the book's fifteen chapters, the Problems for Further Study have been largely recast with a view to making them a more integral part of the teaching function of the text proper. The Oral Activities and Speaking Assignments also are in many cases new, and the Suggestions for Further Reading have been updated and made more useful with brief annotations suggesting their respective contents.

But while *Principles of Speech Communication*, Seventh Brief Edition, has been thus extensively revised and thoroughly updated, readers familiar with earlier editions will find many of the long-standing features of the book essentially intact—carefully buttressed where appropriate, of course, by contemporary findings in speech communication theory, psychology, sociology, and other related fields. Specifically, except for the introduction of more timely material and illustrations, the presentation and treatment of the forms of support, motive appeals, types of imagery, methods for beginning and ending a speech, and the motivated sequence appear in their traditional and time-tested form. Also, despite the inclusion of the chapters on person-to-person and small group communication, *Principles of Speech Communication*, Seventh Brief Edition, remains basically a textbook on public speaking, solidly grounded on the traditional principles of rhetoric and well adapted for use in those courses where the student is expected to prepare and present various types of speeches as an important part of his or her class work.

In preparing this revision, the authors were fortunate to have the recommendations and critical suggestions of a number of teachers who have used and were thoroughly familiar with one or more of the prior editions, among them: Robert H. Fogg, Millersville State College; Lowell L. Johnson, Long Beach City College; Ron Lucke, San Antonio College; E. R. Minchew, Louisiana Tech University; John Muchmore, William Rainey Harper College; Richard G. Rea, University of Arkansas; and Ethel Wilcox, University of Toledo. Gregg Porter of The University of Iowa made useful suggestions regarding the contents of Chapter 15.

Grateful acknowledgment is also made to the following colleges and universities who provided materials for pictorial-illustrative purposes: University of Illinois, Purdue University, Eastern Michigan University, The Pennsylvania State University, Colby College, Louisiana State University, The University of New Mexico, University of Colorado, Kendall College, and Northwestern University; and to the following organizations who also cooperated in the illustration program: National Safety Council, National Aeronautics and Space Administration, and ACTION.

A teachers' *Guide to Using Principles of Speech Communication, Seventh Brief Edition, with Suggestions for Teaching the Beginning Course* was prepared by Professor Bruce E. Gronbeck of The University of Iowa and is available from the publisher on request.

If students using this latest edition of *Principles of Speech Communication* learn more fully to appreciate the values of good speech and thereby become more effective communicators in the various kinds of informal and formal speaking situations they encounter, the purpose of this book will have been richly fulfilled.

A. H. M.

D. W. E.

Contents

Speech Communication Materials
for Study and Analysis

COMMUNICATION AND CHANGE

THE MYTHICAL METROPOLIS of Center City is the scene of our story, and a college student named Claire Lumen is the central character.

Center City is a community of 15,000 persons and the home of Victor College, a four-year undergraduate institution with about 2800 students. For many decades, the city was governed by a five-member city council elected by the voters *at large*.

On the whole, this system worked quite well. Some years ago, however, as the students of Victor College became more active in local affairs, they came to realize that many of their legitimate interests as citizens of the community were being ignored. For example, despite repeated requests and petitions, the city council refused to act against a local factory whose smoke and fumes polluted the campus. It also rejected a tenant-landlord code drawn up by students to protect their rights as renters.

Claire Lumen, a senior majoring in political science, decided that the practical remedy was to elect to the municipal council some person whose special concern would be the protection and promotion of student interests. Yet, since the students could at most muster no more than 2800 votes in a city of 15,000, this task would be far from easy.

The solution, Claire concluded, lay in reorganizing the council itself, so that each council member, rather than being elected as a representative-at-large, would be elected by and primarily responsible to the voters of only *one* of Center City's five wards. In this way, since Victor College was located in Ward 5 and since most of the students lived there, they could be assured of electing someone who would speak for their interests.

For a time Claire considered this plan without mentioning it to anyone. Would such a reorganization be possible? Could the students be stirred into translating their grumblings into concrete actions? What were the advantages and disadvantages of the ward-representation system?

At length, after carefully questioning informed members of the college faculty and reading pertinent books and articles, Claire finally felt ready to try out her ideas on others. So one evening, she broached the subject to her roommate, Joan Harmon. To Claire's surprise, she ran into a hornets' nest of objections. The students, Joan argued, despite their dissatisfaction with the present system, would never devote the time and energy needed to push through so drastic a change. The Chamber of Commerce and the Downtown Business Bureau would certainly fight the proposal because it was to their benefit to have a council dominated by business and professional interests. The League of Women Voters and the Citizens' Committee for a Better Center City also would no doubt argue strongly for the present arrangement.

Claire and Joan tossed arguments back and forth far into the night, but reached no basic agreement. In the days that followed, Claire talked with numerous other persons in an effort to "sell" her idea. She buttonholed friends on campus, at meals, in the union building—anywhere she could find someone who was willing to listen or argue back. Gradually a little knot of opinion favoring the plan began to emerge. The campus newspaper, *Victor Victorious*, carried several editorials favoring the idea, and the proposal was discussed tentatively at a meeting of the Student Senate.

As a result of these developments, Claire felt confident enough to propose that a special committee of the Student Senate be appointed to explore the possibility and to recommend whether the idea should be dropped or pursued. After a lengthy debate, such a committee was appointed, with Claire as chairperson.

This five-person committee engaged in a long series of informal discussions. In preparation, each committee member studied the matter independently and laid before the group the results of this private research. In the discussions themselves, the group attempted to consider the problem in an orderly fashion, but without a strong initial commitment to any one position and without resorting to set speeches or saddling the group with a rigid set of rules and procedures. Under Claire's impartial leadership, all facets of the subject were explored, witnesses were called in to testify, and alternative courses of action were weighed. Eventually a consensus was reached, and Claire's committee as a whole decided to endorse the idea and to recommend a *public* meeting to which all citizens of Center City, students and nonstudents alike, were invited.

At this public gathering, the members of the committee reviewed their deliberations and reported and defended their conclusion that, in the interest of fairness to the students as voters residing in the city, the council should be reorganized on the ward system. Opposition was strong—but there was also evidence of strong support for the idea. Working under the rules of parliamentary procedure, members of the audience made speeches *pro* and *con*, and the issues were hotly debated. By the end of the evening, however, the recommendation of the committee appointed by the Student Senate

was endorsed by a narrow margin, and the assemblage of students and townspeople voted to continue to explore the idea.

For this purpose, small discussion groups were formed in neighborhoods throughout the city. This time, however, the purpose of the discussions was not so much to bring forth recommendations for action as to inform the voters of the nature of the problem and to examine the alternatives offered. In citywide meetings, public speakers presented the issues and vigorously debated the proposal. Other speakers, favoring or opposing reorganization of the city council, appeared before service clubs, civic organizations, and campus groups. Opinions and attitudes both in the city and at the college began to grow and to undergo change.

At this point, Claire and her committee circulated a petition favoring a public referendum on the ward system of council representation, and it was signed by some 6000 persons — enough to require that the question be brought to a vote at a special municipal election.

Meanwhile, conversations between individuals and interaction among persons in small groups meeting on social and business occasions continued at an accelerated pace. So also did the public speeches before clubs and organizations. The facilities of the local radio and television stations were utilized to make pertinent announcements, and talks and discussions on the subject were frequently broadcast.

In due time, the referendum was held; and of the 9300 votes cast, a majority favored representation by wards. Consequently, that form of government is now in effect in Center City, and the students as well as the townspeople are satisfied that a fair and equitable decision has been reached.

Although our story is fictional, it nonetheless illustrates how the speech communication *process* characteristically "works" to effect social and political changes in democratic organizations and institutions. It also serves to demonstrate the various *forms* that speech communication takes: in some cases, that of one individual talking to another; in others, a small number of persons thinking and conversing together in an informal discussion group or a structured committee meeting; in still others, of one woman or man speaking to an audience of many in an effort to inform or persuade them.

In the chapter immediately following, we shall first take a closer look at the *elements* or *factors* involved in the oral communication process and next at the ways in which these factors *interact*. Then, in subsequent chapters, we shall explore the *principles* that should be observed and the *practices* that ought to be followed if the process is to carry ideas clearly and effectively from speaker to listener — and back again.

Chapter 1

The speech communication process

T HINK BACK FOR A MOMENT about Claire Lumen and the mythical metropolis of Center City. As the students and townspeople pondered a change in their form of government, you will recall, they engaged in three quite different kinds of speaking situations. In some cases, one person talked about the proposal with another in a two-party or *person-to-person* interchange. In other instances, the matter was discussed more or less informally by *small groups* of individuals meeting for social conversations or for committee work-sessions. In still other instances, supporters and opponents of the change made *public speeches* before live audiences or over radio or television.

The kinds of speaking which the students and townspeople of Center City did in these situations, you may be sure, differed greatly. Sometimes the speakers stood, sometimes they sat; sometimes they talked in a restrained and formal manner, sometimes they used the relaxed tones of casual conversation. The messages which the speakers framed also varied, ranging from carefully organized speeches to the briefest of chance comments and questions. On some occasions, the listeners responded immediately and overtly by raising objections to the speaker's views, or perhaps by showing — through applause, changes in facial expression, and the like — that they agreed with what was said. In other instances, their reactions were delayed and expressed only weeks or months later when they cast their ballots in the citywide referendum. When the interchange took place face-to-face, light and sound waves carried the message directly from speaker to listener. When talks were given on radio or television, electronic channels were employed.

FACTORS IN THE SPEECH COMMUNICATION PROCESS

In spite of these and other differences among the various speaking situations we have described, note that these occasions also had certain factors or elements in common. In each case, a *speaker*, finding himself or herself in a certain *situation*, originated a *message* which was transmitted over a *channel* to one or more *listeners* who then responded by sending feedback to the speaker in the form of visual or verbal signals. Indeed, had any of these factors been absent, no act of speech communication could have occurred.[1] These factors and the way they interact to create a *speech transaction* are illustrated in the following diagram:

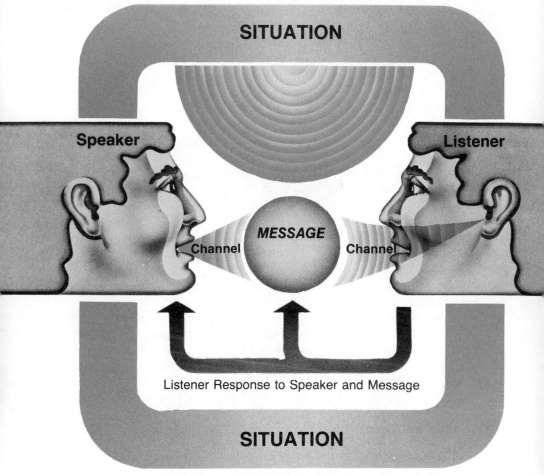

Figure 1. A Speech Communication Transaction: *Basic Factors and Relationships*[2]

Let us examine each factor more fully.

[1]See, in this connection, Lloyd Bitzer, "The Rhetorical Situation," *Philosophy and Rhetoric* I (January 1968): 1–14.

[2]Other diagrams of the oral communication transaction may be found in Raymond S. Ross, *Speech Communication: Fundamentals and Practice,* 3rd ed. (Englewood Cliffs, N.J.: Prentice-Hall, Inc., 1974), pp. 12–15.

THE SPEAKER

Insofar as the speaker is concerned, all speech transactions are conditioned by four factors: communicative purpose; knowledge of subject and command of speech skills; attitude toward self, listeners, and subject; and level of competence and credibility.

Speaker's purpose

Every speaker—whether in a person-to-person, group, or public situation—seeks to achieve some purpose or satisfy some desire. Except in the rarest of instances, we do not speak to others out of accident or whimsy. We speak to achieve some purpose or attain some goal. Our purpose may be as simple as the wish to be sociable or to befriend a stranger. We may, at the other extreme, seek to alter our listeners' most cherished values or move them to a course of action fraught with uncertainties and dangers. Our purpose may be to reinforce an existing attitude, to reduce dissonance, or to heighten the saliency of an issue. We may wish to provide entertainment, call attention to a problem, test an idea, refute an assertion, ward off a threat, establish or maintain status, or achieve any number of similar ends. Sometimes our communicative behaviors are primarily defensive; sometimes they are aggressive and threatening. In every case, however, we communicate with others because consciously or unconsciously we have an end we seek to achieve or a desire we wish to fulfill.

Speaker's knowledge of subject and command of speech skills

In every speaking situation—whether person-to-person, group, or public—the speaker's knowledge of the subject and command of speech skills condition in a significant way the nature of the message and the effectiveness with which it is transmitted. In casual conversations, no less than in formal speeches and addresses, if we have only a surface knowledge of what we are talking about, our ideas are likely to be thin and ill-digested, and we will probably present them in ways that are cloudy and confusing. When, on the other hand, we have a broad and thorough knowledge of a subject, the chances are strong that we will present significant ideas in a clearer and more orderly fashion.

In addition to a thorough knowledge of the subject matter, a command of the fundamental skills of vocal and physical delivery likewise is important. Mumbled or inaudible words, a monotonous and unexpressive pitch pattern, a harsh or breathy voice, an awkward posture, or forced and unnatural gestures always detract in a major way from any kind of oral message. We will consider these matters in detail in Chapters 4 and 5.

Speaker's attitudes

In every speaking situation — whether person-to-person, group, or public — the speaker's attitude toward self, listeners, and subject significantly affects what is said and how it is said.

Speaker's attitude toward self. All of us carry about with us a picture of ourselves as persons — a self-conception or image of the kind of individual we are and of how others perceive us.[3] We think of ourselves as successful or unsuccessful, as liked or disliked, as someone whose opinions are respected or discounted, as competent or incompetent to discuss a given topic or make a judgment concerning it.

The form our self-image takes influences how we are likely to behave in a given speaking situation. If we have a low estimate of our ability or are unsure of ourself or our subject, we tend to advance ideas diffidently and often in a random or confused manner. Usually, our voice is weak and unsteady, our body stiff and restrained, and our gaze directed toward the floor or ceiling rather than toward the persons addressed. We may, because of timidity or fear, weaken or qualify the opinions we advance and, as a result, state them less strongly than the supporting facts or circumstances warrant.

In contrast, if we have an exaggerated idea of our knowledge or abilities, we are more likely to adopt a strong and overbearing manner, to disregard the need for facts and proofs, and to state our ideas without regard for the opinions and feelings of others. In both instances, our self-image exercises a major, negative influence on the content and the style of our message and, to a considerable extent, determines in advance how our ideas will be received.

Speaker's attitude toward listeners. A second important influence on speaking behavior, regardless of the situation in which it occurs, is our attitude toward our listeners. Each time we speak, we do so from a certain status- or role-position — that of seller or buyer, parent or child, teacher or student, boss or employee, creditor or debtor, doctor or pa-

---

[3]On the self-concept and how it affects communication, see especially William D. Brooks, *Speech Communication* (Dubuque, Iowa: Wm. C. Brown Company, 1971), pp. 63 – 76; Gail E. Myers and Michele Tolela Myers, *The Dynamics of Human Communication* (New York: McGraw-Hill Book Company, 1973), pp. 95 – 112.

tient, stranger or friend. And as our role-positions change, so also do our attitudes toward the persons we are addressing. As a result, we talk in one way to individuals we know well and in quite a different way to casual acquaintances or strangers.

Similarly, our speaking manner changes as we communicate with those who stand above or below us in a social or professional hierarchy. The middle-management executive uses a deferential manner when talking to the "big bosses," an open and relaxed style when conferring with other middle-management persons, and an authoritative tone when addressing executives in a lower range or shop foremen.

In addition to social position and role-relationship, how we regard the person or persons we are talking to influences our speaking behavior in subtle ways. Admiration or contempt, sympathy or indifference, love or hatred, patience or impatience, approval or annoyance are mirrored not only in the tone and inflectional patterns of the voice but also in facial expression, muscle tension, and bodily posture. Although for a time we may successfully dissemble or conceal these states of mind, sooner or later such attempts break down; and listeners are able to read the telltale signs we are attempting to hide.

Speaker's attitude toward subject. Finally, our behavior as speakers inevitably is influenced to a greater or lesser degree by how we feel about the subject we are discussing. Whether we believe or disbelieve what we are saying, whether we regard it as interesting or boring, pertinent or irrelevant, crucial or trivial, our attitude not only conditions the ideas we present and the language in which we express them, but it is reflected also in the same subtle cues of voice and appearance that disclose our attitudes toward ourselves and toward our listeners.

Speaker's credibility

In every speaking situation — whether person-to-person, group, or public — the speaker's success in winning agreement, inspiring confidence, or promoting action depends in large measure upon the listeners' estimate of his or her worth and competence as a person. Knowledge of the subject, though important, is not the only factor on which personal effectiveness in speaking depends. If we wish to have our ideas accepted or our proposals endorsed, we must possess other qualities as well. Prominent among these are reputation, character, personality, competence, and dynamism.

Speakers who have acquired a reputation for unreliability or shady dealings, whose personalities are drab and colorless, who by nature are withdrawn and phlegmatic, or whose motives are suspect have little hope of winning adherents. On the other hand, speakers who are known to be of good character, who have warm and colorful personalities, who are alive and alert, and who are genuinely interested in their listeners are always more readily attended to and believed.

Traditionally, the persuasive force residing in the reputation and personality of the speaker was called "ethical proof," after the Greek word *ethos*, meaning "character." Today it is more often referred to as *source-credibility*. Of all the means of persuasion, source-credibility is perhaps the strongest and — if appropriately reinforced — may retain its potency for extended periods of time. For these reasons, it constitutes an indispensable component of any speech transaction.[4]

THE MESSAGE

In all speech communication — whether person-to-person, group, or public — the message which the speaker transmits is made up of the same three variables of content, structure, and style.

Content

That the messages which we as speakers wish to transmit to our listeners have a content — are about something we want them to be aware of — is self-evident. What we say may take the form of an assertion, a question, or an exclamation; it may report an observation, express a feeling, or prescribe a course of action; it may or may not be accompanied by visual or auditory cues that enhance or detract from our meaning. In every case, however, the message has a thought-content or subject matter of some kind.

Structure

Any message we transmit, whether long or short, simple or complex, is of necessity structured or organized in some way. Its structure may be dictated by the nature of the ideas themselves or may, as in the case of the marriage ceremony or pledge of allegiance, be imposed upon the ideas by a socially or institutionally approved formula. The structure

---

[4]An excellent analysis of source-credibility or *ethos*, based upon current research findings, is presented in Kenneth E. Anderson, *Persuasion: Theory and Practice* (Boston: Allyn & Bacon, Inc., 1971), Chapter 12. See also Stephen Littlejohn, "A Bibliography of Studies Related to Variables of Source Credibility," *Bibliographic Annual in Speech Communication: 1971*, ed. Ned A. Shearer (New York: Speech Communication Association, 1971), pp. 1–40.

may be direct or circuitous, loose or compact, clear or confusing. It may, at one extreme, entail no more than the ordering of a few sentences, or — at the other — require the strategic structuring of large-scale units of thought. But because we can express only one idea at a time, we always must make a choice as to what to say first, second, or last; and in so doing, we inevitably give the message a certain structure.

Style

The third variable in every spoken message is style. Just as we must make choices in the selection and arrangement of units of thought, so also must we make choices in the selection and arrangement of words to express those thoughts. One word must be used rather than another, and must be placed in the sentence in one position rather than another. Depending on the choices we make, our style may be plain or elevated, smooth or awkward, rhythmical or jumpy, pleasing or irritating. In communicating ideas through the use of words, however, we always must choose and arrange them in some way and, therefore, give our message a certain language pattern or style.

THE LISTENERS

In all forms of speech communication, the listeners — like the speaker — have a goal or purpose in mind. Moreover, the way in which a message is received and responded to varies according to the listeners' (1) knowledge of and interest in the subject; (2) level of listening skill; and (3) attitude toward self, speaker, and the ideas presented.

Listeners' purpose

The listener — whether in a person-to-person, group, or public situation — wishes to achieve some purpose or satisfy some desire. Listeners, no less than speakers, enter into the speech transaction in search of rewards. Otherwise, they wouldn't listen. They may wish to be *entertained* or *informed*, or they may seek *advice* or *guidance*. But always, consciously or unconsciously, they have a purpose in mind — an end or goal they seek to attain as a result of the listening experience.

Listeners' knowledge of subject and command of listening skills

In every speech transaction — whether person-to-person, group, or public — the listeners' knowledge of and interest in the subject condition in a significant way how the message will be received and responded to. Whether listeners find a speaker's ideas easy or difficult to understand depends in part upon how much they already know about the subject under consideration. Whether they find those ideas interesting or pertinent depends in part upon their personal needs and concerns at the time the speech encounter occurs. When they already have some knowledge of and interest in the subject being discussed or when that subject touches directly upon their health, happiness, or financial security, the speaker's task is easier; when these elements are lacking, the task becomes proportionately more difficult. At times, the listeners' previous knowledge of a subject may be so deficient that there can be no communication at all.

Listeners' knowledge and interest are not, however, the only relevant variables. People also differ considerably in their skill as listeners. Some are able to follow a chain of ideas more easily than others; some are quicker to catch errors in inference or note deficiencies in evidence. How much of this difference in listening skills is the result of differences in training and how much of it reflects differences in native ability remain open questions. Listening ability does, however, differ from person to person and is, therefore, an important variable.[5]

Listeners' attitudes

In every speech encounter — whether person-to-person, group, or public — the listeners' attitudes toward self, speaker, and subject significantly affect how the message will be interpreted and responded to. Just as a speaker's behavior in sending a message is influenced by his or her attitude toward self, subject, and listener, so these same factors influence how a listener responds to the message. Listeners who have poor images of themselves and little confidence in their own judgments tend to be swayed more easily than those whose self-esteem is higher. Listeners also tend to be more readily influenced by views which confirm opinions they already hold. Finally, listeners, as a rule, seek out speakers whose positions on issues they already agree with; and they retain longer and more vividly ideas of which they strongly approve.[6]

---

[5] For more complete discussions of listening, refer to Chapter 2, pages 20–33. See also Larry L. Barker, *Listening Behavior* (Englewood Cliffs, N.J.: Prentice-Hall, Inc., 1971); Ralph G. Nichols and Leonard A. Stevens, *Are You Listening?* (New York: McGraw-Hill Book Company, 1957).

[6] Cf. the personality analysis of a receiver as described in Michael Burgoon, *Approaching Speech Communication* (New York: Holt, Rinehart & Winston, Inc., 1974), pp. 64–69.

THE CHANNEL

All speech communication — whether person-to-person, group, or public — is conditioned to a greater or lesser extent by the channel over which the message is transmitted. When the participants in a speech transaction meet face-to-face, two channels usually are employed, the speaker's message being communicated in part by what is said (the oral channel) and in part by gestures, facial expression, and posture (the visual channel). When, as with messages transmitted by radio or telephone, the speaker cannot be seen, the vocal mechanism alone must do the work it normally shares with the rest of the body. Always, however, there must be a channel or pathway over which the message is carried from originating source to intended destination. Chapter 4, "Using the Body to Communicate," and Chapter 5, "Using the Voice to Communicate," will treat in detail the oral and visual channels of speech communication.

THE COMMUNICATIVE SITUATION

All speech communication — whether person-to-person, group, or public — is conditioned by the physical setting and social context in which it occurs.

Physical setting

The physical setting in which a speech act occurs affects to a considerable extent the listeners' anticipations or expectancies as well as their readiness to respond. Persons waiting in the quiet solemnity of a great cathedral for the service to begin have quite a different expectancy than do theatergoers gathered to witness the opening of a new Broadway play or musical revue. Similarly, listeners at an open-air political rally held in the midst of an exciting campaign have a different expectancy than students gathered to hear a scholarly lecture on political theory presented in a college classroom.

The furniture and decor of the room in which speaker and listeners find themselves also make a difference. Words of love are best spoken in soft light or before an open fire. Comfortable chairs and pleasant surroundings tend to put the members of a discussion group at ease and to promote a more productive interchange. The executive who talks to an employee from behind a large desk set in the middle of an impressively furnished office with the title "President" on the door gains a natural advantage not only because of a superior position in the corporate hierarchy, but also because of the physical setting.

Social context

Even more important than physical setting in determining how a message will be received is the social context in which it is presented. Custom and good manners decree, to a considerable extent, the kind of message and the style of presentation appropriate under a given set of circumstances. To engage in "shop talk" at a social gathering or to dwell on a subject that is of interest to only one or two members of a group is usually considered poor taste. At business luncheons, serious discussion of the matter at hand often is delayed until the conferees have finished eating. Committee meetings frequently are opened with a few moments of general conversation of a personal or incidental nature. In the public situation, memorial services and award dinners are not considered proper places at which to launch attacks upon a political opponent or to engage in discussions of philosophical questions.

Besides influencing structure and content of the messages framed by the speaker, social context also is influential in determining how the listeners will receive the messages. Remarks that win the evident approval of respected individuals sitting or standing near a listener are more likely to win the approval of that listener also. When people are in the company of others—especially large numbers of others—they generally are more highly suggestible, and therefore more easily swayed, than when they are alone. Persons in the middle of an audience tend to respond more readily than those on the periphery. Persons crowded closely together or sitting elbow-to-elbow tend to react as a unit; a handful of listeners scattered at random throughout a large auditorium show less uniformity of response. Facts reported or opinions expressed at a party often are taken less seriously than the same facts or opinions stated at a congressional hearing or as part of a formal lecture. Advice offered in moments of crisis usually is accepted more readily than advice offered under less pressing circumstances.

The overt responses that individuals make as they listen to a message likewise vary from situation to situation. Persons who will listen patiently to a long speech or lecture with which they thoroughly disagree and then applaud politely at its close may, when participating in a business or social conversation, be among the first to register displeasure with an idea they disapprove of. At a political rally, vigorous applause or shouted approval of the speaker's ideas is expected; at a church service, such overt forms of response generally are avoided. In these and similar ways, the behavior of listeners—no less than that of speakers—is conditioned by the physical, the psychological, and the socio-cultural circumstances surrounding the speech act.[7]

INTERACTION OF THE SPEECH COMMUNICATION FACTORS

All speech communication—whether interpersonal, group, or public—entails a complex pattern of interaction among the five factors: speaker, message, listeners, channel, and situation. The nature of a given speech transaction is conditioned not only by forces playing upon it from without, but also by a complex pattern of interaction among the elements or variables of which it is composed.

The personality, values, and aims of the speaker, together with the physical surroundings and social context in which the speech act occurs and the channel over which it is transmitted, influence the content, structure, and style of the message. The message as thus framed and communicated alters or fails to alter the listeners' beliefs or behavior, and changes or confirms their attitudes toward the speaker and the message. The listeners' responses, as fed back to the speaker, influence the way in which subsequent portions of the message are presented. The physical setting and social context, in addition to influencing the content of the message transmitted, influence the language or style in which the content is couched and how the speaker's ideas will be received by the listener. The nature of the channel, in turn, limits the kind of message that can be transmitted, determines the range of auditory and visual stimuli which the speaker may utilize, and affects the listeners' expectations and patterns of response-behavior.

Numerous and intricate as they are in themselves, these patterns of interaction are rendered still more complex by the fact that a given speech transaction, while itself a discrete unit of thought or action bounded by a definite beginning and ending, has antecedents that

---

[7]The effects of physical setting and social context on the reception of an oral message are discussed in Gary Cronkhite, *Persuasion: Speech and Behavioral Change* (Indianapolis: The Bobbs-Merrill Company, Inc., 1969), pp. 148–154; H. L. Hollingworth, *The Psychology of the Audience* (New York: American Book Company, 1935), pp. 161–183; Howard H. Martin and C. William Colburn, *Communication and Consensus: An Introduction to Rhetorical Discourse* (New York: Harcourt Brace Jovanovich, Inc., 1972), pp. 82–84; Albert L. Furbay, "The Influence of Scattered Versus Compact Seating on Audience Response," *Speech Monographs* XXXII (June 1965): 144–148; Gordon Thomas and David C. Ralph, "A Study of the Effect of Audience Proximity on Persuasion," *Speech Monographs* XXVI (November 1959): 300–307. A chapter entitled "Situational Geography" in C. David Mortensen, *Communication: The Study of Human Interaction* (New York: McGraw-Hill Book Company, 1972), pp. 289–320, is also especially helpful.

stretch into the indefinite past and consequents that reach into the indefinite future. What the speaker says and how he or she chooses to say it are influenced not only by the demands of the immediate speaking situation, but also by the accumulation of many years of personal growth and conditioning—years in which knowledge has been acquired, judgments formed, attitudes shaped, and speech skills and habits learned. The background of knowledge, the attitudes, and the listening skills which listeners bring to the speech encounter likewise are the result of a long process of conditioning. Even the mold and structure that a message takes and the channel over which it may appropriately be transmitted have histories that influence both its content and the manner in which it is presented. For centuries, sermons have opened with a reference to a Biblical text and proceeded to an explanation of its significance or an appropriate hortatory appeal. In social introductions younger persons are presented to older ones and men to women. News of the death of a loved one is nearly always communicated to an individual in a face-to-face meeting rather than over the telephone.

In sum, a speech transaction is not an isolated event. It is heavily conditioned (1) by outside forces operative at the time it occurs, (2) by the past experiences of the communicators—experiences extending back into their life histories almost from the moment of birth, (3) by what follows the communicative interchange, (4) by the way other persons visible to the communicator and receiver are reacting during the communication, etc. As a unitary phase of the speech communication process, a speech transaction is merely a moment in an ongoing chain of events, a single discrete occurrence within a total universe of experience. It is embedded in a situation that affects the expectancies of those who hear it, and is in many instances governed by a convention or custom of long standing.[8]

A communication transaction: a model of interactions and relationships

Near the beginning of this chapter we presented a simplified diagram showing the basic factors and relationships involved in a speech transaction. Now that we have examined each of these factors more fully, let us review and summarize them by referring to a more elaborate model of the interactions involved, as follows:

---

[8]The interactive nature of the speech communication process is discussed at greater length in Thomas M. Scheidel, *Speech Communication and Human Interaction* (Glenview, Ill.: Scott, Foresman and Company, 1972), pp. 25–49.

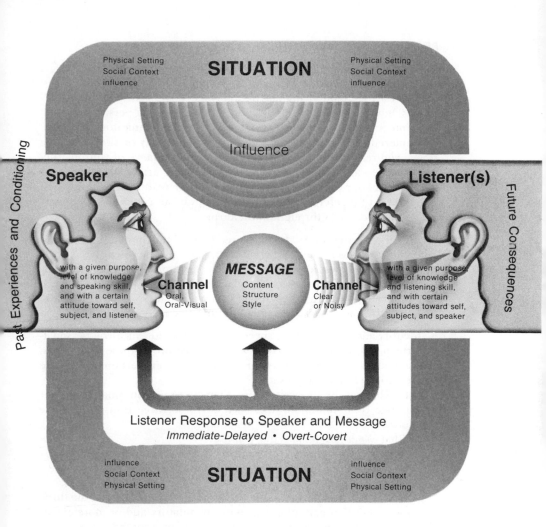

Figure 2. The Speech Communication Transaction: *A More Fully Developed Model*

A *Speaker,* influenced by past conditioning, present *Situation,* communicative purpose, level of knowledge and speaking skill, and attitudes toward self, subject, and listener(s), transmits a *Message* which has content, structure, and style, over a *Channel* which limits or shapes the message to one or more *Listener(s)* whose reception of the message is, in turn, influenced by conditioning, purpose, listening skill, situation, and attitudes toward self, subject, and speaker. The *listener(s)* responds to the speaker and message with cues that cause the speaker to modify subsequent portions of the message or to alter his or her verbal or nonverbal behavior. Insofar as a communication transaction affects the beliefs or behaviors of speaker or listener(s), it has consequences for their future thought and action.

PROBLEMS FOR FURTHER STUDY

1. Countless communicators daily attempt to get a piece of your energy, your time, and your pocketbook via the mass electronic and printed media; via the "mini-media" of bumper stickers, T-shirts, buttons, billboards, mimeographed handouts, and the like; and via person-to-person encounters. List the apparent *purposes* of the communicators you have encountered through all such media over the last day or two; recall the *reasons* you read or listened to them. Under the guidance of your instructor, prepare—as a class—a master list of purposes arrived at, media employed, and your own reasons for listening to or reading these messages. Keep this list for reference as you engage in various communicative exercises and experiences throughout the term.

2. Recognizing that every day you are "bathed" in communicative messages, do you nevertheless attach any special significances to *speech* communication? How would you compare *speech* communication to *printed* or *visual* communicative transactions? In your opinion, what are speech communication's inherent advantages? disadvantages? What does "talk" do better than any other kind of communicative media?

3. Identify and describe three speech transactions in which you personally participated during the past week. In at least two of these encounters, you should have been the speaker initiating the interaction. Formulate answers to the following questions:
   a. In which of the three situations — person-to-person, small group, or public communication — did each of these three transactions take place?
   b. What *channel* or *channels* did you use?
   c. What was your *communicative purpose* in each case?
   d. To what extent do you feel you *accomplished* your communicative purpose in each transaction? Why?
   e. What was the extent of your *message-preparation* in each of the three instances? If preparation was more mandatory and/or more extensive for one situation than for others, explain why this was so.
   f. Show how, in one of these transactions, the *physical setting* probably influenced what happened. In another, explain how the *social context* tended to affect the outcome.

4. Analyze your own background of knowledge and interests:
   a. List your principal curricular and extracurricular interests, your hobbies and enthusiasms, and the business or profession you intend to enter. How much of what you already know about these areas is firsthand, and how much is a result of reading or talking with others?

b. Make a list of subjects connected with your interests or your vocational objective—subjects upon which you would like to speak but need more information.
c. List several social, economic, or political principles which you believe in and would be willing to defend.
d. Select from the foregoing lists five or six topics upon which you might speak in class during the term; narrow down each topic so that it could be covered in a four- or five-minute speech.

5. A communication model is an attempt to stop the highly complex communication process long enough to (1) identify its constituent factors, (2) see interrelationships among those factors, and (3) emphasize the role(s) of each factor within the process. In this chapter, you were presented with a communication model (see p. 15)—only one possibility among many such descriptions. Examine some of the books named in the "Suggestions for Further Reading"—particularly the Mortensen and Ross books—for other attempts at building communication models. From your own experiences, comments made by your instructor, and additional readings, design your own model of the communication process. Identify the factors and explain the interrelationships as you see them. Why do you prefer your model to others you have seen?

6. In a notebook set aside for the purpose, start a Personal Speech Journal. The contents will be seen only by you and your instructor, who will call for the journal at intervals during the term. After thoughtful analysis, prepare an inventory of your personal speech needs and your abilities as a speaker. Include an evaluation of your past experience in individual and group situations. Outline your personal goals and desires for the course.

Your instructor may ask you to include in this journal any of the written work you have done in regard to other study questions, or may make other assignments of a written, observational, or evaluative nature. At any rate, make regular entries at least weekly bearing upon your own communicative behavior. Involved in these entries also could be your perceptions of and reactions to the pertinent communicative behaviors of other class members; analyses of your feelings about your own communicative efforts and the consequences growing out of these efforts; your instructor's remarks or feedback with regard to your classroom speeches and their presentation; and, finally, the effectiveness of class activities in contributing to your personal growth as an oral communicator.

7. In general, our knowledge of speech communication is derived from various disciplines or fields of knowledge. What, for example, does the study of history tell us about communication settings and effects? What does the study of psychology teach us about perception and attitude-

formation? Of what relevance are philosophical discussions of ethics? Do the ways that authors present material in chemistry textbooks illustrate any important communication principles? Answer these and similar questions about other fields of study.

ORAL ACTIVITIES AND SPEAKING ASSIGNMENTS

1. Participate actively in a general class consideration of the subject "Things That I Like (Dislike) in a Speaker." As you and the other members of the class mention your likes and dislikes, your instructor may want to list them in two columns on a chalkboard. At the conclusion of this oral consideration, help your instructor summarize by formulating a composite picture or list of those speaker traits or qualities to which the majority of the class members would respond *favorably* and those traits or qualities to which the majority would respond *unfavorably*. Finally, if you (as a class—collectively) find many traits or qualities which you cannot classify in some absolute manner, ask yourself why. Are there variables within situations or contexts, within our perceptions of "proper" social roles, etc., which make absolute categorization impossible? What are some of these variables?

2. To the extent that the physical facilities of the classroom permit, your instructor will arrange for members of the class to seat themselves in a large circle or—as an alternative—in smaller groups around two or three separate tables. This setting should be as comfortable and relaxing as possible; informality should be the keynote in this particular activity. After the instructor has briefly introduced himself or herself to the others, the student at the instructor's right will orally provide a self-introduction more or less in terms of the following general pattern:

"My name is ————————————————————————.
My major (or my major interest) is ————————————————.
I am in college because ——————————————————————.
In addition to a grade credit, what I hope to get from this course in speech communication is ——————————————————————."

When the first speaker has concluded his or her self-introduction, the next one begins—and so on around the circle or table until everyone present has had a chance briefly to introduce himself or herself to all of the others.

3. An interesting variation of the preceding exercise is for each student to work with another member of the class, more or less as follows: Present information about yourself to another student who, in turn, will

prepare a speech-of-introduction about you. You, of course, will do like-wise for the student with whom you are paired. Each member of the class then offers a short introduction of someone else. In this way, the exercise becomes one wherein you must practice obtaining, selecting, and ordering information about another person.

SUGGESTIONS FOR FURTHER READING

Quintilian, *Institutio Oratorica,* XII.1, "The Orator Must Be a Good Person." An interesting, well-conceived classical view of the ethical roots of effective speechmaking.

Lloyd Bitzer, "The Rhetorical Situation," *Philosophy and Rhetoric* 1 (January, 1968): 1–14. Reprinted in Douglas Ehninger, *Contemporary Rhetoric: A Reader's Coursebook* (Glenview, Ill.: Scott, Foresman and Company, 1972), pp. 39–48. A provocative introduction to ways in which situations constrain and control what is "fitting" for speakers to say.

Stephen Littlejohn, "A Bibliography of Studies Related to Variables of Source Credibility," *Bibliographic Annual in Speech Communication: 1971,* ed. Ned A. Shearer (New York: Speech Communication Association, 1971), pp. 1–40. Perhaps the best available starting point for further investigation of the effect of the speaker's self upon communication processes and outcomes.

C. David Mortensen, *Communication: The Study of Human Interaction* (New York: McGraw-Hill Book Company, 1972), especially Chapter 2, "Communication Models," and Chapter 8, "Situational Geography." A good review of various communication models and their significances, and of the roles of situation and context affecting communication procedures and outcomes.

Raymond S. Ross, *Speech Communication: Fundamentals and Practice*, 3rd ed. (Englewood Cliffs, N.J.: Prentice-Hall, Inc., 1974), especially Chapter 1, "The Communication Process." An enlightening introduction to various communication models and to the various roles of perception in the communication process.

Chapter 2

Listening:
Speaker-audience interaction

Too often we assume that the speaker bears the major, if not the entire, responsibility for effective communication. As we have repeatedly emphasized in the preceding chapter, however, speech communication is a two-way transaction in which the listener as well as the speaker plays an active role and must successfully discharge certain important obligations.[1] In this chapter, we shall look at the listener's obligations in more detail.

LISTENING AS A COMMUNICATIVE RESPONSIBILITY

On a given day, *more than 40 percent* of the time the average adult spends in communication activity is spent in listening.[2] Despite the large amount of time devoted to listening, however, most persons do not listen efficiently. In a recent experiment, for example, a group of college students who listened to a ten-minute lecture were able to remember only about 50 percent of what was said; two weeks later their accuracy of recall had dropped to about 25 percent.[3] If these figures are typical, a great many of us are failing to meet one of our major responsibilities as listeners—that of simply remembering what we are told.

But in addition to the responsibility of remembering material that we hear, as listeners we also have other obligations which must be discharged if the communication transaction is to be of maximum usefulness to all concerned. These include making a genuine effort to under-

---

[1]For a more detailed consideration of the role and responsibilities of the listener in effective speech communication, see the materials developed by Richard L. Johannesen in "Listening, Evaluation, and Ethical Judgment," Chapter 17, Alan H. Monroe and Douglas Ehninger, *Principles and Types of Speech Communication,* Seventh Edition (Glenview, Ill.: Scott, Foresman and Company, 1974), pp. 447–466.

[2]See studies reviewed in Larry L. Barker, *Listening Behavior* (Englewood Cliffs, N.J.: Prentice-Hall, Inc., 1971), pp. 3–4.

[3]Ralph G. Nichols, "Do We Know How to Listen? Practical Helps in a Modern Age," *The Speech Teacher* X (March 1961): 120.

stand the meaning which the speaker wishes to transmit, judging the worth or cogency of the ideas presented, and returning to the speaker in the form of *feedback* some indications of how we are receiving the message. With these duties in mind, two experts on listening, Ralph G. Nichols and Leonard Stevens, have concluded:

> It seems that we shall eventually come to believe that the responsibility for effective oral communication must be equally shared by speakers and listeners. When this transpires we shall have taken a long stride toward greater economy in learning, accelerated personal growth, and significantly deepened human understanding.[4]

IMPROVING YOUR LISTENING SKILLS

Although listening admittedly involves a number of skills which many persons perform poorly, research has shown that it can be improved through guided practice, and that any particular act of listening can be made more productive if the listener will bring to it a correct physical adjustment and a proper mental attitude.[5]

How can you become a better listener? We suggest in five ways:
1. Rid yourself of poor listening habits.
2. Prepare for the listening experience.
3. Learn how to listen for enjoyment.
4. Learn how to listen for understanding.
5. Learn how to listen for evaluation.

Rid yourself of poor listening habits

Over a period of time most persons have developed one or more listening habits which hinder full concentration on the ideas the speaker is presenting or which result in a partial or incorrect reception of the message. Among poor listening habits, the following are common:[6]

---

[4]Ralph G. Nichols and Leonard A. Stevens, *Are You Listening?* (New York: McGraw-Hill Book Company, 1957), pp. 221–222.

[5]See, for example, Colin Cherry, *On Human Communication* (New York: John Wiley & Sons, Inc., 1957), p. 276; Charles E. Irwin, "Motivation in Listening Training," *Journal of Communication* IV (Summer 1954): 42–44; Paul W. Keller, "Major Findings in Listening in the Past Ten Years," *Journal of Communication* X (March 1960): 29–38; Paul T. Rankin, "The Importance of Listening Ability," *English Journal* XVII (October 1928): 623–630.

[6]The discussion of poor listening habits is adapted in part from Larry L. Barker, *Listening Behavior* (Englewood Cliffs, N.J.: Prentice-Hall, Inc., 1971), pp. 61–66; and from Ralph G. Nichols and Leonard A. Stevens, *Are You Listening?* (New York: McGraw-Hill Book Company, 1957), pp. 89–112.

Private planning. While the speaker is talking, some listeners are engrossed in their own problems or in planning forthcoming activities: what they will be doing next weekend, what they will say to the speaker if they get the chance, etc. They cannot, of course, listen attentively to the speaker while doing their private planning.

Self-debating. A listener may carry on a continuous, private argument with himself or herself about the soundness and worth of what the speaker is saying, rather than merely noting that an aspect or element of the message is questionable and delaying full evaluation until later.

Yielding easily to distractions. Distractions take innumerable forms: loud noises or uncomfortable conditions in the environment, daydreams about being in more pleasant and preferred circumstances, etc. A fleeting word, a half-heard phrase, a glimpsed image, or some other stimulus may trigger a lengthy recall of past personal experiences. Inattention to the speaker is the inevitable result.

Avoiding difficult listening. Too many of us like to avoid complex or challenging subjects. We prefer to say, "Oh, that's not for me," and close our ears. When we do this, however, we lose valuable opportunities to *exercise* our concentrative skills and thereby improve our listening abilities.

Prematurely dismissing a subject as uninteresting. We should realize that some seemingly dry subjects are nevertheless important and that a knowledge of them can become valuable to us personally. Rather than "shutting off" the speaker, focus patiently on the message, recognizing as you do so that the real relevance of the topic may not emerge until the speech has been more fully developed.

Being overly critical of the speaker's delivery and physical appearance. Sometimes we are unnecessarily critical of the speaker's mode of dress, vocal and bodily delivery, or other nonverbal factors. We allow ourselves to be "turned off" by these negative impressions and thus obscure the necessity of evaluating the intrinsic merits of the message as such. Nonverbal elements are significant, of course; but if we are to listen well, we must give close attention to *both* the verbal and the nonverbal behaviors of speakers.

Listening just for isolated facts. Too often we listen only for the "bits and pieces" of a speech—only the "things that interest us." At such times, we tend to ignore the substance as a *whole* and overlook the structural relationships and emphases accorded the various parts. As a result, we fail to get the entire picture and, therefore, are in a poor position to judge the worth or usefulness of the message as a whole.

Allowing emotionalism to hinder listening. Often we react positively or negatively and in a strong manner to certain emotionally laden words or ideas. Positive attitudes triggered by a specific word or phrase may cause us to lower our evaluative standards and thereby produce an uncritical, unreflective response. Negative attitudes so triggered may lead us to reject—without fair and total judgment—*everything* the speaker says. We should be *aware* of the nature of our own emotional tendencies and not allow them to affect adversely our reception of a message.

Allowing basic convictions or prejudices to hinder listening. A very human tendency is to allow prejudices; stereotypes; and basic beliefs, attitudes, values, and motives to impair the accuracy of our understanding or fairness of evaluation. The admonition to "know thyself" is directly applicable to effective listening.

Being dogmatic. A closed-minded person with a tunnel vision of *the* truth does not strive to *understand* various or conflicting points of view before selecting one as preferable. He or she does not wait to "hear the speaker out" before evaluating and deciding.

Mental "wool-gathering," internal debate, giving in to distractions, dodging subjects and materials difficult to listen to, premature evaluation of subject and speaker, trying to "absorb" isolated facts rather than the whole picture, emotional distortion, prejudice, and dogmatism—these are among the "culprits" that cause us to be poor listeners. To rid ourselves of these habits, we need to learn to listen with both an open ear and an open mind.

Prepare for the listening experience

As we observed in Chapter 1 (pages 9–10), the listener, like the speaker, has a purpose to achieve by participating in the communicative transaction. This purpose may be (1) simply *to enjoy* what the speaker is saying; (2) *to understand*—to acquire new information or insights; or (3) *to evaluate*—to judge critically the worth of the ideas or arguments presented. Although one of these purposes is usually primary, good listening often includes all three. Under no circumstances is it passive or indifferent. Good listeners always approach the listening situation with a positive rather than a negative attitude. They listen because they want to, not because they have to.

The concentration reflected on the faces of these listeners attests to the *transactional* nature of the speech communication process in which the listener, like the speaker, plays an active role and shares the responsibility for the success of the interchange.

Top, Eastern Michigan University Photo; *left,* Photo by University of Colorado Information Services.

In order to achieve your purpose as a listener, whenever possible prepare yourself in advance for the speech or lecture you are going to attend. Study the topic to be discussed; find out what you can about the speaker and his or her beliefs; investigate the group or organization sponsoring the speech event. When you arrive at the place where the speech is to be given, seat yourself where you can see and hear easily, and throughout the program remain alert physically and mentally. Finally, when the speaker has concluded, review in your own mind what was said, discuss the speaker's ideas with friends, and—if the subject is an important one—study it further. In this way, you will be able to receive maximum benefit for the time and effort you have expended.

Learn to listen for enjoyment

If the speaker's purpose is to entertain rather than to inform or persuade, your purpose as a listener may be simply to derive enjoyment from the speech. Under such circumstances you usually can increase your pleasure and appreciation by following these suggestions:

1. Relax physically and mentally. Sit in a comfortable, relaxed position. Insofar as possible, free your mind from other interests and from vexing problems and worries.

2. Cultivate a receptive attitude. Do not spoil your pleasure by being too analytical or hypercritical. This does not mean that you should be completely undiscriminating, but that you should view the speaker in a warm and friendly light and should anticipate the message with pleasure.

3. Use imagination and empathy. Enter into the spirit of the occasion freely and fully. Give your imagination enough play so that you can join with the speaker in reliving the events or experiences that are described. If you can imagine yourself a participant in such situations, their vividness will be enhanced and your pleasure in the speech will grow accordingly.

Learn to listen for understanding

Sometimes your primary purpose as a listener is to learn new facts, more clearly understand an idea, or more fully comprehend a subject. When that is the case, you may benefit from the following guides:

1. Identify the speaker's major or leading ideas, and concentrate closely on each as it is expressed. Unless you take care to identify each major idea as it is stated and to separate it from the developmental material that is associated with it, you may fail to grasp the speaker's dominant thesis or point of view and may carry away from the listening experience nothing more than a confused mass of data.

2. Identify the structure or arrangement of the major ideas. Determine whether the speaker is organizing his or her material according to one or more of the standard patterns of arrangement—chronological, spatial, cause-effect, problem-solution, and the like. By identifying and bearing in mind the speaker's organizational pattern, you will be able to follow the explanations more easily and remember the main points more accurately.

3. Examine critically the details used to develop and support the major ideas. As you identify each major idea and observe how it fits into the pattern of the speech as a whole, note also the materials by which this idea is exemplified or supported. What additional light is thrown on the idea by the illustrations or comparisons which the speaker supplies? Does this piece of explanation or that set of statistics point up some implication or inference that you have previously overlooked? Do certain of the speaker's quotations confirm or throw doubt on the idea as originally presented? By asking such questions, you can appreciably increase your comprehension of the idea and its place in the speech.

4. Relate the major ideas to your own previous knowledge and interests. Try to determine *why* the information presented by the speaker is important to you or *why* you should want to make it a permanent part of your storehouse of knowledge. What is the relation of the information to your needs and goals? In what ways can you use or apply it? Where and how might you obtain additional material on the subject?

Learn to listen for evaluation: Lines of inquiry

Evaluative listening requires the skills necessary when listening for understanding and comprehension, but it goes beyond them. When your aim is to *evaluate* a speech performance, you will strive for something approaching a total assessment of communicative strengths and weaknesses, societal worth, effectiveness, and ethics of the speaker's subject, purpose, and methods. This, clearly, is a complex and often subjective task. To help structure the evaluative process, we shall raise and discuss a number of questions. In this way we hope to identify potential dimensions for evaluation which you may apply to the speech you are assessing.

1. What seem to be the speaker's general and specific purposes? To entertain, to present information and increase understanding, to reinforce existing beliefs and attitudes, to change beliefs and attitudes, or to secure overt action? To what degree is the purpose appropriate for the speaker, audience, and occasion? How might factors in the occasion or prevailing ideological climate have influenced the speaker's purpose and/or methods? To what in particular does the speaker seem to be responding? Given the audience and relevant circumstances, does the speaker's purpose seem realistic and achievable?

2. How does the speaker arouse and maintain your attention and interest? Are such interest-factors as conflict, suspense, curiosity, action, novelty, and humor capitalized upon?[7] Is interest heightened through analogies, narration, vivid descriptions, contrasts, factual and hypothetical examples, and illustrations?

3. Does the speaker try to make sure that you, as a listener, clearly understand the message as intended? Do you know exactly what the speaker is asking of you, and how he or she intends to implement that idea or proposal? What patterns of organization does the speaker use to promote unity and clarity?[8] If the speech lacks structure, is this due to speaker ineptness or to the nature of the subject being discussed? How does the speaker employ such devices as repetition, restatement, association with the familiar, examples and illustrations, questions and answers, statistics, and definitions?[9] How does the speaker employ audiovisual aids and vocal and physical delivery skills to increase understanding?

4. Do you view the speaker's proposal (idea, belief, policy) as reasonable? Are evidence and reasoning used to demonstrate that the proposal actually will work, will solve the problem, will be efficient, and will not be too costly? Is the proposal feasible despite such potential limitations as minimal finances, time, or manpower?

5. Do you feel there is a legitimate connection between the speaker's idea or purpose and your relevant needs, motives, and goals? Do you see a personal stake in the outcome? Has the speaker exaggerated the connection or appealed to irrelevant needs?

---

[7]The factors of attention and interest are examined fully in Chapter 10, pp. 207–211.

[8]Some possible patterns of speech organization are presented and exemplified in Chapter 7, pp. 137–140.

[9]These and other forms of supporting materials are considered in some detail in Chapter 6, pp. 109–123.

6. Is the speaker's idea consistent with your relevant beliefs and attitudes? If not, is there reason for you to reexamine some of your related beliefs and attitudes?

7. Is the speaker's idea sanctioned by your relevant values? How does it measure up to your conceptions of the Good or the Desirable? Does the speaker's idea conflict in any way with your basic values? Are the values you are using to judge the proposal the most appropriate ones?

8. What is the speaker's apparent attitude toward you as a listener? Do the ideas, language, and delivery reflect such attitudes as respect, sincerity, humility, aloofness, objectivity, coercion, aggressiveness, deference, defensiveness, or conciliation?

9. Do you perceive the speaker as a credible source on this subject? To what degree and in what ways do you view the speaker as expert, experienced, educated, trustworthy, sincere, dependable, and concerned? How and to what extent has the speaker's credibility fluctuated during the presentation of the speech? What factors of content and delivery contributed to your assessment of credibility? Is the speaker *representing* a credible person or group?

10. Can you discern any unstated assumptions in the speech? What unspoken beliefs, values, premises, stereotypes, etc., implicitly undergird the speaker's ideas? Should these assumptions have been made explicit? How do these assumptions reflect the speaker's conception of reality, truth, goodness, or the essential nature of humankind?

11. In what ways does the speaker's language usage (style) contribute to clarity and persuasiveness? Is the language easy to understand? Is it vivid? Is it appropriate to the subject and to the occasion on which the speech is presented? What does the speaker's style reveal about him or her personally or about his or her view of the audience? If the use of metaphors is a major stylistic characteristic, are they trite or fresh? Is there a dominant or thematic metaphor woven throughout the speech? Does the speaker rely heavily on "god terms" or "devil terms," on concepts with intense positive or negative denotations and connotations? If so, are such terms justified by the speaker's subject and purpose? Do they contribute to the persuasive impact of the address?

12. Do the nonverbal elements in the speech reinforce or conflict with the speaker's verbal meaning? Do the speaker's vocal and physical delivery tell you one thing and the words another? If so, which should you believe, and why? How do the nonverbal elements of the speaker's delivery contribute to clarity and persuasiveness?

As yet, you may not have the information and experience necessary to evaluate a speech in accordance with all of the terms and facets singled out in the foregoing questions. However, by the time you have familiarized yourself with the substance of the succeeding chapters, where these matters are explained and elaborated upon, very probably you will have sharpened your evaluative skills and will have had numerous opportunities to improve your listening capabilities.

PROVIDING LISTENER FEEDBACK

As we have repeatedly pointed out, because the speech transaction is essentially a circular process, its success depends not only on the signals the speaker sends to the listeners, but also on the signals the listeners return to the speaker in the form of *feedback*. The good listener, therefore, does more than maintain an attentive, responsive attitude; he or she also helps to complete the communication circuit by actively transmitting to the speaker warranted signs of comprehension or puzzlement, acceptance or rejection, approval or disapproval, etc.

Obviously, no one expects a listener to be insincere or to reward a dull, uninspiring speech with false signs of enthusiastic endorsement. Moreover, in those informal situations where an active verbal interchange between speaker and listeners is in order, courteous objections may be raised or reservations noted. On the other hand, nothing is more discouraging to a speaker than to confront minute after minute a group of stony-faced, impassive auditors—auditors who, as the saying goes, "sit on their hands" no matter how hard the speaker tries to interest or arouse them.

When listening to a speech, maintain a critical attitude and reserve the right to judge objectively the accuracy and worth of what you hear. But suppress open signs of strong disagreement (you may argue with the speaker later during a question period or after the meeting has been adjourned), and respond warmly to ideas and proposals that merit your approval. You will find that in this way the speech encounter can be made a more enjoyable and more productive experience both for you and for the speaker.[10]

---

[10]For additional information on feedback and its role in the speech transaction, see Michael Burgoon, *Approaching Speech Communication* (New York: Holt, Rinehart & Winston, Inc., 1974), pp. 74–80; and R. Wayne Pace and Robert R. Boren, *The Human Transaction* (Glenview, Ill.: Scott, Foresman and Company, 1973), pp. 286–290.

PROBLEMS FOR FURTHER STUDY

1. As you have seen, listening is a complex process, perhaps even more complex than this chapter has indicated, given the fact that you "listen" not only to words and ideas but also to rate, pitch, volume, pauses, the speaker's sense of timing, etc. In your journal, make an objective analysis of yourself as a listener: *(a)* Are you able to keep your own thoughts and prejudices from interfering with your reception of the speaker's message? *(b)* Do you listen for signposts the speaker sets up, for the main ideas and transitions around which the content of the talk is organized? *(c)* Are you able to subordinate supporting material so as to keep the speaker's dominant ideas clearly in mind? *(d)* Are you sensitive to the emotional overtones provided by specific kinds of phrasing? *(e)* Do you include reactions to delivery and voice in your overall judgment of the speaker? When you have answered these questions, prescribe for yourself methods by which you can improve your listening ability — methods drawn along the lines suggested in this chapter. With the assistance of your instructor, try to work out a day-by-day program which will help ensure your implementation and mastery of these methods.

2. What, to your mind, is the importance of physical setting in aiding or discouraging good listening? How do you react to noises, uncomfortable temperatures in a room, seating which makes a view of the speaker difficult, etc.? Does the arrangement of chairs (pews in church, circles of chairs in kindergarten, across-the-desk seating for conferences) affect your listening habits? Do you listen in one manner when seated in front of a lecturer, in another when talking to a friend at a crowded party? Are there any generalizations you can make regarding the ways in which the speech situation affects the ease or efficiency with which you listen?

3. With several other members of the class, attend a speech or lecture held on campus or in the community. Attempt to determine individually *(a)* the speaker's purpose, *(b)* the major ideas of the speech, and *(c)* the types and adequacy of the supporting materials that are used. Compare your findings with those of others in the class. On what kinds of judgments is there unanimity of opinion? On which, divergence? Why?

4. Attend the presentation of a public speech, and seat yourself where you can observe closely the reactions of various members of the audience as they listen to the speaker. Do some appear to listen intently throughout? Do others seem to allow their attention to wander and, if so, at what points in the speech? Does the speaker appear to react or adjust to such audience feedback? How? What kinds of physical cues or signs did you rely on in answering these questions? Do you as a speaker rely on similar cues when adjusting to the listener feedback?

ORAL ACTIVITIES AND SPEAKING ASSIGNMENTS

1. After everyone in class has completed Problem 2 above, participate in a general class discussion on the question "In what ways do aspects of the physical setting affect listening habits?" Focus your attention on this question by considering the following examples:

(a) When Adolf Hitler wanted to stage a particularly successful mass rally, he held it at night, so as to shut out the rest of the world; he surrounded the audience with flags, martial music, flickering torches, loudspeakers; he packed the crowd together, arranging for them to sing for nearly an hour before he himself appeared; and, he raised the speaker's stand well above the audience.

(b) The automobile salesperson starts you ambling through selected cars on the showroom floor while making small talk; then he shows you cars in stock, often guiding you on a "tour" of the entire car lot; next, he takes you on a test drive, during which time he explains technical and mechanical aspects of the machine; finally, with the comment, "Let's go into my office and talk," he ushers you into a wood-paneled cubicle, surrounded with plaques, citations, specification sheets, and pictures of the salesperson's family, and tells you why this car at this price is the one for you.

(c) Delegates attending national political conventions are expected to vote on platforms, select major candidates, and charge themselves up for the hard work of vote-mongering. They meet in bars, hotel caucus rooms, committee rooms, and on the convention floor itself. They discuss candidates, issues, group and individual stands, and their chances for victory in the upcoming election; they listen to supportive, patriotic, actuative, and celebratory messages as they move from setting to setting, from intimate conversation to the mass hysteria of a floor demonstration.

(d) In a church, the congregation usually sits in pews facing the front; liturgical ceremonies are carried out on a raised platform, and a sermon or message is delivered from an elevated pulpit or lectern. The members of the congregation are surrounded on all sides by religious symbols, paintings, and/or icons; often they engage in songs, chants, and/or responsive readings.

As a group, attempt to arrive at generalizations about the effects of these settings on listening habits.

2. As a check on listening abilities, participate in a class discussion on a highly controversial topic which generates strong disagreements among members of your class. Conduct the discussion with a single rule: Before anyone can speak, he or she first must summarize — *to the satisfaction of the previous speaker* — what that speaker has said. As a result of the activity,

what conclusions can you draw about: *(a)* people's ability to summarize accurately and satisfactorily, and *(b)* the manner in which good listening and feedback reduce the amount and intensity of disagreement?

SUGGESTIONS FOR FURTHER READING

Quintilian, *Institutio Oratoria,* VI. 2, "Necessity of Studying the Temper of the Judges." A classical pedagogue's attempt to demonstrate that emotions control listening habits.

Larry L. Barker, *Listening Behavior* (Englewood Cliffs, N.J.: Prentice-Hall, Inc., 1971). Currently the most comprehensive review of research on listening behavior.

Charles M. Kelley, "Emphatic Listening," in *Concepts in Communication,* ed. Jimmie D. Trent *et al.* (Boston: Allyn & Bacon, Inc., 1973), pp. 263–272. A review of industrial listening studies, distinguishing between the listener-as-receiver and the listener-as-critic.

Ralph G. Nichols and Leonard A. Stevens, *Are You Listening?* (New York: McGraw-Hill Book Company, 1957). The near-classic textbook on the art of accurate listening.

Brent D. Peterson, Gerald M. Goldhaber, and R. Wayne Pace, *Communication Probes* (Chicago: Science Research Associates, Inc., 1974), "Your perceptions may be a prime obstacle to effective communication," pp. 24–34. A provocative collection of cartoons, articles, and excerpts from textbooks probing the components of effective listening.

Carl Weaver, *Human Listening: Processes and Behavior* (Indianapolis: The Bobbs-Merrill Company, Inc., 1972). A solid, readable introduction to the psychodynamics of listening.

Chapter 3

Planning and preparing the speech

M<small>ORE THAN ANY OTHER SINGLE FACTOR</small>, a successful speech depends on careful planning and preparation. Should the talk you are to give be memorized, read from a manuscript, or delivered extempore? What guidelines should you follow in selecting a subject, determining a purpose, analyzing the audience, and organizing the ideas you wish to present? These are among the important questions which you should consider every time you are called on to prepare a speech of any kind.

METHODS OF SPEAKING

First, what method should you use in presenting your speech? As you probably have observed, you have four choices. Your speech can be: (1) *impromptu*, (2) *memorized*, (3) *read from a manuscript*, or (4) *extemporized*.

The impromptu speech. An impromptu speech is one delivered on the spur of the moment. No specific preparation is made; the speaker relies entirely on previous knowledge and skill. The ability to speak impromptu is useful in an emergency, but you should limit your use of this method to situations in which you are unable to anticipate your possible involvement. Too often the "moment" arrives without the "spur." Whenever possible, therefore, try to avoid the rambling, incoherent "remarks" which the impromptu method so often produces.

The memorized speech. As its name implies, this type of speech is written out word for word and committed to memory. A few speakers are able to use this method effectively, but it does present certain problems. Usually memorization results in a stilted, inflexible presentation; the speaker may be either excessively formal and oratorical, or may tend to hurry through the speech — pouring out words with no thought as to their meaning. Moreover, with this method it is difficult to adapt the speech to changing audience reactions during the presentation.

The read speech. Like the memorized speech, the read speech is written out word for word, but in this method the speaker reads it from a manuscript . If extremely careful wording is required — as in the President's messages to Congress, where a slip of the tongue could undermine domestic or foreign policies, or in the presentation of scientific reports, where exact, concise exposition is required — the read speech is appropriate. Many radio and television speeches also are read from manuscript because of the strict time limits imposed by broadcasting schedules. The ability to read a speech effectively is valuable as a specialized skill useful in certain situations. But this method should not be employed when it is neither useful nor necessary. No matter how experienced you may be, when you read your message, you will almost inevitably sacrifice some of the necessary freshness and spontaneity.

The extemporaneous speech. Taking a middle course between the memorized or read speech and the speech that is delivered impromptu, the extemporaneous speech requires careful planning and a detailed outline. Sometimes you may want to write out a complete draft, but you should not commit the words to memory. Instead, working from an outline, practice the speech aloud, expressing the ideas somewhat differently each time you go through it. Use the outline to fix the order of ideas in your mind, and practice various wordings to develop accuracy, conciseness, and flexibility of expression. If the extemporaneous method is used carelessly, the result will resemble an impromptu speech — a fact which sometimes leads to a confusion of these two terms. A proper use of the method, however, will produce a speech which is nearly as polished as a memorized one and certainly more vigorous, flexible, and spontaneous. With few exceptions, the speeches you deliver in your classroom will probably be extemporaneous.

THE ESSENTIALS OF SPEECH PREPARATION

Whether your speech is to be memorized, read from manuscript, or presented extemporaneously, the *process* of preparation beyond this point will be much the same. You will need to select and narrow your subject, determine your purpose, analyze the audience and occasion, gather material, make an outline, and practice aloud.[1]

---

[1]When preparing a speech to be given as part of your work in the classroom, in addition to other considerations, always make certain that it fulfills the specific assignment you have been given. Each of the speeches your instructor asks you to make will have a definite goal: to teach you how to organize ideas, how to prove a point, how to maintain interest, etc. Keep this goal clearly in mind. Do not, for instance, prepare a speech to inform when the assignment calls for a speech to persuade; do not support a point with explanation and examples when you have been asked to use statistics. Failure to follow your instructor's directions in these and similar respects will reduce greatly the benefits to be derived from a carefully planned sequence of speech experiences.

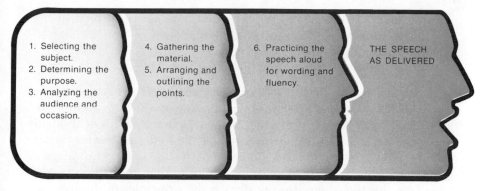

1. Selecting the subject.
2. Determining the purpose.
3. Analyzing the audience and occasion.

4. Gathering the material.
5. Arranging and outlining the points.

6. Practicing the speech aloud for wording and fluency.

THE SPEECH AS DELIVERED

Figure 1. Steps in Planning, Preparing, and Presenting the Speech

Selecting and narrowing the subject

On many occasions, the subject of your speech will be determined for you—at least in part—by the group you are invited to address. You are, for instance, a water-resources expert who is asked to speak to a local service club on means of controlling pollution in a nearby river. Or, after an extensive trip through East Africa, you are invited to describe for a women's study group the social and economic conditions as they now exist in some of the newly emerging nations in that area. At other times, of course, the subject on which you will speak is left to your discretion. Nearly always, however, you will be free to select the particular phase or aspect of the subject you wish to emphasize.

When confronted with the task of choosing a subject or determining which aspect of a more general topic to stress, observe the following guidelines:

Select a subject about which you already know something and can find out more. In a speech, as elsewhere, there is no substitute for knowledge that is thorough and authoritative. In addition to drawing on your own accurate observations, read widely and talk with experts.

Select a subject that is interesting to you. If you are not interested in what you are talking about, you will find preparation a dull task, and your speaking is likely to be listless and ineffective.

Select a subject that will interest your audience. The more interest your listeners already have in the subject, the less you will have to worry about holding their attention when you speak. A subject may be interesting to an audience for one or more of the following reasons:

A. It concerns their health, happiness, prosperity, or security.
B. It offers a solution to a recognized problem.
C. It is new or timely.
D. There is conflict of opinion concerning it.

Select a subject that is neither above nor below the comprehension level of your listeners. A speech about the value of a savings account in a local bank would be appropriate for an audience of grade-school children, but a discussion of the workings of the Federal Reserve System would not. On the other hand, do not underestimate the knowledge or capacity of your listeners by selecting a subject that makes you seem to be talking down to them. Do not discuss the principles of double-entry bookkeeping before an audience of CPAs, or tell a group of professional journalists how to write a good news story.

Select a subject that you can discuss adequately in the time at your disposal. In a ten-minute speech, refrain from reviewing "The Causes and Consequences of the Vietnam War." Instead, describe some of the major decisions leading to U.S. involvement, or discuss the principal terms of the settlement that resulted in our withdrawal. Remember that even though you have been *assigned* a subject, you will probably still need to limit it—to select some phase or aspect that you can discuss effectively within the time limits you have been given.

Determining the purpose

The general purpose. As we pointed out in Chapter 1, whether in a person-to-person, group, or public situation, we speak to others because we have a purpose or goal we wish to achieve. When giving a speech, this purpose usually falls into one of three general classes. We speak because we want our listeners (1) to enjoy themselves, (2) to understand something, or (3) to believe or act in a certain way. In the first case, the purpose of our speech is *to entertain;* in the second, *to inform;* in the third, *to persuade* or *to actuate;* thus:

GENERAL PURPOSE	AUDIENCE RESPONSE SOUGHT
To entertain	Enjoyment
To inform	Clear understanding or comprehension
To persuade or to actuate	Acceptance of and/or actuation by ideas

To entertain. To entertain, amuse, or divert is frequently the purpose of an after-dinner speech, but talks of other kinds also may have the enjoyment of the listener as their principal end. Often a travel lecture, although it also presents a great deal of factual material, has as its overall purpose entertaining the audience with exciting or amusing tales of adventures in a strange land. Club meetings, class reunions, and similar gatherings of friends and associates also provide occasions for speeches to entertain. In these situations, the speaker may depend chiefly on humor or merely present interesting anecdotes or curious bits of information. Heavy discussions and controversial issues are avoided, however; and if facts and figures are presented, they are offered in a verbal setting that is unique and exceptional—in a way that is unlikely to be anticipated by the listeners.

To inform. When your overall objective is to help the members of your audience understand an idea or comprehend a concept or a process, or when you seek to widen the range of their knowledge, the general purpose of your speech will be to inform. Such is the goal of the scientist who reports the results of her research to a group of colleagues, of the college lecturer or the work supervisor, or of the public figure who addresses community groups on a subject in which he or she is an acknowledged expert.

To evoke a response of understanding, you must change the level or quality of information possessed by your audience. By providing examples, statistics, illustrations, and other materials of an instructive nature, seek to expand or alter their reservoir of knowledge. That change alone, however, may not be sufficient to ensure a response of understanding. For not only must an informative speech provide raw data, but also the message and supporting data must be structured and integrated in such a way that listeners will clearly and quickly perceive the import of the whole. For example, an informative speech on how to build a stereo set not only must include the necessary information, but also must present that information in an orderly sequence of steps. Understanding in this instance will depend not only on learning *what* to do, but also on knowing *when* to do it and *why.* Many of your listeners may already be familiar with much of your information and still lack understanding. No one has ever "put it all together" for them; no one has shown them exactly how to proceed step by step in order to achieve the end desired.

In short, in order to communicate an informative message successfully, you must relate your ideas to the existing knowledge of the audience; you must organize them so they are easy to follow and remember, and you must present enough concrete examples and specific data to raise appreciably the perceptual and informational levels of the persons addressed.

To persuade or to actuate. The purpose of a speech to persuade or to actuate is to influence listener belief or action. While it may be argued that all speeches are in some degree persuasive, there are numerous situations in which the speaker has outright persuasion as his or her primary and most insistent purpose. Promoters and public relations experts attempt to create belief in the superiority of certain products, personages, or institutions; lawyers seek to convince juries; ministers exhort their congregations to lead nobler lives; politicians debate campaign issues and strive to influence voters.

Usually, as a persuasive speaker you will seek only to influence the beliefs and attitudes of your listeners. Sometimes, however, you will want to go a step further and attempt to move them to *action*. You may want them, for instance, to contribute money, sign a petition, organize a parade, or participate in a demonstration. The distinguishing feature of a persuasive speech of this type is that instead of stopping with an appeal to their beliefs or attitudes, you ask your listeners to demonstrate their convictions and feelings by *behaving* or *acting* in a specified way.

Whether or not you seek immediate and overt action from the members of your audience, however, you invariably imply that what they believe should influence how they feel. Thus an attorney who wants a jury to believe that a client acted while insane also wants the jurors to feel a certain way about that client, to feel perhaps that the accused is deserving of pity or mercy. Conversely, a speaker who seeks to engender strong feelings about a subject also seeks to intensify listener beliefs and encourage certain kinds of behavior. For instance, in an acceptance speech a presidential candidate not only strives to arouse feelings of loyalty to person and party, but also seeks to reinforce our beliefs about our country's strengths and weaknesses, and to convince us to vote — preferably for him or her — as an act of patriotic behavior. Therefore, although listener acceptance of the speaker's ideas remains the general end of a speech to persuade, the effective speaker will realize that to gain this response from listeners, their beliefs, attitudes, and inclinations to act must be changed in some significant way.

Because the speech to persuade or to actuate characteristically is designed to influence or alter the beliefs and action-tendencies of listeners, you should fill it with well-ordered arguments supported by facts, figures, and examples. In order to persuade successfully, however, you must do more than provide factual data; you must make your listeners *want* to believe or act as you propose. Therefore, in addition to evidence and arguments, you must also introduce strong motive appeals; you must show how the proposal you advocate is related to your listeners' interests—how it will satisfy certain of their basic drives, wishes, or desires. (This matter will be explored in detail in Chapter 11.)

To entertain, to inform, and to persuade are, then, the *general* purposes a speech may have. To attempt to speak without a more precise objective in mind, however, would be foolhardy. The broad, overall purpose of a talk must be narrowed and made more *specific* before you can hope to communicate successfully.

The specific purpose. We may define the specific purpose of a speech as the *precise response* desired from the audience by the speaker. Formulated into a clear, concise statement, the specific purpose delineates exactly what you want the audience to do, feel, believe, understand, or enjoy. The following examples will illustrate the relationship of the subject of a speech to its general purpose and its specific purpose:

Subject: Accident insurance for students.
General purpose: To persuade—evoke action.
Specific purpose: To get members of the student council to approve the group policy offered by the ABC Accident Insurance Company.

Subject: The effects of weightlessness.
General purpose: To inform.
Specific purpose: To explain the effects of weightlessness on the body and the mind of the astronaut.

Subject: The tribulations of an umpire.
General purpose: To entertain.
Specific purpose: To share with the audience the humorous and not-so-humorous experiences of my brief career as a baseball umpire.

The formation of a clear and concise specific purpose is essential to effective speaking not only because it focuses the thinking of the audience, but also because it forces you to clarify in your own mind the exact point you wish your listeners to understand or the exact belief, attitude, or action you wish them to endorse or initiate as a result of your message.

In choosing the specific purpose of a speech, take account of both internal and external factors. By *internal factors* we mean those considerations which relate only to you as the speaker. What aspect of the subject do you know most about? What part of it interests you most? What are your honest beliefs concerning it? Such questions are important because, if you are to speak effectively, you must center your purpose on those things you know best and in which you are most interested.

Equally essential, however, to the wise choice of a specific purpose are a number of *external factors.* These include the *occasion* on which the speech is to be given; the *time limit* assigned; and the *type, attitude,* and *authority of the audience* to be addressed. Because such external considerations are often overlooked by speakers, they deserve emphasis. Be sure, for instance, that both your purpose and your subject fit the spirit of the occasion on which you are to speak. The celebration of a football victory is hardly the place for a serious discussion of nuclear fallout or the necessity for tax reform, and a commemorative or memorial service is not a proper place to promote your candidacy for a local office. Do not be humorous when the situation calls for seriousness, or serious when it calls for humor. Do not urge the adoption of a policy when its adoption is clearly beyond the province of your audience. Fit your purpose to the expectancy of your listeners, as that expectancy is determined by the occasion on which they are gathered.

Analyzing the audience

As we emphasized in both Chapters 1 and 2, the communication process involves a *listener* as well as a speaker and a message. Talking to hear your own voice may be pleasurable or may help you confirm your identity,[2] but it is not to be confused with the quite different aim of communicating ideas or feelings to others. Often speakers forget this important fact. They become so engrossed in their own interests, so impressed by ideas that seem important to them, that they forget

---

[2] See Charles T. Brown and Charles Van Riper, *Speech and Man* (Englewood Cliffs, N.J.: Prentice-Hall, Inc., 1966), pp. 35–36.

they are communicating with people whose interests and attitudes may be quite different from their own. It is a fairly safe assertion that more speeches fail for this reason than for any other.

The most important lesson you as a speaker can learn, therefore, is to see things from the standpoint of your listeners, to take what is sometimes described as a "receiver orientation."[3] You must continually ask yourself, "How would I feel about this if I were in their place?" To answer this question accurately requires a thorough analysis of the audience and occasion because, obviously, an argument which would convince some people would leave others unmoved, and ideas that might be appropriate on one occasion would be inappropriate on another.

But how are you to find out these things? The best way, of course, is to talk with persons who are planning the program or who will be members of your audience. If you do not know any such persons, often you can inquire of others who have had dealings with them. When these methods are impracticable, you will be forced to infer the attitudes and beliefs of your listeners and to gauge the nature of the speaking occasion from whatever factual data you can gather. Information concerning the listeners, for example, might include data on: (1) the *demographic composition of the audience members,* (2) their *probable knowledge of the subject,* (3) their *fixed beliefs and values,* (4) their *attitude toward the speaker,* (5) their *attitude toward the subject,* and (6) their *attitude toward the speech purpose.*

Composition of the audience. The following factors should be considered when analyzing the general makeup of an audience:

Size. Will it be a small and highly homogeneous group of fifteen or twenty people, or a large and diversified mass numbering in the hundreds?

Age levels. Are the members of your prospective audience in the same age-range, or of widely divergent ages? Age is an important factor in determining listeners' needs and interests and also suggests the span of their experience with people and events. For a group of young people to understand certain aspects of World War II, lengthy explanations may be necessary; for an older audience, passing references probably would suffice.[4]

---

[3]In this connection, see especially David K. Berlo, *The Process of Communication* (New York: Holt, Rinehart & Winston, Inc., 1960), pp. 52, 62.

[4]On the effect of age on audience attitudes, see Aristotle, *Rhetoric,* p. 1389a. A discussion of many of the factors determining the social composition of an audience is presented in Paul D. Holtzman, *The Psychology of Speaker's Audiences* (Glenview, Ill.: Scott, Foresman and Company, 1970).

An accurate analysis of the audience and occasion is basic to speech planning. Of especial importance in this regard is an awareness of the fixed beliefs, values, and attitudes of the auditors.

Consider the various ways in which the listeners/
receivers, social contexts, and physical settings
represented here might influence the messages which
would be prepared for them.

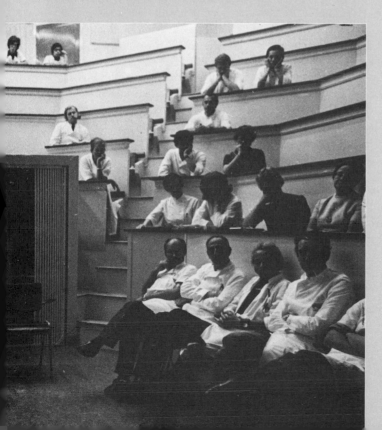

Sex. Is it to be a mixed audience, or are all of the listeners of the same sex? Although in most respects the concerns of men and women overlap, in other respects they are quite distinct.[5] As a result, some subjects that are of interest to one sex may be less appealing to the other or to a mixed audience. Be sure, then, that you know the makeup of your audience in this regard and that you take it into consideration as you plan your speech.

Occupational and vocational interest. Occupation tends to suggest the interests and types of knowledge people have. A speech addressed to the members of a county medical association will doubtless differ in purpose and content from one presented to a local teachers' union. A reasonably accurate idea of the income level of your listeners also can be inferred from a knowledge of their vocations.

Extent of education. Both formal education and education acquired through experience can be important indexes to audience composition. A Chicago cabdriver may not have had broad formal training, but through her work she may have gained a profound knowledge of human nature and of the conditions in her city. To gain clearer insights into the nature of your listeners, remember to consider both schooling and experience.

Membership in social, professional, and religious groups. Rotary International, the Adult Education Association, the American Legion, the National Association for the Advancement of Colored People, the League of Women Voters, the United Auto Workers, B'nai B'rith, the Junior Chamber of Commerce, the National Organization of Women, the Association of Christian Athletes—these organizations suggest, in a general way at least, the types of people involved, as well as their points of view, interests, and special action-tendencies. Whenever you learn that a sizable part of your audience is affiliated with some special group, you have gained a valuable clue to their attitudes and concerns.[6]

Cultural and ethnic background. The American "melting-pot" ideal of cultural assimilation is being increasingly challenged by the ideal of a truly multi-ethnic society. An appreciation of ethnic heritage, contributions, and abilities is an increasing motivation for various societal

---

[5]See Thomas M. Scheidel, "Sex and Persuasibility," *Speech Monographs* XXX (November 1963): 353–358; Irving L. Janis and Peter B. Field, "Sex Differences and Personality Factors Related to Persuasibility," *Personality and Persuasibility*, ed. Carl I. Hovland and Irving L. Janis (New Haven, Conn.: Yale University Press, 1959), pp. 55–68.

[6]For a fuller discussion of the influence of group membership on private opinions, see Elihu Katz and Paul Lazarsfeld, *Personal Influence* (Glencoe, Ill.: The Free Press, 1955).

groups. Before planning your speech, you would be well advised, for example, to discover whether members of your audience perceive themselves as Black, Negro, Chicano, Latino, Japanese-American, Chinese-American, American Indian, etc. The ethnic and cultural self-image held by your hearers will influence their interests and the assumptions they will use to evaluate the implicit or explicit appeals you make.

The audience's fixed beliefs and attitudes. As soon as children begin to receive impressions of their environment, they start to form opinions and attitudes toward the persons and objects that compose or influence it. These opinions and attitudes may be modified by later experience; but by the time the infant has grown to adulthood, some of them have become the bases for firmly held beliefs and predictable conduct.[7]

The speaker who knows what settled beliefs and attitudes lie at the basis of the hearers' thinking can avoid arousing needless hostility and often can use these beliefs as pegs upon which to hang an argument or a proposal. A speaker also may avoid misunderstanding or negative judgment by being aware of the stereotyped perceptions and images reflected in beliefs, attitudes, and opinions. If a speaker can show how his or her ideas coincide with those already established in the minds of the audience, or how a proposal accords with one of their existing principles, often the chance of audience acceptance will be increased.

Finally, a crucial point to remember as you analyze your audience is that all beliefs and attitudes are not equally susceptible to change through speech communication. Be optimistic, of course. But you must also be *realistic* as you plan your speech in the light of knowledge gleaned about the audiences you will be addressing. Do not attempt to accomplish too much. Remember that unexpected, uncontrollable "outside" events or counter-messages from other communicators may be at

---

[7]A *belief* may be defined as any proposition or statement which one accepts as true, and which becomes accepted on such bases as evidence, authority, firsthand experience, faith, etc. An *attitude* can be defined as a predisposition, based on a set of beliefs, to respond positively or negatively to an idea, person, object, or situation. An *opinion* may be viewed as the verbal expression of a belief or attitude. As Daniel Katz points out in "The Functional Approach to the Study of Attitudes," *Public Opinion Quarterly* 24 (1960): 163–204, beliefs and attitudes may serve a variety of psychological functions for those who hold them. Some beliefs and attitudes aid in maximizing rewards and minimizing punishments from those with whom a person must deal directly. Some protect a person from acknowledging harsh truths about himself or his environment. Other beliefs and attitudes reinforce an individual's self-concept and value system. Still others provide standards for structuring and making sense out of the chaotic experience surrounding the person.

work in the minds of your hearers and so diminish the impact of what you plan to say. Moreover, your listeners may not possess the power or the means to make the changes you desire. Remember, too, that all *conditions* are not equally amenable to change through speech communication. For example, no matter what you say, your audience may persist in what appears to be a virtually unshakable "frame of mind." However, underlying many of the established beliefs, attitudes, and behaviors characteristic of a society are what are often described as "the fundamental values"; and a brief examination of some of them should provide additional insights into why audiences think, react, and behave as they do.

The audience's values. A *value*, as a type of belief, may be defined as a conception of the Good or the Desirable. Honesty, justice, honor, efficiency, progress, economy, courage, prudence, and patriotism are all examples of values. A value may function either generally as a goal motivating an individual's behavior or specifically as a standard the person uses to assess the acceptability of means to ends. We might, for instance, recognize that a program is efficient and economical, but reject that program for being dishonest and inhumane. Dominant values for a person or group frequently are reflected in slogans or mottoes: "Liberty, Equality, Fraternity"; "Duty, Honor, Country"; "Law and Order"; "Law and Order and Justice"; "Freedom Now!"; "All Power to the People!"; "Peace with Honor."

In the 1960s and early 1970s a variety of labels have been used to characterize the predominant value-orientations of American society: Puritan Ethic, Protestant Ethic, Establishment, Traditional, Middle American, Silent American, Old Culture, Consciousness II, Essentialist Stance, etc. Other labels have been used to mark the value-orientations seen as to some degree in conflict with the Establishment: Counterculture, New Culture, Hip Culture, Humanistic Ethic, Consciousness III, Existentialist Stance, and the like.[8]

As a communicator whose task it is to understand listeners and to relate harmoniously and productively with them, you must be fully sensitive to these distinctions in value-orientations within our society. Un-

---

[8]For discussions of predominant value-orientations in American society, see Robin M. Williams, *American Society: A Sociological Interpretation,* 3rd ed. (New York: Alfred A. Knopf, Inc., 1970), Chapter 11. Williams has analyzed possible shifts in saliency and intensity of his value-orientation categories in his "Changing Value Orientations and Beliefs on the American Scene," in *The Character of Americans: A Book of Readings,* rev. ed., Michael McGiffert, ed. (Homewood, Ill.: Dorsey Press, 1970), pp. 212–230. The Yankel-

less you can recognize the significant differences, you cannot hope to cope effectively in a communicative sense with the conflicts and controversies such cultural discrepancies are almost certain to generate. Unless you can discover common ground between and among them, your best communicative efforts will almost surely be doomed to failure.

The audience's attitude toward the speaker. The attitude which an audience will have toward you as a speaker will be based in part upon *(a)* your known reputation and, in part, upon *(b)* your behavior during the speech. Regarding your prior reputation, two factors are especially important: (1) the degree of your listeners' *friendliness* toward you, and (2) the degree of their *respect* for you and your knowledge of the subject. The potency of these factors may vary widely. A mother's affection for her small son, for instance, may be very strong; but her respect for her son's judgment may not be. On the other hand, the mother may have the greatest respect for the judgment of a neighbor even though she dislikes her as a person. Respect and friendliness are two different attitudes, but as a speaker you must take both into account.

Regardless of your prior reputation, as you begin to speak and throughout the entire time you are talking, the audience consciously or subconsciously assesses you from many points of view. Among other things, they ask: (1) Are you a *competent* speaker? Do you give evidence of intelligence and expertise? (2) Are you *admirable?* Do you appear to be a good person? (3) Are you *trustworthy?* Do you seem honest, just, fair, and sincere? (4) Are you *dynamic?* Are you energetic, alert mentally? (5) Are you *potent?* Do you seem to have strength and firmness? The audience does not demand perfection in all of these respects; indeed, some will be more important in one situation than in another. Rather, these are various *dimensions* of behavior, each of which can influence the audience's attitude toward you as a speaker. Collectively, these factors point up the need to know your subject thoroughly, to respect your audience, and to deliver your speech with sincerity and vigor.

The audience's attitude toward the subject. People are *interested* in a subject, or they are *apathetic* about it. In either case, the orientation of their interests will have considerable impact on their perception of and

---

ovich public-opinion survey reported in Otis M. Walter and Robert L. Scott, *Thinking and Speaking: A Guide to Intelligent Oral Communication,* 3rd ed. (New York: The Macmillan Company, 1973), pp. 110–111, indicated that most Americans who were surveyed ascribed to the values of hard work, thrift, strength of character, organized religion, competition, private property, law and order, and compromise as essential for progress. See also Frank E. Armbruster, *The Forgotten Americans: A Survey of the Values, Beliefs and Concerns of the Majority* (New Rochelle, N.Y.: Arlington House, Inc., 1972).

response to a communication. Some researchers place *prior audience atti-tude* among the most crucial variables that determine speaking success.[9] If, for instance, the listeners are unfavorably disposed toward the speaker's subject or purpose, they may: *(a)* distort the substance of the message, *(b)* psychologically or physically leave the field, *(c)* discredit the communicator, or *(d)* use a host of similar defense mechanisms to avoid accurate perception of the speaker's intent and message-content.

Apathy or neutrality is usually present in an audience if its members see no connection between the speaker's subject and their own affairs. When your analysis indicates that your listeners will be apathetic, you will need to show them how they are directly concerned with the problem you are discussing; or you will need to arouse their curiosity about some novel aspect of the subject. Utilize all available means for holding and involving their attention. (See pages 205–211.) Even when members of your audience are already interested, you cannot neglect entirely the problems of commanding and holding attention; but when your listeners are apathetic, you must make a special effort to retain their interest.

Interest (or the lack of it) is only one aspect of an audience's attitude toward your subject. *Expectancy* is another. For example, as soon as we hear that a speech will be about the Gay Lib movement, we begin to form favorable or unfavorable attitudes toward the speaker and the subject. As a general rule, the more the listeners know about your subject or the stronger the beliefs they hold concerning it, the more likely they are to have well-defined expectations. Very often these expectations are troublesome, for frequently they operate as listening barriers or as filters which distort the meanings that your audience assigns to your message. The introduction of your speech presents a special opportunity to create or to correct the expectations which the audience should hold. Throughout the entire time you are talking, however, the problem of listener expectation must be borne in mind and adaptations made accordingly.

The audience's attitude toward the speech purpose. If, with no pre-liminaries at all, you told the members of your audience the specific purpose of your speech, what would be their reaction or response? This "attitude toward speech purpose" is not the frame of mind you hope your audience will hold at the end of your speech, but rather the

---

[9]See, for example, Muzafer Sherif and Carl I. Hovland, *Social Judgment* (New Haven, Conn.: Yale University Press, 1961).

one that exists *before you begin*. Since audience predisposition is seldom uniform, many different shades of attitude may be represented. It is best, therefore, to determine—by prior analysis, if possible—what attitude is *predominant* and to adapt your speech to that view while making allowances for variations in the character or intensity of listener belief.

When the general end of your speech is *to entertain* or *to inform*, the attitude of your listeners toward either of these purposes will be governed largely by their attitude toward the subject; that is: *(a)* interested or *(b)* apathetic. When your general purpose is *to persuade*, the listeners' attitude toward the speech purpose will be governed also by their attitude toward the specific belief or action which is urged; hence, their attitude will be one of the following: *(a)* favorable but not aroused; *(b)* apathetic to the situation; *(c)* interested in the situation but undecided what to do or think about it; *(d)* interested in the situation but hostile to the *proposed* attitude, belief, or action; or *(e)* hostile to any change from the present state of affairs.[10]

Having determined the predominant attitude of your audience toward your subject and purpose, you should be guided by this knowledge in selecting your arguments and determining the structure and content of your message. If your listeners are apathetic, begin your speech on a point of compelling interest or startling vividness; show them how your subject affects them. If they are hostile to the proposal, you may wish to introduce it more cautiously, emphasize some basic principle with which you know they agree, and relate your proposal to it. If they are interested but undecided, provide plenty of proof in the form of factual illustrations, testimony, and statistics. If they are favorable but not aroused, try to motivate them by using appeals which touch directly their desires for pleasure, independence, power, creativity, ego-satisfaction, and the like. (See pages 228–234 in Chapter 11.)

No analysis of an audience made prior to a speech is certain to be fully correct; and even if it is, audience attitudes may change even while you are speaking.[11] Hence, you must watch listeners' reactions

---

[10]Traditionally, it has been assumed that audiences hostile to the speaker's proposal or opposed to any change in the existing state of affairs are most difficult to persuade. For qualifications of this point of view, however, see Wayne N. Thompson, *Quantitative Studies in Public Address and Communication* (New York: Random House, Inc., 1967), pp. 38–39.

[11]Often such changes during the course of a speech are dramatic. See Robert D. Brooks and Thomas M. Scheidel, "Speech as Process: A Case Study," *Speech Monographs* XXXV (March 1968): 1–7.

closely when your subject is announced and continue to do so throughout your entire speech. The way your hearers sit in their seats, the expressions on their faces, their audible reactions — laughter, applause, shifting about, whispering, etc. — all are clues to their attitude toward you, your subject, or your purpose. The conscientious communicator will develop a keen sensitivity to these signs of *feedback* on the part of the audience and will adapt his or her remarks accordingly.[12]

Analyzing the speech occasion

To this point, we have emphasized the necessity of analyzing the *audience* for whom your speech is designed. An equally important aspect of your preparation is an analysis of the *occasion* on which you will be speaking. (Indeed, aspects of the two are often inseparable.) In making such an analysis, you should consider carefully and in some detail the following key questions:

What are the nature and purpose of the occasion? Is yours a voluntary or a captive audience? A voluntary audience attends a speechmaking event primarily because of their interest in the speaker or the subject. A captive audience is required to attend, perhaps at the explicit instruction of the boss or under threat of a failing grade for course work. In general, the more "captive" your audience, the less initial interest they will show and the greater will be their resistance to accepting your information or point of view.

Are people interested in learning more about your subject, in taking some positive action concerning it, or have they perhaps come to heckle or embarrass you? Are your subject and purpose in line with the reason for the meeting, or are you merely seizing the occasion to present some ideas which you think are important? Are you one in a series of speakers whom the audience has heard over a period of weeks or months? If so, how does your speech subject relate to those subjects which have been previously presented? These also are important questions you will need to answer when you are analyzing the nature and purpose of the occasion.

What rules or customs will prevail? Will there be a regular order of business or a fixed program into which your speech must fit? Is it the custom of the group to ask questions of the speaker after the address? Do the listeners expect a formal or informal speaking manner?

---

[12]On adapting to feedback, see Paul D. Holtzman, *The Psychology of Speakers' Audiences* (Glenview, Ill.: Scott, Foresman and Company, 1969), pp. 33 – 36, 117.

Will you, as the speaker, be expected to extend complimentary remarks to some person or persons or to express respect for some traditional institution or concept? Knowing these facts will help you avoid feeling out of place and will prevent you from arousing antagonism by some inappropriate word or action.

What will precede and follow your speech? At what time of day or night will your speech be given? Immediately after a heavy meal or a long program, both of which may induce drowsiness and reduce listener interest? Just before the principal address or event of the evening? By whom and in what manner will you be introduced to the audience? What other items are on the program? What are their tone and character? All these things will, of course, influence the interest the audience may have in your speech. In some instances, you will be able to use the other events on the program to increase interest or belief in your own remarks; sometimes they will work against you. In any case, you must always consider the effect which the program as a whole may have on your speech.

What will be the physical conditions affecting the occasion? Will your speech be given out-of-doors or in an auditorium? Is weather likely to be hot or cold? Will the audience be sitting or standing; and, if sitting, will the members be crowded together or scattered about? In how large a room will the speech be presented? Will an electronic public-address system be used? Will facilities be provided for the audiovisual reinforcements you will use, or must you bring your own? Will you be seen and heard easily? Are there likely to be disturbances in the form of noise or interruptions from the outside? These and similar environmental factors have an effect on the temper of the audience, their span of attention, and the style of speaking you will have to employ as you make adjustments to the speech environment or situation.

A SAMPLE ANALYSIS OF AN AUDIENCE AND OCCASION

Keeping in mind the foregoing guidelines for analyzing audiences and speech occasions, study the following step-by-step analysis prepared by a coed for a speech on behalf of an intercollegiate athletic program for women. Observe how the speaker used the facts at her disposal to draw a picture of the persons making up the audience she would confront, and how she planned to adapt her remarks to their concerns and attitudes:

I. *Title:* FROM SPECTATOR TO PARTICIPANT: ATHLETICS FOR WOMEN.
II. *Subject:* Intercollegiate Athletic Competition for Women Students.
III. *General Purpose:* To actuate.
IV. *Specific Purpose:* To get the Board in Charge of Intercollegiate Athletics to institute a program of intercollegiate sports for women students.
V. *Specific Audience:* The Board in Charge of Intercollegiate Athletics, consisting of the Director of Athletics, the Assistant Director of Athletics, Director of Men's Intramural Sports, Director of Women's Intramural Sports, six coaches of men's varsity sports, five elected faculty members, and five elected student representatives. One intramural director, one faculty member, and one student representative are women.
VI. *Analysis of Occasion:*
   A. *Nature:* Annual meeting of the Board to approve the budget for the coming year.
   B. *Prevailing Rules:* A strict time limit of five minutes for every speech made to the Board, plus any time needed for questions by Board members.
   C. *Precedents and Consequences:* Speech will be given late in the afternoon, after Board has heard many other requests. Board members probably will be tired. After all requests have been heard, the Board will still have to draw up the budget.
   D. *Physical Environment:* Board will meet at tables set up in an auxiliary gymnasium, surrounded by athletic equipment.
VII. *Analysis of Audience:*
   A. *Composition:*
      1. *Size:* Twenty Board members, plus additional spectators.
      2. *Age:* Five members are of college age; fifteen members are between 30 and 55.
      3. *Sex:* Seventeen males, three females.
      4. *Occupation:* Collegiate personnel with special interests and qualifications in athletics.
      5. *Education:* One third were physical education majors in college, most with advanced degrees; one third are undergraduates; one third are Ph.D.'s in arts or sciences.
      6. *Membership in groups:* All are members of Board as well as of general academic community. The factors influencing both groups can be made salient in the speech.
      7. *Cultural-Ethnic Background:* Two Board members are black (but this not a factor here).
   B. *Knowledge of Subject:* Board members have:
      1. Specialized knowledge of nature of intercollegiate competi-

tion in sports.

    2. General knowledge of present women's intramural athletic program.

    3. Probable knowledge of current campus controversy over question of an intercollegiate sports program for women.

  C. *Beliefs, Attitudes, and Values:*

    1. *Political:* Board is undoubtedly aware of general charge of sexism in the athletic program and wishes to avoid politicizing its functions.

    2. *Professional:* Board members believe strongly in values of college athletics generally.

    3. *Economic:* Board undoubtedly is worried about increased cost of intercollegiate athletic program, yet well aware that a portion of its money comes from student fees.

  D. *Attitude Toward Speaker:* Probably suspicious.

  E. *Attitude Toward Subject:* Interest mixed with uneasiness and uncertainty about extent and nature of program to be proposed.

  F. *Attitude Toward Speech Purpose:* Most Board members are probably undecided; a few may be hostile.

VIII. *Proposed Adaptation to Audience and Occasion:*

  A. Introduce speech with thanks for fine intramural program now available to women. Make reference to surrounding facilities and equipment.

  B. Keep language of speech positive, but not so strong as to polarize neutral or undecided listeners.

  C. Stress primarily the values of intercollegiate competition for women. Mention—but with this predominantly male audience, do not overemphasize—the matter of equality between the sexes.

  D. Show a knowledge of the financial problems faced by the Board. Ask only for women's field and track competition for coming year, with more sports to be added later. Demonstrate how maximum participation may be realized at minimum cost.

  E. Be prepared to answer Board's possible questions concerning number of women interested, neighboring schools which could furnish competition, estimated cost of proposed program, available locker-room facilities, equipment, etc.

Gathering the speech material

Having carefully considered the subject and purpose of your speech and analyzed the audience and occasion, you are now ready to begin gathering your material. Ordinarily you will start by drawing together what you already know about the subject and deciding roughly what ideas you want to include. Nearly always, however, you will find that what you already know is not enough. You will need to gather additional information—facts, illustrations, stories, and examples—with which you can develop your speech. Some of this information may be acquired through interviews and conversations with persons who know something that you do not know about the subject. Other materials will be gathered from newspapers, magazines, books, and government documents, or will come from radio or television programs. In particular, such sources as the "News of the Week in Review" section of *The New York Times, U.S. News and World Report, Wall Street Journal, Harper's,* and *The Observer* should be consulted by a speaker who plans to deal with a current question of public interest. Many magazines of general interest are indexed in the *Readers' Guide to Periodical Literature;* numerous encyclopedias, yearbooks, government reports, and other reference materials will be found in your college library.

Making an outline

Early in your preparation you may want to make a rough sketch of the points you wish to include in your speech. A complete outline, however, cannot be drawn up until you have gathered all of the necessary material. When this material is at hand, set down in final order the principal points you expect to present, together with the subordinate ideas which will be necessary to explain or to prove these points.

In Chapter 7, you will find a number of specific patterns by which the ideas in a speech may be arranged. There, too, you will find the form which a complete outline should take. For the present, remember two simple but important rules: (1) arrange your ideas in a clear and systematic order, and (2) preserve the unity of your speech by making sure that each point is directly related to your specific purpose.

A SAMPLE OUTLINE

Notice in the following sample outline the clear and orderly manner in which the speaker describes the responsibilities of a school newspaper staff. Observe also that instead of wandering off into a vague discussion of the characteristics of a good editor or the necessity for adequate sponsorship, the speaker holds strictly to the announced purpose of explaining the division of responsibility on a school newspaper staff.

Such clarity of organization, unity of subject matter, and tenacity of purpose will make the speech easy to understand and remember.

SPECIFIC PURPOSE: To explain the duties of a college newspaper staff.

I. To produce a successful college newspaper requires the exacting performance of specific duties by a publisher, editor, advertising manager, circulation manager, production manager, and faculty adviser.
   A. The publisher's duties include:
      1. Setting broad policy guidelines for the newspaper to follow.
      2. Keeping the paper on a sound financial footing.
   B. The editor's duties include:
      1. Selecting members of the editorial staff.
      2. Making assignments to reporters.
      3. Planning the page layouts.
      4. Supervising the preparation of copy.
   C. The advertising manager's duties include:
      1., 2., 3. *(develop as above)*
   D. The circulation manager's duties include:
      1., 2., 3. *(develop as above)*
   E. The production manager's duties include:
      1., 2., 3. *(develop as above)*
   F. The faculty adviser's duties include:
      1., 2., 3. *(develop as above)*

Summary: *(Important duties of each of the above-named staff members briefly reviewed.)*

Practicing aloud

With your outline completed, you are ready for the final step in preparation: practicing your speech for oral presentation. You probably will find that the best method is to talk the outline through aloud, following the planned sequence of ideas. Do this until you have learned this sequence thoroughly and until you can express each idea clearly and fluently. Then, laying the outline aside, think the speech through silently, point by point, to make certain that the ideas are fixed in your mind. Next, go through the speech aloud once again, but this time do not look at the outline at all. On your first oral trial you may inadvertently omit some points and interchange others, but do not let this worry you. Practice until all the ideas are expressed in their proper order and until the words flow easily. The more surely you command your material, the more poise and confidence you will have as you stand before the audience. The self-assurance every speaker desires comes in large measure from always knowing exactly what to say next.

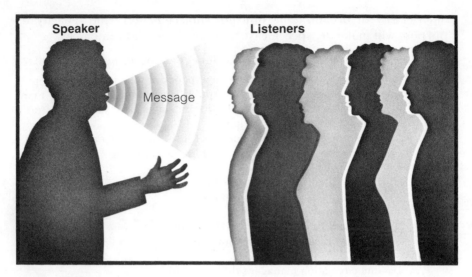

Speaker

Listeners

Message

Figure 2. Communicating in Public

When you can go through the speech several times without forgetting any point or without hesitating unduly in putting your thoughts into words, you may consider your preparation completed. As you practice speaking from your outline, however, preserve a mental image of your listeners and project your speech as though you were actually talking to them. The good speaker talks *with* people, not *at* them.

To summarize, then, the planning and preparation of a speech requires six specific steps in three general areas:

Surveying the problem	1. Selecting and narrowing the subject. 2. Determining the purpose. 3. Analyzing the audience and the occasion.
Building the speech	4. Gathering material. 5. Making an outline.
Practicing the speech	6. Putting your ideas into words and practicing the speech aloud.

It may not always be possible, or perhaps even advisable, to arrange your work in the precise order recommended here. Of course, you will always have to survey the problem before you can start building your speech, and you will have to build the speech before you can practice it, but the order in which you take up the steps within each of these general areas should remain flexible.[13] For example, sometimes your analysis of the audience will determine your selection of a subject and, therefore, step 3 will precede rather than follow step 1.

A SAMPLE STUDENT SPEECH

The following speech by Joyce Miller, a senior at the University of Iowa, was prepared to fulfill an assignment similar to Speaking Assignment 3 at the end of this chapter.

Mrs. Miller chose to discuss "Why Ice Floats" not only because it reflected one of her own interests as a chemistry major, but also because the subject met three other requirements of a good speech: (1) it was something she could talk about with confidence; (2) it was appropriate to the occasion — the warm June afternoon on which the speech was delivered; and (3) it could be covered adequately in the time allotted. The specific purpose of the talk as stated on the prepared outline was: "To get my listeners to understand why ice floats."

Why Ice Floats[14]
Joyce Miller

On these hot summer days, there's nothing I like better than a tall glass of iced tea. Now, I'd be willing to wager almost anything that when I put an ice cube in my tea, it will float at the top of the glass rather than settle to the bottom. This shouldn't surprise any of you.

But do you know *why* ice floats? "That's easy!" you say. "Because ice is less dense, and therefore lighter than water." But why is ice less dense than water? We know that as a rule compounds expand when heated, and contract when cooled. We observe this phenomenon every time we look at a thermometer and see the mercury rise with the temperature. In very hot weather, the concrete on our highways expands until it buckles and cracks. On the other hand, butter and shortenings, gasolines

---

[13]For detailed examples of the preparation process applied to extemporaneous speeches, see Janice W. Noyes and Charles W. Dickson, Jr., *Core Knowledge for Successful Speech: A Workbook in Oral Communication* (Glenview, Ill.: Scott, Foresman and Company, 1969), Part IV, "Samples of Complete Speech Preparations."

[14]Presented June 26, 1967. Text supplied through the courtesy of Mrs. Miller.

and oils all contract when they solidify. Water, too, expands with heat and, upon cooling, contracts at all temperatures except for the range between 0° centigrade and 4° centigrade, where it acts in an exactly opposite manner. Why, then, is water so different from other compounds in this temperature range?

The answer to this question lies in a phenomenon known as *hydrogen bonding*. To understand hydrogen bonding, we must look at the structure of a water molecule. As you undoubtedly know, a molecule of water consists of two atoms of hydrogen and one atom of oxygen. The two hydrogen atoms are attached to the oxygen in such a way that they form an angle of approximately 105°. In fact, a molecule of water looks a little bit like Yogi Bear, his face being the oxygen atom and his two ears stuck out at the 105° angle being the hydrogen atoms.

Because oxygen is a larger atom than the hydrogen, and also for other reasons founded in chemical bonding theories, the oxygen side of the molecule has a slightly negative charge, while the hydrogen side bears a slightly positive one. Now, we all know that like charges repel and unlike charges attract. Therefore, the slightly negative oxygen side of one molecule is attracted toward the slightly positive hydrogen side of a neighboring molecule. This attraction between molecules is known as hydrogen bonding. Hydrogen bonding occurs to a certain extent in water at all temperatures; and heat must be applied to break these bonds, which explains the high boiling point of water when compared with boiling points of chemically similar compounds. When water turns to vapor, all the hydrogen bonds have been broken.

Picture, if you can, fifty members of a marching band standing in a tight group. They don't take up a great deal of space. But when the drum major blows his whistle and says, "Line up," everyone takes his place — with one man in front, one behind, and one on either side, and with a specified distance between them. Now the fifty members of the band are spread out and take up much more space.

The same thing happens in a group of water molecules when water is freezing. The drum major says, "All right, you molecules, line up," and they do. Each molecule of water now is surrounded by four other molecules arranged so that the oxygen atom of one molecule is next to the hydrogen atoms of its neighbor, thus forming a pyramid-shaped crystal with an empty space in the middle. As the ice thus spreads out and takes up more room, it becomes less dense and floats. The molecules begin lining up at a temperature of 4° centigrade and continue lining up until all the molecules are lined up at the temperature of 0° centigrade and the water is frozen. Actually, ice expands to a volume 9% greater than the volume of water. In other words, if you want to freeze 10 quarts of water in a closed container, it would be well to have a container with a volume of 11 quarts.

Finally, let us reverse the process by taking a piece of the ice out of our tea and applying some heat to it. As we do so, some of the hydrogen bonds will be broken and the molecules set free so that they can squeeze more closely together. As a result, the liquid becomes denser than the ice crystals it replaces. This process continues until the temperature of 4° centigrade is reached, the temperature at which water is the densest. At this point, the water begins to act as most other compounds do and expands with increasing temperature.

This is why the ice cube always floats in your glass of iced tea.

Sources

L. B. Leopold, K. S. Davis, and the Editors of *Life*, "Water," *Life Science Library* (New York: Time, Inc., 1966).

W. J. Moore, *Physical Chemistry*, 3rd ed. (Englewood Cliffs, N.J.: Prentice-Hall, Inc., 1962).

C. R. Noller, *Textbook of Organic Chemistry*, 2nd ed. (Philadelphia: W. B. Saunders Company, 1958).

PROBLEMS FOR FURTHER STUDY

1. Assume you are a sanitary engineer specializing in air-pollution control. Describe how you would go about explaining or defending your activities to the following audiences: *(a)* the Chamber of Commerce, some members of which are manufacturers whose firms resisted smoke-control ordinances; *(b)* a high-school ecology class; *(c)* the League of Women Voters; and *(d)* a church-sponsored club of retired men and women. Indicate the general and specific purpose of the speech you would present in each of these four instances, and suggest the particular ideas you would plan to incorporate in each of these speeches. Suggest an appropriate title for each speech.

2. Select a suitable subject and use it to frame a specific purpose for a five-minute speech to persuade *(a)* an audience that is favorable but not aroused, *(b)* an audience that is interested but undecided, *(c)* an audience that is apathetic, *(d)* an audience that is hostile toward the proposition or recommendation, and *(e)* an audience that is opposed to any change from the present situation.

3. Using as a guide the various factors listed in the outline on pages 54–55, make a complete audience analysis of the members of your speech class. Perhaps your instructor will help by having each student prepare a "value-ladder," a pencil-and-paper survey in which he or she

ranks a series of value concepts (e.g., equal justice, public truth, love, belongingness, scientific investigation, law and order, humaneness, wealth, sincerity, etc.). For other useful lists, see again page 48 and also the Rokeach and Lystad material cited in "Suggestions for Further Reading" at the close of this chapter. Your instructor will collect the rankings, calculate the average scores, and present the results so that you may include them in your audience analysis. Record the completed analysis in your journal and use it in selecting topics and purposes for future classroom speeches.

4. Prepare carefully a "belief/attitude/value" analysis on the topic of your next speech. That is, inventory as clearly as possible your own beliefs, attitudes, and general values as they will affect what you plan to say. Where might they be coincident or divergent with those of your audience members? How will you reconcile potential differences, and how will you use whatever common ground you have with them? Does the concept of *audience adaptation* mean that you must "sell out" your own beliefs, attitudes, and values? What kinds of commitments are entailed in examining yourself and others before speaking?

5. Attend a speech — campaign speech, campus lecture, church service, etc. — and analyze the speaker's adaptational strategies. What methods were employed for establishing rapport and increasing credibility? What attempts did the speaker make to seek out values consistent with those presumably held by the audience, and to use factual and authoritative materials gathered with this particular audience in mind? You probably cannot cover all of the speaker's strategies in a single analysis, so select certain of these aspects of adaptation for your observation, and report what you find in a paper, your journal, and/or a class discussion.

6. Come to class prepared to discuss the general topic, "The Ideal Physical Arrangements for a Public Speech." Consider such factors as: the size of the room in relation to the size of the audience; the arrangement of chairs around the speaker's stand; the type of chairs in which the listeners sit; the distance between the speaker and the audience; the advisability of positioning the speaker on a platform which raises him or her above the level of the listeners; the acoustics; the lighting arrangements; the ventilation; and the decoration of the room in relation to the subject of the speech. If the class can arrive at a consensus on some of these factors, ask yourselves "Why are certain physical arrangements preferred?"

ORAL ACTIVITIES AND SPEAKING ASSIGNMENTS

1. Hold a small group discussion (45–60 minutes in length) on the question: "To what degree is the conflict in value-orientations between mem-

bers of the so-called Establishment and the Counterculture serious, significant for communication, and reducible?" As partial preparation, read some of the sources listed in footnotes to this chapter and in "Suggestions for Further Reading."

2. The class will be divided into four-person groups before the next round of speeches. Meet with the other members of your group, and talk to them about the upcoming speeches — topics, general and specific purposes, developments of propositions, useful kinds of supporting materials, and the like. Criticize each other's plans and preparation, offering suggestions for changes and more specific adaptations to this particular audience. After thus discussing your speech with a portion of your audience, you should be in a better position to present a successful message to the entire class.

3. Following the principles and guidelines set forth in this chapter, prepare and present a three- or four-minute speech on a subject chosen by you and approved by your instructor. In the preparation, be sure to draw information from *at least three (3) printed sources* for the purpose of supplementing your personal knowledge of the subject. Narrow the focus of your speech by selecting the one or two aspects of the subject that you feel would be of greatest interest and appeal to your classmates.

SUGGESTIONS FOR FURTHER READING

Aristotle, *Rhetoric*, II.1 – 17. The classic statement on character, emotions, and kinds of men provides a still-interesting, insightful view of audiences.

Paul D. Holtzman, *The Psychology of Speakers' Audiences* (Glenview, Ill.: Scott, Foresman and Company, 1970). A work particularly strong in its use of demographic audience analysis.

Mary Lystad, *As They See It: Changing Values of College Youth* (Cambridge, Mass.: Schenkman Publishing Co., Inc., 1973). An attempt to describe and assess the roots and routes of changing values.

Howard H. Martin, "Communication Settings," in *Speech-Communication: Analysis and Readings*, ed. Howard H. Martin and Kenneth A. Andersen (Boston: Allyn & Bacon, Inc., 1968), pp. 58 – 84. A useful consideration of the factors over which a speaker has control in various communication settings.

Milton Rokeach, *The Open and Closed Mind* (New York: Basic Books, Inc., Publishers, 1960), Chapters I – IV, "The Theory and Measurement of Belief Systems," pp. 3 – 100. A useful, referential basis for preparing the "value-ladder" called for in Problem 3, pages 61 – 62.

Chapter 4

Using the body to communicate

THE EFFECTIVENESS of your speaking depends both on what you say and on how you say it. Without solid content, you will not have anything worth communicating; without effective delivery, you cannot transmit your thoughts clearly and vividly to others. Just as a pitcher can give a ball direction and power by the way he throws it, so you can give your speech strength and vitality by the manner of your delivery.

The best single assurance of good delivery is straightforward sincerity. Effectiveness does not depend on applying mechanically a predetermined set of rules; it comes from practice under the direction of a competent instructor who can help you smooth out rough spots and develop points of strength.

Since in the usual speaking situation the audience both sees and hears the speaker, a consideration of delivery involves two basic elements: the speaker's *physical behavior on the platform* (the subject of the present chapter), and the speaker's *use of the voice* (the subject of Chapter 5).

ASPECTS OF NONVERBAL COMMUNICATION

In recent years a growing body of research has emphasized anew the important role that physical or nonverbal behavior plays in effective oral communication.[1] When you communicate orally, recognize that

---

[1] See, for example, Haig Bosmajian, ed., *The Rhetoric of Nonverbal Communication* (Glenview, Ill.: Scott, Foresman and Company, 1971); Paul Ekman, "Differential Communication of Affect by Head and Body Cues," *Journal of Personality and Social Psychology* II (November 1965): 726–735; Julius Fast, *Body Language* (New York: M. Evans & Co., Inc., 1970); Edward T. Hall, *The Silent Language* (New York: Doubleday & Company, Inc., 1959); Mark L. Knapp, *Nonverbal Communication in Human Interaction* (New York: Holt, Rinehart & Winston, Inc., 1972); Albert Mehrabian, "Communication Without Words," *Psychology Today* II (September 1968): 52–55; B. G. Rosenberg and Jonas Langer, "A Study of Postural-Gestural Communication," *Journal of Personality and Social Psychology* II (October 1965): 593–597.

your listeners read meanings into your facial expression, into the way you stand and walk, and into what you do with your head, arms, shoulders, and hands. Often a slight shrug of the shoulder or an expressive movement of the hand is more revealing than a hundred words. Moreover, listeners are quick to see any discrepancy between your actions and your ideas. Vigorous ideas expressed in a languid manner, or trivial ideas propounded with great force or dignity produce an unconvincing if not ludicrous effect. Finally, remember that since, as a speaker, you are seen before you are heard, it is through visual rather than auditory impressions that the audience makes its initial estimate of your sincerity, your friendliness, and your energy.[2]

Contact with the audience

In their classic study of nonverbal communication, psychologists Jurgen Ruesch and Weldon Kees assert: "All cooperative activities begin with the acknowledgement of the participants' perception of each other; this marks the signal for subsequent communicative exchanges."[3] The first thing you must do, therefore, when addressing an audience is to make its members feel that you are talking to them personally. Listeners are repelled by a speaker who seems unaware of their identity as individuals. They value a sense of close personal relationship, such as exists in an informal conversation.[4]

As a means of establishing personal contact with an audience, nothing is quite so important as the simple device of looking at individuals directly. For this reason, reading a speech or even using notes too obviously invariably detracts from a speaker's effectiveness. Since it is impossible to look at each member of the audience at the same time, do as you would in an informal conversation: Pick out one person and talk directly to him or her for a few seconds, looking your listener in the

---

[2]See N. Compton, "Personal Attributes of Color and Design Preferences in Clothing Fabrics," *Journal of Psychology* LIV (1962): 191–195; G. Thornton, "The Effect of Wearing Glasses Upon Judgments of Personality Traits of Persons Seen Briefly," *Journal of Applied Psychology* XXVIII (1944): 203–207.

[3]Jurgen Ruesch and Weldon Kees, *Nonverbal Communication: Notes on the Visual Perception of Human Relations* (Berkeley: University of California Press, 1964), p. 82. For an interesting treatment of nonverbal communication and particularly eye behavior, see Flora Davis, "How to Read Body Language," *Glamour* (1969); reprinted in Bosmajian, ed., *The Rhetoric of Nonverbal Communication*, pp. 5–6.

[4]Steven A. Beebe, "Eye Contact: A Nonverbal Determinant of Speaker Credibility," *The Speech Teacher* XXIII (January 1974): 21–25.

eye as you do so; then shift to someone else. Be careful, however, that you pick out people in various parts of the audience, and that you stay with each one long enough to avoid the appearance of simply pivoting or wagging your head.

Posture

In speech delivery, posture is of prime importance. How do you stand when you talk to people? Are you erect? comfortable? alert? Does your position seem natural, or does it call attention to itself because it is awkward or unusual? There is no one best way to stand when delivering a speech, but there are several errors which you should avoid. Do not cower behind a speaker's stand or slouch to one side of it. Stand erect behind it or move away from it altogether. Avoid letting the weight of your body fall on your heels; let it rest on the balls of your feet. Avoid bouncing up and down or swaying from side to side. Stand so that you are comfortable without being slouchy, erect without being inflexible or stiff. Give the impression that you are awake and "on your toes." Show the self-assurance which comes only when you are in command of the situation and of yourself.[5]

Bodily movement

The eye instinctively follows moving objects and focuses upon them. A speaker can often awaken a sleepy audience by the simple expedient of shifting from one part of the platform to another. As long as your movement is natural, easy, and purposeful, it will help you hold attention, maintain interest, and convey your thoughts more clearly.

How much movement about the platform is desirable? How often should you change your position? The best guide is to follow your natural impulses. Move about when you feel a desire to do so. Of course, you should avoid continuous and aimless pacing back and forth. But you should also avoid standing glued to a single spot throughout your entire speech. If you are earnestly trying to communicate an important idea to an audience, sooner or later you will feel the desire to move. It will seem natural to change your position as a means of letting your

---

[5]See F. Deutsch, "Analysis of Postural Behavior," *Psychoanalytic Quarterly* XVI (1947): 195–213; W. James, "A Study of the Expression of Bodily Posture," *Journal of General Psychology* VII (1932): 405–436; Albert Mehrabian, "Significance of Posture and Position in the Communication of Attitude and Status Relationships," *Psychological Bulletin* LXXI (1969): 359–372; Ruesch and Kees, *Nonverbal Communication*, p. 38.

hearers know that you have finished one idea and are ready to start another, or to step forward as a means of stressing an important point.

Remember also that the way you walk to the platform and the way you leave it are important. Instead of ambling up to the speaker's stand in a nonchalant, meandering fashion, walk briskly and purposefully. Let your manner show confidence; do not tiptoe timidly, as though you were afraid the audience might see or hear you. Once in position, do not begin your speech immediately. Take time to compose your thoughts and to look at your listeners; *then* begin to talk. When you have finished speaking, do not rush to your seat. Pause at the end of your talk long enough to let your final words take effect; then walk off in a relaxed but dignified way.

Finally, not only when and how you move, but where you stand or come to rest may enhance or impair the effectiveness of your message. In their study of nonverbal behavior, Ruesch and Kees point out that in appraising the friendliness and warmth of others, physical distance provides us with major clues. If you stand too close to persons, you may offend them by invading their sense of "privacy" or personal "space," whereas standing too far away frequently lends an air of indifference or impersonality to your talk.[6] In general, it is a good idea to speak from a position fairly close to your listeners; and when you come to a point you particularly want to emphasize, take another step or two forward. Except under very unusual circumstances, you should never back away from an audience. Nor, as a rule, should you stand behind a table, desk, or lectern that blocks the audience's view of you. Often, objects such as these not only restrict your movements, but they also erect major psychological barriers to full and free communication. In sum, the visual channel between you and your listeners must be kept constantly open.

Gestures

Gestures may be used to clarify or to emphasize the ideas in a message. By gestures we mean *purposeful* movements of some part of the body—head, shoulders, arms, or hands—to reinforce or demonstrate what is said.[7] Fidgeting with coat buttons or aimlessly rearranging books or

---

[6]Ruesch and Kees, *Nonverbal Communication*, p. 82. See also Hall, *The Silent Language*, p. 163.

[7]In this connection, see Michael Argyle, *Social Interaction* (New York: Lieber-Atherton, Incorporated, 1969).

papers on the speaker's table are not gestures; they are not purposeful, and they distract rather than support the ideas you are expressing.

Gestures have aptly been described as "silent words."[8] They serve as "shorthand" ways of communicating matters which it would take many words to express. A simple experiment will demonstrate how important gestures are to communication. Think of a location—a possible destination—several blocks away. Then try to give directions to a stranger who wants to find the place. Notice how necessary it is to point the way and to show turns in the route by movements of the hands, arms, or head. Or observe two persons in a heated argument and notice how often their hands come into play to emphasize the points they are making.

Besides their usefulness as shorthand methods of clarifying and stressing ideas, gestures—like other movements—are valuable in helping to capture and hold listeners' attention. Just as we watch more readily the speaker who occasionally changes position rather than the one who remains rooted in a single spot, so we listen with greater attention to the communicator whose verbal and gestural messages coincide and reinforce one another. Unless a speaker compensates for the lack of gestures by unusually compelling ideas or rich and colorful language, listeners tend to respond sluggishly, even indifferently, to the essential message. On the other hand, a physically active speaker usually is able to stimulate more lively attention and sustain the interest of an audience.

In emphasizing the importance of gestures, we are not implying that you should deliberately adopt a forceful, dynamic mode of delivery if as a person you are habitually quiet and reserved. Again, as in the case of movement, gestures should spring from an inner impulse and should be a natural and appropriate correlate to the ideas you are communicating. Do not decide in advance that at a certain place in your speech you will point your finger at the audience and, at another time, shake your fist. The effect will be, at best, mechanical; at worst, absurd. If gestures are to be effective, they always must reflect your inner states of earnestness, enthusiasm, or emotion.

Gestures of the hands and arms. Gestures of the hands and arms fall into two broad classes: conventional and descriptive gestures.

---

[8]An interesting discussion of the symbolism of gesture may be found in Maurice H. Krout, "The Symbolism of Objects and Movements," *Introduction to Social Psychology* (New York: Harper & Row, Publishers, 1942); reprinted in Bosmajian, *The Rhetoric of Nonverbal Communication,* p. 25.

Conventional gestures are signs or symbols which, though meaningless in themselves, have had meanings assigned to them by convention or custom. Commonly encountered codes or systems of conventional gestures include the hand-and-finger language of deaf-mutes, the arm signals of the football referee, or the arm motions employed by the platoon sergeant in directing his men under fire.[9]

Through long usage certain hand and arm movements employed by public speakers also have acquired conventional meanings. Thus, the pointed finger is usually interpreted as a sign of accusation or challenge; the clenched fist suggests strong feeling; an arm extended with the palm of the hand turned downward is a sign of rejection.

Descriptive gestures, as distinguished from conventional gestures, carry meaning not by common custom or agreement, but because they

---

[9]Mario Pei in *The Story of Language* (New York: J. B. Lippincott Company, 1949) presents some interesting facts concerning the history and use of conventional gestures as systems of sign language. See also Paul Ekman and Wallace V. Friesen, "Hand Movements," *Journal of Communication* XXII (December 1972).

Vigor and naturalness mark the platform manner of Constantine A. Doxiadis, of Athens, Greece, and Washington, D.C., who has written and lectured widely on architecture and city planning. The dynamic speaker was photographed during an appearance at Kendall College, Evanston.

depict or describe more or less directly the idea to be communicated. You may, for example, describe the size, shape, or location of an object by very specific movements of your hands and arms. You may show how vigorous a punch was by striking the air with your fist, the height of a younger brother by holding out your arm, or the details of a complicated manipulation of a toy by performing the manipulative motions required.

Gestures of the head and shoulders. Shrugging the shoulders and shaking the head have the same implications in public speech that they have in conversation; and here, as elsewhere, they are frequently used to help clarify an idea or to lend emphasis. Like arm gestures, moreover, such bodily activities should not be planned or executed consciously. Unless they spring from a genuine desire to communicate more effectively, they will appear artificial or awkward, impairing rather than enhancing the speaker's message.

Facial expressions. Psychologist Albert Mehrabian has devised a formula to account for the emotional impact of a speaker's message. Words, he says, contribute 7 percent, vocal elements 38 percent, and

facial expressions 55 percent.[10] But not only are facial expressions powerful carriers of feelings; they also communicate them with considerable accuracy, regardless of the cultural and educational backgrounds of the receivers. In a carefully controlled study made some years ago, Delwin Dusenbury and Franklin Knower found that, despite significant differences among individuals and groups, the facial expressions associated with emotional tendencies and attitudes often could be interpreted with a high degree of reliability.[11]

Here, as in so many other instances, however, the findings of research merely reinforce what is obvious. Facial expressions — especially when they form part of a total communicative context — reveal much about a speaker's convictions and feelings. Do not plan facial expressions in advance of your message any more than you would plan gestures or the details of other bodily movement. If, however, you are well disposed toward your audience, are genuinely interested in the subject you are discussing, and are enthusiastic about communicating, your face will reflect your state of mind and will help greatly to support the ideas and feelings you express.

Sometimes you may want to make an illustration or a story more vivid by acting and talking as if you yourself were the person directly involved in it. In this imitative process your posture, movements, gestures, and facial expressions are combined to create a picture of the character in the story — to *impersonate* him. Your shoulders droop, and you develop a slight limp; your hand trembles as you knock on the door, and your face shows surprise at what you see when the door opens — together, these actions portray a character and tell what the character is doing. Such detailed imitation or "acting out" of a point, however, should be done only infrequently and with the greatest caution. A representation which is too vivid or dramatic may center the attention of the audience on the action rather than on the idea the speaker is trying to express, and thus defeat its purpose. Moreover, it is essential that

---

[10]Flora Davis, "How to Read Body Language," *Glamour* (1969); reprinted in Bosmajian, ed., *The Rhetoric of Nonverbal Communication*, pp. 5–6. See also Paul Ekman, Wallace V. Friesen, and Phoebe Ellsworth, *Emotion in the Human Face: Guidelines for Research and an Integration of Findings* (New York: Pergamon Press, Inc., 1972); E. C. Izard, *The Face of Emotion* (New York: Appleton-Century-Crofts, 1971).

[11]Delwin Dusenbury and Franklin H. Knower, "Experimental Studies of the Symbolism of Action and Voice — I: A Study of the Specificity of Meaning in Facial Expression," *Quarterly Journal of Speech* XXIV (October 1938): 424–435. See also F. Williams and J. Tolch, "Communication by Facial Expression," *The Journal of Communication* XV (March 1965): 17; J. Tolch, "The Problem of Language and Accuracy in Identification of Facial Expression," *Central States Speech Journal* XIV (February 1963).

you maintain audience contact and that you preserve your image as a thoughtful, responsible person.

Characteristics of good gestures. Although you can perfect your gestures only through practice, you will obtain better results if, as you practice, you keep three characteristics of good gestures in mind: *relaxation, vigor and definiteness,* and *proper timing.*

Relaxation. When your muscles are strained or tense, you have difficulty expressing yourself naturally, and awkward gestures result. One of the best ways to break your tension is to move about. "Warm up" by taking a few easy steps or by unobtrusively arranging your notes or papers. To avoid stiffness and awkwardness, make a conscious effort to relax your muscles *before* you start to speak.

Vigor and definiteness. Good gestures are alive and vigorous. Put enough force into them to make them convincing. A languid shaking of the fist is a poor way to support a threat or issue a challenge; an aimless or hesitant movement of the arm confuses rather than clarifies. Do not pound the table or saw the air constantly; exaggeration of minor points is ludicrous. Vary the nature of your gestures as the ideas in your speech demand, but always make them vigorous enough to show your conviction and enthusiasm.

Timing. The comedian gets many laughs from an audience by mistiming gestures or by timing them in an unexpected way. Try making a gesture after the word or phrase it was intended to reinforce has already been spoken, and observe the ridiculous result. The stroke of a gesture—that is, the shake of the fist, the movement of the finger, or the break of the wrist—should fall exactly on, or should slightly precede, the point the gesture is used to emphasize. If you practice making gestures until they have become habitual and then use them spontaneously as the impulse arises, you will have no trouble on this score. Poor timing is often the result of an attempt to use "canned" or preplanned gestures.

ADAPTING NONVERBAL BEHAVIOR TO THE AUDIENCE AND SUBJECT

Just because a certain type of speech delivery is effective for one subject or with one audience, you must not assume that it will suit all subjects and occasions. Good speakers vary their physical behavior according to the size of their audience, the nature of the ideas they are communicating, and the setting in which the speech is delivered.

These four speakers, though
employing different bodily
movements, are alike in that their
gestures clearly spring
spontaneously from an inner
state or feeling, and enhance the
communication of their ideas
and attitudes.

Clockwise from upper left: Paul Fusco/
MAGNUM PHOTOS; Vilms/JEROBOAM,
INC.; Jerry Shrader/STOCK BOSTON;
Eastern Michigan University Photo.

The size of the audience

Generally speaking, the larger the audience, the broader and more pronounced your gestures should be. What might seem to be a wild swing of the arm to a person close at hand appears quite appropriate to an audience of several hundred. Conversely, small gestures of the arms or slight changes in facial expression, while effective in conversation, seem weak and indefinite to a large group of listeners. By experimenting, you can determine the degree of projection needed.

The nature of the subject and the occasion

Subjects on which feelings run strong or which require weighty and immediate decisions usually motivate speakers to more vigorous bodily action than do subjects which are less moving or crucial. Moreover, occasions such as memorial services or dedications call for dignity of movement as well as of expression, whereas political meetings or pep rallies require more energetic and enthusiastic physical activity.

PRACTICING TO ACHIEVE SKILL IN NONVERBAL COMMUNICATION

In the beginning, you may find that although you recognize fully the role that responsive bodily behavior plays in communicating your ideas and feelings effectively to others, when you actually confront those others, you are restrained or immobile. This is because you still are not as much at home in the speaking situation as you should be. The only sure way to gain the ease in gestural activity and bodily responsiveness you desire is through practice.

Therefore, speak and move and gesture as often as you can; and when you do move and gesture, do not be afraid to let yourself go for fear that you will do something wrong. If your instructor or classmates tell you that you are pacing aimlessly or are using too many gestures, make sure they do not really mean that your movements or gestures lack variety. Instead of reducing the amount of activity, vary it more. Later, after you have gained greater confidence in yourself, you may want to reduce the number of gestures you use, or to move about less frequently. For the present, however, move and gesture as the impulse directs you. With practice you will find that gradually the kind and amount of bodily activity appropriate to you, to your ideas, and to your particular communicative situation will come to you naturally. Your physical behavior as you face your audience will be forgotten and will, without conscious effort on your part, help clarify and reinforce the ideas and feelings you wish to communicate.

PROBLEMS FOR FURTHER STUDY

1. In this chapter the statement was made that words account for 7 percent, vocal elements 38 percent, and facial expression 55 percent of the emotional impact of an oral message. Defend or attack that assertion on the basis of your own experience with communication. In what speech communication situations would you expect these percentages to be largely valid? In what situations would you question them? Further, how might the percentages have to be adjusted when discussing descriptive information rather than matters of emotional impact? Why?

2. Listen to some speaker on the campus or in your community, and write a brief report on your observations regarding his or her platform behavior. Before you attend, make a short outline of the suggestions and warnings contained in this chapter, and use it as a checklist against which to compare the speaker's physical behavior. Your commentary on both strong and weak qualities in the speaker's physical contact with the audience can perhaps be centered on two important questions: (a) Did the speaker's posture, movements, and gestures reinforce or detract from your comprehension of his or her message? (b) Did the speaker's posture, movements, and gestures reinforce or detract from the emotional impact of his or her message? Observe particularly patterns of emphasis, bodily tension, gestures which depicted qualities or shapes, and—in general— movement which seemed to draw in or repel the audience.

3. "Body language" is a term often used to describe much of what is considered in this chapter. Drawing upon "Suggestions for Further Reading," enlarge your understanding of this subject, and prepare a short report for your instructor, your journal, or your class.

ORAL ACTIVITIES AND SPEAKING ASSIGNMENTS

1. Using descriptive as well as conventional gestures, try to communicate the following ideas silently—by means of physical actions alone:
   a. "Get out of here!"
   b. "Why, Tom (or Mary)! I haven't seen you in ages!"
   c. "I'd like to get to know you better."
   d. "Come on! Give her a chance to explain."
   e. "Every penny I had is gone."

f. "Let's get out of here."

g. "If we're going to get what we want, we'll have to fight for it and fight hard."

2. Divide the class into teams and play "charades." (Those needing rules for classroom games should read David Zauner, "Charades as a Teaching Device," *Speech Teacher* 20 [November 1971]: 302.) A game of charades not only will loosen you up psychologically but should help sensitize you to the variety of small but perceptible cues you "read" when interpreting messages.

3. Make a two- or three-minute speech explaining to the class how to do something, such as driving a golf ball, bowling, doing a sleight-of-hand trick, cutting out a dress, tying some difficult knots, or playing a musical instrument. Use movement and gestures to help make your ideas clear. Do not use the chalkboard or previously prepared diagrams.

4. Prepare a short speech describing some exciting event you have witnessed — an automobile accident, a militant protest march, a political or campus rally, a sporting event. Use movement and gestures to render the details clear and vivid; that is, the audience should be able to "see" and "feel" the event, as you seek to integrate words/ideas and movements/actions for maximum impact. Successful completion of this assignment should demonstrate to you your ability to function as a *whole* or *total communicator*.

5. Without words, communicate to the classroom audience a clear picture of each of the following:

   a. A nervous pedestrian crossing a street through heavy traffic.

   b. An irate motorist changing a tire on a hot day.

   c. A panhandler asking several different people for a coin for a cup of coffee.

   d. A sailor marooned on an island and trying to catch the attention of the crew on a passing ship.

   e. A pedestrian trying to rescue a child who has dashed into the path of an oncoming, fast-moving automobile.

SUGGESTIONS FOR FURTHER READING

Rhetorica Ad Herennium, III.26–27, "Physical Movement." The classic analysis of movements and gestures appropriate to various vocal styles.

Haig A. Bosmajian, ed., *The Rhetoric of Nonverbal Communication* (Glenview, Ill.: Scott, Foresman and Company, 1971). A collection of readings covering a wide range of topics such as prenatal movement, street demonstrations, etc.

Julius Fast, *Body Language* (New York: M. Evans & Co., Inc., 1970). A popularized, readable treatment of nonverbal messages in everyday life.

Edward T. Hall, *The Hidden Dimension* (New York: Doubleday & Company, Inc., 1966). A fascinating discussion of the social consequences of the ways societies use space.

Mark L. Knapp, *Nonverbal Communication in Human Interaction* (New York: Holt, Rinehart & Winston, Inc., 1972). A solid introduction to the systematic study of nonverbal communication.

C. David Mortensen, *Communication: The Study of Human Interaction* (New York: McGraw-Hill Book Company, 1972), Chapter VI, "Nonverbal Interaction," pp. 209–253. A useful review of research into nonverbal communication.

Chapter 5

Using the voice to communicate

Aᴆᴛᴇʀ ʟᴏɴɢ ᴇxᴘᴇʀɪᴇɴᴄᴇ in public life Benjamin Disraeli, the British statesman, declared, "There is no index of character so sure as the voice." It is true that often we tend to judge a person by his or her voice. We regard as crude and rough a man whose voice is harsh or guttural. Likewise, we think of a woman whose tones are sharp and nasal as a shrew. A thin, breathy voice, characterized by the frequent use of upward inflections, suggests a lack of conviction or decisiveness.[1]

In addition to projecting a desirable image, a good voice enables a speaker to make a message clearer and more interesting. Listen to a child at a church or school program rattle off a poem or speak lines in a play. Even though every word may be clearly audible, the child's vocal expression often is so drab and monotonous that the author's ideas are imperfectly conveyed. On the other hand, recall a play-by-play account of a football or baseball game broadcast by a skilled sports announcer. Did not the vividness of his description depend in large measure upon the way he used his voice?

How can you as a speaker acquire an effective voice? As in bodily communication, improvement results chiefly from practice. Improper practice, however, may do more harm than good: repeatedly doing the wrong thing merely fixes a bad habit more firmly. To make practice worthwhile, you should first acquaint yourself with the characteristics of a good speaking voice and with some of the methods by which you may acquire these characteristics.

---

[1]See in this connection, David W. Addington, "The Relationship of Selected Vocal Characteristics to Personality Perception," *Speech Monographs* XXXV (November 1968): 492–503; L. S. Harms, "Listener Judgments of Status Cues in Speech," *Quarterly Journal of Speech* XLVII (April 1961): 164–168; Robert Hopper and Frederick Williams, "Speech Characteristics and Employability," *Speech Monographs* XL (November 1973): 296–302; James D. Moe, "Listener Judgments of Status Cues in Speech: A Replication and Extension," *Speech Monographs* XXXIX (November 1972): 144–147.

CHARACTERISTICS OF A GOOD SPEAKING VOICE

A good speaking voice has three essential properties: (1) it is reasonably pleasant to listen to; (2) it communicates the speaker's ideas easily and clearly; and (3) it is capable of expressing the fine shades of feeling and emotion which reveal the speaker's attitude toward self, subject, and listeners. Technically, we refer to these three properties as *quality, intelligibility,* and *variety.* As you proceed to consider each of these characteristics in greater detail, bear in mind that at the close of this chapter you will find a number of specific exercises designed to help you develop or improve your speaking voice accordingly.

Voice quality

The basic component of a good voice is a pleasing tone or quality. This is the overall impression your voice makes on those who hear it — whether they regard it as harsh, nasal, thin, mellow, resonant, or full-bodied. Sometimes, because your vocal mechanism is in a poor state of health or because you habitually abuse it, your voice may be excessively thin or husky or nasal or breathy. In such cases, a special program of training under the direction of a competent instructor may be necessary. Usually, however, by reducing excessive tensions in the neck and throat area and learning to preserve a proper balance between oral and nasal resonance, you will gradually acquire the best or optimum quality of which you are capable.

The quality of your speaking voice is also affected by your attitude or state of mind. Listeners usually are quick to detect whether you are angry, happy, confident, fearful, or sad. Similarly, they are able to tell with a surprising degree of accuracy whether you are sincere or insincere in what you are saying. For these reasons, you should not attempt to vary the quality of your voice artificially or try to simulate an attitude or feeling you do not actually possess. Believe strongly in what you are saying; strive earnestly to make your ideas clear and convincing to your listeners, and in most instances you will find that your voice responds in the appropriate manner.

Intelligibility

The intelligibility or understandability of your speech normally depends upon five separate but related factors: (1) the overall level of loudness at which you speak; (2) the duration of sounds within the syllables you utter; (3) the distinctness with which you articulate words and syllables; (4) the standard of pronunciation you observe; and (5) the vocal stress you give to a syllable, word, or phrase.

Adjusting the loudness level. Probably the most important single factor in intelligibility is the loudness level at which you speak as related to the *distance* between you and your listeners and the amount of *noise* that is present.[2] Obviously, the farther away your listeners are, the louder you must talk for them to hear you well. Most of us make this loudness-level adjustment unconsciously when projecting our voices over extended distances. What we often forget is that a corresponding adjustment is required when the listeners are only a few feet away. You must realize also that your own voice will always sound louder to you than to your listeners because your own ears are closer to your mouth than theirs are.

In addition to distance, the amount of surrounding noise with which you must compete has an effect on the required loudness level. Even in normal circumstances some noise always is present. For example, the noise level of rustling leaves in the quiet solitude of a country lane (10 decibels) is louder than a whisper six feet away. The noise in empty theaters averages 25 decibels, but with a "quiet" audience it rises to 42. In the average factory, a constant noise of about 80 decibels is characteristic. This is just about the same level as very loud speaking at a close range.

How can you determine the proper strength of voice to use in order to achieve sufficient loudness for the distance and noise conditions of a particular speech situation? While apparatus is available to measure the intensity of sounds with considerable accuracy, you probably do not have access to it and would not want to carry it around with you if you did. You can, however, always use your eyes to see if your auditors appear to be hearing you; or, even better, you can *ask* them. Get your instructor's advice on this point. Ask your friends to report on the loudness of your voice as you talk in rooms of various sizes and under varying noise conditions. Listen to the sound of your voice so

---

[2]The term *loudness* is here used synonymously with *intensity* because the former term is clearer to most people. Technically, of course, loudness—a distinct function in the science of acoustics—is not strictly synonymous with intensity. To explain the exact relationships between the two terms is beyond the scope of this book because the explanation involves many complicated psychophysical relationships. For a full discussion of these relationships, see Stanley S. Stevens and Hallowell Davis, *Hearing: Its Psychology and Physiology* (New York: John Wiley & Sons, Inc., 1938), p. 110ff.

that you can begin to correlate your own vocal production with their reports. You will soon learn to gauge the volume you must use in order to be heard.

Syllable duration. The second factor that affects a listener's ability to understand what you say is the duration of sound within the syllables you utter. Generally, a slower rate of speaking is more easily understood than a fast one, but merely slowing down is not enough. How well you are understood depends also on two other elements: *quantity,* or the duration of sound within a syllable; and *pause,* or the silent interval between sounds. A slow, staccato utterance, for example, is not much more intelligible than a faster staccato utterance, but talking at a moderate rate *while prolonging the sounds uttered* improves intelligibility markedly.[3]

This does not mean that everything you say should be spoken in a slow drawl. It *does* mean, however, that a rapid, "machine-gun" utterance often is hard to understand and should, therefore, be avoided. When the momentum of a fast-moving narrative is more important to your purpose than exact listener comprehension of every word you say, naturally you will want to speak with more speed. But when you want to be sure your listeners understand precisely what you are saying on some important point, take time to dwell on every significant word long enough to be sure it will be heard and understood.

Practice, then, until you can prolong your syllables without losing the rhythm and emphasis of your sentences; but be careful not to over-do this manner of speaking when neither noise nor distance requires you to do so.

Distinctness of articulation. Besides increasing the loudness of utterance and giving individual syllables greater duration, you may improve the intelligibility of your speech by exercising greater care in articulation. Good articulation is chiefly the job of the jaws, tongue, and lips. Only by using the muscles which manipulate them with skill and energy can you achieve crisp, clean-cut speech. Some Oriental people move their jaws very little in speaking; in their language, so much of the meaning is conveyed by variation in pitch that scarcely any jaw movement is necessary. In English, however, failure to open the jaws adequately while speaking is a serious fault because meaning is largely conveyed by consonant sounds, and these cannot be made effectively

---

[3]Gilbert C. Tolhurst, "Effects of Duration and Articulation Changes on Intelligibility, Word Reception, and Listener Preference," *Journal of Speech and Hearing Disorders* XXII (September 1957): 328–334.

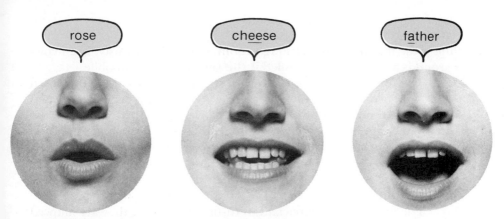

Contrasting movements, especially of the lips and jaw, produce and distinguish each of these vowel sounds from the others: the *o* in *rose,* *ee* in *cheese,* and *a* in *father.*

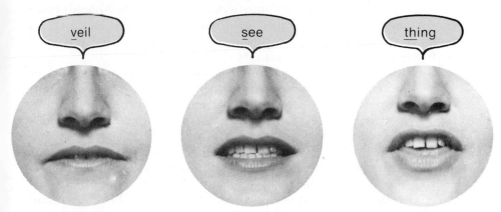

Note characteristic positioning of the articulators, particularly of the lips, tongue, and teeth, for proper formation of these sounds: *v* in *veil,* *s* in *see,* and *th* in *thing.*

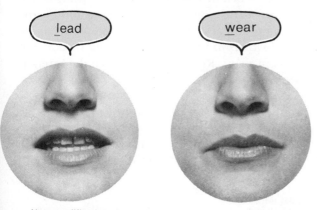

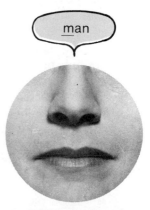

Note modifications in the position of the lips and tongue for the formation of sounds represented by the *l* in *lead* and *w* in *wear.*

Prominent use of the articulators is required for formation of *m* in *man.*

unless the tongue is given enough room to move vigorously. Even vowel sounds are likely to be muffled if the jaws are kept immobile.

The tongue has more to do with the distinct formation of speech sounds than does any other organ. Even when the jaws are opened adequately, the sounds produced cannot be sharp if the tongue lies idle or moves sluggishly. All the vowels depend partly on the position of the tongue for their distinctive qualities. Try saying "ee, ay, ah, aw, oor" and notice how the tongue changes its position. A great many consonant sounds, such as *d, th, ch, g,* and *k,* also depend upon the active movement of the tongue.

The lips, too, are important to distinct speech. If they are allowed to become lazy, the result will be a mumbled articulation, particularly of sounds such as *p, b, m,* and *f,* which depend chiefly on lip position. Of course, when talking directly into a microphone, you should avoid violent and explosive utterance of consonant sounds. However, in ordinary speaking—and especially in public speaking—use lips decisively to cut and to mold the sounds.

When you talk on unfamiliar subjects requiring the use of terms—particularly technical terms—which are strange to your listeners, talk more slowly, prolong your syllables, and articulate more carefully. Wherever possible, try also to choose words that cannot be mistaken in context. In particular, be careful about using similar-sounding words close together in sentences where the meaning of the first word may influence the meaning of the second. The story is told of a reporter who interviewed a farmer by telephone and reported in his newspaper that the farmer had just purchased "2008 pigs." The farmer had actually told him that he had bought "two sows and eight pigs." Although errors of this magnitude do not often occur, frequently a listener may be confused about a certain word or sentence until something is said later in the discussion to clarify the point; and in the meantime the effectiveness of the intervening remarks may have been reduced. Be careful, therefore, to think of words in terms of the way they *sound* and not only of the way they look in print. Remember, it is what the listeners *think* they hear that counts.

Acceptable pronunciation. The fourth factor that contributes to the intelligibility of vocal utterance is adherence to an accepted standard of pronunciation. *If you fail to pronounce words acceptably, your listeners will not be able to grasp easily and quickly the meaning or significance of what you say.* Even if your words are recognized, any peculiarity of pronunciation is almost sure to be noticed by some of the people who hear you; and the mistake not only may distract their attention from your line of thought, but may also discredit your knowledge and authority as a speaker.

Standards of pronunciation differ, of course, sometimes making it difficult to know what is acceptable. Ordinarily, the best criterion is the usage of the educated people of your own community. For most words, a dictionary provides a helpful guide; but dictionaries can become outdated and for this reason should not be followed too slavishly. Moreover, most dictionaries do not take sufficient notice of regional differences in dialect. A native of Louisiana pronounces words differently from a person who lives in Montana, and the speech of a Chicagoan is easily distinguished from that of a Bostonian. The standard of an up-to-date dictionary, modified to agree with the usage of educated people in your community, should, therefore, be the basis of your pronunciation.

A common fault of pronunciation is to misplace the accent in words—to say "genu-*ine*," "*de*-vice," "the-*ay*-ter," "pre-*fer*-able," instead of the more accepted forms, "*gen*-uine," "de-*vice*," "*the*-ater," "*pref*-erable." Other errors arise from the omission of sounds (as in the pronunciation "guh'mnt" for *government*), from the addition of sounds ("athalete" for *athlete*), and from the substitution of sounds ("git" for *get*). Furthermore, the way words are spelled is not always a safe guide to pronunciation, for English words contain many silent letters (of*t*en, *is* land, mor*t*gage), and many words containing the same combinations of letters require different pronunciations (bou*gh*, rou*gh*, thr*ough;* call*ed,* shout*ed,* gasp*ed*). In addition, the formality of the occasion exerts considerable influence. Many omissions acceptable in social conversation, informal interviews, or business conferences become objectionable in formal address.

Do not be so labored and precise as to call attention to your pronunciation rather than to your ideas, but do not take this admonition as an excuse for careless speech. Avoid equally pronunciation that is too pedantic and that which is too provincial. Use your ears: listen to your own pronunciation and compare it with that of educated people in your community and with that of speakers on television and radio. If your pronunciation is faulty, record in a personal speech journal or a notebook a list of the words you mispronounce, and practice their acceptable pronunciation frequently.

Vocal stress. The intelligibility of a word or phrase often depends on how it is stressed. Consider the word *content,* and note the change of meaning produced by shifting the stress from one syllable to the other.

The rules of stress, however, are by no means inflexible when words are used in connected speech. Emphasis and contrast often require the shifting of stress for the sake of greater clarity of meaning. For example, notice what you do to the accent in the word *proceed* when you use it in this sentence: "I said to proceed, not to recede." Many words change considerably in sound when they are stressed; especially is this true of short words such as pronouns, articles, and prepositions. For example, if you are speaking in a casual context, you might say, "I gave 'im th' book." But if you stress the third word, or the fourth one, you will say, "I gave *him* th' book," or "I gave 'im *the* book." In short, the requirements of contrast and emphasis, as well as the conventional rules of accent, influence the placing of stress in words.

Variety

#20. Variety in speech is obtained through four ways...

Although your speech may be easily intelligible, it may yet be dull and monotonous to listen to. Moreover, it may fail to communicate to the audience the full measure of thought and feeling you wish to transmit. This may happen if your voice is not flexible enough to express the fine shades of attitude or emotion upon which accurate and pleasing expression depends.[4]

How may you vary your voice so as to make it more lively or colorful and, at the same time, communicate your feelings and attitudes more precisely? How can you make important ideas stand out from those that are less significant? These are some of the questions with which we shall be concerned as we discuss in order the "vocal fundamentals" of *rate, force, pitch,* and *emphasis.*

Rate. Most persons speak an average of 120 to 180 words a minute; however, they usually do not maintain a uniform rate. In normal speech, the speed of utterance corresponds to the thought or feeling the speaker is attempting to transmit. Weighty, complex, or serious ideas tend to be expressed more slowly; light, humorous, or exciting matters more rapidly. Observe how fast the sports announcer talks when describing a completed forward pass or a quick double play. In contrast, observe the slow, dignified rate at which a minister reads the

---

[4]See Donald Dew and Harry Hollien, "The Effect of Inflection on Vowel Intelligibility," *Speech Monographs* XXXV (June 1968): 175–180; Charles F. Diehl, Richard C. White, and Paul H. Satz, "Pitch Change and Comprehension," *Speech Monographs* XXVIII (March 1961): 65–68; Stafford H. Thomas, "Effects of Monotonous Delivery on Intelligibility," *Speech Monographs* XXXVI (June 1969): 110–113.

wedding or burial service. A temperamentally excitable person tends to talk fast all of the time, while a stolid person characteristically talks in a slow drawl. The enthusiastic but poised individuals who are in complete command of their material and of the speaking situation *vary* their rate of speech, using this variation to express the intensity of their convictions and the depths of their feelings. Such speakers tell a story, lay out facts, or summarize arguments at a lively pace; but they present their main ideas and more difficult points slowly and emphatically so that their importance may be fully grasped by the listeners.

Pause. In addition to varying the rate of utterance as changes in thought or mood require, the skilled speaker—whether in a dyadic, group, or public situation—knows how to use pauses effectively. *Pauses punctuate thought.* Just as commas, semicolons, and periods separate written words into thought groups, so pauses of different lengths separate spoken words into meaningful units. In a speaking situation, the haphazard use of pauses is as confusing to the listener as the haphazard use of punctuation in printed matter is to the silent reader.

Often a pause may be used for emphasis. Placed immediately after an important statement, it suggests to your listeners: "Let this idea sink in." A pause before the climax of a story helps to increase suspense. A dramatic pause introduced at the proper moment may express the depth of your feeling more forcefully than words.

Many speakers are afraid to pause. Fearing they will forget what they want to say or that silence will focus attention on them personally, they rush on with a stream of words or vaguely vocalize the pause with *and-er-ah.* These random and meaningless syllables not only draw attention away from the ideas being expressed, but also are extremely annoying to the listener. Remember that a pause seldom seems as long to the hearer as it does to the speaker. Indeed, the ability to pause for emphasis or clarity is an indication of poise and self-control. Do not be afraid to pause whenever a break in utterance will help clarify an idea or emphasize an important point. Concentrate on the thought or emotion you are trying to communicate and let your voice respond accordingly. But above all, when you do stop, stop completely. Do not fill the gap with *er, uh,* or *um.* These intrusive vocalizations defeat entirely the purposes a pause should serve.

Force. As we already have suggested, as a speaker it is your basic responsibility to use adequate vocal force or energy—to talk loudly enough to be heard easily. A certain amount of force will also help you communicate your ideas and remarks with confidence and vigor. Talking too softly suggests that you are not sure of yourself or that you do not believe deeply in what you are saying. On the other hand, continuous shouting wears out your audience and dissipates attention. With force, as with rate, variety should be your guiding consideration.

Degree. Variations in the force or energy of speech have as their primary purpose the adding of emphasis. By increasing the loudness of a word or phrase or by pointedly reducing its loudness, you may make an idea stand out as if it had been underscored. Moreover, changing the degree of force is an effective way to reawaken lagging interest. A drowsy audience will sit up quickly if a speaker suddenly projects an important word or phrase with sharply increased energy. Remember, however, that the effect is produced not so much by the force itself as by the *change* in degree; a sudden reduction may be quite as effective as a sharp increase.

While you are practicing to develop variety in vocal force or energy, take care not to alter the pitch and quality of your voice. The natural tendency for most speakers is to raise their pitch when they try to increase their loudness. This happens because the nerves which control the speaking mechanism tend to diffuse their impulses to all of the muscles involved, and the resulting general tension is likely to produce a higher pitch, as well as more force. Sometimes this tension is so great that it simultaneously creates a harsh quality. Practice, however, should enable you to overcome this tendency. Just as you have learned to wiggle one finger without moving the others or to wink one eye without the other, so you can learn to apply force by contracting the breathing muscles without tightening the muscles of the throat and thus unnecessarily raising the pitch of your voice. A good way to begin is by repeating a sentence such as "That is absolutely *true!*" Hit the last word in the sentence with a greater degree of vocal energy and at the same time lower your pitch. When you are able to do this, say the entire sentence louder, and *LOUDER*, and LOUDER, until you can shout it without allowing your pitch to go up, too. As you practice, sustain the tone, use a long quantity, and try to maintain a full resonance. By learning to control the force of your voice, you will do much to make your speaking more emphatic and to convey to your audience an impression of power in reserve.

Pitch. Just as singers' voices differ, some being soprano or tenor and others contralto or bass, so do people in general vary in the normal pitch level at which they speak. Except when you are impersonating a character to embellish a story or an anecdote, it is best to talk in your normal pitch range. Otherwise, there is danger of straining your voice. Fortunately, you will find that there is considerable latitude within your normal range. In fact, few beginning speakers take advantage of the possibilities offered by their normal range. Instead, they tend to hit one level and stay there. Nothing reflects the animation and vivacity of speech so much as effective pitch variation.

Habitual pitch level. As we have indicated, the habitual pitch level at which people speak varies considerably from person to person. Nearly everyone, however, can easily span an octave, and many people have voices flexible enough to vary more than two octaves without strain. Within this range, the key-level at which you habitually speak may create a very definite impression of you as a person. Ordinarily, a pitch that is continuously high suggests weakness, excitement, irritation, or extreme youth; a lower key-level suggests assurance, poise, and strength. For this reason, your customary pitch should be in the lower half of your natural range. In particular, be careful when you are applying increasing degrees of force not to let your voice get out of control, going to a higher and higher key until it cracks under the strain. If you feel tension, pause for a moment and lower your pitch. At times, of course, you will be excited, and your voice naturally will rise to a high key to match your emotion. Remember, however, that a somewhat restrained emotion makes a more favorable impression on listeners than does emotion which has gone completely out of control.

Steps and slides. In connected speech, pitch is changed in two ways: by steps and by slides. Suppose, for example, that someone has made a statement with which you agree and you answer by saying, "You're exactly right!" The chances are that you will say it something like this:

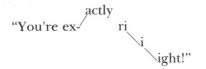

Notice that a complete break in pitch level occurs between the first and second syllables of the word *exactly*. This abrupt change in pitch is what we mean by a *step*. On the word *right,* however, a more gradual pitch inflection accompanies the production of the sound. Such a continuous change of pitch within a syllable is a *slide*. Both steps and slides may go upward or downward, depending on the meaning intended. Slides also may be double, the pitch going up and then down or vice versa, as when one says:

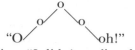

"O oh!"

to express the meaning, "I didn't realize that!"

In general, an upward step or slide suggests interrogation, indecision, uncertainty, doubt, or suspense, whereas a downward inflection suggests firmness, determination, certainty, finality, or confidence. Thus if you were to say, "What shall we do about it? Just this . . . ," a rising inflection in the question would create suspense; a downward inflection of the last phrase would indicate the certainty with which you were presenting your answer. A double inflection, as indicated by the example above, suggests a subtle conflict or contradiction of meaning, and is frequently used to express irony or sarcasm, or to suggest innuendo. Steps and slides are primarily useful in communicating thought content rather than expressing emotional tone or color. By mastering their use, you will be able to make your meaning clearer and more precise.

All this does not mean that when you are about to speak to another individual or a group of individuals you should say to yourself: "This sentence requires an upward inflection," or "I shall use a *step* between these two words and a *slide* on that one." Such concentration on the mechanics of utterance would destroy communicative contact with your listeners. Rather, in private and in class exercises, practice reading aloud selected passages which require extensive pitch inflection and which encourage the habit of flexibility to grow in your speaking. Then, when you speak to others, your voice will tend to respond more or less appropriately and spontaneously to the ideas and moods you wish to convey.

Intonation patterns. In all kinds of speech the rhythm and swing of phrase and sentence weave themselves into a continuous pattern of changing pitch. As the individual's thought or mood changes, the intonation pattern changes also. The use of a monotonous intonation pattern, however, is just as deadly as staying at one pitch level all of the time. Beware, therefore, of seesawing back and forth in a singsong voice. Avoid also the tendency of many inexperienced speakers to end nearly every sentence with an upward inflection. Assertions, when inflected in this way, sound more like *questions;* and you may sound doubtful even though you feel certain. A downward inflection at the close of each sentence is almost as bad, for it suggests an intolerance or dogmatism to which most listeners react unfavorably. If you can develop *variety of pitch inflection,* your melody pattern normally will adjust itself to the thought and mood you intend to express. Be careful, however, not to get into a vocal rut, unconsciously using the same pattern for everything you say.

Emphasis. Obviously, all forms of vocal variety help provide emphasis. Any change in rate, force, or pitch serves to make the word, phrase, or sentence in which the change occurs stand out from what precedes or follows it. This is true regardless of the direction of the change. Whether the rate or force is increased or decreased, whether the pitch is raised or lowered, emphasis will result. And the greater the amount of change or the more suddenly it is effected, the more emphatic will the statement be. In addition, emphasis is increased by pause and contrast: a pause allows the audience to "get set" for or to think over an important idea; contrast makes the idea seem more important than it otherwise would be.

Two warnings, however, should be noted: (1) Avoid *over*-emphasis. (2) Avoid *continuous* emphasis. If you emphasize a point beyond its true value or importance, your audience will lose faith in your judgment. If you attempt to emphasize everything, nothing will stand out. Be judicious. Pick out the ideas that are really important and give them the emphasis they deserve.

THE IMPORTANCE OF PRACTICE

In this chapter we have studied the characteristics of a good speaking voice. We have suggested ways in which you can make your speech more intelligible and have reviewed the standard of pronunciation to which you should adhere. In addition, we have pointed out the importance of having a voice that is varied as well as clear, and have shown how variety depends upon a proper use of rate, force, pitch, and emphasis. Do not assume that you will be able to master in a day or a week all of the vocal skills that have been described. Take time to review and digest the ideas presented.

Above all, *practice.* Practice the exercises which are given in the following pages. Return to these exercises again and again, even after you have mastered them, so that your skills will not become rusty through disuse. Remember that any vocal skill, before it can be natural and effective with listeners, must be so much a habit that it will work for you without conscious effort when you begin to speak and will continue to do so throughout the utterance of your message.

EXERCISES FOR VOICE PRACTICE

Voice quality

To improve control of breathing

1. Practice expelling the air from your lungs in short, sharp gasps; place your hand on your abdomen to make sure that there is a sharp inward contraction of the muscle wall synchronous with the chest contraction on each outgoing puff.
   a. Then vocalize the puffs, saying "hep! — hep! — hep!" with a good deal of force.
   b. In the same way, say "bah, bay, bee, bo, boo" with staccato accents and considerable vigor.

2. Fill your lungs; then exhale *as slowly as possible* until the lungs are empty. Time yourself to see how long you can keep exhaling without a break. (Note that the object here is not to see how much air you can get into the lungs but how slowly you can let it out.)
   a. Filling your lungs each time, vocalize the outgoing breath stream first with a long continuous hum, second with an *oo* sound, and then with other vowel sounds. Be careful not to let the sound become "breathy"; keep the tone clear.
   b. Place a lighted candle just in front of your mouth and repeat the series outlined above. The flame should just barely flicker.

3. On the same breath, alternate the explosive and the slow, deliberate exhalations outlined in Exercises 1 and 2. Practice until you can shift from one to the other easily both in silent breathing and in vocalized tones.

To induce relaxation of the throat

4. Repeat the following sequence several times in succession:
   a. Keeping your eyes closed and your neck and jaw muscles as relaxed as possible, raise your head easily to an upright position and then yawn with your mouth open as wide as possible.
   b. While your mouth is thus open, inhale deeply and exhale quietly two or three times; then intone "a-a-a-ah" very quietly.
   c. Say "m-m-a-a-ah" several times slowly, each time nodding the head forward gently and without tension.

To improve the quality of the tone

5. Intone the following words quietly at first, then louder, and louder; try to give them a ringing quality; put your fingertips on the nose and cheekbones to see if you can feel a vibration there. Avoid breathiness.

one	home	tone	alone	moan
rain	plain	mine	lean	soon
ring	nine	dong	moon	fine

6. Read aloud the following passages in tones as clear and resonant as you can produce. Be sure that you open your mouth wide enough and that you use only enough air to make the tones vibrate. Do not force the tone. If you notice any tension in your throat or harshness in your voice, repeat the exercises until the tension and harshness disappear.

from THE RIME OF THE ANCIENT MARINER

> Alone, alone, all, all alone,
> Alone on a wide, wide sea!
> And never a saint took pity on
> My soul in agony.
>
> *Samuel T. Coleridge*

from THE RAINY DAY

> The day is cold, and dark, and dreary;
> It rains, and the wind is never weary;
> The vine still clings to the mouldering wall,
> But at every gust the dead leaves fall,
> And the day is dark and dreary.
>
> *Henry W. Longfellow*

The selected passages which follow are intended for further practice in improving voice quality. Some of them are included because of the emotional tone they portray; others because of the vocal control they require. All of them, however, call for a clear, resonant quality. Study them first for their meaning; try to understand fully what the author is saying. Then absorb the feeling; allow yourself to follow the author's mood. Finally, read the passages aloud, putting as much meaning and feeling into your reading as you can.

from THE MAN WITH THE HOE[5]

> Bowed by the weight of centuries he leans
> Upon his hoe and gazes on the ground,

---

[5]Copyright by the author.

The emptiness of ages in his face,
And on his back the burden of the world.
Who made him dead to rapture and despair,
A thing that grieves not and that never hopes,
Stolid and stunned, a brother to the ox?
Who loosened and let down this brutal jaw?
Whose was the hand that slanted back this brow?
Whose breath blew out the light within this brain?

Edwin Markham

from THE BARREL-ORGAN[6]

There's a barrel-organ carolling across a golden street
    In the City as the sun sinks low;
And the music's not immortal; but the world has made it sweet
And fulfilled it with the sunset-glow;
And it pulses through the pleasures of the City and the pain
    That surround the singing organ like a large eternal light;
And they've given it a glory and a part to play again
    In the Symphony that rules the day and night.

Alfred Noyes

from APOSTROPHE TO THE OCEAN

Roll on, thou deep and dark blue Ocean, roll!
    Ten thousand fleets sweep over thee in vain;
Man marks the earth with ruin — his control
    Stops with the shore; — upon the watery plain
    The wrecks are all thy deed, nor doth remain
A shadow of man's ravage, save his own,
    When for a moment, like a drop of rain,
He sinks into thy depths with bubbling groan,
Without a grave, unknelled, uncoffined, and unknown.

George Gordon, Lord Byron

Intelligibility

To test the intelligibility of your speech

7. Following are twenty lists of sixteen words each which may be used in class to test whether your speech is intelligible to others.[7] Your scores will not be as accurate as if these tests were conducted under scientifically controlled conditions, but they will provide a measure of the relative intelligibility of your speech as compared with your classmates' and will show you what happens under various conditions. Proceed with the test as follows: (a) Read silently the list of words which is assigned to you. (b) Stand in a corner of the classroom with your back to the class. Read the first four words; then pause long enough for your classmates to write down the four words before going ahead to the next group of four words. Continue in this manner until you have read the complete list. (c) To determine your score, count the total number of words understood correctly by all listeners. Divide this total by the number which is the product of the number of listeners times sixteen (the number of words spoken). The result will be your percentage of intelligibility on this test.

    a. Three, flap, switch, will——resume, cold, pilot, wind——chase, blue, search, flight——mine, area, cleared, left.

    b. Iron, fire, task, try——up, six, seven, wait——slip, turn, read, clear——blue, this, even, is.

    c. Nan, flak, timer, two——course, black, when, leave——raise, clear, tree, seven——search, strike, there, cover.

    d. List, service, ten, foul——wire, last, wish, truce——power, one, ease, will——teeth, hobby, trill, wind.

    e. Flight, spray, blind, base——ground, fog, ceiling, flame——target, flare, gear, low——slow, course, code, scout.

    f. Tall, plot, find, deep——climb, fall, each, believe——wing, strip, clean, field——when, chase, search, select.

    g. Climb, switch, over, when——this, turn, gear, spray——black, flare, is, free——runway, three, off, red.

    h. Thing, touch, marker, sleeve——find, top, leave, winter——skip, free, have, beach——meet, aid, send, lash.

    i. Try, over, six, craft——green, victor, yellow, out——trim, X ray, ramp, up——speed, like, believe, sender.

    j. Dim, trip, fire, marker——wave, green, rudder, field——climb, to, plot, middle——speed, like, straight, lower.

    k. Smooth, mike, four, catch——strip, park, line, left——leg, wheel, turn, lift——time, baker, orange, look.

---

[7]From a test used by Gayland L. Draegert in an experiment reported in *Speech Monographs*, XIII, 50–53. Reprinted by permission of the Speech Communication Association.

l. Wake, other, blue, been——size, wish, black, under——field, down, empty, what——ship, strip, land, fire.

m. Leg, on, strip, leave——ground, trip, plot, area——speed, blue, will, ramp——wheel, blind, sector, nan.

n. Tail, when, through, at——climb, off, tower, rain——time, gear, cloud, pass——loaf, three, crash, direction.

o. Station, left, reply, read——final, blue, field, out——wind, west, marker, fire——tower, ground, gear, time.

p. Sighted, toward, finder, search——red, blind, each, weather—— tall, after, while, wide——close, hole, mark, signal.

q. Neat, warm, beam, where——side, leader, bell, map——view, face, trap, well——seem, feed, clutch, vine.

r. Circle, beach, up, that——port, even, catch, pad——reach, heat, break, safe——still, put, enter, iron.

s. Chamber, wait, hair, open——wind, keep, sector, free——light, home, take, will——base, eleven, headphone, by.

t. Service, flat, have, on——bay, wait, fade, cold——tire, horn, bill, sad——feel, cave, set, limit.

To develop an adequate degree of loudness and syllable duration

8. Practice saying the words in the above lists with a voice loud enough—

   a. to be barely understood (score below 50%) in a quiet classroom.
   b. to be perfectly understood in a quiet classroom.
   c. to be understood in a quiet classroom with your listeners' ears plugged with cotton (to simulate distance).
   d. to be understood above the noise of two, three, or four other students who are all reading aloud from different pages of the textbook.

9. Practice saying the words in the lists above with varying degrees of syllable duration under the conditions listed in the problem above.

10. Devise variations of these conditions with whatever recording or public-address systems are available to your class.

11. Prepare sentences requiring precise understanding of the component words and practice saying them with the loudness and syllable length required for:

   a. a small group in a small room.
   b. a class in a fairly large lecture room.
   c. an audience in your college auditorium.
   d. a crowd in your football stadium.

Here are a few sample sentences to use:

"Just ten minutes from now, go in single file to room 316."
"In 1985, the population of Panama may be one and two fifths what it was in 1948."
"Hemstitching can be done by machine operation, using strong thread."
"Oranges, nuts, vegetables, and cotton are raised on the Kingston ranch."

To increase distinctness of articulation

12. Stretch the muscles of articulation:
   a. Stretch the mouth in as wide a grin as possible; open the mouth as wide as possible; pucker the lips and protrude them as far as possible.
   b. Stretch out the tongue as far as possible; try to touch the tip of the nose and the chin with the tongue tip; beginning at the front teeth, run the tip of the tongue back, touching the palate as far back as the tongue will go.

13. With vigorous accent on the consonant sounds, repeat "pah, tah, kah" several times. Then vary the order, emphasizing first *pah*, then *tah*, then *kah*. In the same way, practice the series "ap, at, ak" and "apa, ata, aka." Work out additional combinations of this kind, using different combinations of consonants and vowels.

14. Make a list of as many tongue twisters as you can find and practice saying them rapidly and precisely. Here are a few short examples to start on:
   a. She sells seashells on the seashore.
   b. National Shropshire Sheep Association.
   c. "Are you copper-bottoming them, my man?" "No, I'm aluminuming 'em, mum."
   d. He sawed six long, slim, sleek, slender saplings.
   e. Dick twirled the stick athwart the path.
   f. Rubber baby-buggy bumpers.
   g. B—A, Ba; B—E, Be;
      B—I, Bi; Ba Be Bi;
      B—O, Bo; Ba Be Bi Bo;
      B—U, Bu; Ba Be Bi Bo Bu!
   h. Twenty Scots in assorted tartans went to Trenton.
   i. Winds were eastward for the Easter weekend.

15. Read the following passages in a distinct and lively manner; move the tongue, jaw, and lips with energy:

from THE CATARACT OF LODORE

"How does the water
Come down to Lodore?"
  My little boy asked me
  Thus once on a time;
And moreover he tasked me
To tell him in rhyme.
. . . .
  The cataract strong
  Then plunges along,
  Striking and raging,
  As if a war waging
Its caverns and rocks among;
  Rising and leaping,
  Sinking and creeping,
  Swelling and sweeping,
Showering and springing,
  Flying and flinging,
  Writhing and ringing,
  Eddying and whisking,
  Spouting and frisking,
  Turning and twisting,
  Around and around . . .

And rushing and flushing and brushing and gushing,
And flapping and rapping and clapping and slapping,
And curling and whirling and purling and twirling,
And thumping and plumping and bumping and jumping;
And dashing and flashing and splashing and clashing;
And so never ending, but always descending,
Sounds and motion for ever and ever are blending,
All at once and all o'er, with a mighty uproar —;
And this way the Water comes down at Lodore.

Robert Southey

To encourage acceptable pronunciation

16. Make a list of words which you have heard pronounced in more than
one way. Look them up in a dictionary and come to class prepared to
defend your agreement or disagreement with the dictionary pronunciation. Here are a few words on which to start:

abdomen	creek	gauge	indict	route
acclimated	data	gesture	inquiry	theater
advertisement	deficit	grievous	recess	thresh
alias	drowned	humble	research	vagary
bona fide	forehead	idea	roof	yacht

17. Try to understand the significance of the following passages before you start practicing them. Then begin by reading them as you would before a small, quiet audience; next as you would need to do if the audience were large or there were considerable noise-interference. Remember, however, that exaggerated precision, loudness, syllable duration, etc., beyond the amount clearly required for easy intelligibility in the actual situation will sound artificial to your listeners and is not good speech.

from THE WAR SONG OF THE SARACENS[8]

We are they who come faster than fate: we are they who ride early or
  late:
We storm at your ivory gate: Pale Kings of the Sunset, beware!
Not on silk nor in samet we lie, not in curtained solemnity die
Among women who chatter and cry, and children who mumble a prayer.
But we sleep by the ropes of the camp, and we rise with a shout, and
  we tramp
With the sun or the moon for a lamp, and the spray of the wind in our
  hair.

James Elroy Flecker

from THE SEA AROUND US[9]

For the sea as a whole, the alternation of day and night, the passage of
the seasons, the procession of the years, are lost in its vastness, obliterated in its own changeless eternity. But the surface waters are different.
The face of the sea is always changing. Crossed by colors, lights, and
moving shadows, sparkling in the sun, mysterious in the twilight, its
aspects and its moods vary hour by hour. The surface waters move
with the tides, stir to the breath of the winds, and rise and fall to the
endless, hurrying forms of the waves. Most of all, they change with the
advance of the seasons. Spring moves over the temperate lands of our
Northern Hemisphere in a tide of new life, of pushing green shoots

---

[8]"The War Song of the Saracens" from *Collected Poems* by James Elroy Flecker. Published by Martin Secker & Warburg Limited.

[9]Rachel Carson, *The Sea Around Us*, Oxford University Press, 1961, pp. 28–29.

and unfolding buds, all its mysteries and meanings symbolized in the northward migration of the birds, the awakening of sluggish amphibian life as the chorus of frogs rises again from the wet lands, the different sound of the wind which stirs the young leaves where a month ago it rattled the bare branches. These things we associate with the land, and it is easy to suppose that at sea there could be no such feeling of advancing spring. But the signs are there, and seen with understanding eye, they bring the same magical sense of awakening.

—Rachel L. Carson

Variety

To develop flexibility in vocal manipulation

18. While repeating the alphabet or counting from one to twenty, perform the following vocal exercises (trying throughout to maintain good vocal quality and distinctness of utterance):
   a. Beginning very slowly, steadily increase the speed until you are speaking as rapidly as possible; then, beginning rapidly, reverse the process.
   b. Stretch out the quantity of the vowel sounds, speaking at a slow rate but allowing no pauses between letters or numbers; then shift to short quantity with long pauses. Shift back and forth between these two methods with every five or six letters or numbers you say.
   c. Begin very softly and increase the force until you are nearly shouting; reverse the process. Then practice shifting from one extreme to the other, occasionally changing to a moderate degree of force.
   d. Keeping the loudness constant, shift from an explosive application of force combined with a staccato utterance to a firm, smooth application of force.
   e. Stress alternate letters (or numbers); then change by stressing every third letter, every fourth, etc.; then change back to alternate letters again.
   f. Begin at the lowest pitch you can comfortably reach, and raise the pitch steadily until you reach the highest comfortable pitch; reverse the process. Shift back and forth suddenly from high to low to middle, etc.
   g. Practice slides with the vowel sound *oh*. Try upward slides, downward slides, and those which are double—going up and down or down and up.
   h. Using a half dozen letters or numbers, practice similar pitch changes in steps; then alternate steps and slides.

19. Vary the *rate* with which you say the following sentences in the manner indicated:

a. "There goes the last one."
   (1) Use long quantity, expressing regret.
   (2) Use short quantity, expressing excitement.
   (3) Use moderate quantity, merely stating a fact.
b. "The winners are John, Henry, and Bill."
   (1) Insert a long pause after *are* for suspense; then give the names rapidly.
   (2) Insert pauses before each name as if picking it out.
   (3) Say the whole sentence rapidly in a matter-of-fact way.

20. In the manner suggested, vary the *force* for the following:
   a. "I hate you! I hate you! I hate you!"
      (1) Increase the degree of force with each repetition, making the last almost a shout.
      (2) Say the second "*hate*" louder than the first, and the last one *sotto voce.*
      (3) Shout the first statement; then let the force diminish as if echoing the mood.
   b. "What kind of a thing is this?"
      Repeat the question, stressing a different word each time. Try not to raise the pitch, but to emphasize by force alone.
   c. "I have told you a hundred times, and the answer is still the same."
      (1) Make the statement a straightforward assertion, using sustained force.
      (2) Speak the sentence with a sudden explosion of force, as though you were uncontrollably angry.
      (3) Speak the sentence with deep but controlled emotion, applying force gradually and firmly.

21. Practice varying the *pitch* with which you say the sentences below, following the directions given:
   a. "I certainly feel fine today—that is, except for my sunburn. Now, don't slap me on the back! Ouch! Stop it! Please!"
      Begin confidently in a low key, successively raising the pitch level until the *please* is said near the top of your range. Repeat several times, trying to begin lower each time.
   b. "Oh, yes? Is that so?"
      Say this question as indicated in the following notations. Diagonal lines indicate *slides;* horizontal ones indicate a *level pitch;* and differences in height between the end of one line and the beginning of the next indicate *steps.* Each line represents one word.

      (1) —⎺ ⎯ ⎺ —

      (2) —╱ ⎯ ⎺ ╲

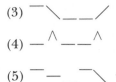

(3)
(4)
(5)

What are the different meanings thus conveyed?

   c. Say the sentences with varied pitch inflections so that it will mean as many different things as possible.

22. Practice reading aloud sentences from prose and poetry that require emphasis and contrast to make the meaning clear. Vary the pitch, rate, and force in different ways until you feel you have the best possible interpretation of the meaning. Here are some examples for practice:

   a. One of the most striking differences between a cat and a lie is that a cat has only nine lives. — *Mark Twain*

   b. So, Naturalists observe, a flea
      Has smaller fleas that on him prey;
      And these have smaller still to bite 'em;
      And so proceed ad infinitum. — *Jonathan Swift*

   c. I have waited with patience to hear what arguments might be urged against the bill; but I have waited in vain: The truth is, there is no argument that can weigh against it. — *Lord Mansfield*

   d. Gentlemen may cry, peace, peace! — but there is no peace. The war has actually begun! I know not what course others may take; but, as for me, give me liberty, or give me death! — *Patrick Henry*

23. Read the following passages so as to give the effect of climax: first practice the climax of increasing force, and then that of increasing intensity of feeling with diminishing force.

   a. There is no mistake; there has been no mistake; and there shall be no mistake. — *Duke of Wellington*

   b. Let us cultivate a true spirit of union and harmony . . . let us act under a settled conviction, and an habitual feeling, that these twenty-four States are one country. . . . Let our object be, OUR COUNTRY, OUR WHOLE COUNTRY, AND NOTHING BUT OUR COUNTRY. — *Daniel Webster*

To increase vocal variety and emphasis

24. Clip a paragraph from a newspaper story describing some exciting incident and read it with appropriate vocal variety.

25. Memorize a section of one of the speeches printed in this book, as assigned by your instructor, and present it in such a way as to make the meaning clear and the feeling behind it dynamic.

26. Find an argumentative editorial or magazine article with which you agree or disagree. In your own words, attack or defend the point of view presented, and do so with all the emphasis, contrast, and vocal variety of which you are capable.

The selected passages which follow are intended for further practice in improving vocal variety. Before you begin to practice a passage, study it carefully to understand its full meaning and determine its dominant mood. Some of the selections are light and fast moving; others are thoughtful and serious; at least one contains a marked climax. Avoid superficial or mechanical manipulation of the voice; read so as to make the meaning clear and the feeling contagious to your listeners. Effective reading requires that you practice enough in private so that before an audience you will not have to keep thinking of your voice but will be able to concentrate on communicating ideas and feelings.

THE DISAGREEABLE MAN

If you give me your attention, I will tell you what I am:
I'm a genuine philanthropist — all other kinds are sham.
Each little fault of temper and each social defect
In my erring fellow-creatures, I endeavor to correct.
To all their little weaknesses I open peoples' eyes,
And little plans to snub the self-sufficient I devise;
I love my fellow-creatures — I do all the good I can —
Yet everybody says I'm such a disagreeable man!
    And I can't think why!
To compliments inflated I've a withering reply,
And vanity I always do my best to mortify;
A charitable action I can skillfully dissect;
And interested motives I'm delighted to detect.
I know everybody's income and what everybody earns,
And I carefully compare it with the income-tax returns;
But to benefit humanity, however much I plan,
Yet everybody says I'm such a disagreeable man!
    And I can't think why!

I'm sure I'm no ascetic; I'm as pleasant as can be;
You'll always find me ready with a crushing repartee;
I've an irritating chuckle, I've a celebrated sneer,
I've an entertaining snigger, I've a fascinating leer;
To everybody's prejudice I know a thing or two;
I can tell a woman's age in half a minute — and I do —

But although I try to make myself as pleasant as I can,
Yet everybody says I'm such a disagreeable man!
And I can't think why!

William S. Gilbert

from A LETTER TO THE CORINTHIANS (1 CORINTHIANS, 13)

Though I speak with the tongues of men and of angels, and have not charity, I am become as sounding brass, or a tinkling cymbal. And though I have the gift of prophecy, and understand all mysteries, and all knowledge; and though I have all faith, so that I could remove mountains, and have not charity, I am nothing. And though I bestow all my goods to feed the poor, and though I give my body to be burned, and have not charity, it profiteth me nothing. Charity suffereth long, and is kind; charity envieth not; charity vaunteth not itself, is not puffed up, doth not behave itself unseemly, seeketh not her own, is not easily provoked, thinketh no evil; rejoiceth not in iniquity, but rejoiceth in truth; beareth all things, believeth all things, hopeth all things, endureth all things. Charity never faileth: but whether there be prophecies, they shall fail; whether there be tongues, they shall cease; whether there be knowledge, it shall vanish away. For we know in part, and we prophesy in part. But when that which is perfect is come, then that which is in part shall be done away. . . . And now abideth faith, hope, and charity, these three; but the greatest of these is charity.

—Paul, the Apostle

PROBLEMS FOR FURTHER STUDY

1. Edward T. Hall identifies four distances at which people can communicate: *intimate distance*—0 to 1½ feet; *personal distance*—1½ to 4 feet; *social distance*—4 to 12 feet; and *public distance*—12 feet or more. Hall argues that all communication variables change from distance to distance. To verify these matters for yourself: *(a)* Read the appropriate section of Hall's *The Hidden Dimension* (New York: Doubleday & Company, Inc., 1966). *(b)* Conduct your own investigation. Purposely place yourself at these distances from others and carry on conversations. Note carefully the changing characteristics of quality, loudness, syllable duration, distinctness of articulation, vocal stress, variety, rate, force, pitch, and emphasis. *(c)* Chart several of these characteristics and compare your conclusions with those of Hall.

2. Listen to a successful speaker addressing a crowd—someone who, because of the extended distance involved, must project his or her voice to

a large audience without a microphone. Chart the vocal characteristics listed in Problem 1 above. Then answer these questions: *(a)* What kinds of sentence structures are spoken easily by someone forced to project vocally? *(b)* What kinds of sentence structures are apparently difficult for listeners to understand in such circumstances? *(c)* Can you discern relationships between vocal quality, loudness, rate, pitch, etc., and the physical behavior of the speaker? Identify these relationships. *(d)* In general, describe some of the relationships among vocal, physical, and verbal characteristics of successful, large-scale, public communication.

3. Are you sensitive to variations in vocal dialects? Do you associate personality types, intelligence, communication mannerism, etc., with a British accent, a German accent, an Oriental accent — or with a Georgia accent, a Texas accent, a Bronx accent, a Minnesota-Scandinavian accent? Why? Bad movies? Limited experiences? Or, do you think members of these cultures and subcultures *actually* think and, therefore, speak differently? How can you be sure?

The power of vocal stereotyping cannot be underestimated. Explore such stereotyping by reading and by making personal contacts with members of various subcultures or cultures other than your own. Take careful, objective notes on what the resulting face-to-face interviews and dialogues reveal.

SUGGESTIONS FOR FURTHER READING

Rhetorica Ad Herennium, III. 19–25, "Vocal Quality." The principal statement by the ancients on the connotations of various vocal patterns.

D. W. Addington, "The Relationship of Selected Vocal Characteristics to Personality Perception," *Speech Monographs* 35 (1968): 492–503. A good example of experimental research into the effects of vocal qualities upon communicative effectiveness.

Bert E. Bradley, *Fundamentals of Speech Communication: The Credibility of Ideas* (Dubuque, Iowa: Wm. C. Brown Company, Publishers, 1974), "Pronunciation" and "Attitude Toward a Nonstandard Dialect," pp. 244–249. A nontechnical and informative exploration of dialects in the United States and their importance in speech communication.

R. W. Fasold and W. Wolfam, "Some Linguistic Features of Negro Dialect," in *Teaching Standard English in the Inner City*, ed. R. W. Fasold and R. W. Shuy (Washington, D.C.: Center for Applied Linguistics, 1970), pp. 41–86. An attempt to correct many of our notions about Black English, and therefore a useful starting point for discussions concerning dialects.

Chapter 6

Supporting one point

THERE ARE MANY communicative situations in which, instead of presenting a long and complex speech, you wish to explain or to prove a single point. The need for such "one-point" speeches may arise in class discussions and informal arguments, or on occasions requiring reports or instructions. Moreover, speeches to entertain frequently consist of a series of humorous stories or unusual anecdotes unified around one worthwhile thought.

Besides being useful in actual speaking situations, the one-point speech is valuable as a learning device. Attempt to explain or to prove just one idea at first, and leave until later the more difficult types of speaking. If, while you talk, you need develop only one point rather than several, you will be less inclined to ramble over a number of unrelated thoughts or to propound vague generalities. Then, too, most long speeches are actually a series of one-point units tied together into a more comprehensive line of explanation or argument. Hence, in learning how to develop a single idea, you are mastering a skill that has wide applications.

THE NEED FOR SUPPORTING MATERIALS

In a one-point speech, as in any other, ideas must be developed and supported if they are to be grasped by the audience. Listeners find it difficult to understand abstract statements; nor will they usually believe a proposition or act upon a proposal in the absence of proof. In giving a speech, therefore, you not only must state the point you wish to communicate, but you also must amplify, illuminate, and support it.

Suppose that the purpose of your speech is to explain to an audience why " 'Bad' money drives out 'good' money," or to prove that "Mechanical failure is the principal cause of automobile accidents." How would the average listener react to each of these statements upon initially hearing it? In the first case, the listener would be almost certain to think, "I do not understand this assertion; please explain it." In the second, he or she might think, "I doubt or disbelieve this statement; prove it." These reactions would arise not because the hearer was dull or obstinate, but because of a natural inability to comprehend an abstract and rather ambiguous statement and an honest reluctance to accept any proposition without some notion of the evidence and reasoning which underlie it. Materials which provide explanation or proof are called *supporting materials* and are of two principal types: *verbal* and *visual*. In this chapter we shall consider each of these types and then illustrate how they may be used to develop a one-point speech.

VERBAL SUPPORTING MATERIALS

The verbal supporting materials commonly found in speeches may be divided into seven classes: (1) explanation, (2) comparison or contrast, (3) illustration (detailed example)—hypothetical or factual, (4) specific instance (undeveloped example), (5) statistics, (6) testimony, and (7) restatement.

Figure 1. Materials for Verbally Supporting and Illuminating an Idea

Sometimes two or more of these kinds of materials are combined, as when statistics are used to develop an illustration, or when the testimony of an authority is given to strengthen or verify an explanation. At other times they are used singly, the speaker's choice of materials depending upon the type of support needed. Comparisons, contrasts, and hypothetical illustrations, for example, can be especially helpful in making ideas clear and vivid. Specific instances, statistics, and testimony usually work effectively as proof. Factual illustrations and restatements serve both purposes.

Explanation

An explanation is an expository or descriptive passage the purpose of which is to make a term, concept, process, or proposal clear and intelligible. Usually, explanation consists of simple exposition or description. It may, however, show the relationship between a whole and its parts. Often, explanation is reinforced by examples, statistics, or other forms of support.

Notice, for instance, how G. R. Bowers, Assistant Superintendent for Instruction, Ohio Department of Education, used explanation to make clear the meaning of the English word *sincerity:*

> To construct some of the early Roman buildings, it was necessary to transport the huge blocks of stone from a distance. In the quarrying and shipping of these stones large chips were sometimes broken out, making the stones unsightly and sometimes unfit for use. To avoid a loss the breaks were filled with wax to camouflage the breaks. After the stones were set and exposed to ravages of the elements, the wax crumbled out leaving the unsightly chips exposed to view, or so weakened the walls that the building itself crumbled to the ground.
>
> This practice of camouflaging became so common that builders would not accept stones not bearing the label *Sine Cera*, meaning "without wax." This phrase guaranteed quality and genuineness. Later it was applied to all things without flaw, to things of genuineness, purity, truth and honesty. It is from this that we get our English word *sincerity*, which Webster defines as being that state or quality of being true or genuine.[1]

[1]From speech "The Future — Brighter in Education" by G. R. Bowers, from *Vital Speeches of the Day*, Volume XXXX (January 15, 1974), p. 222. Reprinted by permission of Vital Speeches of the Day.

Although explanation is a good way to begin to make an idea clear, be careful not to make your explanations too long or involved. Many audiences have been put to sleep by long-winded expositions and descriptions full of abstract details. Keep your explanations simple, brief, and accurate; and combine them with other forms of support when necessary.

Comparison and contrast

Comparisons point out similarities between something that is known, understood, or believed and something that is not. Contrasts, on the other hand, clarify or support an idea by emphasizing differences.

Comparisons. Dr. Louis Hadley Evans, minister-at-large of the Presbyterian church, made clear the meanings of the abstract terms *deist* and *theist* by comparing the former with a clock and the latter with a car:

> To you this world is what: a clock or a car? Is it a huge clock, that God once made, that He wound up at the beginning and left to run of itself? Then you are a *deist.*
>
> Do you believe that it is rather a car that God once made, but that does not run without His hand on the wheel, without His ultimate and personal control? Then you are a *theist.*[2]

When, during the darkest days of the Civil War, critics attacked the administration's policies, Lincoln answered them by comparing the plight of the government with that of Blondin, a famous tightrope walker, attempting to cross the Niagara River:

> Gentlemen, I want you to suppose a case for a moment. Suppose that all the property you were worth was in gold, and you had put it in the hands of Blondin, the famous rope-walker, to carry across the Niagara Falls on a tightrope. Would you shake the rope while he was passing over it, or keep shouting to him, "Blondin, stoop a little more! Go a little faster!" No, I am sure you would not. You would hold your breath as well as your tongue, and keep your hands off until he was safely over. Now the government is in the same situation. It is carrying an immense weight across a stormy ocean. Untold treasures are in its hands. It is doing the best it can. Don't badger it! Just keep still, and it will get you safely over.

---

[2]Excerpt from "Can You Trust God?" by Dr. Louis Hadley Evans. Reprinted by permission of the author.

Contrasts. Contrasts often take the form of telling what a thing is not. Thus a speaker who wished to make clear the nature of the British parliamentary system of government might do so by contrasting it with the federal system we have here in the United States. At other times, as in the following passage from a speech by Gus Turbeville, president of Coker College, a series of brief contrasts may be used to throw a line of thought into sharp relief:

> Without evil, there would be no good; without darkness, there would be no light; without ugliness, there would be no beauty; without the valleys, there would be no mountains. Personalizing this, without others you would have no self-conception. You would not know if you were moral, or attractive, or intelligent, or superior unless there were others by whom you could measure your own attributes. Without a sense of self you could not be evil, sinful, mean, selfish, or attracted by all the temptations flesh is heir to. And without a self you could not be good, generous, kind, considerate, and godly. Although it is terrifying to think that Hitler formed a self-identity through his reactions with others, it is encouraging to note that so did Schweitzer.[3]

Whatever form it takes, however, at least one of the items used in the contrast should be familiar to the audience and distinct enough from the other so that the difference between them stands out clearly.

Illustration

A *detailed narrative example* of the idea or statement you wish to support is called an illustration. Sometimes an illustration describes or exemplifies a concept, condition, or circumstance; sometimes it shows or demonstrates the results which have been obtained through the adoption of a plan or proposal. Always, however, an illustration is an expanded example presented in narrative form and having about it some striking or memorable quality.

There are two principal types of illustrations: the *hypothetical* and the *factual*. The first tells a story which *could have happened* or *probably will happen;* the second tells what *actually has happened.*

Hypothetical illustration. When addressing the Wisconsin Education Association Council, James D. Koerner, program officer of the Alfred P. Sloan Foundation, introduced a hypothetical illustration in

[3]From "Victory Over Self" by Gus Turbeville, from *Vital Speeches of the Day*, Volume XXXIX (October 1, 1973), p. 763. Reprinted by permission of Vital Speeches of the Day.

ILLUSTRATION 113

the form of a humorous story to show that the answer an investigator finds often depends on the *kind of question* he asks:

> Thus there is significance in the way one asks questions about change in education, as is illustrated in a favorite little story of mine. It concerns two Catholic priests, a Dominican and a Benedictine, both of whom were addicted to tobacco and both of whom found that the prayers they were required to say each day deprived them for considerable periods of time of the pleasure of smoking. So on the occasions when they met they engaged each other in a kind of continuing theological debate as to whether it was permissible for priests to smoke while in the course of their devotions. They were unable to resolve the question and so agreed that both would write the Pope for a decision. Some time later they encountered each other again, whereupon the Benedictine said to the Dominican, "Well, did you write the Pope as we agreed?" "Yes, I did," said the Dominican. "And what did he say?" The Dominican replied, "He said no." "Really?" asked the Benedictine with surprise, "What did you write him?" "Well, of course," said the Dominican, "I wrote and asked if it was all right for me to smoke while I prayed, and he said no." "Oh," said the Benedictine, "you asked the wrong question. I wrote and asked if it was all right for me to pray while I smoked, and he said yes."[4]

Because in a hypothetical illustration aspects of the situation can be manipulated at will, this form of support is an especially valuable means of clarifying an idea or of stimulating interest. Also, it provides a good way to explain a complicated process. Instead of talking in general terms, the speaker may take a person, perhaps herself or a member of the audience, and picture that person going through the various steps which the process entails. As proof, however, the hypothetical illustration is at best of doubtful value. The very fact that the details can be manipulated by the speaker may cause the audience to withhold credence.

Factual illustration. A factual illustration, as we have said, is a narrative that describes in detail a situation or incident that has actually occurred. Because details are brought into the story, the incident is made clear and vivid to the listeners; because the incident actually happened, the illustration frequently has high persuasive value. In the factual illustration which follows, note particularly how Donald Greve has

---

[4]From "Changing Education" by James D. Koerner, from *Vital Speeches of the Day*, Volume XXXX (January 1, 1974), p. 177. Reprinted by permission of Vital Speeches of the Day.

employed the narrative method of development and how he has used direct discourse to lend interest and reality to the story:

> Pop Warner, a football coach, had a bunch of Indians on his football team. He tried to get them in shape. He had them doing calisthenics like all football players do. They didn't like it. He couldn't get them to do it. He didn't say all Indians were lazy because these boys didn't do the calisthenics to get in shape. Instead, Pop Warner went around and talked with some of the Indian parents to find out what could be done. With their help, he figured out a new way to motivate them. He loaded his Indian players on the school bus and went two miles away from the college. He put each one of the players off the bus and handed them a tow sack. He said, "Take this tow sack, go out there and catch two rabbits any way you want to. Then run back to town as fast as you can." They did it! They got in shape. He learned to motivate these fellows based on their background, not based on his. As a direct result, he had a nation's champion in his caliber of football teams. There was one fellow in particular, a 158-pound fullback who was not very big for a fullback, but was a great athlete. His name was Jim Thorpe. I doubt that Jim Thorpe could have become the outstanding athlete that he was if Pop Warner had not learned to motivate him based on his background.[5]

Guidelines for choosing illustrations. Three considerations should be kept in mind when choosing an illustration, hypothetical or factual. *First, is it clearly related to the idea it is intended to support?* If you have to labor to show its connection, the illustration will be of little use. *Second, is it a fair example?* An audience is quick to notice unusual circumstances in an illustration; and if you seem to have picked only the exceptional case, your example will not prove convincing. *Third, is it vivid and impressive in detail?* The primary value of an illustration is the sense of reality which it creates. If this quality is absent, the advantage of using an illustration is lost. Be sure, then, that your illustrations are pointed, fair, and vivid.

Specific instance

A specific instance is an *undeveloped illustration or example.* Instead of describing a situation in detail, it merely mentions the person or event in question. Carroll G. Brunthaver, Assistant Secretary of Agriculture,

---

[5]From "The American Indian" by Donald Greve, from *Vital Speeches of the Day,* Volume XXXVI (February 15, 1970), p. 278. Reprinted by permission of Vital Speeches of the Day.

used the following series of specific instances to account for the recent increase in world demand for American farm products:

> We are living in a period of rapid and significant change. Things are happening right now around the globe that are changing the world we live in. In Taiwan, a farmer is buying a tractor that will increase his productivity. His sons are studying to become engineers.
>
> In Korea, they're building a subway for their capital city of Seoul. It will be in operation before the subway in Washington, D.C.
>
> The once-sleepy country of Spain now has the fastest-growing economy in the industrialized world.
>
> In Russia, the government is giving top priority to satisfying consumer demand—a sharp departure from its traditional concern with heavy industry.
>
> Mainland China is buying Western technology—petrochemical plants, jetliners, and machine tools—aimed at bringing the Chinese economy up to date.
>
> In the developing countries of the world, kids are learning to read and their parents are learning new skills.
>
> All over the world, doctors and medicines are helping people live longer, healthier lives.
>
> All of these changes are part of what I consider a major phenomenon of our times—a basic shift in the world's demand curve.[6]

If the persons or events referred to are common knowledge, the mere mention of them may be sufficient. On subjects with which the audience is not familiar, however, or on subjects concerning which listeners have marked differences of opinion, you should supplement specific instances with illustrations or other more fully developed supporting material.

Statistics

Not all figures are statistics; some are merely numbers. Statistics are figures used to show relationships among things: to point out increases or decreases, to emphasize largeness or smallness, or to show how one phenomenon is correlated with another. Because statistics are capable of summarizing great masses of specific facts or data, they are useful in

---

[6]From "What's Happening to Demand?" by Carroll G. Brunthaver, from *Vital Speeches of the Day*, Volume XXXX (March 1, 1974), p. 307. Reprinted by permission of Vital Speeches of the Day.

making clear the nature of a complex situation, in substantiating a potentially disputable claim, or in predicting future developments.

In the following example, Arthur H. Doerr, vice-president for Academic Affairs at the University of West Florida, amassed a body of statistical data to impress upon his audience the thoughtless way in which we are depleting our resources and polluting the environment:

Some examples of resource-use and environmental impact are seen in the following statements:

1. We are currently destroying agricultural land at the rate of 1,000,000 acres per year.
2. We discard, use, or discharge into the environment each year:
   a. 48,000,000,000 cans
   b. 26,000,000,000 bottles
   c. 142,000,000 tons of smoke
   d. 61,000,000 tons of carbon monoxide
   e. 16,000,000 tons of hydrocarbon gases
   f. 7,000,000 junked automobiles
   g. 6,000,000 tons of nitrogen oxide
   h. 210,000 tons of lead

We use each day 4 gallons of oil, 300 cubic feet of natural gas, 15 pounds of coal, and smaller amounts of energy from other sources per person—eight times the world average.[7]

At another point in the same speech, when Mr. Doerr wished to show how we in the United States compare to the rest of the world in population and the consumption of raw resources, he translated the relevant data into somewhat more personalized terms. Note that he did not merely cite figures; he emphasized their significance by establishing some unique *relationships* among them:

Suppose world population was compressed into a single city of 1000 people. In this imaginary city, 55 of the 1000 people would be American citizens, and 945 would represent all other nations. Of these 945 people, 215 would be citizens of the People's Republic of China. The 55 United States citizens would receive more than 40 percent of the town's income. These 55 people, representing 5½ percent of the population, would consume almost 15 percent of the town's food supply; use, on a per capita

---

[7]From "The Bounds of Earth" by Arthur H. Doerr, from *Vital Speeches of the Day*, Volume XXXX (February 1, 1974), p. 230. Reprinted by permission of Vital Speeches of the Day.

basis, 10 times as much oil, 40 times as much steel, and 40 times as much general equipment.[8]

Comparative statistics of this nature are especially desirable when the import of a large body of figures needs to be communicated or when the numbers involved are unusually large. Remember that figures by themselves tell little; you must establish trends—increases, decreases, variations, etc.—in order to create understanding or affect belief. Remember, too, that masses of figures or unusually large or small numbers often are difficult for an audience to comprehend and should, therefore, be translated into more immediately understandable terms. For example, to help make clear the immense age of the earth, Richard Carrington, a science writer, presented this comparison:

> If the earth's history could be compressed into a single year, the first eight months would be completely without life, the next two would see only the primitive creatures, mammals wouldn't appear until the second week in December, and no *homo sapiens* until 11:45 P.M. on Dec. 31. The entire period of man's written history would occupy the final 60 seconds before midnight.[9]

Other ways of making statistics more readily understandable include stating very large figures in round numbers (say "nearly 4,000,000," rather than "3,984,256"), breaking totals down on a per capita basis, writing figures on the chalkboard as you discuss them, pointing to prepared charts or graphs on which the data are presented, handing out mimeographed material summarizing the statistics you are presenting, and slowing down your rate of delivery. (For a discussion of the use of visual supporting materials, see pages 122–124.)

When effectively and honestly interpreted, statistics are invaluable in explanation or proof. You must, however, be careful to avoid the misuses and fallacies to which they are prone. Remember that a median or mean can be a deceiving figure, since it tells little or nothing about any one of the individual items on which it is based. Remember, too, when drawing comparisons, that the units compared must actually be of the same sort; and that in order to establish a trend, the figures must cover a reasonably lon_ period of time.

---

[8]*Ibid.*, p. 229.

[9]Quoted in the *Des Moines Register* September 16, 1965, p. 6.

Testimony

When speakers cite the opinions or conclusions expressed by others, they are said to be using *testimony* Sometimes the purpose of testimony is merely to add weight or impressiveness to an idea; at other times it is intended to supply proof for an assertion.

In the following passage from a speech by Professor Waldo W. Braden, chairman of the Department of Speech at Louisiana State University, testimony serves the first of these purposes:

> At the heart of successful communication is an attitude, an understanding, a sympathy for listeners and an eagerness to reach and help them. Kenneth I. Brown, former head of the Danforth Foundation, expresses this spirit in these words:
>
> "No man is an island, neither can he live within an all-inclusive government of one. He needs that sensitiveness to the incipient emotions and heart-longings of others if he is to live as a responsible member of the human race. He needs a special competence in those media of communication which are more difficult than the spoken language— the troubled eye, the quivering mouth, the withheld presence. Love is not alone the giving of self, even though that giving be generous and abundant. Love is the giving of self to another's need, and that need of the other can be learned not from generalizations about mankind , . . but through the sensitive outreach of a human spirit touching gently another human spirit."[10]

An example of testimony used as proof or support for an assertion comes from a lecture by another professor of speech, Dr. Robert T. Oliver, former chairman of the department at Pennsylvania State University:

> The manner in which mind and language are related has intrigued human curiosity at least as far back as the beginnings of recorded history—and still we do not know the answer with any certainty. Is all our thinking grammar-bound and limited to the extent of our vocabulary? Do we think in words? Does an individual increase his general mental powers as he improves and extends his mastery of language? The precise nature of the relationship is speculative; but the fact that there is a relationship is unquestionable.

---

[10]From "Beyond the Campus Gate" by Waldo W. Braden, from *Vital Speeches of the Day,* Volume XXXVI (July 1, 1971), p. 574. Reprinted by permission of Vital Speeches of the Day.

Max Muller, in his *Lectures on the Science of Language,* says flatly: "To think is to speak low. To speak is to think aloud." Edward Sapir, in *Language,* declares that "thought is nothing but language denuded of its outward garb." Charleton Laird, in his *Miracle of Language,* defines man as "a languagized mammal," and concludes that "when we study language, we are, to a remarkable degree, studying human nature." A. D. Ritchie, in *The Natural History of Mind,* writes: "As far as thought is concerned, and at all levels of thought, it is a symbolic process. . . . The essential act of thought is symbolic." Susanne Langer, author of *Philosophy in a New Key,* believes that the discovery or invention of language marked "a whole day of creation" between man and lower animals and was "the real beginning of mentality."[11]

Tests of authority. All testimony should meet the twin tests of *pertinence* and *audience acceptability.* When used to prove a statement, rather than merely to add weight or to clarify, testimony also should satisfy four more specific criteria:

1. *The person quoted should be qualified by training and experience, as an authority.* He or she should be an expert in the field to which the testimony relates.
2. Whenever possible, *the statement of the authority should be based on firsthand knowledge.*
3. *The judgment expressed should not be unduly influenced by personal interest.* The authority must not be prejudiced.
4. *The hearers should realize that the person quoted actually is an authority.* They should respect his or her opinion.

When citing testimony, watch particularly the tendency to use big names simply because they are well known. A movie star's opinion on the nutritive value of a breakfast food is less reliable than the opinion of your physician. The best testimony always comes from subject-matter experts whose qualifications your listeners recognize.

Restatement

Restatement is reiteration of an idea in different words. Therefore, it is to be distinguished from mere repetition, in which the words remain the same.

---

[11]From "Mind and Language" by Robert T. Oliver, from *Vital Speeches of the Day,* Volume XXXI (October 15, 1964), p. 22. Reprinted by permission of Vital Speeches of the Day.

Although they provide no real proof, restatement and repetition often have persuasive impact. Advertisers realize this fact and spend millions of dollars annually repeating essentially the same message in magazines, on billboards, and over radio and television. "Let Hertz put you in the driver's seat." "Hallmark cards . . . When you care enough to send the very best." "Wouldn't you really rather have a Buick?" Slogans such as these have been repeated until they are familiar to almost everyone.

Up to a certain point, of course, repetition of the same words or restatement of the same ideas may persuade the listener; beyond that point, however, they become monotonous and boring. Be careful to avoid this danger. Be sure also that you plan your restatements so that they reformulate the phrasing of the original idea as clearly and precisely as possible.

In the speech cited earlier, Professor Braden used a combination of repetition and restatement effectively to drive home the idea that communication is a process in which the listener as well as the speaker plays a vital role:

> Let me remind you. We communicate—not by what we are, but by what listeners understand. We communicate—not by what we intend to say, but by what listeners see, hear and are willing to accept. We communicate—not by what we say, but by what listeners hear.[12]

In an effort to make clear the kind of leader he thinks is required in present-day America, Dr. Ralph Eubanks of the University of West Florida employed a somewhat different kind of restatement or redefinition of his concept of the "new leadership." Notice how he has rephrased the essential idea in four different ways:

> We must, among other things, create a new leadership in America. . . . The leader I shall define as one who can help his group conduct well the ancient search for the "good life in the good society." Put another way, a good leader for our times is one who can hold ever before the members of his group a truly human vision of themselves. In slightly different terms, he is one who can help his group find their way to honorable, human goals and can teach them how to "care for persons" in the

---

[12]From "Beyond the Campus Gate" by Waldo W. Braden, from *Vital Speeches of the Day*, Volume XXXVI (July 1, 1971), p. 573. Reprinted by permission of Vital Speeches of the Day.

process. In still different terms, he is one who can help us live up to the ancient definition of ourselves as *Homo Sapiens,* or Man the Wise.[13]

Explanation, comparison and contrast, illustration, specific instance, statistics, testimony, and restatement—these, then, are the common forms of verbal supporting materials. Fill your speeches with them. Avoid abstract, unsupported statements. Amplify your ideas, illuminate them, and make them concrete.

VISUAL SUPPORTING MATERIALS

Thus far we have discussed only the verbal materials that you may use to explain or to prove a point—what you may *say* about it. Equally important, sometimes even more so, are the visual materials that you may use to *show* what you mean. Whereas in explanatory talks, visual materials help clarify ideas, in persuasive speeches, they may actually help win acceptance of a contention by making the supporting facts more vivid and impressive.

These visual materials, which include *maps, diagrams, charts, pictures, small working models,* or even *full-scale equipment,* supplement the spoken forms of support and help to make your ideas clearer and more convincing. If, for example, you are explaining how to use a complicated camera, it undoubtedly will help if you hold the camera before your listeners, show them its parts, and demonstrate the adjustments required for different kinds of pictures. Similarly, the advantages of a new kind of tape recorder or pocket calculator can best be made clear by demonstration. If the actual equipment or object is not available or is too big to bring into the room where the speech is to be made, a small scale model may be used. Model airplanes, for instance, are employed in teaching aerodynamics. Maps are helpful in explaining the layout of a city, a state's road system, or a flood-control project. Diagrams show structural elements of an organization or parts of a mechanism and suggest their operation. Line, bar, and pie graphs clarify statistical data. Pictures, including slides and films, are especially valuable when you are describing unusual persons, places, objects, or events.

---

[13]From a speech before Annual Leadership Conference by Dr. Ralph Eubanks, from *Vital Speeches of the Day,* Volume XXIX (May 15, 1963), p. 479. Reprinted by permission of Vital Speeches of the Day.

Clockwise from upper left: Arnold Ogden/ University of Colorado; Elaine F. Keenan, NEST, S.F.; Michael D. Sullivan.

When carefully prepared and properly used, visual supporting materials can be valuable aids to the speaker who seeks to clarify a difficult concept, show the structure of an object, or display the workings of a device or mechanism.

Guides for using visual materials

Four important rules should be kept in mind when you are using visual aids. First, *do not stand between your listeners and what you wish to show them.* When pointing to a map or diagram, place yourself to one side of the visual material, and talk to the audience directly. Second, *be sure your visual material is large enough to be seen easily from all parts of the room.* Third, *use only visual materials that are closely related to the point you are presenting,* and refer only to those parts of the aid that are relevant. Avoid the temptation to explain details that are not necessary to the development of your speech. Fourth, *present in visual form only data which are simple enough to be comprehended at a glance.* If your listeners must stop to "puzzle out" what a chart or diagram means, they will not be able to follow you as you move on to new ideas in your speech. In preparing your visual materials, therefore, use few and simple words; avoid a mass of meandering or crisscross lines; employ vivid colors instead of weak pastels. Put only one idea or one closely related set of ideas on each chart or graph.

The use of supporting materials to explain

How should you assemble supporting materials in a short talk designed to explain a single point? Usually it is best to divide such a speech into three parts or steps. First, state in a clear, concise sentence the point you wish to explain; second, bring in your supporting materials—especially explanations, illustrations, comparisons, and visual devices; third, restate the point you have explained. In the second step the verbal and visual materials may be presented separately or together. That is, you may *first* tell your listeners and *then* show them; or you may show them *while telling them.*

A SAMPLE OUTLINE FOR A ONE-POINT SPEECH

In the following outline note how the speaker has combined verbal and visual materials to establish and develop the main point:

HOW WE BREATHE

Explanation I. The human breathing mechanism may be likened to a bellows which expands to admit air and contracts to expel it.
   A. When we inhale, two things happen.
      1. Muscles attached to the collarbone and shoulder bones pull upward and slightly outward.

2. Muscles in the abdominal wall relax, allowing the diaphragm—a sheet of muscle and tendon lying immediately below the lungs—to fall.

B. This permits the spongy, porous material of which the lungs consist to expand.

   1. A vacuum is created.

   2. Air rushes in.

C. When we exhale, two things happen also.

   1. Gravity causes the rib cage to move downward.

   2. Muscles in the abdominal wall contract, squeezing the diaphragm upward.

D. The space available to the lungs is thus reduced.

   1. The lungs are squeezed.

   2. Air is emitted.

Comparison

E. The similarity between the breathing mechanism and a bellows is represented in this diagram:

Visual Aid

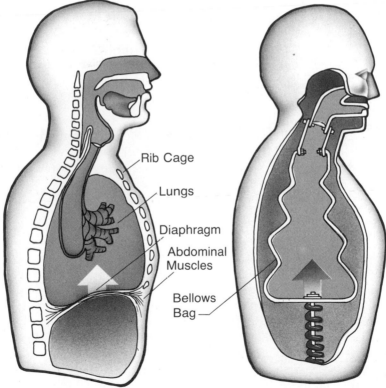

Rib Cage

Lungs

Diaphragm

Abdominal Muscles

Bellows Bag

Restatement F. In summary, then, to remember how the human breathing mechanism works, think of a bellows.
  1. Just as increasing the size of the bellows bag allows air to rush in, so increasing the space available to the lungs allows them to admit air.
  2. Just as squeezing the bellows bag forces air out, so contracting the space the lungs can occupy forces air to be emitted.

THE USE OF SUPPORTING MATERIALS TO PROVE

When supporting materials are used to prove a point, they may be organized in either of two ways: (1) the *didactic method* or (2) the *method of implication*.

The didactic method

The didactic method utilizes a pattern similar to that employed in the expository speech outlined above. In using this method you first state and clarify the proposition you wish to prove, then you present the proof in the form of concrete supporting materials, and finally you restate the proposition as an established conclusion. The steps in this pattern, therefore, are as follows:

  1. State your point.
  2. Make it clear (by explanation, comparison, illustration, or through the use of models or diagrams).
  3. Prove it (by specific instances, testimony, statistics, or additional factual illustrations).
  4. Restate your point as an established conclusion.

The method of implication

The method of implication consists of presenting your facts first, and then stating the conclusion toward which these facts inevitably lead. You do not bring out the point to be proved until you have made clear the evidence upon which your contention rests. This method, sometimes called the "natural" method of argument, more nearly coincides with the way in which people arrive at conclusions when thinking things through for themselves. For this reason, though often not so clear or so easy to use as the didactic method, the method of implication may be more persuasive. Because it works by indirection or inference rather than frontal assault, it always is to be preferred when talking to a skeptical or hostile audience. This implicative method usually entails four separate steps:

1. Present a comparison or illustration which *implies* the point you wish to make.
2. Offer additional illustrations, instances, statistics, or testimony which point inevitably toward this conclusion without actually stating it.
3. Show specifically how these facts lead to the conclusion; use explanation if necessary.
4. Definitely state your point as a conclusion.

A SAMPLE OUTLINE USING THE DIDACTIC METHOD

Study the sample speech outline below. Note that although the didactic method is used, if the general statement were to be omitted, this organizational form would illustrate equally well the method of implication.

CABLE TELEVISION — AT YOUR SERVICE!

Main Idea

I. Cable television soon will revolutionize your everyday life.

First Supporting Statement: Hypothetical Illustration

A. Suppose, on a rainy day a few years from now, you decide to "run" your errands from your living room.

Specific Instances Within the Illustration

1. You turn on your two-way communication unit, and begin your round of errands:
   a. On Channel 37, your bank's computer verifies the amount of a recent withdrawal.
   b. On Channel 26, you ask the telephone company to review last month's long-distance charges.
   c. On Channel 94, a supermarket lets you scan products, prices, and home-delivery hours.
   d. On Channel 5, you study a list of proposed changes in the city charter.
      (1) You can "call in" for further information.
      (2) You can vote from your own home.
   e. Channel 115 gives you access to resource personnel at the public library.

Restatement

2. Thus — with "cable television at your service" — you

have accomplished your day's errands with minimum expenditure of time, gas, and parking-meter money.

B. These possibilities, once thought of only as dreams, are becoming actualities across the United States.

1. New York City already has a channel which gives citizens direct access to city officials.
2. San Francisco's "public-access channels" already are filled with local talent and ethnic programming.

3. Ann Arbor, Michigan, has been leasing channels to private firms and public-utility companies.

C. Cable television soon will be available to virtually every household in the United States at a reasonable cost.
1. Because the cost is shared by licensee and householder alike, no one bears an excessive burden.

   a. Commercial users find that leasing a channel costs little more than their computer-accounting systems and print/electronic advertising services.
   b. Studio facilities for the public-access channels are made available at cost in most cable television contracts — normally about $30 per hour.

   c. Current installation charges range from $15 to $50.
   d. Monthly rental fees per household seldom exceed $6.
2. The technical characteristics of cable television render it inexpensive.
   a. Some existent telephone lines and equipment can be used.
   b. The conversion box mounts easily on a regular television set.
   c. Studio costs are minimal.
      (1) Relatively inexpensive ½" videotape and broadcasting equipment can be used.
      (2) Engineering and production personnel need minimal training for cable systems.

<table>
<tr><td>Restatement</td><td>D. Given actual and potential uses, plus the positive cost-benefit ratio, cable television will revolutionize your daily life.</td></tr>
<tr><td>Comparison</td><td>1. Just as the wheel extended our legs and the computer our central nervous system, so will cable television extend our communicative capabilities.</td></tr>
<tr><td>Testimony Used
as Restatement
of Main Idea</td><td>2. In the words of Wendy Lee, communication consultant to new cable-television franchises: "We soon will be a nation wired fully for sight and sound. We will rid ourselves of the need for short shopping trips; we will cut the lines in doctors' offices; and we will put the consumer and the constituent into the front offices of his or her corporate suppliers and political servants. The telephone and the motor car will become obsolete."</td></tr>
</table>

Although the proof of a single point may not require the use of supporting materials as numerous or varied as those employed in this sample outline, they are presented here to show how a number of different forms may be combined.

THE USE OF SUPPORTING MATERIALS TO ENTERTAIN

As we pointed out in Chapter 3, in a speech to entertain, your general purpose is not to explain or to prove something to your listeners, but simply to amuse them—to cause them to sit back and enjoy themselves. Although you may assemble the supporting materials around a central theme in much the same way as in a speech to inform or persuade, you should choose them not so much to clarify or to add substance as to divert or amuse. Allow careful explanation and solid proof to give way to lively descriptions and novel facts; replace statistics with humorous anecdotes and tales of your own or someone else's experiences; introduce exaggerated descriptions, puns, irony, and unexpected turns of phrase.

Whereas humor is usually a primary element, a good speech to entertain is more than a string of unrelated jokes. Let one story or observation lead naturally into the next, and see that all serve to bring out a central point around which your talk is built. Use stories and anecdotes to develop a common theme—some sentiment of loyalty or appreciation for the group addressed or a serious thought concerning your subject.

Arranging speech materials to entertain

A speech to entertain, then, should consist of a series of illustrations, quips, and stories following one another in rapid order and developed around a central idea that has at least some significance or merit. The following is a good way to arrange such a talk:

1. Relate a story or anecdote, present an illustration, or quote an appropriate verse.
2. State the essential idea or point of view implied by your opening remarks.
3. Follow with a series of additional stories, anecdotes, or illustrations that amplify or illuminate this central point. Arrange these items in the order of increasing interest or humor.
4. Close with a striking or novel restatement of the central point you have developed.

By organizing your talk in this way, you not only will provide your listeners with entertainment, but you also will help them remember your central idea.

A SAMPLE OF A SPEECH TO ENTERTAIN

The speech printed below illustrates the four steps we have described. In addition, it shows how light and humorous materials may be used to develop a potentially serious thought.

A Case For Optimism[14]
Douglas Martin

Poem embodying contrast used as opening

I'm sure you have heard the verse that runs:

'Twixt optimist and pessimist
The difference is droll:
The optimist sees the doughnut,
The pessimist, the hole.

Statement

The longer I live, the more convinced I am of the truth of this poem. Life, like a doughnut, may seem full, rich, and enjoyable, or it may seem as empty as the hole in the middle. To the pessimist, the optimist seems foolish. But who is

---

[14]Based in part on material taken from *Friendly Speeches* (Cleveland: National Reference Library).

foolish—the one who sees the doughnut or the one who sees the hole?

Contrast

Somebody else pointed out the difference between an optimist and a pessimist this way: An optimist looks at an oyster and expects a pearl; a pessimist looks at an oyster and expects ptomaine poisoning. Even if the pessimist is right, which I doubt, he probably won't enjoy himself either before or after he proves it. But the optimist is happy because he always is expecting pearls.

Illustration

Pessimists are easy to recognize. They are the ones who go around asking "What's good about it?" when someone says "Good morning." If they would look around, they would see *something* good, as did the optimistic merchant whose store was robbed. The day after the robbery a sympathetic friend asked about the loss. "Lose much?" he wanted to know. "Some," said the merchant, "but then it would have been worse if the robbers had got in the night before. You see, yesterday I just finished marking everything down 20%."

Illustration

There is another story about the happy-go-lucky shoemaker who left the gas heater in his shop turned on overnight and upon arriving in the morning struck a match to light it. There was a terrific explosion, and the shoemaker was blown out through the door almost to the middle of the street. A passerby, who rushed up to help, inquired if he were injured. The shoemaker got up slowly and looked back at the shop, which by now was burning briskly. "No, I ain't hurt," he said, "but I sure got out just in time, didn't I?"

Testimony (pro and con)

Some writers have ridiculed that kind of outlook. You may recall the fun Voltaire made of optimism in *Candide:* "Optimism," he said, "is a mania for maintaining that all is well when things are going badly." A later writer, James Branch Cabell, quipped: "The optimist proclaims that we live in the best of all possible worlds; the pessimist fears this is true."

These writers, I suppose, couldn't resist the urge to make light of optimists; but I, for one, refuse to take *them* seriously. I like the remark by Keith Preston, literary critic and journalist: "There's as much bunk among the busters as among the boosters."

Beginning the summary

Optimism, rather than the cynicism of Voltaire, is the philosophy I like to hear preached. There was a little old lady who complained about the weather. "But, Melissa," said her friend, "awful weather is better than no weather." So quit complaining, I say, and start cheering; there is always something to cheer about. And stop expecting the worst. An optimist cleans his glasses before he eats his grapefruit.

Give in to optimism; don't fight it. Remember the doughnut. And, as Elbert Hubbard advised:

As you travel on through life, brother,
Whatever be your goal,
Keep your eye upon the doughnut
And not upon the hole.

In this chapter we have discussed the various types of supporting materials, both verbal and visual; and we have demonstrated how these materials may be assembled to explain or to prove the points that a speaker wishes to make. We also have suggested how to develop a single idea into a speech to entertain. We have, moreover, emphasized the usefulness and wide applicability of one-point speeches and have urged that in preparing them, you should be sure to state in a simple, straightforward manner the central idea you want to establish; choose supporting materials that are clear and substantial or light and entertaining; and arrange these materials so that they develop and emphasize the theme of your speech.

PROBLEMS FOR FURTHER STUDY

1. Your instructor will assign each member of the class a list of three or four magazines or journals. In the Reference Room of your college library, find published indexes which include materials from the periodicals you have been assigned. Check into such indexes as *The Readers' Guide to Periodical Literature, The International Index, The Education Index, The Essay Index,* and the like. While in the Reference Room, ask to see such research helps as *Psychological Abstracts, Speech Index, The New York Times Index, The Bibliographic Index, United Nations Document Index, Vertical File Index,* and also more specialized indexes in fields of your own interest. Enter in your journal a brief description of each index you examine; refer to these notes before you begin your research on your next speech.

2. Read at least six recent public speeches in *Vital Speeches of the Day* or some other suitable source, and tabulate the supporting materials employed by the speakers. Which forms of support are used most frequently? Which least frequently? Considering the subjects with which the speeches deal and the purposes for which they were delivered, try to explain the findings you have noted. Finally, comment critically on the sup-

porting materials you have uncovered: Were the forms used appropriately and effectively? Why or why not? What changes would you suggest? Why?

3. List five general subject-areas on which you would like to speak. For each of these subject-areas, first frame a specific purpose suitable for a short, one-point speech, and then frame a specific purpose suitable for a longer and more fully developed speech. Be ready to defend your choice of purposes and to tell why each is suitable for a one-point development or for a more fully detailed, multi-point treatment.

4. Nonverbal supporting materials capture appropriate moods, clarify potentially complex subjects, and sometimes even carry the thrust of a persuasive message. Look around you; examine magazine advertisements, "how-to-do-it" articles in magazines, store windows, special displays in museums and libraries, and slide-projection lectures in some of your other college classes. *(a)* Using the *types* considered in this chapter, classify the nonverbal supporting materials you have encountered. *(b)* Assess the *purposes* these materials serve—clarification, persuasion, attention-focusing, mood-setting, and others you may wish to cite. *(c)* Evaluate the *effectiveness* with which each of the nonverbal supporting materials you have examined is doing its job. *(d)* Prepare a class report, a paper, or an entry in your journal on the results of your experiences and observations.

5. Consider some of the circumstances (the nature of the subject, attitudes of the audience toward the subject and toward you, the time available, etc.) under which you probably would choose to organize a single-idea speech according to the *didactic pattern* and some of the circumstances under which you would select the *method of implication.* Which of these circumstances affect your decision most directly and strongly? Which seem most deeply rooted in audience expectations? Are some speakers "allowed" by status, position, or circumstances to appear more didactic, whereas others seemingly have more to "prove" about themselves and therefore *must* use the method of implication?

ORAL ACTIVITIES AND SPEAKING ASSIGNMENTS

1. Because supporting materials can be used by communicators fairly or fallaciously, you would be well advised to arm yourself against the trickster and manipulator. Each member of the class will be asked to prepare a report on a chapter from Darrel Huff's *How to Lie with Statistics* (New York: W. W. Norton & Company, Inc., 1954) or Martin Gardner's *Fads and Fallacies in the Name of Science* (New York: Dover Publications, Inc., 1957; orig. *In the Name of Science,* 1952). In preparing your report, clearly

identify the trick or fallacy being described by the author. Integrate appropriate visual aids with your presentation.

2. Following presentations for Oral Activity 1, your instructor will divide the class into groups of four or five students each. Each group should meet and discuss the topic "Pitfalls in Proof." Concern yourselves with the sanctity with which we view statistical data in our technological age, the credibility we seem to grant to scientists and their research, and even the role of smooth and self-assured delivery in giving force to apparent "proofs." Then assemble as a whole class to compare the conclusions of the different groups.

3. Following the suggestions offered in this chapter, prepare and present a two- or three-minute, one-point speech to inform, to prove, or to entertain. For possible subjects, check your speech journal or lists of subjects provided at the ends of Chapters 10 and 11, specifically, pp. 223–226 and 263–264.

4. Present to the class a five-minute, one-point speech, the purpose of which is to explain or clarify a term, concept, process, plan, or proposal. Use at least three different forms of supporting material in developing your ideas, and employ at least one chart, diagram, map, picture, or other nonverbal support. If you have difficulty selecting an appropriate subject, check the list of subjects referred to in Activity 3 above.

5. Using the four-step procedure laid out on page 130, prepare and present to a classroom audience a one-point speech to entertain, based on one of the following topics or a similar one:

> You can't take it with you.
> How to swallow a pill.
> What this country really needs is _____.
> Gentlemen prefer blonds — and brunettes and redheads.
> Professors I have known.
> The inevitables of life.

SUGGESTIONS FOR FURTHER READING

Fenelon, *Dialogues on Eloquence* (1718). The classic statement on "verbal portraiture" and its role in intensifying ideas.

Donald C. Bryant and Karl R. Wallace, *Fundamentals of Public Speaking*, 4th ed. (New York: Appleton-Century-Crofts, 1969), Chapter VII, "Development of Materials in Informative Speaking," pp. 85–113. An expanded discussion of the types of supporting materials described in this chapter.

Nicholas Capaldi, *The Art of Deception* (Buffalo, N.Y.: Prometheus Books, 1971). A readable discussion of formal and substantive fallacies and the means of correcting them.

James C. McCroskey, "A Summary of Experimental Research on the Effects of Evidence in Persuasive Communication," *Quarterly Journal of Speech* 55 (April 1969): 169–176. Reprinted in Jimmie D. Trent, Judith S. Trent, and Daniel J. O'Neill, eds., *Concepts in Communication* (Boston: Allyn & Bacon, Inc., 1973), pp. 167–179. A review of research investigating relationships of evidence to attitude-change, source-credibility, sources of evidence, delivery, media of presentation, and the speaker's prior knowledge of the subject.

Walter A. Wittich and Charles F. Schuller, *Audio-Visual Materials: Their Nature and Use,* 2nd ed. (New York: Harper & Row, Publishers, 1957). A useful discussion of nonverbal supporting materials, their uses and preparation.

Chapter 7

Arranging and outlining related points

I N THE PRECEDING CHAPTER we examined the kinds of materials from which speeches are built. Moreover, we saw how these materials may be used to explain or to prove a single point. Most speeches, however, contain more than one point; so we must now consider how to put longer speeches together in an orderly manner. Our chief concerns in this chapter will be how to organize the main points of a speech, how to arrange the subordinate ideas and the supporting materials, and how to state the plan of the entire speech in outline form.[1]

TYPES OF ARRANGEMENT

Always arrange the points of your speech in a systematic sequence so that one idea leads naturally into the next. Not only will such an order make it easier for you to remember what you planned to say, but it also will enable your audience to follow your thoughts more readily. There are several standard patterns or sequences for organizing a speech so that each point leads logically into the one that follows.

Time sequence

One method of organization is to begin at a certain period or date and to move forward chronologically. The climate of Alaska, for example, may be described by considering the weather conditions as they exist in the *spring, summer, fall,* and *winter;* the refining of petroleum, by tracing the development of the refining process from the earliest attempts down to the present; or the manufacture of an automobile, by following the process on the assembly line from beginning to end. Note the time sequence in the following outline of a speech about American flights in outer space:

---

[1]For discussions of the special problems involved in organizing speeches to inform and to persuade or actuate, see Chapter 10, "Speaking to Inform," pp. 212–221; and Chapter 11, "Speaking to Persuade," pp. 241–262.

I. On May 5, 1961, Lieutenant Commander Alan Shepard became the first American to enter outer space.
II. On December 21–27, 1968, Frank Borman, James A. Lovell, Jr., and William A. Anders were the first humans to escape earth's gravity.
III. On July 20, 1969, Neil Armstrong and Edwin Aldrin were the first Americans—and the first Earthmen—to land successfully on the moon.
IV. On February 8, 1974, the crew of America's Skylab 3—Gerald Carr, Edward Gibson, and William Pogue—completed a record-breaking space flight lasting eighty-four days.

In rare cases, in order to make progress or development seem more striking and vivid, you may arrange the items in your outline to move *backward* from a chosen point in time, beginning with the most recent one and ending with the earliest. Whether you move forward or backward, however, be certain to preserve the actual chronological or reverse-chronological sequence of events in ordering the key points of your outline. If you jump haphazardly from date to date or from event to event, without regard to their chronological occurrence, you will create an unclear picture and confuse your listeners.

Space sequence

When using the space sequence, arrange your materials by moving systematically from east to west, from north to south, from the bottom upward, from the center to the outside, or in some similar space-relation pattern. For example, you might discuss the problem of flood control in our nation by considering in turn the various geographical areas affected; you might describe the plans for a building, floor by floor; or you might explain the layout for a city park by proceeding from entrance to exit. The following outline for a speech about Midwest farmers illustrates *space sequence:*

I. Iowa farmers grow huge crops of corn and soybeans.
II. Kansas farmers produce vast quantities of wheat for bread and other bakery goods.
III. Wisconsin farmers contribute endless supplies of eggs and dairy products.
IV. Michigan farmers provide a wealth of excellent fruits and vegetables.

Cause-effect sequence

When using a cause-effect sequence, you may begin by enumerating certain forces or factors and then point out the results which follow from them. Or you may first describe conditions or events and then discuss the forces which caused them. For example, you might start by recounting recent developments in the control of communicable diseases and then show that *as a result* widespread epidemics in those areas no longer are a serious threat; or, reversing the process, you might first point to the absence of widespread epidemics and then attribute their elimination to recent developments in the control of communicable diseases.

Using the cause-effect pattern, a speech relating our shortages of energy to wasteful practices in the past might be arranged in either of these ways:

Cause	I. For many years, we have used our most valuable forms of energy wastefully and without thought of the future.
Effect	II. As a result of this wastefulness, we must now face the most serious shortages in our history.

OR

Effect	I. We now face serious shortages of our most valuable forms of energy.
Cause	II. A major cause of these shortages is that for many years we have used energy wastefully and without thought of the future.

Problem-solution sequence

Sometimes you can best organize a speech by dividing it into two major parts: (1) a description of a problem (or related problems) and (2) the presentation of a solution (or solutions) to that problem. For instance, you might first point to the immense technical difficulties involved in building the Mackinac Bridge connecting the Upper and Lower Peninsulas of Michigan, and then explain how these difficulties were overcome. The problem-solution sequence is especially effective when you are exploring a problem that directly concerns the audience. Thus you might point to declining interest in an important campus activity and then try to convince your listeners that they should adopt one or more ways of reversing this trend. Or you might outline the problems involved in protecting the consumer against false or misleading advertising and then suggest possible solutions for those problems. Here is how one speaker employed this sequence in discussing urban crime:

Stating the problem.	I. Each year the problem of crime in our major cities grows more serious.
Emphasizing the extent and seriousness of the problem.	A. Capital crimes such as murder and kidnaping are on the increase. B. The juvenile crime rate has grown alarmingly.
Proposed three-way solution to the problem.	II. We must solve this problem in three ways: A. Begin a nationwide crime-prevention program. B. Remove certain laws and regulations which now hamper the police in their work. C. Free our courts from political ties and pressures.

Special topical sequence

Certain types of information fall into categories with which your listeners are already familiar. For example, they could customarily expect financial reports to be arranged by assets and liabilities or income and expenditures, or talks about our national government to be divided according to its three branches: the executive, the legislative, and the judicial. When such partitions are established by tradition or are specifically suggested by the subject matter to be presented, take advantage of such listener-expectations and use them as the basic pattern or plan of your speech. You may also arrange in special topical sequence a description of qualities or functions, or a series of arguments supporting or opposing a course of action. A special topical sequence for a talk on "food groups" might, for example, take this form:

    I. Meat provides protein, fat, iron, and B-complex vitamins.
   II. Vegetables and fruits supply roughage, carbohydrates, and A and C vitamins.
 III. Cereals contain carbohydrates and B-complex vitamins.
 IV. Dairy products are rich in protein, fat, iron, and A and D vitamins.

CONSISTENCY OF ARRANGEMENT

Sometimes you may want to choose one method of arrangement for the main points of your message and another method for the subordinate ideas. On no condition, however, should you shift from one method to another in the presentation of the main points themselves, for this would confuse your listeners. The following outline illustrates how space, special topical, and time sequences might be combined in a talk on the major cities of India.

I. The major cities of *western* India include Bombay and Ahmadabad.
   A. Bombay.
      1. Early history.
      2. Development under the British.
      3. Condition today.
   B. Ahmadabad.
      1., 2., 3. *(Develop as above.)*
II. The major cities of *central* India include Delhi and Hyderabad.
   A. Delhi.
      1. Early history.
      2. Development under the British.
      3. Condition today.
   B. Hyderabad.
      1., 2., 3. *(Develop as above.)*
III. The major cities of *eastern* India include Calcutta and Madras.
   A. Calcutta.
      1. Early history.
      2. Development under the British.
      3. Condition today.
   B. Madras.
      1., 2., 3. *(Develop as above.)*

Note that in this outline space sequence is used for the main points, special topical sequence for subpoints A and B, and time sequence for sub-subpoints 1, 2, and 3.

Or a talk on discrimination against women in business and the professions might employ a special order emphasizing pay, professional advancement, and social equality, thus:

I. Women usually earn less than men holding comparable positions.
II. Women frequently are denied advancement to the executive level.
III. Women suffer many subtle forms of social discrimination in the course of their daily work.

At times it is wise to let the anticipated responses of your listeners, rather than the nature of your subject matter, determine the arrangement of a speech. If you know in advance that certain important questions or objections are likely to be raised concerning your idea, you may plan your entire speech to meet these objections. Suppose, for example, that you are advocating some form of public aid for private schools and colleges and you know your listeners are likely to ask, "What advantages does your proposal hold for me as a taxpayer, as the parent of a college-age student, or as a concerned citizen?" You might plan your speech in this way:

  I. Public aid will enable many hard-pressed private colleges to survive in a time of constantly increasing costs.
  II. Public aid will help relieve the heavy enrollment pressures on our state-supported universities.
  III. Public aid will ensure that students can choose from many different kinds of colleges the one that is exactly right for them.

PHRASING MAIN POINTS

For reasons of emphasis as well as of clarity, you should word the main points of your speech carefully. While illustrations, explanations, quotations, and the like constitute the bulk of any talk, the main points tie these supporting details together and, therefore, most directly convey the message you wish to communicate. In order to achieve maximum effectiveness in the statement of your main points, keep in mind these four characteristics of good phrasing: *conciseness, vividness, immediacy,* and *parallelism*

Conciseness

State your main points as briefly as you can without distorting their meaning. A simple, straightforward declaration is easy to grasp; a long and complex statement tends to be vague and confusing. Avoid clumsy modifying phrases and distracting subordinate clauses. State the essence of your idea in a short sentence which can be modified or elaborated as you subsequently present the supporting material. Say, "Our state taxes are too high," not "Taxes in this state, with the exception of those on automobiles, motor boats, and trucking lines, are higher than is justified by existing economic conditions." The second statement may express your idea more completely than the first, but it contains nothing that your supporting material could not clarify, and its greater complexity makes it less crisp and emphatic.

Vividness

Whenever possible, state the main points of your speech in attention-provoking words and phrases. If your principal ideas are drab and colorless, they will not stand out from the supporting materials which surround them, nor will they be easy to remember. Because they are your main points, you should make them the punch lines of your speech. Notice how much more vivid it is to say, "We must cut costs!" than to say, "We must reduce our current operating expenditures." Vivid phrasing should not, of course, be overdone or used to distort the truth; nor should the sort of language suitable for a pep rally or political meeting be used on a more dignified occasion. Within these limits, however, vividness of phrasing is desirable. (Note: The quality of vividness — and other matters pertaining to the wording of the speech — will be examined more extensively in the following chapter.)

Immediacy

Try to word your main points so they will appeal directly to the immediate interests and concerns of your listeners. Remember that you are speaking not merely *about* something, but *to* somebody. Instead of saying "Chemical research has helped to improve medical treatment," say "Modern chemistry helps the doctor make you well." Rather than saying "Air travel is fast," say "Air travel saves you time."[2]

Parallelism

Whenever possible, use a uniform type of sentence structure and similar phraseology in stating your main points. Since these points represent coordinate units of your speech, word them so they sound that way. Avoid unnecessary shifts from active to passive voice or from questions to assertions. Use prepositions, connectives, and verb forms which permit a similar balance, rhythm, and direction of thought. *Avoid* this kind of wording for a series of main points:

    I. The amount of your income tax depends on the amount you earn.
   II. You pay sales taxes in proportion to the amount you buy.
  III. Property tax is assessed on the value of what you own.

Instead phrase the main points like this:

---

[2]See in this connection the discussion of audience interests and desires, pp. 42–52.

I. The amount of money you earn determines your income tax.
II. The amount of goods you buy determines your sales tax.
III. The amount of property you own determines your property tax.

Observe that in this series a part of each statement ("The amount of . . . you . . . determines your . . . tax.") is repeated, whereas the remainder of the statement is changed from point to point. Such repetition of key words may help your listeners remember the major ideas in your message.

ARRANGING SUBORDINATE IDEAS AND SUPPORTING MATERIALS

When you have selected, arranged, and phrased the main points of your speech, you are ready to organize your subordinate ideas and supporting materials in such a way as to give substance and orderliness to the whole message.

Subordinating the subordinate ideas

A "string-of-beads discussion," in which everything seems to have equal weight—tied together as it usually is by *and-uh, and next, and then, and so* —not only lacks purposive form, but also obscures meaning. Because everything receives equal emphasis, nothing seems important; and the speech soon becomes tiresome. Regardless of how well you have chosen, arranged, and worded the main points, they will not stand out unless your lesser ideas are properly subordinated. Avoid giving the subpoints the emphasis due only to your principal thoughts, and avoid listing under such main thoughts ideas that are not subordinate to them.

Types of subordinate ideas

Subordinate ideas commonly fall into one of five classes: (1) *parts of a whole,* (2) *lists of functions,* (3) *series of causes or results,* (4) *items of logical proof,* and (5) *illustrative examples.* While other types might also be listed, these five are certainly among the most important.

Parts of a whole. If a main point concerns an object or a process that has a number of parts or refers to a total composed of many items, the subpoints then take up and treat those parts or items. For example, the grip, shaft, and head are the parts you would discuss in describing the manufacture of a golf club; or the number of television stations in England, Scotland, Ireland, and Wales are the subtotals you would refer to when showing that the number of television stations in the British Isles has increased.

Lists of functions. If a main point suggests the purpose of some mechanism, organization, or procedure, the subordinate ideas may list the specific functions it performs. The purpose of a municipal police department, for example, may be made clear by discussing its responsibilities for traffic control, crime detection, and safety education.

Series of causes or results. If a main point states that a cause has several effects, or that an effect results from a number of causes, the various effects or causes may be listed as subordinate ideas. For example, the causes of crop failure may be enumerated as drought, frost, and blight; or its effects as high food prices, deprivation, and possible riots.

Items of logical proof. In a speech designed to influence belief, the subordinate ideas under a main point may consist of a group of separate but related arguments or of the successive steps in a single, coordinated line of reasoning. In either case, you should be able to relate the subordinate ideas to the main point by the word *because* (i.e., the main point is true because the subordinate ideas are true). You might support a plea for a new high school in your community with this series of separate but related arguments: "We need a new high school *(a)* because our present building is too small, *(b)* because our present building lacks essential laboratory and shop facilities, and *(c)* because the growth of our city has made it difficult for many students to get to our present building." Conversely, you should be able to proceed from the subpoints to the main point by using the word *therefore.* For example: "Our present high school building *(a)* is too small, *(b)* lacks necessary facilities, and *(c)* is in a poor location; *therefore,* we should construct a new building."

Illustrative examples. If a main point consists of a generalized concept or assertion, the subordinate ideas may illustrate it with specific cases or examples. You may use this method in both exposition and argument, the examples providing clarification in the first case, and proof in the second. For instance, you may explain the theory of reciprocal trade agreements by showing your listeners how such agreements work in actual cases involving specific goods and products; or you may, by citing the results obtained in certain communities which have added fluorine to their water supply, support the contention that fluorine in a community's drinking water helps in the prevention or the reduction of tooth decay.

Coordinating the subordinate ideas

Subordinate ideas not only should be directly related to the main point under which they fall, but they should also be coordinate with each other—that is, they should be equal in scope or importance. To list poor teachers, the lack of adequate textbooks, and a broken Coke machine as the reasons for poor scholarship among the students in a large high school would indicate that your analysis of your subject is in some way faulty: you are treating as equal three items which obviously are not equal in importance. Either the broken Coke machine is symptomatic of a greater evil—careless administration, a dilapidated school building, etc.—and therefore should be placed *under* this head, or it is irrelevant and should be eliminated from the speech altogether. To treat it as a factor equal to poor teaching and the lack of textbooks is to confuse a less important idea with more important ones and to create an unconvincing and incongruous effect.

Arranging the subordinate ideas

Subordinate ideas, no less than main points, must be arranged in an orderly and purposeful fashion. Parts of a whole, functions, or causes—even items of proof or illustrative examples—often can be listed according to the patterns already discussed for ordering the main headings. You can put your subordinate ideas in a time, space, causal, or topical sequence—whichever pattern seems most appropriate. You may want to use one sequence for the items under one main point and a different sequence for those under another; do not, however, alter the sequence of the subordinate ideas *within* the same coordinate series, for this may seriously confuse your listeners. Above all, be sure to employ some systematic order; do not crowd the subordinate ideas in haphazardly just because they are subordinate. Moreover, be careful not to let the process of subordination become too intricate or involved, or your listeners will not be able to follow you; but however far you go, keep your subordination consistent and logical.

Supporting the subordinate ideas

The important role that supporting materials play in making a speech effective was discussed in Chapter 6. The general rule should be: *Never make a statement in a speech without presenting some facts or reasoning to clarify, illustrate, or prove it.* Too often speakers think that if they divide every main point into two or three subordinate ideas, they have done enough. In reality, however, such divisions add only to the skeleton of the speech. They do not supply the supporting materials upon which understanding or belief ultimately depends. The real *substance* of any talk lies in explanations, statistics, illustrations, instances, comparisons, and testimony. Within reasonable limits, the more of these materials you have, the stronger your speech will be.

We have now considered the principles that should govern the arrangement of ideas within a speech and have surveyed several patterns by which the main points may be ordered and by which the subordinate points may be coordinated. Even with a thorough grasp of these principles and patterns, however, you probably will be unable to work out all of the details of a speech entirely in your mind. To develop a tangible, overall view of the structure as well as the content of a talk, you will find it necessary to follow some kind of orderly procedure for setting ideas and facts down on paper. For this purpose, most speakers find it best to prepare an outline.

REQUIREMENTS OF GOOD OUTLINE FORM

The amount of detail you include in an outline will depend on your subject, on the speaking situation, and on your previous experience in speech composition. But regardless of these factors, any good outline should meet the following basic requirements:

Each unit in the outline should contain only one idea. If two or three ideas are run together under one symbol, the relationships they bear to one another and to other ideas in the outline will not stand out clearly. Notice the difference between the following examples:

Wrong

I. You should ride a bicycle because bicycling is an ideal form of convenient and inexpensive transportation and because it is also an excellent form of healthful recreation and is fun.

Right

I. You should ride a bicycle.
   A. Bicycling is an ideal form of transportation.
      1. It is convenient.
      2. It is inexpensive.

B. Bicycling is an excellent form of recreation.
   1. It is healthful.
   2. It is fun.

Less important ideas in the outline should be subordinate to more important ones. Because a subordinate idea is a subdivision of the larger heading under which it falls, it should rank *below* that heading in scope and importance. It should also directly support or amplify the statement made in the superior heading.

Wrong

I. The cost of medical care has skyrocketed.
   A. Operating-room fees may be as much as $200 or $300.
      1. Hospital charges are high.
      2. A private room may cost as much as $150 a day.
   B. X rays and laboratory tests are extra.
   C. Complicated operations may cost several thousand dollars.
      1. Doctors' charges constantly go up.
         a. Office calls usually cost between $10 and $15.
      2. Drugs are expensive.
      3. Some antibiotics cost 80 or 90 cents per dose.
   D. The cost of non-prescription drugs has mounted.

Right

I. The cost of medical care has skyrocketed.
   A. Hospital charges are high.
      1. A private room may cost as much as $150 a day.
      2. Operating-room fees may be as much as $200 or $300.
      3. X rays and laboratory tests are extra.
   B. Doctors' charges constantly go up.
      1. Complicated operations may cost several thousand dollars.
      2. Office calls usually cost between $10 and $15.
   C. Drugs are expensive.
      1. Some antibiotics cost 80 or 90 cents per dose.
      2. The cost of non-prescription drugs has mounted.

The logical relationship between units of the outline should be shown by proper indentation. Normally, your main points will be the most general as well as the most important statements in your speech. As such, they should be placed nearest the left-hand margin of your outline, with less important statements ranged beneath and to the right of them in the order of increasing specificity. In your finished outline, therefore, the broadest and most central statements will lie farthest to the left; the narrowest and most particular ones will lie farthest to the right. If a statement is more than one line in length, the second line should be aligned with the first. (For example, see item I., B. in the outline below.)

A consistent set of symbols should be used throughout the outline. An acceptable set of symbols is exemplified in the outlines printed in this chapter. But whether you use this system or some other, be consistent. Items comparable in importance or scope always should be assigned the same type of symbol.

The four requirements just named apply to any outline you may make. An additional requirement, however, applies to the final draft of a complete, formal outline: *All the main points and subordinate ideas in such an outline should be written out as full sentences.* Especially as you prepare outlines for your classroom speeches, you will find that putting the items of the outline into sentence form will help clarify in your mind the meaning of each point and will show its exact relation to the other points. You will also find that a carefully framed statement of each point and a recognition of its place in the overall structure of your speech are invaluable aids in helping you remember what you want to say when it is time to speak.

STEPS IN PREPARING AN OUTLINE

An outline, like the speech it represents, should be developed gradually through a series of stages. While the process of preparing an outline may vary, certain steps should always be included:

   I. Select and limit the subject of your speech.
      A. Phrase your specific purpose.[3]
      B. Consider your purpose in the light of the limiting factors of time, audience, and occasion.
      C. Restate your purpose so that it fits these conditions.
  II. Develop a rough draft of your outline.
      A. List the main points you expect to cover.

---

[3]Review at this point the discussion of the specific purpose of a speech, pp. 41–42.

B. Rearrange these main points into a systematic sequence.

C. Insert and arrange the subordinate ideas that fall under each main point.

D. Note the supporting materials to be used under each point.

E. Check your rough draft to be sure it covers your subject and fulfills your purpose.

F. If you are dissatisfied, revise your rough draft or start over.

III. Put the outline into final form.

A. Write out the main points as complete sentences.

1. State them concisely, vividly, and — insofar as possible — in parallel phraseology.

2. Direct them to the needs and interests of your listeners.

B. Write out the subordinate ideas as complete sentences.

1. Be sure they are subordinate to the point they are intended to develop.

2. Be sure they are coordinate to the other items in their series.

C. Fill in the supporting materials in detail.

1. Be sure they are pertinent.

2. Be sure they are adequate.

IV. Recheck the entire outline.

A. Be sure it represents good outline form.

B. Be sure it adequately covers the subject.

C. Be sure it accomplishes your purpose.

In order to see how this process may be followed in a specific situation, let us apply the principles we have just discussed to the selection and limitation of a subject, the development of a rough draft, and the preparation of an outline in final form.

Selecting and narrowing the subject

Suppose that your instructor has asked you to prepare an informative speech on a subject in which you are interested. You decide that you will talk about life in a medieval university; you already know a good deal about the subject from a course in the history of education; you are interested in the similarity between medieval university life and your own college life, and you think the subject would appeal to the present-day university students who compose your classroom audience. Your broad topic area, therefore, is:

Life in a Medieval University

In the eight or ten minutes you have to speak, however, you obviously will not be able to cover everything you might say on this subject. Therefore, recalling what you learned in Chapter 3 about fitting your material to your listeners, you decide to focus your discussion on how the students lived and worked rather than on such matters as quarrels among the faculty, the slight attention paid to creative scholarship, etc. Consequently, you limit your topic as indicated below:

LIFE IN A MEDIEVAL UNIVERSITY

(A brief description of who the students were, how they lived, what they studied, and what they did in their spare time.)

Developing the rough draft

In determining the limits of your subject, you already have made a preliminary selection of some of the principal ideas to be dealt with in your speech. Now you set these points down on paper to see how they may be modified and fitted into a suitable sequence. Your list may look something like this:

A typical school day
Vacations
Living arrangements
Initiation of freshmen
Discipline
Academic work

This list covers a number of the things you want to be sure to include, but the order seems random, and several important aspects of the subject still are missing. As you supply these additional items—composition of the student body, life outside the classroom, etc.—you successively discard time, space, and causal sequence as patterns for organizing your speech, and decide instead that a *topical* order would best enable you to present the information you wish to convey.

You begin, therefore, to arrange your ideas in this way:

Composition of the student body
How the students lived
The rules by which they were governed
What and how they studied
Extracurricular life

Certainly, this arrangement is an improvement over your earlier random listing. Yet it is still not entirely satisfactory. Were you to make each of these five items a major point of your speech, you would have more leading ideas than the audience might easily remember. Moreover, upon further analysis you realize that how the students lived, the rules by which they were governed, and the discussion of extracurricular activities and pastimes all relate to life outside the classroom, and therefore may be grouped as subpoints under this all-inclusive head. Consequently, you decide to make a threefold rather than a fivefold division of your material, using as your principal topics:

1. The students
2. Academic work and studies
3. Extracurricular life and pastimes

With the major points, or "heads," of your speech thus chosen and arranged, you next proceed to phrase them more precisely, then to place under each major point the subordinate ideas by which it is to be explained or amplified. This additional development enables you to test the appropriateness of the main points and to see how they "hang together" when the details are added.

After inserting and arranging the subordinate ideas, you next sketch in the necessary supporting materials in the form of examples, statistics, comparisons, and the like. You also rework your title in an effort to make it more accurate and interesting.

At this point, examine your rough draft carefully to be sure (1) that you have included all the points you want to cover, (2) that you have not unbalanced your discussion by expanding unimportant items too greatly or skimping on important ones, (3) that you have followed the principles of systematic arrangement and subordination, and (4) that you have assembled sufficient supporting materials in the form of illustrations, comparisons, and the like. When you are satisfied on these matters, recast your outline into final form.

Putting the outline into final form

This task consists primarily of examining what you have already done and adjusting the details. Sometimes, however, you may want to combine or rearrange certain of the points as they appear in your rough draft, or perhaps even to drop several of them. Finally, you will now need to restate all of the items in your outline as complete sentences—

sentences which convey your meaning clearly and exactly—and to see that your outline form meets the requirements listed on pages 147–149.

Usually the process of revision will follow the procedure suggested in step IV on page 150. Begin by working on your main points, rephrasing them so that they are clear and vivid. Then taking each main point in turn, restate the subordinate ideas which fall under it, striving for proper coordination and subordination. As you do this, fill in the supporting materials in detail, testing them for pertinence and adequacy. After all parts of the outline are complete, go back and review the whole, checking its *form*, its *coverage* of the subject, and its *suitability* for your purpose.

A SAMPLE OUTLINE: FINAL DRAFT

By now your outline—revised, polished, and showing the full development of the three main points (II, III, and IV below) of the *body* of your speech—will appear more or less as follows:

MEDIEVAL UNIVERSITY LIFE: A MIRROR OF THE TIMES

Introduction[4]

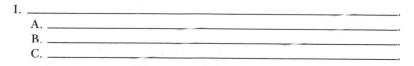

I. _____.
   A. _____.
   B. _____.
   C. _____.

Body

II. The students in a medieval university were a mixed lot.
   A. The students varied greatly in age.
      1. Most undergraduates were between 13 and 18 years of age.
      2. Sometimes boys of 7 or 8 were admitted.
      3. Many students in the graduate schools of law, theology, and medicine were 30 or more.
   B. The students were a cosmopolitan group.
      1. Famous universities attracted young men from many countries.

---

[4]In order to make the basic structure of the body of the speech stand out more clearly, those portions of the outline which show the development of the *introduction* and the *conclusion* have been omitted here, but have been developed in some detail in Chapter 9, "Beginning and Ending the Speech." See especially pp. 197–199.

       a. The University of Paris was a center for the study of philosophy and theology.

       b. Bologna was famous for its law faculty.

       c. Salerno had the best-known school of medicine.

    2. Students from the same country banded together into groups called "Nations."

       a. The Nations provided fellowship for young men far from home.

       b. They protected the rights of aliens living in a foreign country.

       c. They provided channels through which student opinion could make itself felt in the government of the university.

C. The students came from all classes of society.

    1. The sons of great noblemen lived luxuriously.

       a. They had retinues of servants.

       b. They were surrounded by paid "companions."

    2. Some students were so poor that the university licensed them to beg on the streets.

    3. The majority came from upper-middle-class backgrounds.

       a. They were the sons of knights, tradesmen, or minor government officials.

       b. They were supported by their parents or by benefactors.

D. The students' preparation for university work varied widely.

    1. No standard course of schooling was required for admission.

    2. The ability to read and speak Latin with some facility was the only prerequisite.

E. The students differed greatly in interest and industry.

    1. A small percentage worked diligently.

    2. Many wasted their time in taverns.

    3. Thousands left the university without taking even the lowest degree.

III. Academic work was much different than it is today.

A. The curriculum was rigidly prescribed.

    1. It consisted chiefly of the study of the "seven liberal arts."

       a. The "trivium" of grammar, rhetoric, and logic was emphasized.

       b. The "quadrivium" of music, arithmetic, geometry, and astronomy also received attention.

    2. Advanced students read the *Ethics, Physics,* and *Metaphysics* of Aristotle.

    3. In the graduate or professional schools, the students studied law, medicine, and theology.

    4. Instruction in the French language sometimes was offered.

      a. A knowledge of French was thought useful for the future diplomat or churchman.

      b. Instruction in French was not allowed to interfere with the regular course of studies.

B. Textbooks were few and expensive.

  1. They consisted of manuscripts copied by hand.

  2. Many students had no textbooks at all.

  3. Elaborate sets of lecture notes were circulated to supplement the small supply of books.

C. Teaching methods were dull and unimaginative.

  1. Lectures were the principal form of instruction.

      a. They were delivered in Latin.

      b. They were devoted to commenting line by line on the works of Aristotle and a few other standard authors.

      c. They were presented slowly and monotonously.

      d. They sometimes lasted for as long as three hours.

      e. Questions and class discussion were not allowed.

  2. Lectures were reviewed and students quizzed in informal sessions called Repetitions.

      a. Repetitions were held in the afternoon or evening.

      b. They were presided over by tutors.

  3. Examinations for degrees were conducted orally.

      a. They tested the student's knowledge of prescribed books.

      b. They tested his ability to advance and maintain a "thesis" against attack.

      c. The student was required to swear that he would not harm the examiners if they failed him.

  4. Advanced students disputed on subjects drawn from philosophy and theology.

      a. These disputations followed a rigid pattern.

         (1) A set order of speaking was preserved.

         (2) All arguments had to be stated in syllogistic form.

      b. Decisions were handed down by professors or fellow students.

D. The lecture rooms were bleak and uncomfortable.

  1. They were unheated in winter.

  2. Artificial light was lacking.

  3. Glass windows were rare.

  4. The students sat in straw spread on the floor.

E. The school day was long.

  1. The students arose at 5:00 A.M.

  2. Morning devotions lasted from 5:30 to 6:30.

      a. Prayers and meditation came first.

      b. Mass was at 6:00 A.M.

    3. Lectures and study occupied the hours from 7:00 A.M. until noon.

    4. During the afternoon, the morning's lectures were reviewed and independent studies pursued.

    5. At 8:30, evening chapel was the last required event of the day.

IV. Medieval students lived a carefree and colorful life outside the classroom.

  A. Housing arrangements were casual.

    1. Groups of students banded together to rent houses from the townspeople.

      a. The university exercised little or no supervision over these living arrangements.

      b. Each house had an elected Head or Principal.

        (1) The Principal was usually an upperclassman or graduate student.

        (2) His only powers were those voluntarily granted him by the occupants.

    2. The houses later became the Halls or Colleges of our modern European universities.

  B. Discipline was relaxed.

    1. Prior to the fourteenth century, university statutes interfered very little with the private life of the students.

      a. Bands of students roamed the town at will.

      b. Tavern brawls were common.

    2. Later, a few rules were imposed to regulate conduct.

      a. The carrying of arms was restricted.

      b. Gambling and borrowing from any unauthorized money-lenders were forbidden.

      c. Women were not permitted within the college grounds.

      d. The amount of money which could be spent in celebrating a degree or other academic accomplishment was severely limited.

      e. Dogs could not be kept in students' rooms.

    3. Punishments were geared to the nature of the offense.

      a. For minor infractions the student might be required to supply his professors or his companions with a certain quantity of wine.

      b. More serious offenses could result in suspension or expulsion.

      c. The records give no hint of corporal punishment prior to the fifteenth century.

4. Punishments were entirely under the control of university authorities.
    a. Civil courts had no jurisdiction over students.
    b. When local officials attempted to restrain the students, the university came to their defense.
C. Accounts of extracurricular life have a familiar ring.
  1. Freshmen were called "bejauns" or "yellow bills."
      a. Upperclassmen subjected them to various indignities.
      b. They were required to provide feasts for faculty members and other students.
  2. Riots and other mass disturbances occurred frequently.
      a. Some arose out of disputes between the Nations.
      b. Others involved differences between "town" and "gown."
          (1) These disturbances were particularly violent.
          (2) The riots sometimes lasted for several days.
          (3) They usually resulted in physical injuries.
          (4) Occasionally persons were killed.
      c. Often faculty members as well as students participated.
  3. Pranks and practical jokes abounded.
      a. They often were of a crude or violent nature.
      b. They sometimes represented the organized efforts of large groups of students.
  4. On certain public occasions, students were permitted to deride the faculty.
      a. Their remarks sometimes were exceedingly scurrilous.
      b. Only in the most extreme cases did expulsion result.
  5. Traditions passed from one generation of students to the next.
      a. If a professor did not complete a lecture on time, the students were free to leave.
      b. If a professor did not cover an entire course during the assigned period, he might be fined.
      c. Students vociferously indicated their approval or disapproval of a lecture.
          (1) They would shout or whistle.
          (2) They would shuffle their feet noisily.
      d. Attendance records were based on students' oaths that they had been present at the required sessions.
      e. A rudimentary honor system existed.
          (1) Students were honor-bound to report infractions of the rules which they observed.
          (2) Infractions on the part of the faculty were not exempt.

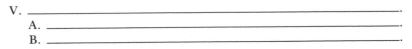

Conclusion[5]

V. _____ .
   A. _____ .
   B. _____ .

From the foregoing example, you can see that arranging and out-lining the related points of a speech are not simple tasks which can be tossed off in a few moments. Time and effort are required to do the job well. Allow yourself the time and exert the effort; the greater clarity and force of expression which will result will more than compensate you. Remember, too, that skill in outlining develops with experience. If you lack practice in outlining, the task may take you longer than it takes the experienced speaker. As you continue to make outlines, how-ever, your skill and speed will increase. Begin now by carefully outlin-ing every speech you make, in or out of class.

PROBLEMS FOR FURTHER STUDY

1. By themselves, perhaps, organizational arrangements are static repre-sentations of clearly structured ideas. But their purpose is more than in-tellectual; they also serve important *rhetorical functions.* Organizational arrangements or patterns not only clarify ideas, but—perhaps more im-portantly—help you decide how to structure a speech *for a particular audi-ence.* Essentially, a speech must start "where the audience is" and then, step by step, advance the listeners intellectually and emotionally through the topic to the point at which the speaker wishes them to be. A speaker's selection of a particular organizational pattern, then, should reflect *(a)* the speaker's specific purpose, *(b)* the supporting materials accumulated by the speaker for this audience, *(c)* the level of the audience's knowl-edge, and *(d)* the state of mind of the audience.

Suppose, for example, you decided to speak about your college's ca-reer-counseling program. *(a)* For what kinds of purposes, audiences, etc., would you select a *time sequence* (founding and original functions, key pe-riods of the program's development, its functions and services today)? *(b)* For what kinds of purposes and audiences might you employ a *problem-solution sequence* (today's harsh job market and services provided by the program)? *(c)* When might you want to use a *special topical pattern* (divisions of careers and opportunities in the program)? *(d)* Could you, perhaps, build a speech around job-market data collected by the pro-

[5]Ibid., pp. 198–199.

gram, using an *effect-cause sequence* (current job scene and the program's analysis of causes)? Select an organizational pattern for a speech on a subject of your choice by asking yourself such questions.

2. Subject your next classroom speech to the kind of analysis described in Problem 1. In packaging your ideas and materials for that speech, ask yourself these questions: *(a)* What is my purpose, and how should I reveal it? *(b)* Are there natural divisions in my supporting materials, and are those divisions appropriate for my purpose and for my audience? *(c)* How much does my audience already know about this topic? How much more background do they require? How quickly can I move them through the needed steps of analysis-of-causes/description-of-effects/proposal-of-solutions/call-for-action? *(d)* Is this audience enthusiastic, neutral, hostile, etc.? How far, how quickly, can I move them emotionally? Answers to these questions should help you determine the appropriate organizational pattern and the most utilitarian development for each part of your talk.

3. Using as a source this textbook, recent issues of *Vital Speeches of the Day,* or other sources suggested by your instructor, select three speeches for organizational analysis, and make a complete outline of each. Which of the three was easiest to outline? Which was the most difficult? How do you account for these differences? Would you want to rework the most difficult outline if you gave a speech on the same topic? How and why? (Or why not?)

4. During the next round of classroom speeches, try to outline each talk as it is given. After listening to the speech, compare your outline with the one prepared by the speaker.

5. For a speech entitled "Making Reading Your Hobby," rearrange the following points and subpoints in proper *outline form:*
    Low-cost rental libraries are numerous.
    Reading is enjoyable.
    It may lead to advancement in one's job.
    Books contain exciting tales of love and adventure.
    Many paperback books cost only 95¢ to $1.25.
    People who read books are most successful socially.
    Reading is profitable.
    One meets many interesting characters in books.
    Nearly every town has a free public library.
    Through books, one's understanding of human beings and the world is
        increased.
    The new and stimulating ideas found in books bring pleasure.
    Reading is inexpensive.

ORAL ACTIVITIES AND SPEAKING ASSIGNMENTS

1. Read Chapter 4, pages 49–54, of Thomas Olbricht, *Informative Speaking* (Glenview, Ill.: Scott, Foresman and Company, 1968), where "branching outlines" are discussed. Following the instructions which Olbricht sets forth, prepare a branching outline on a subject of your choice. Down the left-hand side of your paper, lay out your basic outline. Then, down the right-hand side, indicate additional "branches"—materials which further develop, illustrate, and/or prove subpoints in the speech. In presenting the speech, you will find that the branching outline can aid you in adapting to unexpected situations—puzzled looks on the faces of listeners, the strong inner feeling that an idea has been misunderstood, the realization that you have chosen the wrong examples initially, or the sinking feeling you have when a timekeeper signals "one minute to go." Try using a branching outline, with essential material on one side, supplemental or developmental material on the other. Practice the speech with varying amounts of supporting material, and enter actual speaking situations with a knowledge of your own flexibility.

2. After all class members have completed Problems 1 and 2, pages 158–159, participate in a general class discussion on the topic "Strategies for Choosing Among Organizational Arrangements." See if you and your classmates can distinguish between situations in which *cause-effect* is preferable to *effect-cause*, when *time sequences* should be used, and why *special topical* seems to be the arrangement used most frequently.

3. Prepare a five- to seven-minute speech on a subject of your choice for presentation in class. As part of your preparation, draw up a detailed outline in accordance with the sample form provided in this chapter. Hand your speech outline to your instructor at least one week before you are scheduled to speak. The instructor will check this material and return it to you with suggestions for possible improvement. Carefully rewrite the outline and hand the improved version back to your instructor just before you begin the actual presentation of your speech.

SUGGESTIONS FOR FURTHER READING

Rhetorica Ad Herennium, II.16–18, "Arrangement." An interesting discussion of general arrangement principles as well as strategies for placing materials within an outline.

Loren J. Anderson, "A Summary of Research on Order Effects in Communication," in *Concepts of Communication*, ed. Jimmie D. Trent *et al.* (Boston: Allyn & Bacon, Inc., 1973), pp. 128–138. The most recent summary of research relative to one aspect of organization: the order in which ideas are arranged.

Carl Hovland *et al.*, *The Order of Presentation in Persuasion* (New Haven, Conn.: Yale University Press, 1957). A series of now-classic studies of the effect of organization upon attitude-change.

Glen E. Mills, *Message Preparation: Analysis and Structure* (Indianapolis: The Bobbs-Merrill Company, Inc., 1966), Chapter 5, "Outlining and Patterns of Arrangement," pp. 37 – 46. A series of useful examples of various outlining patterns.

C. David Mortensen, *Communication: The Study of Human Interaction* (New York: McGraw-Hill Book Company, 1972), from Chapter 5, "Verbal Interaction," esp. pp. 184 – 193. A recent review of experimental literature relative to the effect of organization upon learning and attitude-change.

Walter F. Terris, *Content and Organization of Speeches* (Dubuque, Iowa: Wm. C. Brown Company, Publishers, 1968), Chapter 3, "The Fundamental Organizational Patterns," pp. 25 – 42, and Chapter 6, "The Subsidiary Patterns of Organization," pp. 69 – 86. A logical and psychological approach to organization.

Chapter 8

Wording the speech

A N OUTLINE sets forth the structure of your speech and the material to be used in supporting that structure, but it is only the skeleton of your finished talk. The problem of phrasing the ideas in vivid and compelling language and of making clear and graceful transitions from one point to another still confronts you. In this chapter, we shall consider some of the principles that underlie the effective use of words and shall offer specific guidance for their selection and arrangement.

ACCURACY OF MEANING

In order to express your meaning precisely, you must choose words carefully. The man who tells the hardware clerk that he has "broken the hickey on his hootenanny and needs a thing-ma-jig to fit it" expresses his meaning vaguely; but his vagueness is only a little greater than that of the orator who proclaims, "We must follow along the path of true Americanism." Because words are merely symbols which stand for the concepts or objects they represent, your listener may attach to a symbol a meaning quite different from the one you intend. *Democracy*, for example, does not mean the same thing to a citizen of the United States that it does to a citizen of Soviet Russia. An *expensive* meal to a college student may seem quite moderate in price to a wealthy man. A mode of travel that was *fast* in 1875 is painfully slow today. Nor are all of the persons or things designated by a class name alike: Frenchman A differs from Frenchmen B and C; one Ford may be old and rusty; another is new and shiny. Students of General Semantics continually warn us that many errors in thinking and communication arise from treating words as if they were the actual conditions, processes, or objects and — as such — fixed and timeless in meaning.[1]

---

[1]For a more extended treatment of this subject, see Irving J. Lee, *Language Habits in Human Affairs* (New York: Harper & Row, Publishers, 1941); Wendell Johnson, *People in Quandaries* (Harper & Row, Publishers, 1946); Doris B. Garey, *Putting Words in Their Places* (Glenview, Ill.: Scott, Foresman and Company, 1957); and Roger Brown, *Words and Things* (Glencoe, Ill.: The Free Press, 1958).

To combat vagueness in definitions and elsewhere, choose words which express the exact shade of meaning you wish to communicate. Although dictionary definitions are not infallible guides, they do represent commonly accepted usages stated as precisely as possible. Observe, for example, the distinctions a good dictionary makes among related words, such as *languor, lassitude, lethargy, stupor,* and *torpor.* In a book of synonyms (such as Roget's *Thesaurus*) among those listed for the verb *shine* are *glow, glitter, glisten, gleam, flare, blaze, glare, shimmer, glimmer, flicker, sparkle, flash, beam.* The English language is rich in subtle variations. To increase the precision of your expression, make use of this range of meaning in your choice of words.

SIMPLICITY

No matter how accurately a word or phrase may express your meaning, it is useless if the audience cannot understand it. For this reason, expression not only must be exact, but also must be clear and simple. "Speak," said Lincoln, "so that the most lowly can understand you, and the rest will have no difficulty." This rule is as valid today as when Lincoln uttered it; and because modern audiences as created by the electronic media are vaster and more varied than any Lincoln dreamed of, there is even more reason for contemporary speakers to follow it. Say "learn" rather than "ascertain," "after-dinner speech" rather than "postprandial discourse," "large" rather than "elephantine." Never use a longer or less familiar word when a simpler one will do.

In particular, choose words that are concrete rather than abstract. Herbert Spencer, in *The Philosophy of Style,* illustrates the importance of this advice by comparing two sentences:

> (1) "In proportion as the manners, customs, and amusements of a nation are cruel and barbarous, the regulations of their penal code will be severe."

— How much better to have said —

> (2) "In proportion as men delight in battles, bullfights, and combat of gladiators, will they punish by hanging, burning, and the rack."[2]

Billy Sunday, the famous evangelist, gave this example:

---

[2]Herbert Spencer, "The Philosophy of Style," in *Representative Essays on the Theory of Style,* ed. William T. Brewster (New York: The Macmillan Company, 1911), pp. 173–174.

If a man were to take a piece of meat and smell it and look disgusted, and his little boy were to say, "What's the matter with it, Pop?" and he were to say, "It is undergoing a process of decomposition in the formation of new chemical compounds," the boy would be all in. But if the father were to say, "It's rotten," then the boy would understand and hold his nose. "Rotten" is a good Anglo-Saxon word, and you do not have to go to the dictionary to find out what it means.[3]

Use short words; use simple words; use words that are concrete and specific; use words with meanings that are immediately obvious. The able speaker, regardless of the range of his or her experience, invariably devotes painstaking attention to matters of simplicity, specificity, and vividness in the actual phrasing of a speech. Examine this short manuscript, "Eulogy for the Astronauts," written and presented by Eric Sevareid on CBS Evening News, January 31, 1967, and note how he has employed the principles of effective word choice and the careful polishing of his text:

Grissom and White and Chaffee -- ~~the men~~/who ~~aspri~~ mortals aspired

to the moon and ~~space and~~ eternal space -- were returned to the

earth today from which they came and to which we all belong.

They had lived more intensely ~~than most of us in their~~

~~few years~~ in a very few years than most of us do in our lifetimes

and they shall be remembered far longer ~~than nearly all the rest of~~

~~us~~.

They were among the men who wield the cutting edge of history

and by this sword they died.

Grissom and Chaffee were buried near the grave of ~~Liettenant~~

[3]Quoted in John R. Pelsma, *Essentials of Speech* (New York: Crowell Collier and Macmillan, Inc., 1934), p. 193.

[4]"Eulogy for the Astronauts" by Eric Sevareid. Copyright 1967 by Eric Sevareid. Reprinted by permission of The Harold Matson Company, Inc.

Lieutenant Thomas Selfridge, the first american military pilot to
be killed in an airplane crash ~~nearly sixty years ago - what he
was attempting~~ nearly sixty years *ago,* ~~ago was then as~~ Then, the
air above the ground was as ~~uncharted~~ unfamiliar as the space above the air.

The men who go first are accounted heroes and rightly so,
whatever the age, whatever the new element and horizon. Space, said
the late president kennedy, is our new ocean and we must sail
upon it.

It was truly the hazards of the unknown oceans and territories
that ~~killed~~ took the lives of earlier heroes, ~~the two men~~ like
Magellan or Captain Cook, men who went first and were killed by
~~the wild~~ inhabitants of the Pacific.

It was not precisely the unknown hazards of space that killed our
astronauts; it was the ha ards of fallible man's calculations.
It w as not a technical failure; all technical failures are human
failures. It was the familiar, never totally escapable failure
of the human brain to cope with ~~certainty with~~ the complexities
it has arranged.

A slight miscalculation, a single slip, ~~and~~ then a spark,
a flame and the end of three remarkable ~~o~~ products of those
infinitely more complex mysteries, genetic inheritance and

environment. The process that occasionally produces ~~human~~

personalities like grissom and white and chaffee -- men who

are brave but not brash; proud but not self-conscious;

thoughtful but not brooding. Men of a health, a wholeness

we all aspire to but so few attain.

We are told they will be replaced. This only means that

other such men will take their places. The three ~~They~~ cannot be replaced.

There never was a replaceable human being.

walter

APPROPRIATENESS

Besides being accurate and clear, your language should be appropriate to the subject on which you are speaking and to the situation in which your speech is delivered.

Serious or solemn occasions call for diction that is restrained and dignified; light or joyful occasions, for diction that is informal and lively. Just as you would never use slang in remarks at a funeral service or in a speech dedicating a church or memorial, so you should never phrase a humorous after-dinner speech in a heavy or elevated style. Suit your language to the spirit and tone of the occasion; be dignified and formal when formality is expected, and light and casual when informality is called for.

See to it also that your language is appropriate to the audience you are addressing—that the terms you employ and the allusions you make are within the realm of the listeners' understanding. In her book *North to the Orient,* Anne Morrow Lindbergh skillfully fulfills this latter requirement in her vivid description of a church service for Alaskan Eskimos:

> . . . nothing distracted the congregation. Men, women, and children leaned forward earnestly watching the minister. Many could not understand English. Even those who had learned it in school were bewildered by psalms sung by a shepherd on a sun-parched hillside.

" 'We have gone astray like sheep,' " began the reading. Sheep, what did that mean to them? I saw stony New England pastures and those gray backs moving among blueberry bushes and junipers.

"Like the reindeer," explained the minister, "who have scattered on the tundras." The listening heads moved. They understood reindeer.

" 'Your garners will be filled.' " Big red barns, I saw, and hay wagons rumbling uphill. But the Eskimos? "Your meat cellars," the minister answered my question, "will be full of reindeer meat."

" 'Your oxen will be strong,' " read the next verse. "Your dogs for your dog teams will pull hard," continued the minister. " 'The Power of God.' " How could he explain that abstract word *Power*?

"Sometimes when the men are whaling," he started, "the boats get caught in the ice. We have to take dynamite and break up the ice to let them get out. That is power—dynamite—'the dynamite of God.' "

"For Thine is the Kingdom, 'the dynamite,' and the Glory forever and ever. Amen," I said over to myself.[5]

IMAGERY

We receive our impressions of the world around us through sensations of sight, smell, hearing, taste, and touch. If your listeners are to experience the object or state of affairs you are describing, you must, therefore, appeal to their senses. But you cannot punch them in the nose, scatter exotic perfume for them to smell, or let them taste foods which are not present. The primary senses through which you as a speaker can reach your listeners *directly* are the visual and the auditory: they can see you, your movements, your facial expressions, and objects you use as "visual aids"; and they can hear what you say.

Despite this limitation, however, you can *indirectly* stimulate all of the senses of your listeners by using language that has the power to produce imagined sensations, or which causes them to recall images they have previously experienced. Through image-evoking language, you can help your hearers create many of the sensory "pictures" and "events" that you yourself have experienced or encountered. Through vivid words, you can project the desired image swiftly into the "mind's eye" of your listeners. The language of imagery falls into seven classes, or types, each related to the particular sensation that it seeks to evoke.

---

[5]From *North to the Orient*, copyright, 1935, © 1963, by Anne Morrow Lindbergh. Reprinted by permission of Harcourt Brace Jovanovich, Inc.

TYPES OF IMAGERY

The seven types of imagery are:

1. Visual *(sight)*	a. Texture and shape
2. Auditory *(hearing)*	b. Pressure
3. Gustatory *(taste)*	c. Heat and cold
4. Olfactory *(smell)*	6. Kinesthetic *(muscle strain)*
5. Tactual *(touch)*	7. Organic *(internal sensations)*

Let us examine briefly each of these types.

Visual imagery

Try to make your audience actually "see" the objects or situations you are describing. Mention *size, shape, color,* and *movement.* Recount events in vivid language. In the following passage from his speech "On Capital Punishment," the French writer Victor Hugo uses visual imagery to portray the horror aroused by the public execution of a man by guillotine:

> Here is a man condemned, wretched, who is dragged on a certain morning into one of our squares—there he finds a scaffold. He rebels, he pleads, he will not die; he is still young, hardly twenty-nine years old—great heavens! I know what you will say—"He is an assassin!" But listen! Two executioners seize him; his hands are bound, his feet fettered; still he pushes them back. A horrible struggle ensues. He twists his feet in the ladder, and uses the scaffold against the scaffold. The struggle is prolonged; horror takes possession of the crowd. The executioners, the sweat of shame on their brows, pale, breathless, terrified, desperate with I know not what terrible despair—borne down by the weight of public reprobation that must confine itself to condemnation of the death penalty, but that would do wrong in harming its passive instrument—the headsman—the executioners make savage efforts. Force must remain with the law, that is the maxim! The man clings to the scaffold and demands mercy; his clothing is torn away; his bare shoulders are bloody; he resists all the while. At last, after three quarters of an hour of this awful contest, of this spectacle without a name, of this agony, agony for every one—do you realize it?—agony for those present as well as for the condemned; after this age of anguish, gentlemen of the jury, the poor wretch is carried back to prison. The people breathe again.[6]

---

[6]Victor Hugo, "On Capital Punishment," tr. Mary Emerson Adams, *The Library of Oratory Ancient and Modern,* ed. Chauncey M. Depew (New York: E. R. Du Mont, 1902), XII, pp. 16–17.

Auditory imagery

All of us are acquainted with how poets often use words to make us actually "hear" what they are describing. In his translation of Homer's *Iliad*, for example, Alexander Pope has the following lines:

> Loud sounds the air, redoubling strokes on strokes;
> On all sides round the forest hurls her oaks
> Headlong. Deep echoing groan the thickets brown,
> Then rustling, crackling, crashing, thunder down.

In prose passages and in speeches also, auditory imagery may frequently be used with great effect. Note, for example, how Alfred Lansing describes the last moments of a wooden ship caught in the ice floes of the Antarctic:

> There were the sounds of the [ice] pack in movement—the basic noises, the grunting and whining of the floes, along with an occasional thud as a heavy block collapsed. But in addition, the pack under compression seemed to have an almost limitless repertoire of other sounds, many of which seemed strangely unrelated to the noise of ice undergoing pressure. Sometimes there was a sound like a gigantic train with squeaky axles being shunted roughly about with a great deal of bumping and clattering. At the same time a huge ship's whistle blew, mingling with the crowing of roosters, the roar of a distant surf, the soft throb of an engine far away, and the moaning cries of an old woman. In the rare periods of calm, when the movement of the pack subsided for a moment, the muffled rolling of drums drifted across the air.[7]

Gustatory imagery

Help your audience imagine the *taste* of what you are describing. Mention its saltiness, sweetness, sourness, or its spicy flavor. Observe how Charles Lamb in his "Dissertation upon Roast Pig" describes that delicacy:

> There is no flavor comparable, I will contend, to that of the crisp, tawny, well-watched, not over-roasted, *crackling*, as it is well called—the very teeth are invited to their share of the pleasure at this banquet in overcoming the coy, brittle resistance . . . the tender blossoming of fat

---

[7]From *Endurance* by Alfred Lansing. Copyright 1959 by McGraw-Hill Book Company. Used with permission of McGraw-Hill Book Company.

. . . the lean, not lean, but a kind of animal manna—or, rather, fat and lean so blended and running into each other, that both together make but one ambrosian result . . . too ravishing for mortal taste.[8]

Olfactory imagery

Make your audience smell the odors connected with the thing or circumstance you describe. Do this not only by mentioning the odor itself but also by describing the object that has the odor or by comparing it with more familiar items. Example:

> To the boy Henry Adams, summer was drunken. Among senses, smell was the strongest—smell of hot pine-woods and sweet-fern in the scorching summer noon; of new-mown hay; of ploughed earth; of box hedges; of peaches, lilacs, syringas; of stables, barns, cow-yards; of salt water and low tide on the marshes; nothing came amiss.[9]

Tactual imagery

Tactual imagery is based upon the various types of sensation that we get through physical contact with an object. Particularly it gives us sensations of *texture* and *shape, pressure,* and *heat* and *cold.*

Texture and shape. Enable your audience to feel how rough or smooth, dry or wet, or sharp, slimy, or sticky a thing is.

Pressure. Phrase appropriate portions of your speech in such a way that your auditors sense the pressure of physical force upon their bodies: The weight of a heavy trunk borne upon their backs, the pinching of shoes that are too tight, the incessant drive of the high wind on their faces.

Heat and cold. These sensations are aroused by what is sometimes called "thermal" imagery.

Effective use of tactual imagery is well demonstrated by the blind Helen Keller in explaining how the sense of touch enabled her to experience the world about her:

> When water is the object of my thought, I feel the cool shock of the plunge and the quick yielding of the waves that crisp and curl and ripple about my body. The pleasing changes of rough and smooth, pliant and

---

[8]Charles Lamb, "A Dissertation upon Roast Pig," *The Complete Works and Letters of Charles Lamb* (New York: Modern Library, Inc., 1935), pp. 110–111.

[9]From *The Education of Henry Adams.* Copyright 1918. Reprinted by permission of Houghton Mifflin Company.

rigid, curved and straight in the bark and branches of a tree give the truth to my hand. The immovable rock, with its juts and warped surfaces, bends beneath my fingers into all manner of grooves and hollows. The bulge of a watermelon and the puffed-up rotundities of squashes that sprout, bud, and ripen in that strange garden planted somewhere behind my finger tips are the ludicrous in my tactual memory and imagination.[10]

Kinesthetic imagery

Kinesthetic imagery describes the sensations associated with muscle strain and neuromuscular movement. Word suitable portions of your speech in such a way that your listeners may feel for themselves the stretching, tightening, and jerking of muscles and tendons, the creaking of their joints. The following description of a person making a parachute jump is rich in kinesthetic imagery:

> The earth and sky become a whirling maelstrom as you plummet downward, somersaulting, the force of the air against your heavy body as it is pulled as by an invisible, all-powerful hand. Then suddenly your chute opens, billowing out above you like a white cloud, and you are stopped with a force which seems more than you can stand. The press and pull of the harness seems to crush your chest and leave your legs momentarily separated from your body. You gasp for breath, like a man who has just surfaced after an "eternity" under water, your right hand clutching tightly around the ring of the emergency chute. Slowly you drift toward the earth.[11]

Organic imagery

Hunger, dizziness, nausea—these are a few of the feelings organic imagery calls up. Observe this example from H. G. Wells:

> That climb seemed interminable to me. With the last twenty or thirty feet of it, a deadly nausea came upon me. I had the greatest difficulty in keeping my hold. The last few yards was a frightful struggle against this faintness. Several times my head swam, and I felt all the sensations of falling. At last, however, I got over the well-mouth somehow and staggered out of the ruin into the blinding sunlight.[12]

---

[10]Helen Keller, *The World I Live In* (New York: The Century Company, 1908), p. 11.

[11]From *The Speaker and His Audience* by Martin P. Andersen, Wesley Lewis, and James Murray. Copyright © 1964. Reprinted by permission of Harper & Row, Publishers, Inc.

[12]H. G. Wells, "The Time Machine," *The Complete Short Stories of H. G. Wells* (London: Ernest Benn, Ltd., 1927), p. 59.

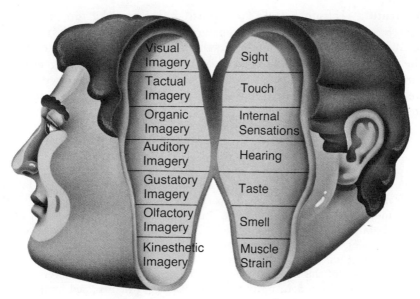

Visual Imagery	Sight
Tactual Imagery	Touch
Organic Imagery	Internal Sensations
Auditory Imagery	Hearing
Gustatory Imagery	Taste
Olfactory Imagery	Smell
Kinesthetic Imagery	Muscle Strain

Figure 1. Perceptual "Doorways to the Mind"

USING IMAGERY

The seven types of imagery which we have just considered — *visual, auditory, gustatory, olfactory, tactual, kinesthetic, and organic* — have been aptly referred to by Victor Ketcham as "The Seven Doorways to the Mind."[13] These are the doorways which, as speakers, we must open with our words if we expect our listeners to understand or believe us. When speaking to others, we must always remember that because *people differ in the degree to which they are sensitive to different types of imagery,* we must try to build into our messages as many of these perceptual "doorways" as possible.

Supply vivid, detailed word-pictures

When employing imagery, remember that although you can speak only one word at a time, your listeners normally are able to receive a large number of different and detailed sensations simultaneously. If you are

[13]Victor Alvin Ketcham, "The Seven Doorways to the Mind," in *Business Speeches by Business Men,* ed. William P. Sandford and W. Hayes Yeager (New York: McGraw-Hill Book Company, 1930).

to create a realistic picture, you must therefore take time to *describe many aspects* of an object, person, or event. A famous passage from Daniel Webster's opening statement in the White Murder Case exemplifies the importance and effectiveness of such details in drawing *word-pictures*. Note how Webster, in relating how the crime occurred, makes detailed mention of every movement and circumstance to render the description especially vivid:

> Deep sleep had fallen on the destined victim, and on all beneath his roof. A healthful old man, to whom sleep was sweet, the first sound slumbers of the night held him in their soft but strong embrace. The assassin enters, through the window already prepared, into an unoccupied apartment. With noiseless foot he paces the lonely hall, half lighted by the moon. He winds up the ascent of the stairs, and reaches the door of the chamber. Of this he moves the lock, by soft and continued pressure, till it turns on its hinges without noise, and he enters, and beholds his victim before him. The room is uncommonly open to the admission of light. The face of the innocent sleeper is turned from the murderer, and the beams of the moon, resting on the gray locks of his aged temple, show him where to strike. The fatal blow is given, and the victim passes, without a struggle or a motion, from the repose of sleep to the repose of death! It is the assassin's purpose to make sure work; and he plies the dagger, though it is obvious that life has been destroyed by the blow of the bludgeon. He even raises the aged arm, that he may not fail in his aim at the heart, and replaces it again over the wounds of the poniard! To finish the picture, he explores the wrist for the pulse! He feels for it, and ascertains that it beats no longer! It is accomplished. The deed is done. He retreats, retraces his steps to the window, passes out through it as he came in, and escapes.[14]

Use loaded words skillfully but ethically

In a lecture on "Mind and Language," Dr. Robert T. Oliver, Professor Emeritus of Speech at Pennsylvania State University, reminds us:

> The labelling function of words . . . is only a part of their service and of their influence. What language does to us and what we can do with it extends far beyond the simple process of identifying objects by naming them.

---

[14]From "The Murder of Captain Joseph White" by Daniel Webster from *The Great Speeches and Orations of Daniel Webster.* Copyright 1894 by Little, Brown & Company.

Words are also *incitements;* they are stimulants. Words are used much as a red flag is used to arouse the anger of bulls or as bait is used to attract fish. In the heat of a presidential campaign, the words "Democrat" and "Republican" are used less as labels than as inducements to loyalty or to enhance antagonism. "I love you" is not only a label for an emotion but also an invitation to reciprocity. "Communist" and "Nazi" are words used to arouse dislike; "patriotism" and "duty" are used to stir up loyal devotion. Much of our use of words is aimed less to define meanings than to create or magnify attitudes. And attitudes are not attributes of fact-items as they exist in the exterior world but are personal preferences. They assume forms and serve functions determined by the mind rather than prescribed by the fact-items to which they refer.[15]

Words which "create or magnify attitudes," which express the preferences and prejudices of the speaker and attempt to impress these upon the listeners, are generally known as "loaded words." For example, note the different response that you yourself make to each of the following: *man, fellow, guy, person, savage, cheapskate, piker, chiseler, sportsman, father, dad, baron, miser, dictator.* Although all of these words denote a human being, what different types of human beings they suggest and how strongly some of them convey approval or disapproval!

Because of the responses which they can call up, loaded words must be used with caution. When employing them, be sure you can answer these two questions affirmatively: (1) Will the audience understand the meaning I intend to convey? (2) Do I have sound facts and reasoning to support my position so that the use of these words is justified? Select words which will add vividness to your speaking, but take care to employ them accurately and fairly.

Meaning derived from association. Many words become "loaded" as a result of the experiences with which they are associated. After the repeal of national prohibition, for example, places where liquor was sold came to be called *taverns* in order to avoid the unpleasant mental image associated with the old saloon. The word *politician* suggests to many people a scheming, dishonest man, making promises which he does not expect to keep and uttering pious platitudes while he secretly accepts illegal pay from "special interests"—a picture repeatedly painted by cartoonists and novelists and by opposing politicans. Yet the in-

---

[15]From "Mind and Language" by Robert T. Oliver, from *Vital Speeches of the Day,* Volume XXXI (October 15, 1964), p. 26. Reprinted by permission of Vital Speeches of the Day.

trinsic meaning of the word only denotes one who is occupied in the management of public affairs or who works in the interest of a political party. Since different people have had different experiences, the connotation of a word may vary greatly; and you must be tactful in adapting it to your particular audience. Shoe clerks, for example, tell a woman: "Madam, this foot is slightly smaller than the other," instead of "That foot is bigger than this one." Observe in the following example how Dr. Ernest Tittle, in his description of words as such, uses language that is freighted with meaningful associations:

> There are colorful words that are as beautiful as red roses; and there are drab words that are as unlovely as an anemic-looking woman. There are concrete words that keep people awake; and there are abstract words that put them to sleep. There are strong words that can punch like a prize-fighter; and weak words that are as insipid as a "mama's boy." There are warm, sympathetic words that grip men's hearts; and cold, detached words that leave an audience unmoved. There are warm, sympathetic words that lift every listener, at least for a moment, to the sunlit heights of God; and base words that leave an audience in the atmosphere of the cabaret.[16]

Meaning derived from the sound of the word. The meaning of such words as *hiss, crash, rattle, slink, creep, bound,* and *roar* is suggested by the way they sound. The poems of Edgar Allan Poe and of Vachel Lindsay abound in words of this kind — *clanging, tinkle, mumbo-jumbo.* As H. A. Overstreet has said, "There are words that chuckle; words that laugh right out; words that weep; words that droop and falter."[17] A proper appreciation of the sound values of words will help make your speaking clearer and more vivid.

Avoid trite, overworked, and slangy expressions

Words and expressions which are powerful or vivid in themselves may be rendered ineffective and colorless by overuse. A once-powerful phrase is stripped of its significance by thoughtless repetition and serves only to display a lack of originality in the person who employs it. Thus, when we say that "he sat down to a sumptuous repast," or "a ta-

---

[16]From a commencement address by Ernest F. Tittle, delivered at the Northwestern University School of Speech, June 1924.

[17]H. A. Overstreet, *Influencing Human Behavior* (New York: W. W. Norton & Company, Inc., 1925). For advice on the use of words, see pp. 50–70, 96–107, 125–139.

ble loaded with delicacies," we not only are violating the rule of simplicity but are using worn-out phrases as well. The words *gorgeous, fabulous, terrific,* and others have been so overworked that they have lost much of their original effectiveness. Figures of speech in particular are likely to become trite; avoid such expressions as "slept like a log," "dead as a doornail," and "pretty as a picture." On the other hand, beware of unusual combinations and mixed metaphors. The speaker who described a dump heap as a "picturesque eyesore" was original but self-contradictory, while the man who remarked that "The years roll on, drop by drop" combined two quite different figures. Note in contrast the appropriateness of this metaphorical statement by Herbert Read: ". . . meaning is an arrow that reaches its mark when least encumbered with feathers."[18]

Note also the strength and freshness of A. Whitney Griswold's figurative comparison of the free and the unfree mind: "Discovery is the true essence of learning. The free mind travels while the unfree simply looks at the maps. The unfree mind locks the doors, bars the shutters, and stays at home."[19]

On certain occasions, slang words and phrases add succinctness and color to a talk. Usually, however, they should be avoided. College slang especially tends to become trite and to substitute one word for a variety of more specific and effective terms. A young woman, for example, is "out of sight," but so is a football game, a sports car, a dance, a class lecture, or a pair of shoes. To use slang for a particular effect is permissible, but to use it merely to avoid the search for more precise words is slipshod and results in weak or empty expressions.

Make your connective phrases clear and graceful

Unlike written compositions, material which is spoken cannot be divided into units by paragraph indentations or by underlined headings. Instead, the relationships between the points of a speech must be made clear by the wording alone. Preliminary and final summaries are useful in mapping out for an audience the road you intend to follow and in reviewing your speech at its close. But you also must set up signposts

---

[18]Excerpt from *English Prose Style* by Herbert Read. Copyright 1952. Reprinted by permission of Pantheon Books, a Division of Random House, Inc.

[19]Quoted from "The Bold Go Toward Their Time" by William C. Lang in a speech by A. Whitney Griswold printed in *Vital Speeches of the Day,* Volume XXVII (March 15, 1961), pp. 333–334. Reprinted by permission of Vital Speeches of the Day.

along the way if you expect your audience to follow you. For this purpose, a variety of connective phrases are useful. The following list contains some of the more common ones:

Not only . . . but also . . .
In the first place. . . . The second point is . . .
In addition to . . . notice that . . .
More important than all these is . . .
In contrast to . . .
Similar to this . . . is . . .
Now look at it from a different angle . . .
This last point raises a question . . .
You must keep these three things in mind in order to understand the importance of the fourth . . .
What was the result of this . . . ? Just this: . . .

Expand your list of such phrases and use them to make easy, smooth transitions from one point to another.

Work systematically to build an ever larger speaking vocabulary

If a speaker is to choose words that are accurate, clear, appropriate, and vivid, he must have a large and constantly growing vocabulary. Reading, close observation of the language used by cultured people, a systematic attempt to "use a new word every day"—all of these methods are helpful in vocabulary development. It is equally important, however, to put into active use the vocabulary you already possess. Most people know the meanings of ten times as many words as they actually use. Work to transfer the words in your recognition vocabulary to your speaking vocabulary. Effective speakers are noted not for the large number of words they employ but rather for the skill with which they combine the simple words of the average man's vocabulary to state even complicated ideas clearly and precisely.

PROBLEMS FOR FURTHER STUDY

1. A speaker's language must serve—often simultaneously—two distinct functions: *clarification* (denotative reference) and *affect* (connotative attitude toward the object or experience). Accuracy and clarity contribute principally to denotative reference; appropriateness and vividness, to connotative affect. For example, compare these three sentences:

a. "He is a quiet person."
b. "He is the strong, silent type."
c. "You can't get a peep out of him."

All three statements are clear, but the first is relatively *neutral;* the second, *positive attitudinally;* and the third, *negative attitudinally.* Reword the following statements, first positively, then negatively:

d. "That is an untruth."
e. "Granola is a different-tasting cereal."
f. "He spoke at great length."
g. "She ran across the park."

2. Find a shorter and simpler word to express each of the following:

maintain	designate	culmination
escalate	perturbation	tenacious
partition	holistic	funereal
investigation	tautology	preferential

3. Read a recent issue of *Vital Speeches of the Day* to find *(a)* passages that illustrate particularly good word-choice (i.e., passages in which the words are accurate, simple, and appropriate); and *(b)* instances of the skillful use of connective words and phrases.

4. What connective phrase might you use to join *(a)* a major idea with a subordinate one, *(b)* a less important idea with a more important one, *(c)* two ideas of equal importance, *(d)* ideas comparable in meaning, and *(e)* contrasting or opposing ideas?

5. Using varied and vivid imagery, describe orally or in writing one of the following:

Sailboats on a lake at sunset.
A mountain stream in the spring.
Traffic at a busy intersection.
Sitting in the bleachers at a football game in 15° weather.
The hors d'oeuvre table at an expensive restaurant.
The city dump.
A symphony concert.

ORAL ACTIVITIES AND SPEAKING ASSIGNMENTS

1. Describe orally in class a personal experience or an event you have recently witnessed—for example, a traffic accident, a memorable meal, the crucial moment in a basketball game, backpacking through the mountains. Employ vivid imagery in an effort to reproduce at least part of that experience or event for your listeners.

2. Individually or in small groups, examine one issue of a college or local newspaper; read news stories, features, and editorials selected at random. For each of these items, make a rough tabulation of the relatively neutral or almost purely descriptive nouns, adjectives, adverbs, and verbs; and the relatively loaded or affective nouns, adjectives, adverbs, and verbs. Typically, you should discover that news stories use predominantly descriptive language (and hence should be judged on their objectivity) and that editorials and features use emotionally weighted words and images (and hence should be judged on their rhetorical effectiveness). Do such patterns appear? If not, why not? As a class, discuss the use of emotional shading and attitude-building in news stories and informative presentations.

3. Write a four- to six-minute speech to be presented orally from manuscript. Revise the manuscript several times to be sure that *(a)* the words and expressions you choose are accurate, simple, and appropriate; *(b)* wherever possible, you have employed lively and vivid imagery; *(c)* you have employed loaded language skillfully but ethically; *(d)* you have avoided trite expressions; and *(e)* your connective phrases are clear and graceful.

SUGGESTIONS FOR FURTHER READING

Cicero, *Orator,* 135 – 139, "The Embellishment of Style." A classic list of thirty-nine figures of speech and thought which the ancients used to teach effective style.

Hubert G. Alexander, *Meaning in Language* (Glenview, Ill.: Scott, Foresman and Company, 1969). A philosophically oriented introduction to language and communication.

James I. Brown, *Programmed Vocabulary: Steps Toward Improved Word Power* (New York: Appleton-Century-Crofts, 1964). A work particularly useful to students who want — by systematic means — to improve their vocabularies and expand their language abilities.

John B. Carroll, *Language and Thought* (Englewood Cliffs, N. J.: Prentice-Hall, Inc., 1964). A psychologically based introduction to the role of language in thought-formation.

Maila Harrell, John Waite Bowers, and Jeffrey P. Bacal, "Another Stab at 'Meaning': Concreteness, Iconicity, and Conventionality," *Speech Monographs* XL (August 1973): 199 – 207. A difficult but rewarding discussion of three dimensions of rhetorically potent language.

Bardin H. Nelson, "Seven Principles of Image Formation," *Dimensions of Communication*, ed. Lee Richardson (New York: Appleton-Century-Crofts, 1969), pp. 53–60. An easy-to-read discussion of ways in which language builds ideas in the mind.

Robert L. Scott, *The Speaker's Reader: Concepts in Communication* (Glenview, Ill.: Scott, Foresman and Company, 1969), D, "Style;" and E, "Tone." An enlightening treatment, particularly of a most difficult subject—verbal "tone."

Chapter 9

Beginning and ending the speech

E very speech, whether long or short, must have a beginning and an end. Too often speakers devote all their time to choosing and arranging the main ideas of a talk and do not plan how to open and close it effectively. Admittedly, the development of the main points deserves the major share of your preparation time and must be worked out before you can sensibly plan how to introduce and conclude your remarks. But it is foolish to leave the introduction and conclusion to the inspiration of the moment, for all too frequently the result is a dull or hesitant beginning and a weak or indefinite ending. The impact of your speech always will be greater if you plan in advance how to direct your listeners' attention to your subject at the outset and how to tie your ideas together in a firm and vigorous conclusion. In this chapter we shall first discuss the aims of an effective introduction and suggest various ways in which these aims may be achieved; then we shall consider the requirements of a suitable conclusion and review several specific methods by which the conclusion may be developed; finally, we shall discuss how to integrate the introduction and conclusion with the body of the speech.

BEGINNING THE SPEECH

The attention of the audience must be maintained throughout a speech, but *capturing* this attention is your principal task at the beginning. Unless people are ready to attend to what you have to say, the most interesting and useful information and the most persuasive appeals will be wasted. Mere attention, however, is not enough; in the first minute or two that you are on the platform, you also must win the good will and respect of your listeners. In many situations your own reputation or the chairperson's introduction will help ensure a fair hearing. But when you are confronted by indifference, distrust, or skepticism, you must take steps to change these attitudes. Finally, you must lead the thinking of your listeners naturally into the subject with which you are concerned. A good introduction, then, should accomplish at least three things: (1) it should gain attention; (2) it should secure good will and respect for you as a speaker; and (3) it should prepare the audience for the discussion that is to follow.

To help you gain these ends, there are a number of well-established means for developing the introduction of a speech, including:

1. Referring to the subject or occasion.
2. Using a personal reference or greeting.
3. Asking a rhetorical question.
4. Making a startling statement of fact or opinion.
5. Using a quotation.
6. Telling a humorous anecdote.
7. Using an illustration.

Referring to the subject or occasion

If the audience already has a vital interest in the subject you are to discuss, you may need only to *state* that subject before plunging into your first main point. The very speed and directness of this approach suggest alertness and eagerness to come to grips with your topic. A speaker once began a talk to a group of college seniors with these words: "I am going to talk tonight about jobs: how to get them and how to keep them."

Arthur R. Taylor, president of the Columbia Broadcasting System, in opening a speech presented as part of a colloquium held on the campus of Amherst College, also referred directly to his subject:

> Within the framework of the theme of this Colloquium, "What's Worth Doing?," I propose to take a hard, critical look at the American corporation—its virtues and vices, its strengths and weaknesses, and most of all its future—and to consider whether or not the modern American corporation is a place worthy of investing one's life. I've worked closely with perhaps twenty-five major U.S. corporations—as an investment banker, as a financial advisor, and more recently as an employee. I'm convinced that, on balance, work for the corporation constitutes work worth doing. Let me try to say why.[1]

---

[1]From "Corporations and the Social Contract" by Arthur R. Taylor, from *Vital Speeches of the Day*, Vol. XXXIX (June 1, 1973), p. 491. Reprinted by permission of Vital Speeches of the Day.

Although such brevity and forthrightness may strike exactly the right note on some occasions, you should not, of course, begin all speeches in this way. To a skeptical audience, a direct beginning may sound immodest and tactless; to an apathetic audience, it may sound dull or uninteresting. When listeners are receptive and friendly, however, reference to the subject often produces a businesslike and forceful opening.

Sometimes, instead of referring to the subject to be discussed, you may in your introduction refer to the *occasion* which has brought the audience together or to the *surroundings* in which your talk is being presented. The first of these possibilities is illustrated by the opening of a speech which John A. Logan, president of Hollins College, delivered at a special convocation celebrating the hundredth anniversary of Western Maryland College, Westminster, Maryland:

> I am honored and delighted to be a part of this significant occasion. Not many colleges in this country have reached the century mark, and admission to that select company is reserved for institutions with special qualities of service and of excellence. I congratulate you on the achievement which this convocation signifies, and thank you for letting me share it.[2]

Using a personal reference or greeting

At times, a personal word from the speaker serves as an excellent starting point. Ms. Joyce Shaw, herself an epileptic, used this method to introduce a speech pleading for a better understanding of the disease and its victims:

> I am a drug addict. Every day I consume enough drugs in the form of "downers," "barbs," "bummers" — what doctors call barbiturates — to help two people come down off of their highs. But I don't have a high to come off of; I have a disease to compensate for. I am an epileptic, and I stay addicted to drugs in order to lessen the symptoms of my disease.
> Because I am epileptic, I want to talk to you about epilepsy.[3]

The way in which a personal-reference type of introduction may sometimes be used to gain a hearing from a hostile or skeptical audi-

---

[2]From "The Liberal Arts College" by John A. Logan, from *Vital Speeches of the Day*, Vol. XXXIV (March 1, 1968), p. 308. Reprinted by permission of Vital Speeches of the Day.

[3]Reprinted from *Winning Orations*, 1971, by special arrangement with the Interstate Oratorical Association, Duane L. Aschenbrenner, Executive Secretary, University of Nebraska at Omaha.

ence is shown by Anson Mount, Manager of Public Affairs for *Playboy* magazine, in a talk presented to the Christian Life Commission of the Southern Baptist Convention:

> I am sure we are all aware of the seeming incongruity of a representative of *Playboy* magazine speaking to an assemblage of representatives of the Southern Baptist Convention. I was intrigued by the invitation when it came last fall, though I was not surprised. I am grateful for your genuine and warm hospitality, and I am flattered (though again not surprised) by the implication that I would have something to say that could have meaning to you people. Both *Playboy* and the Baptists have indeed been considering many of the same issues and ethical problems; and even if we have not arrived at the same conclusions, I am impressed and gratified by your openness and willingness to listen to our views.[4]

Introductions in the form of greetings to the audience are common, and in certain situations practically obligatory. Here is how General James Ferguson, Air Force Systems Command, when speaking at the Air Force Academy to open a two-day conference on "Value Engineering," combined a greeting with reference to the surroundings:

> It is a great pleasure, on behalf of the Air Force Systems Command, to join General Moorman in welcoming each of you to these breathtaking surroundings. It seems to me entirely fitting and proper that so many high-level managers from Government and Industry should be meeting together in this rarefied atmosphere.
>
> The size and caliber of this assemblage are certainly very gratifying to all of us at Systems Command, and we appreciate your overwhelming response to our "Request for Participants." The fact that so many top industrial and military managers would take the time to work with us here for two days speaks volumes about the value that *you* place on Value Engineering. Let us all hope that your example—amplified by the exchange of information and ideas that takes place here today and tomorrow—will ripple and spread throughout the defense and industrial communities.[5]

---

[4]Excerpt from speech presented to Christian. Life Commission of Southern Baptist Convention by Anson Mount, Manager of Public Affairs for *Playboy* Magazine from *Contemporary American Speeches*, 3rd ed. Reprinted by permission of The Christian Life Commission.

[5]From "Value Engineering" by General James Ferguson, from *Vital Speeches of the Day*, Vol. XXXVI (October 15, 1969), p. 29. Reprinted by permission of Vital Speeches of the Day. The "breathtaking surroundings" to which the General refers are located in the especially scenic mountains of Colorado, near Colorado Springs.

If the personal reference or greeting used in the introduction is modest and sincere, it may establish good will as well as gain attention. Effusiveness and hollow compliments, however, should be avoided. Audiences are quick to sense a lack of genuineness on the part of a speaker, and they always react unfavorably toward feigned or falsified sentiments. At the other extreme, avoid apologizing. Do not say, "I don't know why I was picked to talk on this subject when others could have done it so much better," or "Unaccustomed as I am to public speaking . . . ." Apologetic beginnings suggest that your speech is not worth listening to. Be cordial, sincere, and modest, but do not apologize.

Asking a rhetorical question

A third way to open a speech is to ask a question or a series of questions to start the audience thinking about your subject. Jacques Piccard, the well-known marine scientist, used such questions to good advantage when introducing a lecture on the pollution of the oceans:

> Everywhere we hear of pollution, of ecological problems, and of environmental disasters. In every newspaper we read that the sea is about to die, that the atmosphere is poisoning our lungs, that mankind itself may disappear within one or a few generations. Pollution has become the great problem in our century. And as always when a big subject becomes fashionable, all the most dangerous exaggerations are carefully mixed up with the most realistic facts. What should we believe? What should we fear? What is the role played in this by the oceans? I would like to analyze the general problem with you and try to see what can be done to increase the chances of human survival.[6]

Making a startling statement

On certain occasions a speech may be opened with what some writers have referred to as the "shock technique." This method consists of jarring the audience into attention by making a startling statement of fact or opinion, and is especially useful when hearers are distracted or apathetic. Guy O. Mabry, vice-president of the Owens-Corning Fiberglas Corporation, when addressing members of the National Apartment Association on the challenge facing the building industry, used this "shock-technique" introduction:

[6]From "How Modern Technology Is Endangering Our Lives" by Jacques Piccard, from *Vital Speeches of the Day*, Vol. XXXIX (January 1, 1973), p. 179. Reprinted by permission of Vital Speeches of the Day.

Ladies and gentlemen . . . The building industry faces a mission as momentous and as seemingly impossible as landing a man on the moon. The mission is this: the industry must rebuild America in the next thirty years.

For every home that exists, the industry is going to have to create a new home. For every store, a new store. For every office building, a new office building. For every existing apartment house, another apartment house.

It's going to have to build a new Austin, a new Sacramento, a new Indianapolis, a new Albany, a new Youngstown, a new Omaha. And it's going to have to do it in thirty years.

By the building industry, I mean not just builders alone. I mean builders and manufacturers and unions and financial institutions and governmental agencies. I mean everyone concerned.[7]

Using a quotation

If properly chosen and presented, a quotation may be an excellent means of introducing a speech. Wilma Scott Heide, president of NOW, the National Organization of Women, when addressing the organization's sixth national conference, opened her speech by skillfully combining a quotation from Eleanor Roosevelt with the acronym NOW:

Eleanor Roosevelt, who I'd like to think would be with us in spirit, once wrote: "We face the future fortified only with the lessons we have learned from the past. It is today that we must create the world of the future. . . . In a very real sense, Tomorrow is NOW."

We return to the birthplace of NOW in our nation's capital to declare that feminism is a bona fide occupational qualification (b.f.o.q.) for every human endeavor. Every social issue, every public policy, every institution of our society needs feminist analysis and leadership, and we will provide it as a basic requirement for a humanist world. What we are about is a profound universal behavioral Revolution: Tomorrow is NOW![8]

Telling a humorous anecdote

At times you may begin a speech by telling a funny story or relating a humorous experience. But be sure that the story or experience you

---

[7]From "Modular Components" by Guy O. Mabry, from *Vital Speeches of the Day*, Vol. XXXVI (November 1, 1969), p. 61. Reprinted by permission of Vital Speeches of the Day.

[8]From "Tomorrow Is NOW" by Wilma Scott Heide, from *Vital Speeches of the Day*, Vol. XXXIX (May 1, 1973), p. 424. Reprinted by permission of Vital Speeches of the Day.

recount will amuse the audience and that you can tell it well. If your opening remarks fail to arouse interest or to put the audience in a receptive frame of mind, your speech will be off to a poor start. Also be sure that the anecdote contributes to the central purpose of your talk. A joke or story that is unrelated to your subject not only wastes valuable time but channels the thinking of your listeners in the wrong direction. Finally, be sure that what you say is in good taste. Not only do doubtful or "off-color" stories violate the accepted standards of social behavior, but they may also seriously undermine the respect which the members of the audience should have for you as a speaker.

Consistent with the requirements we have just described, Howard J. Aibel, a noted corporate counselor, in talking about antitrust problems as they affect businessmen and women, built his opening remarks around the following anecdote:

> Thank you, Mr. Chairman, ladies, and gentlemen. When I sat down to draw my thoughts together in preparation for these remarks, I thought of a story told about Robert Benchley, the late humorist. As I have heard it, when Benchley was an undergraduate, he was called upon to write an examination in a history course in which he was enrolled but which he had rarely attended. One of the questions on the examination called for a discussion of the naval battle over fishing rights off the Grand Banks of Newfoundland between the French and the British in the War of 1763. As the story goes, Benchley, unprepared, was puzzled as to what to say; but after just a few minutes, he commenced by answering along the following lines: On the one hand, much has been written about this battle from the point of view of the French; on the other hand, even more has been written from the British side of this battle. There has been a paucity of comment, however, about this incident from the point of view of the fish, a deficiency which I will now set about remedying.
>
> I, like Benchley, was puzzled as to what to say to you today since you have all heard enough in recent years from earnest and sincere critics of developments in antitrust law and economics, on the one hand from the hawks and on the other hand from the doves. Inevitably, I came to the conclusion that I might serve you best by discussing competitive measures and competitive facts from the point of view of the fish — the businessmen and the business lawyers faced with the task of advising a client, trying to swim through the nets and seines of antitrust, swirling in the currents and tides of what otherwise might be considered safe waters.[9]

---

[9]From "Antitrust Problems and National Priorities" by Howard J. Aibel, from *Vital Speeches of the Day*, Vol. XXXVIII (April 15, 1972), p. 409. Reprinted by permission of Vital Speeches of the Day.

Using an illustration

One or more real-life incidents, a story taken from literature, or a series of hypothetical illustrations also may be used to get a speech under
way. As in the case of the humorous anecdote, however, any illustration
you employ should not only be interesting to the audience in its own
right, but should also be closely connected with the central idea you
want to communicate. Here is how Gail Bauer, a student at Wisconsin
State University, began a speech criticizing our present child-adoption
laws:

> Picture this: a husband comes to the hospital to pick up his wife and
> new baby. As he passes the nursery door, he reads a sign which says:
> "Parents: No infants released until satisfactory answers can be given to
> these questions—Are you Catholic, Protestant, or Jew? Do both parents
> share the same faith? Do you belong to a church? Please name. Will the
> child receive religious training? Note: Non-believers need not apply."
> An actual sign? Of course not. Incredible? Yes, for couples lucky
> enough to conceive and bear their own children. But for those who seek
> a child through adoption these questions are no laughing matter. For in
> this land of religious freedom, the wrong religion, or—even worse—no
> religion, can be the bar between the happy union of a child who needs
> parents and a couple who want a baby to love.[10]

These, then, are seven useful ways of opening a speech: *a reference
to the subject or occasion, a personal allusion or greeting, a rhetorical question,
a startling declaration, an appropriate quotation, a humorous anecdote,* and *a
striking illustration.* Sometimes one approach may be used alone; at other
times, two or more of them may be combined. Whether used singly or
in combination, however, the materials comprising your introduction
always should be aimed at the same objective: arousing the attention
and winning the good will and respect of your listeners. Moreover,
those materials should be relevant to the purpose of your speech and
should lead naturally into the first of the major ideas you wish to present. To establish a common ground of interest and understanding
and to point the audience toward the conclusion you ultimately hope to
reach—these are the functions your introductory remarks always should
serve.

---

[10]Reprinted from *Winning Orations,* 1971, by special arrangement with the Interstate
Oratorical Association, Duane L. Aschenbrenner, Executive Secretary, University of Nebraska at Omaha.

ENDING THE SPEECH

The principal function of the ending or conclusion of a speech is to *focus the thought of the audience on your central theme and purpose.* If you are presenting a one-point speech (see Chapter 6), you will usually restate that point at the end in a manner that makes your meaning clear and forceful. If your speech is more complex, you may bring its most important points together in a condensed and uniform way; or you may spell out the action or belief which these points suggest.

In addition to bringing the substance of the speech into final focus, your conclusion should *aim at leaving the audience in the proper mood.* If you want your listeners to express vigorous enthusiasm, you should stimulate that feeling in your closing remarks. If you want them to reflect thoughtfully on what you have said, you should encourage a calm, judicious attitude. Therefore, you should decide whether the response you seek requires a mood of serious determination or lighthearted levity, of warm sympathy or utter disgust, of thoughtful consideration or vigorous desire for action; then you should plan to end your speech in such a way as to create that mood.

Finally, a good ending should *convey a sense of completeness and finality.* Listeners grow restless and annoyed when they are given reason to feel that the speaker has finished, only to hear him or her ramble on. Therefore, avoid false endings. Tie the threads of thought together so that the pattern of your speech is brought clearly to completion, deliver your concluding sentence with finality — and stop.

Some of the means most frequently used to conclude speeches are:
1. Issuing a challenge or appeal.
2. Summarizing.
3. Using a quotation.
4. Using an illustration.
5. Supplying an additional inducement to belief or action.
6. Stating a personal intention.

Issuing a challenge or appeal

When using this method, the speaker openly appeals for support or action, or reminds the listeners of their responsibilities in furthering a desirable end. Such an appeal must be vivid and compelling and should, as a rule, contain within it a suggestion of the principal ideas or arguments presented in the speech. Note how Secretary of State Henry Kissinger employed this type of conclusion in his address opening an international conference on the energy problem held in Washington in February 1974:

> The approach to global cooperation outlined here has prompted the President's invitations to you to join us here today.
> This conception is ambitious, but the need is great.
> Therefore let us resolve:
> — To meet the special challenges and opportunities facing the major consuming nations with a program of cooperation.
> — To bring the developing nations into immediate consultation and collaboration with us.
> — To prepare for a positive and productive dialogue with the producing nations.
> As we look toward the end of this century we know that the energy crisis indicates the birth pains of global interdependence. Our response could well determine our capacity to deal with the international agenda of the future.
> We confront a fundamental decision. Will we consume ourselves in nationalistic rivalry which the realities of interdependence make suicidal? Or will we acknowledge our interdependence and shape cooperative solutions?
> Our choice is clear; our responsibility compelling. We must demonstrate to future generations that our vision was equal to our challenge.[11]

A somewhat different approach to ending a speech, but one which also adroitly utilizes both a challenge and an appeal, was employed by President Richard M. Nixon in concluding his State of the Union address to the Congress for the year 1972:

> Never has a Congress had a greater opportunity to leave a legacy of profound and constructive reform for the nation than this Congress.
> If we succeed in these tasks, there will be credit enough for all—not only for doing what is right, but for doing it in the right way, by rising above partisan interest to serve the national interest.
> If we fail, then more than any of us, America will be the loser.
> That is why my call upon the Congress today is for a high statesmanship—so that in the years to come, Americans will look back and say that because it withstood the intense pressures of a political year, and

---

[11]From "The Washington Energy Conference" by Henry Kissinger, from *Vital Speeches of the Day*, Vol. XXXX (March 15, 1974), p. 325. Reprinted by permission of Vital Speeches of the Day.

achieved such great good for the American people, and for the future of this nation—this was truly a great Congress.[12]

Summarizing

In a summary conclusion, the speaker reviews the main points of the message or draws whatever inferences may be implicit in the material presented. In a speech to inform, a summary ending is nearly always appropriate because it helps to impress upon the listeners those ideas which should be especially remembered. In a speech to inform, such an ending affords a chance to repeat the major items of knowledge or information previously presented which the speaker hopes the listeners will carry away with them. In a speech to persuade, a summary conclusion provides an opportunity to reiterate the principal arguments.

When addressing students of communication at the University of Texas on the subject "Eloquence as a Creative Art," Professor Waldo W. Braden of Louisiana State University offered this summary of the leading ideas he had presented:

> What [then] does eloquence as creative art entail? Let me briefly summarize:
>
> First, the speaker "inwardly and desperately" believes in his cause.
>
> Second, the speaker sees for himself a demanding goal that will stretch his inventive capacities in their achievement.
>
> Third, the speaker has respect for the intellectual integrity of his listeners. He is moved by the belief that his listeners have a right to hear his deep thoughts and sincere convictions.
>
> Fourth, the speaker realizes his social responsibility; he leads, but he does not exploit.
>
> Fifth, eloquence as a creative art demands that the speaker express his thoughts appropriately, but also with a grandeur approaching the qualities of music and poetry.
>
> Sixth, the speaker must exercise a powerful delivery that adds depth and character to what is said.
>
> Seventh, the speaker strives for a lasting impression upon his listeners—both those who hear him and those who may later read him. Eloquence as a creative art is the delivered essence of the democratic spirit.
>
> In summary, let me emphasize the difference between eloquence as a creative art and the present emphasis upon results. The first gives more attention to goals, preparations, and methods; it demands of the speaker

---

[12]From "State of the Union Message, 1972" by Richard M. Nixon, from *Representative American Speeches, 1971–1972.* Published by The H. W. Wilson Company, p. 26.

his very best; the second seeks to gain ends with little attention to means.[13]

Using a quotation

A quotation may be used to conclude a speech if it bears directly on the central idea that has been developed or strongly suggests the attitude or action the speaker wishes the audience to take. Speaking to a group of business leaders on the subject "There Is a Difference Between Right and Wrong," Dr. John A. Howard, president of Rockford College, concluded his remarks with a quotation from the Russian writer, Alexander Solzhenitsyn:

> In summary, I think we have arrived at the moment of truth in our society where we must reassert in our own lives a recognition that there is a vital and moral difference between good and bad, between better and less good, and do everything in our power to convey that difference to our young people in our homes as parents, and in all other segments of society where we can exert influence, with special attention to the schools and colleges.
>
> I want to conclude with a passage quoted from the undelivered speech Alexander Solzhenitsyn prepared as a response to the Nobel Prize which his government would not let him receive. It is ironic that a virtual prisoner of a repressive government must teach us, out in the free world, our opportunities and our obligations, but I guess it was ever thus. Earlier I spoke of false prophets. In Solzhenitsyn, I believe we are blessed with a true and powerful and poetic prophet:
>
> "The spirit of Munich is in no sense a thing of the past, for that was no flash in the pan. I would go so far as to say that the spirit of Munich is the dominant one in the twentieth century. The civilised world quailed at the onslaught of snarling barbarism, suddenly revitalised; the civilised world found nothing with which to oppose it, save concessions and smiles. The spirit of Munich is an illness of the will-power of the well-to-do, it is the usual state of those who have surrendered to the lust for comfort at any price, have surrendered to materialism as the main aim of our life on earth. Such people—and how many there are in the world today—choose passivity and retreat just so that normality can last a bit longer and the onset of brutishness be put off for another day; as for tomorrow, you never know, it may turn out all right. (But it won't! The

---

[13]From "Eloquence as a Creative Art" by Waldo W. Braden, from *Vital Speeches of the Day*, Vol. XXXVIII (April 15, 1972), p. 401. Reprinted by permission of Vital Speeches of the Day.

price of cowardice will be all the higher. Courage and victory come to us only when we are prepared to make sacrifices.)"[14]

Using an illustration

Just as an illustration which epitomizes your leading ideas may be used to open a speech, so may an epitomizing illustration be used at the close. Edward B. Rust, president of the Chamber of Commerce of the United States, provided the following:

> In 301 A.D. the economy of the Roman Empire suffered from the cumulative efforts of many years of government debasement of the currency. In other words, from inflation.
>
> However, the Emperor Diocletian preferred to blame price rises on "unprincipled greed." To solve that problem, he issued the Edict of 301, freezing wages and prices, with death penalties for violations.
>
> The result of his action was described in 314 A.D. by the historian Lactantius:
>
> > "There was much blood shed upon very slight and trifling accounts; and the people brought provisions no more to markets, since they could not get a reasonable price for them; and this led to such shortages that at last, after many had died by it, the law itself was laid aside."
>
> One thousand six hundred and sixty years later, we are still making the same mistake.
>
> Perhaps it's time for a change.[15]

Supplying an additional inducement to belief or action

Sometimes a speech may be concluded by quickly reviewing the leading ideas presented in the body of the talk and then supplying one or more additional reasons for endorsing the belief or taking the action proposed. The following example shows how a speech on the importance of an annual medical checkup might be concluded in this way:

---

[14]From "There Is a Difference Between Right and Wrong" by John A. Howard, from *Vital Speeches of the Day*, Vol. XXXX (February 15, 1974), p. 284. Reprinted by permission of Vital Speeches of the Day. The passage from Solzhenitsyn is from *One Word of Truth*, translated by the BBC Russian Service and published by The Bodley Head, London. The "spirit of Munich," which Solzhenitsyn mentions, is a reference to the conference in Munich in September, 1938, in which Germany, Italy, France, and England agreed to the surrender of the Sudetenland (a part of Czechoslovakia) to Germany. This "spirit" came to be synonymous with "appeasement" or "peace at any price."

[15]From "The Price of Regulation" by Edward B. Rust, from *Vital Speeches of the Day*, Vol. XXXX (February 1, 1974), p. 256. Reprinted by permission of Vital Speeches of the Day.

All in all, then, you will find an annual checkup by a competent physician to be a wise investment, no matter what your age or how well you may feel at the moment. As I have pointed out, in their early stages a number of potentially serious diseases have no symptoms of which the victim is in any way aware. Many other ills if caught in time can be eliminated or brought under control. Finally, the time and money a good checkup will cost you are only a tiny fraction of the time and expense a serious illness entails.

Here, as in other aspects of life, be guided by the old but still pertinent adage, "A stitch in time saves nine." Remember that even though you may be foolish enough to take chances with your own well-being, you owe it to your loved ones and to those dependent on you to take no chances with the most precious of all things — your own good health. Make an appointment for a checkup today!

Stating a personal intention

A statement of the speaker's intention to act as his or her speech recommends is particularly valuable when the speechmaker's prestige with the audience is high. The most famous example of this method of closing a speech, perhaps, is the personal commitment voiced by Patrick Henry: "As for me, give me liberty or give me death!" This type of conclusion also was used by Senator Paul Fannin of Arizona in a speech presented as part of a management-training course sponsored by the General Electric Company:

> I may not agree that everything is right about our present system, but I surely think it is better than anything we could import. I see no major government on the world scene today that I would care to swap for ours. So I shall continue to work on improving this system, to make right those things that are wrong with it, and to preserve those time-tested, honorable principles that are the foundation of our national success.
>
> It is my hope that you view yourself in a similar role.[16]

Regardless of the means you choose — whether you close your speech with *a challenge or appeal,* or with *a summary, quotation, illustration, added inducement,* or *statement of personal intention* — remember that your conclusion should focus the thought of your listeners on the central theme you have developed. In addition, a good conclusion should be

---

[16]From a speech by Paul Fannin, from *Vital Speeches of the Day,* Vol. XXXIV (May 1, 1968), p. 421. Reprinted by permission of Vital Speeches of the Day.

consonant with the mood or tenor of your speech and should convey a sense of completeness and finality.

FITTING THE BEGINNING AND ENDING TO THE BODY OF THE SPEECH

In Chapter 7 we considered various patterns for developing the body or substance of a speech and the principles to be followed in outlining that part of it. When the introduction and conclusion are added to the outline, the completed structure should look something like this:

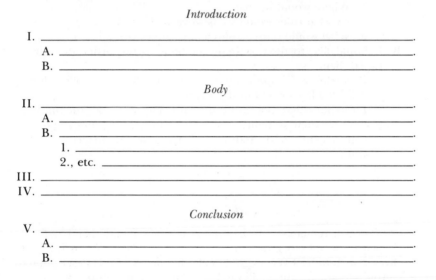

Introduction

I. _____.
    A. _____.
    B. _____.

Body

II. _____.
    A. _____.
    B. _____.
       1. _____.
       2., etc. _____.
III. _____.
IV. _____.

Conclusion

V. _____.
    A. _____.
    B. _____.

A SAMPLE OUTLINE FOR AN INTRODUCTION AND A CONCLUSION

An introduction and conclusion for a classroom speech on the medieval university, as outlined in Chapter 7 (pages 153–158), might take the following form:

MEDIEVAL UNIVERSITY LIFE: A MIRROR OF THE TIMES

Introduction

I. During a recent lecture in his course on World Institutions, Professor Howard Jones of our history department declared: "If you would see the medieval world in microcosm — the values it cherished, the customs it practiced, and the morals it approved—you can do no better than to look at its great universities."

A. Let us by exercising our imaginations take just such a look today.
   1. Let us for the next few moments imagine that, instead of living in the twentieth century, we are living in the thirteenth or fourteenth.
   2. Let us imagine that, instead of being enrolled in our present college, we are students at Oxford, Paris, Salerno, or one of the other famous universities of that day.
      a. What would our fellow students be like?
      b. What studies would we pursue?
      c. Where would we live?
      d. By what rules would we be governed?
      e. What would our customs and pastimes be?

B. I should like to discuss these questions in the order in which I raised them.
   1. By so doing, I hope I can give you some flavor of college life as it existed five or six hundred years ago.
   2. I also hope that as a result of what I shall say about the universities and their students, you will—as Professor Jones suggests—gain a better understanding of medieval life and culture as a whole.

[*Body*][17]

Conclusion

V. As you will remember, in beginning my talk I said that I not only hoped to be able to give you some flavor of college life as it existed five or six hundred years ago, but also by means of this description to throw additional light on all medieval thought and culture.

A. Rather than presenting a formal review of all I have covered, therefore, let me conclude by pointing especially to four ways in which the medieval universities and their students mirror the life of the times.
   1. The wide discrepancies between different classes of students reflect the deep divisions that existed within the entire social structure.
   2. The narrow, tradition-bound curriculum, with its emphasis on theology and the ancient languages, shows the unconcern of the period for science and material progress.

---

[17]For a complete development of the body of the speech, review Chapter 7, "Arranging and Outlining Related Points," especially pp. 149–158.

3. The laborious explication of texts by the lecture method suggests the universal reverence for tradition and authority.
4. The riotous behavior of the students is evidence of the rough and undisciplined nature of society.

B. When we consider these points we can, I think, understand why Professor Jones described the universities as "the medieval world in microcosm."

PROBLEMS FOR FURTHER STUDY

1. On the first page of this chapter, we noted that one of the purposes of an introduction is to "prepare the audience for the discussion that will follow." Such preparation should take into account not only the *intellectual needs* of the subject matter and audience but also the *emotional tone* you wish the speech to project. A humorous anecdote may be appropriate for an after-dinner speech, but hardly for a funeral oration; a personal greeting probably is appropriate if it comes from a visiting dignitary, but perhaps not from an unknown person with no established authority or sponsoring organization. Think about questions of *tone* when preparing your next speech: *(a)* Will an illustration you have found be serious or light enough for your purposes? *(b)* Does a quotation you have discovered come from a source who has authority and status for *this* audience? *(c)* Will a startling statement you have concocted appear too gimmicky? *(d)* Have a significant number of your audience members *really* thought about the rhetorical questions you plan to ask? *(e)* Is the occasion sufficiently significant or unique to merit a reference to it? Ask yourself these and similar questions about your introductions (and, of course, conclusions) as you build your future speeches.

2. Select fifteen or twenty speeches from recent issues of *Vital Speeches of the Day, Representative American Speeches,* or other sources suggested by your instructor. Classify the various ways in which these speeches begin and end. Are certain types of beginnings and endings used more frequently than others? Do some types seem to be more common in speeches to inform and others more common in speeches to persuade? What types appear most frequently in speeches delivered on special occasions — anniversaries, dedications, farewells, etc.?

3. Select ten of the beginnings and endings cataloged in Problem 2. Evaluate these in terms of their suitability to *(a)* the speaker's purpose, *(b)* the subject matter of the speech, and *(c)* the nature and attitudes of the audience (insofar as you can gauge them). Which of the beginnings and endings could have been improved? How? Why?

4. After listening to one or more of the following types of speeches, evaluate the introduction and conclusion which the speaker used in *(a)* a classroom lecture; *(b)* a church sermon; *(c)* an open hearing at a meeting of the city council; *(d)* remarks made at a fraternity, sorority, or dormitory council meeting; and *(e)* a formal address, "live" or televised, made by a political candidate. In reporting your evaluation, supply sufficient information about the speaker and speaking situation so that someone who was not present could understand why you evaluated a particular beginning or ending as you did.

ORAL ACTIVITIES AND SPEAKING ASSIGNMENTS

1. Participate in a class discussion concerning introductions and conclusions to public speeches. The discussion might be structured as follows: One student will lead off by suggesting a topic for a possible speech to this class. A second student will then suggest an appropriate type of introduction and conclusion, justifying those choices. A third student will, in turn, challenge that selection, proposing alternative introductions and/or conclusions. Continue this discussion until everyone has proposed and defended the different types of introductions and conclusions that would be appropriate for various speech topics.

2. Select a subject toward which the members of your speech class probably will hold one of the attitudes described in Chapter 3, pages 49–50: favorable, but not aroused; apathetic; interested, but undecided; hostile to any change; etc. Prepare and present a five-minute speech on a subject of interest to the members of your speech class. Conclude it with an ending designed to leave the audience *(a)* thoughtful or reflective, *(b)* emotionally aroused or excited, or *(c)* determined to take the action you propose. At the conclusion of your presentation, take a quick survey of your listeners to determine the extent of your purpose-fulfillment.

SUGGESTIONS FOR FURTHER READING

Aristotle, *Rhetoric* 1414b–1415b, "The Proem or Introduction," and 1419b–1420b, "The Epilogue." The oldest statements on introductions and conclusions that we possess.

John Waite Bowers and Michael M. Osborn, "Attitudinal Effects of Selected Types of Concluding Metaphors in Persuasive Speeches," *Speech Monographs* XXXIII (June 1966): 147–155. An interesting experimental study of one variable affecting the strength of a conclusion.

Donald C. Bryant and Karl R. Wallace, *Fundamentals of Public Speaking*, 4th ed. (New York: Appleton-Century-Crofts, 1969), Chapter 10, "Framing the Speech and Highlighting the Essentials," pp. 163–176. Another textbook offering an alternative approach to introductions and conclusions.

Bernard P. McCabe, Jr., and Coleman C. Bender, *Speaking Is a Practical Matter*, 2nd ed. (Boston: Holbrook Press, Inc., 1973), "Organize the [Informative] Speech Materials into Purposeful Speech" and "Structure [Persuasive Materials] into Organized-Reasoned Patterns," pp. 166–180, 207–217. A useful attempt to discuss introductions and conclusions exclusively in terms of speakers' purposes.

Wayne Minnick, *The Art of Persuasion*, 2nd ed. (Boston: Houghton Mifflin Company, 1968), Chapter 3, "Getting and Holding Attention." A well-diagrammed discussion of practical problems of gaining listeners' attention in speech introductions.

Chapter 10

Speaking to inform

AN IMPORTANT FUNCTION OF SPEECH is the communication of knowledge. Through informative utterance, people are able to give others the benefit of their learning and experience. In this chapter, we shall consider how to present information in a clear and interesting fashion.

TYPES OF INFORMATIVE SPEECHES

Informative speeches take many forms. Three of these forms — *reports, instructions,* and *lectures* — occur so frequently, however, that they merit special mention.

Oral reports

Scientific reports, committee reports, and executive reports are typical of this kind of informative speech. Experts who engage in special research announce their findings. Committees carry on inquiries and report the results to the organization of which they are a part. Teachers, sales representatives, and businessmen attend conventions and later report to others the information they have obtained.

Oral instructions

In a complex industrial society, job instructions, class instructions, and instructions for special group efforts play a vital role. Teachers instruct students in ways of preparing assignments. Supervisors tell their subordinates how a task should be performed. Leaders explain to volunteer workers their duties in a fund-raising drive or a cleanup campaign. For convenience, such instructions often are given to a *group* of persons rather than to individuals and, even when written, may need to be accompanied by oral explanations.

Lectures

Characteristic of this type of informative communication are lectures on travel and public affairs, classroom lectures, and lectures at club meetings, study conferences, and institutes. Sometimes the speaker is a member of the community who has had special training or experience in the subject he or she covers. At other times, visiting dignitaries or experts talk. Always, however, the purpose is to increase the audience's understanding or appreciation of a particular field of knowledge.

THE PURPOSE OF A SPEECH TO INFORM: TO ATTAIN UNDERSTANDING

Although the main purpose of a speech to inform is to create understanding, you should not view it as an opportunity to parade your knowledge. Instead of trying to see how much ground you can cover in a given time, try to help others grasp and remember the facts or ideas you present.

Remember, too, that people absorb information more easily when it interests them. Therefore, a secondary purpose of your speech should be to make the information interesting to your audience. This secondary intention must, however, be kept subordinate. Too often a speaker rambles from one interesting matter to another without specifically relating them to each other or to his central theme. Your principal goal is to make the conclusions of your report clear, to have your instructions understood, or to ensure a proper grasp of the content of your lecture. All else must be subordinated to these aims.

ESSENTIAL CHARACTERISTICS OF A SPEECH TO INFORM

Three qualities should characterize a speech to inform: (1) *clarity*, (2) *concreteness*, and (3) *the association of new ideas with familiar ones*. The informative speaker must keep these qualities well in mind and develop the means of providing them for listeners.

Clarity

This quality is in large part the result of effective organization. Observe, therefore, the following rules: *(a)* Do not have too many points. Confine your speech to three or four principal ideas, and group the remaining facts and considerations under these headings. *(b)* Clarify the relationship between your main points by observing the principles of coordination set forth in Chapter 7, pages 144–149. *(c)* Keep your speech moving ahead according to a well-developed plan; do not jump back and forth from one idea to another.

While clarity is largely achieved through effective organization, it is aided by the wise selection of reinforcing materials and by the use of certain compositional devices. In Chapter 6, we pointed out how supporting materials may effectively clarify and illustrate a speaker's ideas. In later sections of this chapter, we shall discuss how such devices as initial and final summaries, transitional statements, and definitions also promote clarity.

Concreteness

In a speech to inform, concreteness is as important as clarity. A lecture or report should be packed with facts — with names and references to actual places, events, and experiences. In presenting facts, however, observe these two precepts: (1) Do not multiply details unnecessarily. Present statistics in round numbers, especially if they involve large and complicated sets of data; outline the general course of a historical change or development rather than recount each minute incident; do not belabor a story or illustration until the thinking of your listeners is drawn away from the point you wish to emphasize. Facts are indispensable, but excessively detailed facts are confusing. (2) Again, as we emphasized in Chapter 6, whenever possible, support your presentation of factual information with charts, diagrams, models, or other visual materials. If the members of your audience can see what you are describing, they usually can take in details more readily.

Association of new ideas with familiar ones

Audiences grasp new facts and ideas more readily when they are able to associate them with things that are already known; therefore, in a speech to inform, always try to connect the new with the old. If you are giving instructions or describing a problem, relate your materials to procedures or problems with which your listeners are familiar. A college dean talking to an audience of manufacturers on the problems of higher education presented his ideas under the headings of raw material, casting, machining, polishing, and assembling.

CAPTURING AND HOLDING THE LISTENERS' INTEREST

An informative speech that has the characteristics just described — that is, a speech that is clear and concrete and associates new or strange ideas with old and familiar ones — will naturally tend to be interesting.

Sometimes, however, these qualities are not in themselves sufficient to capture the attention of the listeners and hold it at a level which will ensure understanding. Therefore, it is important that every speaker, regardless of purpose, know something of the relationship between interest and attention and be acquainted with those types of ideas which are especially calculated to arouse and maintain interest in an oral discourse.

Interest and attention

Interest and attention are closely related. People not only pay attention to what interests them, but—conversely—what they pay attention to over a period of time often tends to *become* interesting. Frequently, students begin a required course convinced that they are going to be thoroughly bored. After a while, however, the course begins to interest them and may actually arouse them to the point that they continue for many months or years to investigate the subject matter covered. The important thing in a speech, therefore, is to capture the attention of the audience in the first place and to ensure that listeners give the speaker's message a fair hearing. When this is done—if the speaker is skillful and the message worthwhile—interest grows as the talk proceeds.

What is attention? For our purposes, it may be thought of as a focusing upon one element in a given field, with the result that other elements in that field fade, become dim, and for all practical purposes momentarily cease to exist.[1] Consider, as an example, the baseball fan sitting in the bleachers. The home team is one run ahead in the ninth inning; the visiting team is at bat; the bases are loaded; there are two outs; and the count is three and two. The pitcher wraps his fingers around the ball, winds up, and curls a slider over the corner of the plate. The umpire bawls, "Strike three! You're out!" Only then does the fan lean back, take a long breath, and notice what has been going on around her: that she has dropped her sack of peanuts or thrown off her hat, that her neighbor has been thumping her on the back, that

---

[1]Psychologist Floyd L. Ruch, University of Southern California, describes attention more precisely as "The process of psychological selectivity by which we select, from a vast number of potential stimuli, only those which are related to present interests and needs." He explains: "From among the many stimuli which are within range physiologically, we select—and consciously react to—only those that are related to our present needs and interests. . . . Most psychologists regard attention as having three interrelated aspects, all of which are part of a single complex act. Attention is (1) an adjustment of the body and its sense organs, (2) clear and vivid consciousness, and (3) a set toward action." In *Psychology and Life*, 7th br. ed. (Glenview, Ill.: Scott, Foresman and Company, 1967), pp. 295, 572.

threatening clouds are gathering on the horizon. While all her faculties were focused on the crucial pitch—while, as we say, she was paying attention to it—she was largely unaware of her immediate surroundings. It is this focusing upon one source of stimuli to the greater or lesser exclusion of others that we call *attention*.

How can you as a speaker capture the attention of your listeners? How can you get them to focus on what you are saying rather than listen to the knocking radiator, study the hat of the lady in the first row, or worry about tomorrow's date with the dentist? As we pointed out in Chapters 4 and 5, a great deal depends on how you deliver your speech—on the vigor and the variety of your gestures and bodily movements, on the flexibility and animation of your voice. Your reputation and prestige *(ethos)* also will help secure a degree of attention, and the color and impressiveness of your language or style will contribute, too. *Fundamentally, however, you will capture attention through the types of ideas you present to your hearers.* As the experience of many speakers has shown, some types of ideas have greater attention value than others; people not only are attracted to them in the first place, but—upon listening to these ideas—their interest or concern is further aroused.

Factors of attention

Those types of ideas which have high attention value are sometimes called "the factors of attention" and include the following:

1. Activity or movement	4. Familiarity	7. Conflict
2. Reality	5. Novelty	8. Humor
3. Proximity	6. Suspense	9. The vital

These terms, of course, overlap; and in an actual speech the qualities they represent often are combined. For purposes of explanation, however, let us consider them separately.

Activity. If you were at the theater and one actor was standing motionless while another was moving excitedly about the stage, which one would you look at? The moving one, most likely. Ideas that "move" likewise tend to attract attention. Narratives in which something happens or in which there are moments of uncertainty and crisis nearly always have attention value. Similarly, expository talks hold attention when, for instance, the parts of a machine are described as being in motion or when aspects of a process are introduced.

In addition, your speech as a whole should "move"—should, as someone has said, "march" or press forward. Nothing is so boring as a talk that seems to stand still. For this reason, it is important to make the progress of your speech apparent to your audience by indicating when you have finished one idea and are ready to tackle the next, or by previewing the ground yet to be covered. Do not spend too much time on any one point, and do not elaborate the obvious; constantly push ahead toward a clearly defined goal.

Reality. The earliest words a child learns are the names of "real" objects and of tangible acts related to them. This interest in reality—in the immediate, the concrete, the actual—persists throughout life. The proposition $2 + 2 = 4$ when unrelated to any specific events, persons, or circumstances holds little interest. Instead of talking in abstractions, talk of real-life people, places, and happenings. Use pictures, diagrams, and charts. Tell not what happened to "a certain prominent physician of this city," but to Dr. Fred Smith, who lives at 418 Paine Street. Use all of the various forms of verbal and nonverbal support discussed in Chapter 6. Make your descriptions specific and vivid. Remember always that actual cases are more real to a listener than general trends or broad classifications, particular names and places more interesting than impersonalized, vague allusions.

Proximity. A direct reference to someone in the audience, to some object near at hand, to some incident that has just occurred, or to the immediate occasion on which the speech is being made usually will command attention. A reference to a remark of a preceding speaker or of the chairperson creates a similar effect. If attention lags, call a member of the audience by name or make him or her the central character in a hypothetical illustration. Not only will this awaken anyone who happens to be dozing (heaven forbid!), but it will also tend to increase the attention-level of the other members. As psychologists Floyd L. Ruch and Philip G. Zimbardo point out, "Individuating listeners is one of the most effective means of getting—and holding—attention. When you are talking to a single individual, looking him straight in the eye increases the likelihood that he will look back at you and listen to what you have to say."[2]

Familiarity. Many things are familiar to us because of the frequency with which we meet them in our daily lives. Knives and forks, rain, automobiles, toothbrushes, classes, and a host of other common objects and events are closely built into our experiences. Because they

---

[2]Floyd L. Ruch and Philip G. Zimbardo, *Psychology and Life*, 8th ed. (Glenview, Ill.: Scott, Foresman and Company, 1971), p. 268.

are so much a part of us, these familiar things catch our attention. We say, "Ah, that is an old friend." But, as with old acquaintances, we become bored if we see too much of them and nothing else. In a spoken message, the familiar holds attention primarily when the speaker introduces it in connection with something unfamiliar or when some fresh or unknown aspect of it is pointed out. Stories about Lincoln and Washington, for example, are interesting because we are familiar with their characters; but we don't like to hear the same old railsplitter or cherry-tree tales unless they are given a new twist or application.

Novelty. As an old newspaper adage has it, when a dog bites a man, it's an accident; when a man bites a dog, it's news. Perhaps we should marvel that airplanes make countless flights across the oceans every day, but we take this for granted. Even missile launchings and space travel command less attention than they did a few years ago. Routine occurrences are not news; only novel happenings, dramatic advances, or unusual developments attract wide notice.

Two special types of novelty are *size* and *contrast.* Insofar as *size* is concerned, especially large or especially small objects or amounts attract attention. Reference to a $3000 or $4000 automobile or to a $30,000 home would not stand out as unusual; but reference to a $20,000 automobile or to a $200,000 home would. In a speech on the high cost of national defense, a speaker caught the attention of his listeners with this sentence: "Considering that it costs more than $5000 to equip an average soldier for combat, it is disquieting to learn that in a year his equipment will be 60% obsolete."[3]

Although attention-arousing in themselves, large and small figures become even more compelling when thrown into *contrast* with their opposites. Here is how Henry W. Grady, in an address at the University of Virginia, used novel or startling contrasts to focus attention on the gap between the rich and the poor: "A home that cost three million dollars and a breakfast that cost five thousand are disquieting facts to the millions who live in a hut and dine on a crust. The fact that a man . . . has an income of twenty million dollars falls strangely on the ears of those who hear it as they sit empty-handed with children crying for bread."[4]

---

[3]Neal Luker, "Our Defense Policy," a speech presented in a course in advanced public speaking at the University of Iowa.

[4]From an address by Henry W. Grady, presented to the Literary Societies of the University of Virginia, June 25, 1889.

In utilizing the materials of novelty be careful, of course, not to inject elements that are so different or unusual that they are entirely unfamiliar. As we have emphasized, your listeners must at least know what you are talking about, or their attention will soon waver. They must be able to relate what you say to things they know and — preferably — have a degree of experience with. Best results are achieved by the proper combination of the new and the old, of the novel and the familiar. Note, too, that novelty may gain attention, but it will not necessarily hold it.

Suspense. A large part of the interest which people have in a mystery story arises from uncertainty about its outcome. When giving a speech, create uncertainty by pointing out results which have mysterious or unknown causes or by calling attention to forces which threaten uncertain effects. Introduce suspense into the stories you use to illustrate your ideas. Mention valuable information you expect to divulge later in your talk but which requires an understanding of what you are now saying. Make full use of the factor of suspense; but in doing so, observe two cautions: *(a)* Do not make the information seem so difficult or mysterious that your listeners lose all hope of comprehending it; and *(b)* make sure that the information, when it finally is revealed, is important enough to warrant the suspense you have created.

Conflict. The opposition of forces compels attention — especially if the listeners identify themselves with one of the contending sides. Often conflict, like suspense, suggests uncertainty; but even when there is little doubt of the outcome, the combat itself draws attention. Football games, election contests, the struggle against disease and the adverse elements of nature — all these have an element of conflict within them; and people become interested when the conflict is vividly described. For the same reason, controversy is more interesting than concurrence. A vigorous attack upon some antisocial force — be it gangsterism, graft, or child-neglect — will draw more immediate attention than an objective analysis of it, although the analysis might — in the long run — prove more effective or enduring. Describe a fight, show vividly the opposition between two factions, or launch a verbal attack on somebody or something, and people usually will listen to you. Be cautious, however, of sham battles. If you set up straw men and knock them down, the reality — and hence the effectiveness — of your message may be largely destroyed.

Humor. Laughter indicates enjoyment, and people pay attention to that which they enjoy. Few things, in fact, will hold an audience as well as the speaker's judicious use of humor. It provides relaxation from the tension often created by other factors of attention—conflict and suspense, especially—and thus reduces fatigue while still exercising a measure of control over the perceptions of the listener. When using humor, however, remember that its attention-holding power is likely to be much stronger if you keep two guidelines in mind: *(a) Be relevant.* Beware of wandering from the point under discussion. Any joke or anecdote you may use must reinforce rather than detract from the central idea of your speech. *(b) Use good taste.* Avoid humor on occasions where it would be out of place, and refrain from using those types of humor which might offend the sensitivities of your listeners.

The vital. Finally, people nearly always pay attention to matters that affect their health, reputation, property, or employment. If you can show your audience that what you are saying concerns them in one or more of these ways, the chances are good that they will consider your message vital and will listen to it closely. Pointing out how your subject concerns persons close to them also will command your listeners' attention because people tend to identify themselves with family, friends, and associates. If the other factors of attention are important, an appeal to the *vital* is indispensable.

The vital, humor, conflict, suspense, novelty, familiarity, proximity, reality, and activity and movement—these, in sum, are the magnetic "forces" that beckon us to attention. These nine attention-attractors should be your constant guides when you are assembling, sorting out, and presenting ideas for a speech.

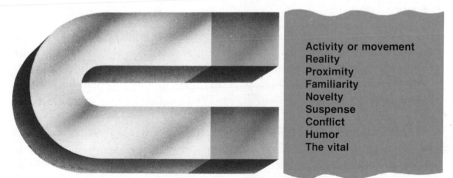

Activity or movement
Reality
Proximity
Familiarity
Novelty
Suspense
Conflict
Humor
The vital

Figure 1. Factors of Attention

THE STRUCTURE OF A SPEECH TO INFORM

When you are organizing a speech to inform, the governing principle is to *lead* the thoughts of your listeners rather than to try to force them. Do not, therefore, plunge into the body of your talk until by means of a carefully planned introduction you have prepared the audience to receive the information you are going to present.

The introduction

In the introduction to a speech to inform, you should accomplish two things: (1) capture the hearers' attention, and (2) point out to them why they need to know something about the subject you are going to discuss. When you are sure that your topic will be of interest, you may be able to command attention simply by referring to it. Usually, however, you will need to use one of the other methods for capturing attention, as outlined in Chapter 9, "Beginning and Ending the Speech" (pages 183 – 190).

Pointing out to your listeners why they need to know what you are about to tell them may be done briefly, but it is exceedingly important. All too often speakers fail because they assume that people are waiting to seize the "pearls of knowledge" which their speeches contain. Unfortunately, this is not always the case. In most instances, you must show your audience that the information you are going to present is valuable to them—that it is something they need to know or act upon. If you suggest how your information will help your listeners get ahead, save money, or do their work efficiently and easily, they will be more willing to listen.

The body

With the audience's attention captured and the importance of your subject made evident, you are ready to move into the body of your speech and to present the information itself. This presentation naturally will constitute the greatest part of a speech to inform—probably three-fourths to nine-tenths of it, and for this reason it must be carefully organized.

To facilitate understanding and retention on the part of your listeners, you will often find it helpful to preface the detailed presentation of the body of your speech with a preview or *initial summary* of the points to be covered. You also should clearly define any *new or special-*

ized terms which you employ, either before or as you present your *detailed information.*

Initial summary. The initial summary provides a skeleton around which to group your facts, and indicates the relationship each idea bears to the others. Thus it helps your listeners to follow your pattern of development—to see exactly where your speech is going. If, for instance, you are explaining cultural activities on your campus, in an initial summary you might say:

> In my review of cultural activities on our campus for the coming year, I shall discuss, *first*, the program of lectures and musical events the Student Affairs Committee has planned; *second*, the program of plays to be offered by the University Theater; and, *third*, the special exhibitions of paintings which will be on view in the Memorial Union.

The initial summary should be brief and simple because a complex statement is difficult to remember and needlessly repetitive of what later will be developed in detail. Moreover, the order of points which it announces should be followed in the presentation of the information, or the listeners will be confused. Obviously, you need not have an initial summary in every informative speech you deliver; but when appropriate and properly developed, such a preview is useful both to your listeners and to you as the speaker.

Definition of terms. In an informative speech you should *define all unfamiliar terms and also any terms that you use in a special sense.* There is no fixed point at which such definitions should be introduced; but when they relate to the entire body of information being presented, they are usually inserted just before or immediately after the initial summary. When the definitions concern only a part of the information, they may be introduced at relevant points in the discussion.

Detailed information. Following the initial summary, present the detailed information of your speech. Explanations, facts, figures, comparisons, and other supportive or elaborative data should be grouped around each main point in a systematic fashion; and, where feasible, such material should be amplified and illustrated by maps, pictures, tables, or diagrams. As we suggested earlier (see pages 140–142), follow a consistent pattern in organizing the subordinate ideas that fall under a main point, and amplify each idea with an abundance of supporting materials. As you advance from one point to the next, use connective sentences or phrases to emphasize the transition; if you use an initial summary, relate each new point to the plan you announce there. Keep the audience constantly aware of where you are, where you have been, and where you are heading.

How you organize your major points in a speech to inform depends on your subject, your purpose in speaking, and the audience to whom your talk is addressed. As we pointed out in Chapter 7, certain subjects may best be presented in a chronological or time order, whereas others fall naturally into a space order or call for a special topical sequence. Besides the subject of your talk, however, you must also consider your purpose in speaking. When your aim is to give instructions, usually you will find it best to divide the body of your speech according to the various steps or operations to be performed and to take up these steps in the proper order. Then under each step you may discuss the materials, tools, or special knowledge required to carry it out. When making a report of an investigation you have conducted, a natural treatment is to retrace the steps you yourself took in reaching your conclusions or recommendations, and then to present the conclusions or recommendations in order.

Always, however, whatever your subject or purpose, in organizing your ideas be sure you keep in mind the *listeners* to whom your speech will be given. This is crucial. How much do they already know about the topic you will be discussing? Are they likely to be interested in it, or will you have to put forth a special effort to arouse their interest before presenting the information itself? Will they, because of their background and experience with similar topics, be able to grasp your ideas quickly, or will you have to proceed slowly and explain each succeeding step in detail? No matter how well informed you yourself may be on a topic or how systematically you have arranged your remarks, unless the pattern you choose is well adapted to the interests and knowledge-level of your listeners, you cannot hope to convey information to them effectively.[5]

The conclusion

When you have presented your information and attained your listeners' understanding of it, you will have accomplished your purpose.

---

[5] On arranging the major points of a speech to inform, see especially Thomas H. Olbricht, *Informative Speaking* (Glenview, Ill.: Scott, Foresman and Company, 1968), Chapter 4, "Structuring the Informative Discourse."

Ordinarily, therefore, you will complete your speech with a final summary.

Final summary. Coming after the detailed data have been presented, the final summary ties the information together and leaves the audience with a unified and coherent picture. This summation usually consists of a restatement of your main points, together with any important conclusions or implications which have grown out of them. Although it is similar to the initial summary in that it states the leading ideas of your speech, the final summary usually is longer and is particularly designed to impress these ideas on the memory of your listeners. Compare the initial summary on page 213 with this final summary:

> From what I have said, you can readily see that for those of you who are interested in cultural events of various kinds, this is going to be a truly exciting year. You will have an opportunity to hear some of the world's best-known lecturers and musical artists. You will be able to see plays by Shakespeare, Molière, and Pinter. And you will be able to visit outstanding exhibits of primitive and modern art.

There are times, of course, when you may wish to encourage further study of the subject you have been presenting. In such cases, by naming one or two specific sources of information or by calling attention to books or printed instructions which your listeners already have in their possession, you may suggest how they can learn more. Then, if you wish, you may close with a brief expression of thanks for their attention; or, if you are addressing a group of employees or campaign workers, you may express confidence in their ability to carry out the procedures which you have explained.

Finally, as we pointed out in Chapter 9, you should conclude your speech in such a way that you focus the thought of the audience on your central theme and purpose, leave the listeners in the proper mood, and convey a sense of finality.

A SKELETAL OUTLINE FOR DEVELOPING AN INFORMATIVE SPEECH

If you develop an informative speech according to the structure just explained, your skeleton plan will look something like the one which appears on the following page. Obviously, each supporting item indicated in this skeletal outline will require details as called for by the purpose of the message and the nature of the speech occasion.

SUBJECT: _____

SPECIFIC PURPOSE: _____

Introduction

Gaining
attention

I. (Opening statement)
   A. (Support)
   B. (Support)

Showing the
listeners why
they need to
know

II. (Statement of need for information)
   A. (Support)
   B. (Support)

Body

Presenting the
information

I. (Statement of purpose)

(Initial
summary)

   A. (Preview of first major division of subject)
   B. (Preview of second major division of subject)

(Detailed
information)

II. (Statement of first major division of subject)
   A. (Support)
   B. (Support)
III. (Statement of second major division of subject)
   A. (Support)
   B. (Support)
   C. (Support)
IV. (Statement of third major division of subject), etc.

Conclusion

(Final
summary)

I. (Summarizing statement)
   A. (Support)
   B. (Support)
   C. (Support)
   D. (Support)
II. (Concluding statement)

A SAMPLE OUTLINE OF AN INFORMATIVE SPEECH

The following outline suggests one way to organize a speech to inform:

TALK WITH ANIMALS[6]

SPECIFIC PURPOSE: To describe recent research on chimpanzee communication and its implications for understanding human communication.

Introduction

I. The idea of talking with animals has always been appealing.

Gaining attention by making concrete references to actual people, events, and experiences

A. Most of us have pets whom we think try to "talk" with us.
1. Jill (a classmate) tells me her cat knows when it is exactly eight o'clock and wakes her up with a particular kind of meow.
2. Brian's collie uses a special whine to tell his master a storm is coming.
3. Jenny's terrier has an easily distinguishable warning bark, play bark, food bark, and illness bark.

B. Stories and fables have been built around this idea.

Using specific instances of general familiarity

1. As children, all of us read *Lassie Come Home* and were impressed with the exploits of the amazing collie.
2. Dr. Doolittle captivated millions of people with the way he could "talk to the animals."
3. "Mr. Ed," the talking horse, and "Flipper," the communicative dolphin, were the stars of popular television series.
4. All of us who are old movie buffs have seen films about Tarzan, the jungle man, and his near-human chimpanzee named Chita.

II. The question "Can animals really talk with us?" is being answered affirmatively in research centers across the country.

Making transition into thesis

A. Chita's relatives are successfully being taught to talk with humans through the use of artificial sign languages.
B. A number of different teaching methods are used.

III. These experiments in chimpanzee communication are important to us for two reasons:

---

[6]Reprinted from *Psychology Today* Magazine, January, 1974. Copyright © 1973 Ziff-Davis Publishing Company. All rights reserved.

Showing the listeners why they need to know

    A. First, they are teaching us much more than we ever knew about the remarkable abilities of these animals.

    B. Second, they are adding significantly to our understanding of the communication process and the resources on which it depends.

       1. As informed persons, we should be interested in learning all we can about chimpanzees—our nearest relatives among the greater primates.

       2. As students of speech communication, we should be especially interested in extending our knowledge of the communication process.

Body

  I. During the course of my speech this morning I should like to do three things:

(Initial summary)

    A. First, explore briefly the origins of present-day research on chimpanzee communication.

    B. Second, examine the three principal methods now being used to teach chimpanzees to communicate.

    C. Third, suggest some of the implications which this research on chimpanzees may have for our understanding of human communication.

(First point in support of thesis)

  II. Prior to 1966, research on chimpanzee communication had met with only limited success.

    A. A few chimps had been taught to speak.

    B. The world's record was held by a chimp named Viki, who had learned four verbalized words.

(Second point in support of thesis)
Making transition from first point to explanation

  III. In June 1966, Beatrice and Allen Gardner at the University of Nevada began working on teaching a gestural language instead of a verbalized language.

    A. The Gardners had several reasons for abandoning the teaching of a verbalized language.

       1. Chimps in the wilds used many more hand signals than verbalized signals.

       2. Chimps lacked sufficient control of their mouths to form many different sounds.

       3. Chimps have an extraordinary capacity to gesture.

(Detailed information)

    B. The Gardners chose a chimp named Washoe for their training experiments.

       1. While in the wilds, Washoe had learned the necessity of using a sign language.

2. Washoe had the development of a one-and-a-half-year-old child—the usual age for early language training.
3. Washoe had the capacity to form strong human attachments.
C. The Gardners chose the American Sign Language (ASL) to teach Washoe.
1. In ASL many of the signs are actual visual representations of the ideas or actions signified.

Combining visual and verbal supporting material

a. This, for example, is the sign for "drink." *(Demonstrate.)*
b. This is the sign for "up." *(Demonstrate.)*
c. These are the signs for "hear" and "see." *(Demonstrate.)*
2. Psychologists could compare these signs as used by Washoe and by deaf children of deaf parents, because the ASL is the language used by the deaf.
D. The Gardners used the following procedure:
1. Washoe first was taught ten individual signs.
2. Next she was taught two-sign combinations expressing basic relationships.
a. She learned the agent-action relationship, "Roger tickle."
b. She learned the location relationship, "in hat."
c. She learned to express feelings, "Washoe sorry."
E. The Gardners' method of teaching Washoe produced highly gratifying results.
1. After twenty-one months, Washoe could use thirty-four signs to communicate meanings.
2. At the end of four years, Washoe had a total vocabulary of 160 signs which she could use in grammatically correct and contextually accurate ways.
F. The Gardners' work with Washoe is currently being carried forward by Professor Roger Fouts at the Institute for Primate Studies, Norman, Oklahoma.

(Third point in support of thesis) (Detailed information)

IV. A second approach to chimpanzee communication is used by Dr. David Premack, professor of psychology at the University of California at Santa Barbara.
A. Dr. Premack uses magneticized plastic shapes and a metallic board as teaching devices.

1. The chimp is required to express ideas and make responses by "spelling them out" with the plastic shapes. (Show some typical shapes.)
2. The chimp is subjected to classic conditioning techniques.

B. Using this method, Sarah — Dr. Premack's star pupil — progressed further and more rapidly than Washoe.
1. She acquired 130 signs in two and one-half years.
2. She learned more sophisticated grammatical constructions.

(Fourth point in support of thesis)

V. A third approach to chimpanzee communication has been taken by Professor Duane Rumbaugh at Georgia State University.

A. Professor Rumbaugh employs a computerized typewriter.

(Detailed information)

1. His pupil, three-year-old Lana, operates a fifty-character keyboard.
   a. Each key has a colored background and a white geometric pattern.
   b. The keyboard is attached to a film projector and a computer.
2. Lana types and a configuration of characters is flashed on a screen.

B. Lana talks to herself on her typewriter.
1. She writes sentences without prodding.
2. She erases mistakes she makes in a sentence.

C. Lana is rewarded when she performs correctly.

D. Lana has learned her "language" in only one year.
1. She can use "language" that is grammatically sophisticated.
2. She can use "language" without the presence of either objects or human beings.

(Fifth point in support of thesis)

VI. This research in chimpanzee communication is important for our understanding of human language usage and development.

A. We may learn more about how we acquire our own language.

B. We may learn better how to teach language to retarded children.

C. We may learn how to teach foreign languages more efficiently.

Conclusion

I. So . . . the next time you see a TV show or a movie full of "talking" animals, be neither a skeptic nor a scoffer.
   A. These animals may be more than merely funny, furry friends.
   B. These animals may aid us in solving our human problems.

II. Ultimately, anthropologists and psychologists who study animal communication may probe *beyond* mere communicative complexities and into fundamental questions of human *survival.*
   A. We may discover vital new facts about all human learning.
   B. We may learn more about our instinctive drives.
   C. We may better understand the artificial social structure in which we spin out our lives.
   D. We may learn to survive—and help the rest of the human race survive—the mistakes we daily make in thinking and speaking.

      1. As Konrad Lorenz points out in his book *On Aggression:* "All the great dangers threatening humanity with extinction are direct consequences of conceptual thought and verbal speech. They drove man out of the paradise in which he could follow his instincts with impunity and do or not do whatever he pleased. . . . Knowledge springing from conceptual thought robbed man of the security provided by his well-developed instincts long, long before it was sufficient to provide him with an equally safe adaptation. Man is, as Arnold Gohlen has so truly said, by nature a jeopardized creature."[7]

Intermingling
humor and the
most serious
point of the
speech

      2. In sum, Washoe and her cousin chimps who—so amazingly—are now actually learning to "talk" may help us make sure that our own "monkey business" does not drive us back into the jungle permanently.

---

[7]Konrad Lorenz, *On Aggression,* trans. Marjorie Kere Wilson (New York: Bantam Books, 1966), p. 230.

PROBLEMS FOR FURTHER STUDY

1. List at least ten situations in which an informative speech seems called for. Then, drawing on this list, answer the following questions: *(a)* Although each situation you identified called for an *informative* speech, could there be lurking beneath the surface some kind of ultimately *persuasive* goal? *(b)* Would you go so far as to argue—as some communication theorists do—that "all communication is persuasive"? (Such theorists believe that an audience is always persuaded toward something—be it toward the usefulness of a thing, the desirability of pursuing some hobby, the competence of a given speaker, or whatever.) *(c)* Furthermore, if one can, in fact, detect persuasive purposes or effects in all pieces of communication, is it even worthwhile to discuss "informative speaking"? Why or why not? Defend your position.

2. Using the list of situations you developed in Problem 1, concern yourself with another group of questions: *(a)* Do speakers in such situations habitually prefer one type of organizational pattern? Why or why not? *(b)* Do speakers in such situations seem to use principally certain types of supporting materials but not others? Why or why not? *(c)* In each of these situations, would you as an audience member expect certain organizational patterns and/or types of supporting materials? *(d)* Does your answer to the last question tell you anything about social-cultural "rules" regarding informative speeches, and about the "obligations" you face as an informative speaker? Defend your answer.

3. Outline an informative speech reprinted in a recent issue of *Vital Speeches of the Day*, and note the psychological structuring devices employed by the speaker. What method has he or she used to gain attention? Does the speaker show the listeners why they need to know the information presented? Are there initial and final summaries?

4. In at least three informative speeches, analyze the use made of the factors of attention. Are some of the factors used more frequently than others? Which seem to you to be most effective?

5. Drawing upon your observations as a listener, discuss the role a speaker's delivery plays in conveying information clearly and interestingly. Can you cite examples in which delivery definitely helped or hindered a speaker?

ORAL ACTIVITIES AND SPEAKING ASSIGNMENTS

1. Participate in a general class discussion on types of organizational patterns (time, space, cause-effect, effect-cause, problem-solution, or special

topical sequences) which you think would be most suitable for an informative speech on each of the following subjects. Defend your choices.

The campus parking problem.
Facilities of the college library.
The fraternity-sorority tradition.
Censorship of the press.
Our city government and services.
Principles and policies of public taxation.
The Head Start program.

2. Prepare a speech to inform for presentation in class. Using one of the topics suggested below (or a similar topic approved by your instructor), select and narrow it appropriately. Use whatever visual aids you think will improve your presentation. Follow the rules of organization and development set forth in this chapter. Suggested topics:

Wonder drugs.
Writers.
Techniques of behavior-modification.
The "open classroom" concept in American education.
Architecture and the problems of the aged.
Functions of your school's placement service.
Recent advances in mass-transit systems and planning.

3. A common problem faced by informative speakers is that of explaining unfamiliar and/or complex concepts and objects. Prepare a short speech for your class on a subject such as:

Transcendental meditation.
The "zone defense" in football.
Game theory in social psychology.
Laser beams.
An automobile's carburetor.
Macramé.
The Library of Congress book-classification system.

Keep in mind, especially, the problems of attention and clarity which you as a speaker face in this assignment.

4. Another problem frequently faced by informative speakers is that of presenting two sides of an issue. The "opposing positions" speech is an exercise in clarity and impartiality, one in which a communicator seeks to explicate and summarize conflicting philosophies, solutions to some problem, or whatever. Prepare and deliver a speech of this type on one of the following topics or a similar one:

The argument over euthanasia.
The pros and cons of birth control.
Suggested alternatives to the piston engine.
The furor over deer hunting.
The strip-mining controversy.
Alternative grading systems.
Genetic control—yes or no?

Keep in mind that your job principally is to organize clearly and fairly the opposing positions, plank by plank, idea by idea.

5. Many of us are called upon from time to time to demonstrate, describe, or explain the operation of a device, the use of a product, or the steps in a process. This kind of speech—often called the "demonstration" speech—represents a highly coordinated effort at using verbal and nonverbal communication to illustrate or explain a manipulatable object or reinforce listeners' understanding of an operational idea. All of us have experienced the need for this kind of communicative skill in presenting information ranging in complexity from how to assemble a simple toy by means of the "Insert a Tab in a Slot" technique to "How to Derive the Pythagorean Theorum from Basic Geometric Axioms." Prepare a five-minute demonstration speech, keeping especially in mind two considerations: *(a)* your listeners will probably understand and internalize your informative material more slowly than you will want to present it and that you must, therefore, watch them closely for signs of positive and negative feedback; and *(b)* the object or the product or the tangible essentials of the process you are demonstrating must be visible to everyone in your audience. Possible topics might include the following:

The basic tennis strokes.
Transplanting seedlings or cuttings.
Basic functions of a slide rule.
Reading cloud formations.
The fundamentals of self-defense.
Sleight-of-hand dexterity for fun and profit.

6. Currently, the kind of informative speech with which you probably are most closely connected is the classroom lecture. Day after day, many of your professors offer structured information orally and expand or illuminate it by using chalkboards, dittoes, and models of materials that are often quite technical or abstract. The principal virtues of good informative lectures are three: *(a) clarity*—to enliven and make information concrete by means of illustrations and demonstrations, *(b) obvious structure*—to facilitate listener comprehension and make outlining easy for note-takers, and *(c) dynamism*—to keep "lecture-hardened" students awake!

No doubt you have on occasion criticized the abstruse, disorganized, dull, classroom lecturer—and justifiably so. However, should you attempt to lecture informatively on the obligatory topics of college professors, you may find that the task is not an easy one. To test this assertion, prepare and present a seven-minute lecture to your classmates on a topic with which most of them probably are not familiar.

Three factors producing the American Revolution.
What is perception?
Research on source-credibility and persuasion.
Ion transfer in nuclei.
Technocracy and social change.
How a convex lens works.
Predicting voting outcomes from demographic data.
Plato's theory of reality.
Ciardi on how a poem "means."

SUGGESTIONS FOR FURTHER READING

Hugh Blair, *Lectures on Rhetoric and Belles Lettres* (1783), Lecture XXXV, "Comparative Merit of the Ancients and the Moderns—Historical Writing"; Lecture XXXVI, "Historical Writing"; and Lecture XXXVII, "Philosophical Writing—Dialogue—Epistolary Writing—Fictitious History. A great rhetorician's treatment of the only forms of discourse that most past theorists considered as informative.

W. A. Mambert, *Presenting Technical Ideas: A Guide to Audience Communication* (New York: John Wiley & Sons, Inc., 1968). A series of solid suggestions for solving communicative problems faced by technicians.

Donovan J. Ochs and Ronald J. Burritt, "Perceptual Theory: Narrative Suasion in Lysias," in *Explorations in Rhetorical Criticism,* ed. G. P. Mohrmann *et al.* (University Park: Pennsylvania State University Press, 1973), pp. 51–74. An interesting analysis of the persuasive effect of "mere" information, together with a case study.

Thomas H. Olbricht, *Informative Speaking* (Glenview, Ill.: Scott, Foresman and Company, 1968). Perhaps the most readable work on informative speaking in print—discussing the speaker-audience "contract" in informative speaking.

Charles R. Petrie, "Informative Speaking: A Summary and Bibliography of Related Research," *Speech Monographs* XXX (June 1963): 79–91. Reprinted in *The Rhetoric of Our Times,* ed. J. Jeffrey Auer (New York: Appleton-Century-Crofts, 1969), pp. 237–254. Though somewhat dated, still the best research summary on informative speaking available.

Chapter 11

Speaking to persuade

SPEECHES TO PERSUADE seek to influence the beliefs or actions of listeners and therefore supply arguments and motivations for thinking or doing as the speaker recommends.

Belief and action, the goals of persuasive speaking, are closely related. If you wish people to act in a certain way, you must first convince them that such behavior is "right," or expedient, or advantageous. Then, if they believe strongly, they will tend to act according to that belief. Many Americans, for instance, when called to serve on a jury in a trial involving capital punishment, proceed to do so because they believe that such service is a citizen's responsibility; others, however, are guided by equally strong convictions and seek to be excused.

Some speeches to persuade urge belief in a principle or point of view which, though it could influence future decisions, calls for no immediate action. ("The causes of the American Revolution were primarily economic.") Other persuasive speeches go a step further and openly appeal for action. ("Contribute to the United Fund Drive today.") Because of the intimate relationship between belief and action, however, all persuasive speeches have the same primary objective—influencing the listeners to make a choice or decision.

Although the purpose of a persuasive speech is to win belief or produce action, an unwilling decision is of little value. Beliefs which people are forced to accept may soon be abandoned; actions done unwillingly are usually done inefficiently and without any sense of reward or accomplishment. To persuade successfully, therefore, not only must you make your listeners believe or do something, but you also must make them *want* to believe or do it. For this reason, two subsidiary purposes of persuasive speaking must be kept in mind: (1) to provide the audience with motives for believing by appealing to certain of their basic needs or desires and (2) to satisfy their understanding by convincing them that the proposition you recommend will make the satisfaction of these desires possible.

ANALYZING THE NEEDS AND DESIRES OF THE LISTENERS

Even though a persuasive speech may contain an abundance of facts and employ sound reasoning, it is likely to fail if it does not make a direct appeal to the people who hear it. Therefore, you must relate your proposal to your listeners' interests and desires. In their book *Strategy in Handling People,* psychologists E. T. Webb and J. J. B. Morgan emphasize the importance of this principle. "From a practical standpoint," they write, "the first precaution in managing people is to discover what they really want, especially the exact nature of the most active wants which touch upon us and our plans."[1] What are these "wants" or "needs" that motivate and impel human behavior, and to which of them should a speaker's arguments and appeals be addressed?

The concept of motivational needs

There have been many disputes among psychologists concerning the nature and number of motive-needs and whether they are inborn or acquired. With the details of these disputes we need not be concerned. It is important for us, however, to note two facts which are commonly agreed upon: (1) much human behavior is goal directed in the way we have just suggested; and (2) although in some instances such behavior may be set into motion by the individual's own physiological or psychological needs, in others it may be triggered by aspects of the environment.

A classification of motive-needs

Of late, the distinction between "biological" and "psychological-social" needs, or between what are sometimes called "maintenance" (homeostasis-oriented) and "actualization" tendencies has received considerable emphasis. In addition, a number of psychologists are attaching greater importance to such social drives as the need for participation and belonging, "competence" in relation to one's environment, achievement, group approval, and the like.

---

[1]E. T. Webb and J. J. B. Morgan, *Strategy in Handling People* (Chicago: Boulton, Pierce and Company, 1931), p. 73.

The classification of fundamental human needs most often cited today is, perhaps, the one developed by the psychologist Abraham H. Maslow.[2] Maslow presents the following categories of needs and wants which impel human beings to think, act, and respond as they do:

1. *Physiological Needs*—for food, drink, air, sleep, sex, etc.—the basic bodily "tissue" requirements.

2. *Safety Needs*—for security, stability, protection from harm or injury; need for structure, orderliness, law, and predictability in one's environment; freedom from fear and chaos.

3. *Belongingness and Love Needs*—for abiding devotion and warm affection with spouse, children, parents, and close friends; need to feel that one is a part of social groups; need for acceptance and approval.

4. *Esteem Needs*—for self-esteem based on achievement, mastery, competence, confidence, freedom, independence; desire for esteem of others (reputation, prestige, recognition, status).

5. *Self-Actualization Needs*—for self-fulfillment, actually to become what one potentially can be; desire to actualize one's capabilities; being true to one's essential nature; what a person *can* be he *must* be.

These "needs," according to Maslow, function as a *prepotent hierarchy;* that is, lower-level needs must be largely fulfilled before higher-level needs become operative. Persons caught up in the daily struggle to satisfy physiological and safety needs will, for example, have little time and energy left to strive for "esteem" or "self-actualization." Once these basic requirements of living are satisfied, however, higher-level drives take over. We should note, moreover, that as individuals we tend to move upward or downward between one level and another as our life progresses or regresses. Maslow's category of basic human needs and the hierarchical order in which they stand may be usefully viewed as a kind of pyramid, as in the diagram on the following page.

---

[2]From "A Theory of Human Motivation" in *Motivation and Personality* by Abraham H. Maslow. Copyright, 1954 by Harper & Row, Publishers, Inc. Copyright © 1970 by Abraham H. Maslow. Reprinted by permission of the publisher.

Figure 1. A Hierarchy of Motivational Needs

Some need-motive relationships

If Maslow is right and if these are indeed humankind's basic needs, then—in terms of persuasive communication—there are certain questions we must answer. In what ways do these needs influence the thinking and behavior of both speakers and listeners? As speakers, how can we translate these underlying needs/wants/desires into specific motivational appeals which we can make to our listeners? Some of the answers, certainly, can be found in the relationships which exist between needs and motives.

Motives—the impulses to believe and to act—arise from the basic human needs we have been noting. These motives, in turn, generate responses and influence the way in which people think and behave.

The strength of the motives thus generated varies, of course, from one individual to another, depending on such factors as past experience, immediate environment, the person's psychological makeup, etc.

Although motives often underlie and impel behavior, the cause-effect relationship is not always a direct and simple one. The complexities of the human organism and the customs and mores of the society in which we live may prevent the immediate fulfillment of a fundamental need. When blocked or frustrated, these needs do not disappear, however; they merely manifest themselves in different ways. These indirect or "manifest" needs may represent only certain aspects of a given motive or combination of motives. But whether direct or indirect, such needs provide the grounds for what we call *motive appeals*. The identifying and shaping of these appeals pose the crux of the challenge facing the speaker who would persuade effectively.

Motive appeals useful to the persuasive speaker

Following is a list of "appeals" which the speaker may make to arouse in the listener a particular feeling, emotion, or desire and thereby stimulate or perhaps set at work one or more of the primary *motive needs*. Any such enumeration must of necessity be incomplete and somewhat "experimental" because there are, of course, an infinite number of human wants, needs, and motives — and combinations thereof. This list does, nevertheless, include some of the specific desires, drives, feelings, and sentiments to which practiced speakers often appeal in order to effectively motivate their listeners toward a given belief or action.[3]

MOTIVE APPEALS

1. Achievement and display.
2. Acquisition and saving.
3. Adventure and change.
4. Companionship and affiliation.
5. Creativity.
   a. Organizing.
   b. Building.
6. Curiosity.

---

[3] For most of the motive appeals listed, some major implications will doubtless be immediately apparent. Those students desiring a somewhat detailed analysis of these matters may wish to read Alan H. Monroe and Douglas Ehninger, *Principles and Types of Speech Communication*, 7th ed. (Glenview, Ill.: Scott, Foresman and Company, 1974), pp. 270–282.

7. Deference.
8. Dependence.
9. Destructiveness.
10. Endurance.
11. Fear.
12. Fighting and aggression.
    a. Anger.
    b. Competition.
13. Imitation and conformity.
14. Independence and autonomy.
15. Loyalty.
    a. To family.
    b. To friends.
    c. To organizations and groups.
    d. To country, region, state, etc.
16. Personal enjoyment.
    a. Of comfort and luxury.
    b. Of beauty and order.
    c. Of pleasant sensory sensations.
    d. Of recreation.
    e. Of relief from restraint.
17. Power, authority, and dominance.
18. Pride.
    a. Reputation.
    b. Self-respect.
    c. Sound judgment.
19. Reverence or worship.
    a. Of leaders.
    b. Of traditions or institutions.
    c. Of a deity.
20. Revulsion.
21. Sexual attraction.
22. Sympathy and generosity.

You may have noticed that this list contains certain appeals which seem to contradict each other: for example, fear against the drive for adventure; deference against the desire for power, authority, and dominance; and so on. Remember, in this regard, that the human being is an inconsistent and changeable creature who, at different times, may pursue quite different ends or goals.

Using motive appeals

In practice, motive appeals—instead of acting singly—often act in combination. Suppose you were deciding whether to buy a particular suit or dress. What would influence your decision? One thing, obviously, would be price—*saving;* another, however, would be comfort and appearance—the *personal enjoyment* to be derived from wearing it; a third consideration might be style—*imitation;* a fourth, individuality of appearance—*independence;* and finally, all these items together would raise the question of *pride:* Would other people think the clothes in good taste; would they envy your selection? Some of these influences might be stronger than others, and some might conflict, but all of them probably would affect your choice, and you would buy the dress or suit which made the strongest total appeal.

Because motive appeals are thus interrelated, it is a good idea to employ them in combination rather than singly when building a speech. However, if the variety is too great, you may dissipate the effect at which you aim. Generally, therefore, try to select the two or three appeals which you think will have the greatest effect on your hearers and concentrate on these, allowing others to be secondary or incidental. Be sure also that you do not inadvertently use conflicting appeals—for instance, urge your listeners to do something because of the *adventure* involved but describe the situation so vividly that they come to *fear* the act or its consequences. To avoid this danger, select as the main points of your speech those ideas that contain strong appeals and then examine them closely for pertinence and consistency.

Recently a representative of a College Union Board, in urging students to take advantage of a Union-sponsored summer tour of Europe, built her talk around these three points:

Acquisition and saving	I. The tour is being offered for the very low price of $600 for three weeks.
Independence	II. There will be a minimum of supervision and regimentation.
Companionship	III. You will be traveling with your friends and fellow students.

In the complete development of her speech, the Union Board representative also emphasized the educational value of the experience *(self-advancement)* and said that a special mountain-climbing expedition was being planned *(adventure).*

Above all, do not let your attempt to motivate your listeners become too obvious, for in all probability this would cause them to react negatively. Do not say, "I want you to *imitate* Jones, the successful banker," or "If you give to this cause, we will print your name in the newspapers so that your *reputation* as a generous man will be known to everybody." Instead, merely suggest these results through the descriptions and illustrations you use. Remember, too, that people generally are ashamed to acknowledge publicly certain motives which privately may be very powerful, such as greed, fear, imitation, or pride. Therefore, when appeals to these and similar motivational factors are used in a speech, they must be carefully framed and supplemented by others which people are publicly willing to admit as the cause of their actions.

Adapting appeals to fixed attitudes and opinions. As you are doubtless aware, either as the result of personal experience or because of repeated assertions by parents, teachers, respected friends, or accepted authorities, people tend to develop strong opinions concerning many aspects of their environment. They are "for" or "against" labor unions, civil rights, military preparedness, professional athletics, fraternities; they consider policemen, politicians, nurses, flyers, lawyers, and Frenchmen as good or bad, unreliable or trustworthy, ignorant or intelligent; they like or dislike popular music, flashy clothes, mathematics, and traveling on buses. Crystallized attitudes and opinions of this kind originally are based on a combination of wants; but over a period of time, the underlying motivation is submerged, and the rigidly held attitude or opinion becomes the dominant influence. Whatever your subject, therefore, you must weigh whether to appeal not only to the more universal types of motive-needs, but also to the specific attitudes and opinions into which these motives may have developed. By associating your ideas and proposals with the value structures and positive attitudes of your audience and by avoiding negative associations, you can make your appeals stronger and more direct. In sum, the choice and the exact phrasing of your motive appeals always should be adapted to the particular beliefs, attitudes, and values of the listeners to whom you are appealing.[4]

---

[4]For information on dominant value structures in contemporary American society, see Frank E. Armbruster, *The Forgotten Americans: A Survey of the Values, Beliefs and Concerns of the Majority* (New Rochelle, N.Y.: Arlington House, Inc., 1972); Roger M. Williams, "Changing Value Orientations and Beliefs on the American Scene," in *The Character of Americans: A Book of Readings*, rev. ed., Michael McGiffert, ed. (Homewood, Ill.: Dorsey Press, 1970), pp. 212–230.

SOUND REASONING

In addition to strong motivation, speeches to persuade should set forth the *reasoning* necessary to prove that the view or policy you recommend will satisfy one or more of the listeners' basic needs or desires. (At times it may also be necessary to prove that these needs or desires actually are threatened.) A brief consideration of the three most frequently used forms of reasoning, therefore, is essential; namely, reasoning from example, from axiom, and from causal relation.

Reasoning from example

This form of reasoning consists of drawing conclusions about a general class of objects by studying certain members of that class. If a shopper were in doubt about the flavor of apples in a bushel basket, she could bite into one of them to test it. If the taste pleased her, she would reason that all or at least most of the apples in the basket had a good flavor. Or perhaps, if she were a bit skeptical, she also might test an apple from the bottom of the basket to make sure that her "sample" was a fair one. This form of reasoning from specific cases to a more general conclusion is employed in much of our thinking, whether the point at issue is big or little. Scientific experiments, public-opinion polls, and many studies of social behavior depend on reasoning from example. Reasoning of this kind should be tested by asking the following questions:

1. *Are the examples extensive enough to support the conclusion offered?* One robin does not make a spring, nor do two or three examples always prove that a general proposition is incontestably true.
2. *Have the examples been fairly chosen?* To attempt to prove that Americans oppose tax relief for the farmers by citing opinions polled in New York, Chicago, and Los Angeles — all large metropolitan areas — would be to reason from selected or weighted samples, since the attitudes of urban dwellers on this problem probably are quite different from those of farmers or persons living in small towns.
3. *Are there any outstanding exceptions to the generalization?* One well-known exception may undermine your general conclusion unless you can show that it is the result of unusual or abnormal circumstances.

Reasoning from axiom

Reasoning from axiom is the opposite of reasoning from example. Instead of inferring a general rule from the study of a representative sample, you apply a general rule or principle to determine the nature of a specific situation. For instance, merchants usually concede that savings may be effected by purchasing merchandise in large lots. When, therefore, you argue that a grocery chain saves money by buying in large quantities, you are merely applying this general rule to the specific case of the grocery chain. Reasoning from axiom may be tested as follows:

1. *Is the axiom, or rule, true?* Many generalizations which are assumed to be true actually are fictions. For example, people once assumed that, as a group, men were more intelligent than women. Before applying an axiom, therefore, test its validity. Also, be sure that its validity is recognized by the audience. Unless the principle used as a premise is accepted as true, the conclusion drawn from it will be rejected.

2. *Does the axiom apply to the specific situation in question?* Too often, axioms which are valid in themselves are loosely or incorrectly applied. Thus, you may argue that because large-scale purchasing effects savings, a grocery chain can buy goods more cheaply than an independent store. You may not, however, argue that the customer always can buy from a chain at a lower price. The inference extends only to the prices at which the grocery chain buys, not to prices at which its stores sell. In order to establish this second contention, you should provide an additional premise.

Reasoning from causal relation

When something new or unexpected happens, we look for its causes; or when we see a force in operation, we speculate about its probable effects. A great deal of our reasoning is based on such cause-effect relationships. The crime rate goes up; and we lay the blame on the drug traffic, on bad housing, on public apathy, or on inept police officials. We hear that our star quarterback is hospitalized with a broken ankle, and we fear for the outcome of Saturday's game. We reason from known effects to probable causes and from known causes to probable effects. No other form of reasoning, perhaps, is used so much by public speakers; nor is any other form so often misused. To test the soundness of causal reasoning, ask these questions:

1. *Has the cause been confused with the effect?* When two phenomena occur simultaneously, it sometimes is difficult to tell which is cause and which is effect. In a period of mounting inflation, do higher wages cause higher prices, or do higher prices force wages to rise?

2. *Is the cause powerful enough to produce the alleged effect?* A small pebble on the railroad track will not derail a freight train, but a large boulder will. Be careful not to mistake a pebble for a boulder.

3. *Has anything prevented the cause from operating?* If a gun is not loaded, pulling the trigger will not make it shoot. Be certain that nothing has prevented the free operation of the cause which you assume has produced the effect.

4. *Could any other cause have produced this effect?* Four possible causes for an unsuccessful speech are poor subject-choice, inadequate preparation, monotonous delivery, and a lack of concrete supporting material. When assigning causes, try to diagnose the situation correctly; do not put the blame on the wrong cause, or all the blame on a single cause if it should be divided.

5. *Does a causal connection actually exist?* Sometimes people assume that because two things occur in sequence, they are causally connected. The appearance of a skin rash after you have touched a leafy plant does not necessarily mean that the contact caused the rash. Do not mistake a coincidence for a true cause-effect relationship.

Whatever form of reasoning you employ, support it strongly with pertinent facts and figures. Present an abundance of instances, illustrations, and comparisons. No other single factor is so important in a speech to persuade as presenting facts, facts, and more facts. Review Chapter 6, where the various types of supporting material are discussed, and employ them liberally whenever you are speaking to persuade.

TYPES OF CLAIMS IN SPEECHES TO PERSUADE

Most persuasive speeches assert that in the opinion of the speaker (1) something should or should not be done; (2) something is or is not the case; or (3) something is desirable or undesirable. Such judgments or recommendations, when formally addressed to others, are called the speaker's *claims*.[5]

Claims of policy

Claims which assert that a given course of action should or should not be followed are known as *claims of policy*. They are so named because they say, in effect, that doing as the speaker recommends would be a good *policy:* "The United States *should* withdraw its military forces from Europe and Asia." "Government expenditures for foreign aid *should not* be increased." "The student senate *ought* to be given control over all extracurricular activities."

Establishing claims of policy. In order to persuade an audience to accept a claim of policy, a speaker usually must cause listeners to answer four questions affirmatively:

1. *Is there a need for the policy or course of action proposed?* If people are not convinced that a change from the present state of affairs is needed, they will not seriously consider—much less approve—a new policy.
2. *Will the proposed policy or plan work?* If people do not believe that a proposal will correct existing evils or improve conditions, they will reject it.
3. *Is the proposed policy free of major disadvantages?* People will not approve a proposal—even though it may correct an existing problem—if it might bring with it other evils in the form of high costs, threats to person or property, and the like.
4. *Is the proposed policy better than any other plan or policy?* People usually will not endorse a policy if they believe some other course of action is better.

Sometimes your listeners will recognize the need for a new policy or program even before you begin to speak. And occasionally they will

---

[5]A fuller discussion of the various kinds of claims and the reasoning that supports them may be found in Douglas Ehninger, *Influence, Belief, and Argument* (Glenview, Ill.: Scott, Foresman and Company, 1974), pp. 27–32, 90–98.

recognize that if the proposed policy is practicable—that is, if it can be put into operation, administered, paid for, etc.—it will bring many advantages. Under such circumstances, answers to questions 1 and 3 may be omitted from your speech or merely mentioned in passing. Generally, however, in order to secure belief or action on a policy, you must deal with all four of the questions listed above.[6]

Claims of fact

When, instead of recommending or opposing a policy, you attempt to persuade your listeners that something is or is not true, you are advancing a *claim of fact*. Do not, however, let the name fool you. A claim of fact is not something that is already accepted as a fact; it is a statement that you are trying to prove is a fact. Observe also that not all factual questions should be dealt with in speeches. Often questions of whether or not something is true may best be settled by personal observation, by conducting a controlled experiment, or by looking up the answer in a reliable printed source. It would be absurd for men to argue the question of whether it is raining outside, or whether the soil in a particular field contains nitrate, or how long it takes to go by plane from Seattle to San Francisco. The first of these questions of fact could be settled by glancing out the window, the second by making appropriate chemical tests, and the third by referring to a timetable.

Other questions of fact, however, do not lend themselves to these methods. Is the United States really making progress in solving the race problem? Is the present government of Eudalia communist-dominated? Is Jones guilty of embezzlement as charged? Because they inquire whether something is or is not so, these questions, too, are questions of fact. But while observation or experimentation or printed data may help us arrive at a decision concerning them, in the end we must depend to a greater or lesser degree upon our own informed judgment—upon reasoning from the best information available to what appears to be the most accurate or fairest answer. It is on factual questions of this kind that we make speeches, trying to persuade others that our opinions or judgments are correct.

---

[6]A speech opposing a policy should, of course, answer one or more of these four questions in the *negative*. That is, it should (1) show there is no *need* for the proposed policy, (2) prove that it would not *work*, (3) point out that it would have *serious evils or disadvantages*, or (4) establish that *some other plan or policy would be preferable*. See in this connection the outline "The Parking Ramp," pp. 257–258.

Claims of value

A statement which asserts that something is desirable or undesirable, or praiseworthy or blameworthy, is called a *claim of value*. This term derives from the fact that claims of this kind evaluate something or declare its worth. "Progressive education is inferior education," "Modern art is decadent," "Despite the criticism to which Harry Truman was subjected, he was one of our great Presidents"—these are claims of value.

   Establishing claims of fact and value. Whereas in establishing a claim of policy, a speaker usually must answer affirmatively the four questions listed on page 238, in establishing a claim of fact or value, only the following two questions are relevant:

1. *Upon what criteria or standards should a judgment concerning this matter be based?* A standard is essential in judging the merit of claims of fact or value. To prove that the air in many of our large cities is polluted, you have to have some criterion for "clean air." In presenting the value statement "Our present grading system is undesirable," you would have to show what you conceive a desirable grading system to be. Otherwise it would be impossible for your listeners to decide one way or the other concerning your contention.

   Be sure also that the criteria you advance are acceptable to your listeners. Is the worth of a particular institution or practice to be judged by economic or by moral standards? By the standards of the expert or by those of the average citizen? Often, you may find that you need to suggest two or three different kinds of criteria which together cover all possible bases for judgment. For example, to determine the quality of a particular college, you might select as criteria the distinction of its faculty, the adequacy of its physical plant, the success of its students in graduate and professional schools, and the reputation it enjoys in its region.

2. *Do the facts and circumstances in question meet the criteria specified?* Just as you would determine whether a product is overpriced or underpriced by comparing it with an established average, so you must judge the worth of a claim of fact or value by measuring the relevant evidence against the standards which have been set up as criteria. What are the standards and practices of our present grading system? Do these standards and practices

meet the conditions of "desirability" as you have designated them? Questions concerning criteria or existing conditions are not always easy to answer, and sometimes definitive answers are impossible. In order to establish a claim of fact or value to the satisfaction of a reasonable listener, however, it is necessary to show that at least a preponderance of the evidence meets the criteria which have been set forth as bases for judgment.

From what has been said about the three types of claims, you should now be able to see the importance of knowing exactly the kind of claim you are seeking to establish in a given persuasive speech. Is it a claim of policy, fact, or value? If it is a claim of policy, do you need to answer all four of the basic questions listed on page 238, or is your audience likely to accept one or more of them without proof? If yours is a claim of fact or value, what criteria should you use as bases for judgment; and how well are they met by the evidence?

Finally, unless there are sound reasons for delay, you should announce early in your speech the claim you are going to support or oppose. If your listeners do not see the precise point on which they will be asked to judge, your strongest arguments and appeals probably will prove useless.[7]

DEVELOPING A PERSUASIVE SPEECH: THE MOTIVATED SEQUENCE

When you have clearly in mind the specific claim of policy, fact, or value for which you wish to gain acceptance, you are ready to begin gathering material and organizing your persuasive speech. Insofar as organization is concerned, the most important principle is similar to the one given in Chapter 10 for informative speaking (page 212): You cannot cram ideas down people's throats, but must lead their thoughts easily and gradually toward the conclusion you desire. A speech is not something to be planned in isolation and then brought out and "displayed" before the audience. Rather, it must be prepared with a particular group of listeners constantly in mind and must be constructed so as to conform with the steps they normally follow in arriving at choices and judgments. To organize a talk otherwise would be as foolish as trying to make a man fit a suit.

---

[7]A full discussion of the logical grounding of claims in evidence and reasoning is presented in Douglas Ehninger and Wayne Brockriede, *Decision by Debate* (New York: Dodd, Mead & Company, 1963).

Some psychological bases for organizing a persuasive speech

Although individuals may vary to some extent, research has shown that most people seek a consistency or *balance* among their cognitions. When confronted with a problem that disturbs their normal orientation, they look for a solution; when they feel a want or need, they search for a way to satisfy it. In short, when anything throws them into a condition of disorganization or dissonance, they are motivated to adjust their cognitions or values, or to alter their behavior so as to achieve a new state of balance.[8]

Many years ago, the philosopher John Dewey drew upon this fact to develop a description of the way in which most individuals, when confronted with a choice or problem situation, systematically think their way through to a decision. *First,* Dewey said, they begin simply by recognizing the specific lack or disorientation which constitutes the problem at hand. *Second,* they examine the problem to determine its nature, scope, and implications. *Third,* they search for a new orientation in the form of a solution. *Fourth,* they compare and evaluate the possible solutions which occur to them. And, *fifth,* they select that solution or course of action which, upon the basis of the foregoing reflection, seems best.[9] Thus they achieve a new state of balance.

Of course, there is no guarantee that everyone, even in his or her most reflective moments, will always think through a problem or arrive at a decision in this fashion. But much observation and testing have made it apparent that, typically, when confronted with a problem, most of us usually do raise questions such as these: Exactly what is the nature of the problem? What is its range, its seriousness? Is an immediate decision called for? What are the possible answers or solutions? If the problem raises a question of fact or value, does the proffered judgment meet the criteria specified? If it involves a policy or course of action, would the proposal be practicable? Would it really work to solve the problem, and do so without introducing new and worse evils? Until they are satisfied on these matters, few people will accept a judgment of fact or value, or be ready to endorse a policy.

---

[8]Useful summaries of "balance theory" may be found in Thomas M. Scheidel, *Persuasive Speaking* (Glenview, Ill.: Scott, Foresman and Company, 1967), pp. 22–23; and in Roger Brown, *Social Psychology* (New York: The Free Press of Glencoe, Inc., 1965), Chapter 11.

[9]John Dewey, "Analysis of Reflective Thinking," in *How We Think* (Boston: D. C. Heath and Company, 1910), p. 72.

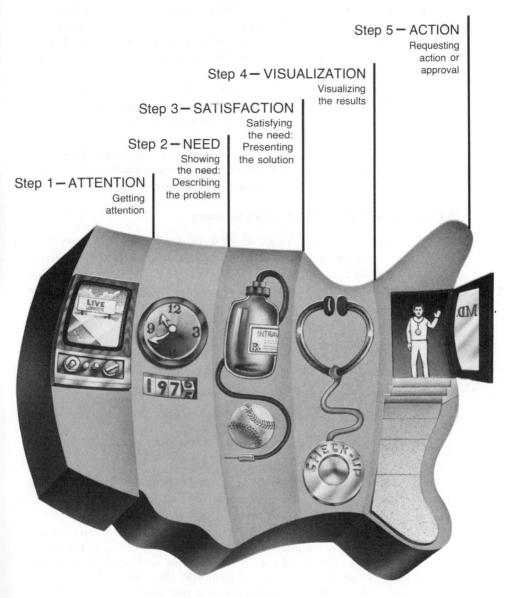

Step 5 – ACTION
Requesting action or approval

Step 4 – VISUALIZATION
Visualizing the results

Step 3 – SATISFACTION
Satisfying the need: Presenting the solution

Step 2 – NEED
Showing the need: Describing the problem

Step 1 – ATTENTION
Getting attention

Figure 2. The Motivated Sequence

Because these questions are so prevalent, they provide a dependable psychological basis upon which you can organize a persuasive speech. Begin by catching the attention of the listeners; direct that attention to a question to be answered or a problem to be solved; next, advance the answer or solution which you believe to be best; then visualize the advantages to be gained from believing or behaving as you recommend; and, finally, ask the audience for agreement or action. By adhering to this general progression from question to answer or from problem to solution, and then on to visualization and action, you can develop your appeals along the thought-line that most people are accustomed to following. Such organization will make your speech easier to understand and will render it more naturally persuasive.

A five-step sequence for motivating listeners

The plan of speech organization which is derived from this analysis of the thinking process may be called *the motivated sequence:* the sequence of ideas which, because it adheres to the steps people naturally follow when systematically thinking their way through problems, *motivates* the listeners to accept the speaker's proposition. As we have already suggested, the motivated sequence consists of five steps:

1. Getting attention. *(Attention Step)*

2. Showing the need: Describing the problem. *(Need Step)*

3. Satisfying the need: Presenting the solution. *(Satisfaction Step)*

4. Visualizing the results. *(Visualization Step)*

5. Requesting action or approval. *(Action Step)*

Observe how these steps were employed for a persuasive purpose in an advertisement, "Motivated Men Made America Great," which appeared in *Fortune* Magazine. Here, in part, is the text:

> 1. [*Attention*] The phonograph, the incandescent light, central electrical power systems, the fluoroscope, moving pictures . . . these are Thomas A. Edison's best remembered contributions to the well-being of the world. There were thousands more. All testify to the genius of a man who worked best under competitive pressure and once explained his success by saying, "*I can only invent under powerful incentives. No competition means no invention. It's the same with the men I have around me. It's not money they want but a chance for their ambition to grow.*"

Motivated Men Made America Great

Thomas A. Edison

Motivating men to sell your product is our business

MARITZ INC.

2. [*Need*] Countries need motivated men. Companies do, too, especially when their success depends on the extra effort of individual salesmen and entire sales organizations.

3. [*Satisfaction*] We help fill this need for companies in all industries. Maritz is the only company in the United States engaged exclusively in the business of motivating men to sell. As specialists, we offer complete sales motivation services including basic planning, program promotion, complete administration and thorough *follow-through.* All are offered in conjunction with distinctive merchandise and glamorous travel awards.

4. [*Visualization*] The combination causes salesmen to work harder, more intelligently, and more successfully. Their increased productivity improves sales and profits for the clients we serve.

5. [*Action*] Your Maritz Account Executive can tell you why salesmen become more productive when rewards for extra achievement are more than monetary. He can also help you plan, announce, and conduct sales motivation programs to meet your company's specific needs. We suggest you contact him. He alone offers you the exclusive services of the leader in the field of sales motivation.[10]

---

[10]"Motivated Men Made America Great" from *Fortune* Magazine (March 1966). Reprinted by permission of Maritz Inc.

The motivated sequence applied to speeches to persuade

Let us now consider a speech which, like the advertisement we have just examined, attempts to motivate the audience by employing the five steps: Attention, Need, Satisfaction, Visualization, and Action. Entitled "Nice People," it was prepared and presented in the annual contest of the Interstate Oratorical Association by Ms. Jan Bjorklund, Mankato State College, Mankato, Minnesota.

"Nice People"[11]
Jan Bjorklund

Attention step

What I am about to say, I have said before; so have many others in many other ways. And that's about it. A great deal has been *said,* but very little has been *done,* so this problem remains a problem. For this reason, I'd like to emphasize the words and the meaning of this speech, hoping that you will react from an understanding of these words.

Need step

An epidemic of contagious disease is threatening the United States at this very minute: one so massive that a new case occurs every 15 seconds, for a total of 7,500 a day.

All age levels are being victimized by this disease, but most selectively young people, ages 16 to 30. This epidemic is capable of spreading undetected inside the bodies of over 700,000 women, allowing them to continue a normal life, causing them no discomfort, no disability, no pain, while robbing them of their ability to bear children.

All the while this disease continues to strike, to spread, and to slay, the means to cure it not only exist, but are relatively inexpensive, relatively simple to administer, and painless to the receiver.

Isn't it strange that our nation, one of the healthiest in the world, should allow such a disease to continue, to multiply into an uncontrollable epidemic? One would think that the halls of government would be echoing with the debate and discussion of possible courses of action to eradicate this festering blight. Yes, one could think that—until realizing this is not the case, due to the small and medically irrelevant fact that the disease in question is *venereal* disease.

---

[11]Reprinted from *Winning Orations,* 1972, by special arrangement with the Interstate Oratorical Association, Duane L. Aschenbrenner, Executive Secretary, University of Nebraska at Omaha.

In 1936, the Surgeon General of the United States Public Health Service, Thomas Parran, stated that the great impediment to the solution of the VD problem was that "nice" people don't have it. Since then, the basis for this statement has disappeared. Oh, Freaks have it, and Blacks, and Jesus People, and urban disadvantaged, and poverty-stricken, and people on welfare: *they* all have it, all right! It's been called "their" disease. But is it theirs alone?

Berkeley, California, is a "nice" place to live. Within the city's limits, we find the University of California and many of its prominent faculty and students. Last year, 2,000 cases of gonorrhea were reportedly found there, too.

Houston, Texas, is a "nice" place, too. Nice enough to attract attention and become the headquarters for our national space program. Last year it also attracted 1,266 cases of gonorrhea for every 100,000 inhabitants.

Atlanta, Georgia, the cultural and commercial capital of the South, also leads the nation in the reported number of cases of gonorrhea. Last year it reported 2,510 cases for every 100,000 inhabitants.

These are only the *reported* cases, estimated to be 25 percent of all cases, for only 1 out of every 4 cases is ever reported.

This would mean that of the 100,000 inhabitants of Berkeley, California, approximately 8,000 contracted VD; that would be 1 out of 12!

This ratio isn't so crucial, though, when you compare it to that in some San Franciscan high schools where a student has 1 chance in 5 of contracting syphilis or gonorrhea before he graduates.

Why? People neglect to get the proper treatment; or when they do, they don't name all their contacts, so the disease continues to spread.

According to *Today's Health* magazine, of the 4 out of 5 cases that are treated by private physicians, only 1 out of 9 is reported. And of the many, many that go by unreported, I'd guess that 90 percent involve nice people.

Syphilis and gonorrhea are infectious diseases outranked in incidence only by the common cold.

. . . .

Venereal disease is especially rampant among young people. As reported in *Newsweek*, January 24, 1972, at least 1 of every 5 persons with gonorrhea is below the age of 20. Last year, over 5,000 cases were found among children between the ages of 10 and 14. Another 2,000 cases were found among children below the age of 9. Dr. Walter Smartt, Chief of the Los Angeles County Venereal Disease Control Division, states that the probability of a person acquiring VD before he reaches the age of 25 is about 50 percent. This would mean that of the number of us here in this room, one half of us have already or shortly will come in contact with VD. Where does that put you? Or me? It's always easy to say it can only happen to someone else, to the other person, but there is only one guarantee that it can't strike me or you.

And that one guarantee is abstinence. But in this day and age, that's hardly a likely possibility. We wouldn't think of stopping tuberculosis by stopping breathing, so how could we think of stopping venereal disease by stopping sex?

Satisfaction step

What is the solution? Many suggestions have been made.

First of all, in the opinion of many experts, syphilis could be brought under control by case-finding. However, in the last few years the number of case-finders has been reduced. The Federal Government is not supporting this effort.

Secondly, there is a deplorable inadequacy in both teaching and courses of instruction concerning VD. We need an educational effort at the earliest feasible age group. Looking at the ages of the patients coming into the clinics, we see we almost have to beat puberty.

Another possibility has been suggested by Dr. John Knox of Houston's Baylor College of Medicine. He predicts that a vaccine for syphilis could easily be developed in 5 years, but at the rate the government is putting out money, it will probably take 105 years. A vaccine for gonorrhea, on the other hand, seems almost impossible at this point. There is a crying need for more research.

Visualization step

I thought for sure that such a complex problem would require a complicated cure. However, I became aware of my mistaken thinking during a visit with my college physician, Dr. Hankerson. He informed me that syphilis and gonorrhea can be brought under control and cured by simple treatments of penicillin or similar antibiotics. If every American would have a regular checkup, and receive treatment if necessary, by 1973 we could begin to send venereal disease the way of typhoid, measles, polio, and the bubonic plague. If each of us would begin with a regular checkup, now.

As you can see, it is a complex problem, and no one solution can completely eliminate it. What we need is a concerted drive that will encompass case-finding, support for an educational effort, and the search for a vaccine, along with the use of penicillin and other similar antibiotics.

But even if this does happen, the effort cannot be successful, for venereal disease will continue to spread as long as it is thought of as dirty and shameful. Dr. McKenzie-Pollock, former director of the American Social Health Association, made the following statement: "Once the public is aware and notified that syphilis and gonorrhea are serious factors in our everyday lives right now, the rest will follow."

Very well, consider yourself *notified* . . . or are you one of those "nice people"?[12]

Observe that in her speech Ms. Bjorklund (1) called attention to her subject by piquing the curiosity of her hearers; (2) pointed out — by means of statistics, specific instances, authoritative testimony, and comparisons — the crucial need to bring venereal disease under control; (3) demonstrated — by means of offering a three-way solution — that this pressing need could be satisfied; (4) visualized briefly the results of carrying out the proposed solution; and (5) concluded by appealing for direct and immediate action in the form of a concerted drive.

USING THE MOTIVATED SEQUENCE IN A SPEECH URGING THE ADOPTION OF A POLICY

Step 1. Getting attention

It has been said that all too frequently the attitude of the persons about to hear someone give a speech is "Ho-hum." Obviously, you must change this attitude at the very beginning if you hope to persuade your listeners to believe or to act. The methods for effecting this change are described in Chapter 9. A review of pages 183–190 will remind you how startling statements, illustrations, questions, and other supportive materials can be used to focus wide-awake attention on what you have to say.

---

[12]Based on factual data from *VD Fact Sheet—1971,* U.S. Department of Health, Education, and Welfare, Public Health Service, page 9; *Today's Health,* April 1971; *VD Statistical Letter,* DHEW, February 1972; *Newsweek,* January 24, 1972; *Minneapolis Tribune,* Wednesday, April 5, 1972; *Sex and the Yale Student,* Student Committee on Human Sexuality, 1970.

Step 2. Showing the need: Describing the problem

When you have captured the attention of your listeners, you are ready to make clear why the policy you propose is needed. To do this, you must show that a definite problem exists; you must point out what is wrong with things as they are and through facts and figures make clear just how bad the situation is. For example, "Last month our plant at Littleton produced only 200 carburetors rather than the 300 scheduled. As a result we have had to shut down our main assembly line at Metropolis three times, with a loss of more than $60,000."

In its full form, a need or problem step requires a fourfold development: (1) *Statement*—a definite, concise statement of the problem. (2) *Illustration*—one or more examples explaining and clarifying the problem. (3) *Ramification*—additional examples, statistical data, testimony, and other forms of support showing the extent and seriousness of the problem. (4) *Pointing*—making clear to the listeners how the problem directly affects them. You will not, however, invariably need to use all four of these developmental elements. "Statement" and "pointing" should always be present, but the inclusion of "illustration" and "ramification" will depend upon the amount of detail required to impress the audience. But whether you use the complete development or only a part of it, the need step is exceedingly important in your speech, for it is here that your subject is first definitely related to the needs and desires of your listeners.

Step 3. Satisfying the need: Presenting the solution

The solution or satisfaction step in a speech urging the adoption of a policy has the purpose of getting your listeners to agree that the program you propose is the correct one. Therefore, this step consists of presenting your proposed solution to the problem and proving this solution practicable and desirable. Five items are usually contained in a fully developed satisfaction step: (1) *Statement*—stating the attitude, belief, or action you wish the audience to adopt. (2) *Explanation*—making sure that your proposal is understood. (Often diagrams or charts are useful here.) (3) *Theoretical demonstration*—showing by reasoning how your proposed solution meets the need. (4) *Reference to practical experience*—supplying examples to prove that the proposal has worked effectively where it has been tried. (Use facts, figures, and the testimony of experts to support this contention.) (5) *Meeting objections*—forestalling opposition by answering any objections which might be raised against the proposal.

Just as certain items may at times be omitted from the need step, so also may one or more of these phases be left out of the satisfaction step if the situation warrants. Nor must the foregoing order always be followed exactly. Occasionally, objéctions can best be met by dealing with them as they arise in the minds of the listeners; in other situations, the theoretical demonstration and reference to practical experience may be combined. If the satisfaction step is developed properly, however, at its conclusion the audience will say, "Yes, you are right; this is a practicable and desirable solution to the problem you pointed out."

Step 4. Visualizing the results

The function of the visualization step is to intensify desire. It should picture for the audience how conditions will be in the future (1) if the policy you propose is adopted, or (2) if the policy you propose is not adopted. Because it projects the thinking of the audience into the future, it might just as correctly be called the "projection" step.

The projection aimed at in the visualization step may be accomplished in one of three ways: by the *positive* method, the *negative* method, or the method of *contrast*.

The positive method. When using this method, you describe conditions as they will be in the future if the solution you propose is carried out. Make such a description vivid and concrete. Select a situation which you are quite sure will arise. Then picture your listeners in that situation actually enjoying the conditions which your proposal will produce.

The negative method. This method describes conditions as they will be in the future if your proposal is not carried out. It pictures for your audience the evils or dangers which will arise from failure to follow your advice. Select from the need step the most undesirable aspects of the present situation, and show how these conditions will be aggravated if your proposal is rejected.

The method of contrast. This method combines the two preceding ones. The negative approach is used first, showing the disadvantages accruing from failure to adopt your proposal; then the positive approach is used, showing the advantages accruing from its adoption. Thus, the desirable situation is thrown into strong contrast with the undesirable one.

Whichever method you use — positive, negative, or contrast — remember that the visualization step must stand the test of reality: the conditions you picture must be capable of attainment. Moreover, they must be made vivid. Let your listeners actually see themselves enjoying the advantages or suffering the evils you describe. The more clearly you can depict the situation, the more strongly the audience will react.

The following excerpt illustrates how a speaker urging home owners to carry adequate property insurance might develop a visualization step by the method of contrast:

> Suppose that while you and your family are watching television some warm summer evening, a tornado warning is suddenly flashed on the screen and you are told to go at once to a safe corner of your basement. You gather your children in your arms and hurry down the steps. As the sky grows dark and the wind howls, you huddle together, hoping against hope that your lives will be spared.
>
> Eventually the storm passes, and you emerge from your shelter. At first you can only think how fortunate you and your family are to have escaped injury. But then you begin to look about you. Although you and your loved ones have survived, in other ways you have not been so lucky. The roof of your house has been entirely blown off and the walls reduced to kindling. Your home is a total loss!
>
> Then with a shock you realize that your insurance will not even begin to cover the damage. In addition to the expense of moving to an apartment and buying new furniture, you will need to purchase another dwelling. Not only will your hard-earned savings disappear, but you will have to go heavily into debt for many years to come.
>
> Suppose, on the other hand, that your house had been fully insured. How different the picture would be! Although the inconvenience and trauma caused by the storm still would be present, one great worry would be taken off your mind. You would know you had the money to buy and furnish a new home, and to do so without any financial sacrifice on your part. So far as money matters were concerned, you would be able to pick up your life and carry it forward exactly as you had planned.

Step 5. Requesting action or approval

The function of the action step in a policy speech is to translate into overt action the desire created in the visualization step. This step commonly takes the form of a challenge or appeal, an inducement, or a statement of personal intention, as described in Chapter 9. A review of pages 191–197, where these endings are discussed, will suggest their appropriateness as methods for developing this actuative phase.

Beware, however, of making the action step too long or involved. Someone has given this formula for successful public speaking: "Stand up; speak up; shut up." It is well here to emphasize the final admonition; finish your speech briskly and sit down.

A SKELETAL PLAN FOR USING THE MOTIVATED SEQUENCE IN A SPEECH TO PERSUADE[13]

If you develop a persuasive speech in the manner just indicated, your skeleton plan will look something like the one shown below. (Bear in mind, of course, that each item and sub-item must be sufficiently *detailed*, as emphasized on the preceding pages, to support the speaker's purpose, the subject under consideration, the occasion, etc.)

SUBJECT: _____

SPECIFIC PURPOSE: _____

Step 1: Attention

   I. (Opening statement)
     A. (Support)
     B. (Support)
  II. (Statement or restatement)

Step 2: Need

    I. (Statement of need)
   II. (Illustration)
  III. (Ramification)
  IV. (Pointing statement—relating need to audience)

Step 3: Satisfaction

    I. (Statement of idea or plan proposed)
   II. (Explanation)
  III. (Theoretical demonstration)

---

[13]In the sample outlines appearing subsequently in this chapter each step in the motivated sequence is point-numbered *separately* because in the textual presentation each step has been considered as a more or less complete entity with its own internal point-structure, thus: "Attention step"—I, II, etc.; "Need step"—I, II, etc. You may choose, however, to begin numbering your outlines with the roman numeral I and continue *consecutively* on through to the end; for example: "Attention step"—I, II; "Need step"—III, IV; "Satisfaction step"—V, VI; etc.

IV. (Reference to practical experience)
V. (Meeting possible objections)

Step 4: Visualization

I. (Statement of negative projection)
  A. (Support)
  B. (Support)
II. (Statement of positive projection)
  A. (Support)
  B. (Support)

Step 5: Action

I. (Request for belief or action)
  A. (Support or recapitulation)
  B. (Support or recapitulation)
II. (Restatement or appeal)

This plan, of course, should be viewed as a *flexible* arrangement; it merely *suggests* the general pattern to be followed. The number of main points within each step and the number and order of subordinate or supporting ideas will vary from speech to speech and cannot be determined in advance. Sometimes the restatement will be omitted from the attention step; sometimes, instead of the method of contrast, you will use only a negative or a positive projection in the visualization step; and sometimes other modifications will be in order.

Once you have determined the general plan, however, write out the points of the outline as complete sentences, following the suggestions for phrasing and outline form given in Chapter 7 (pages 142– 149). See also that each part of the talk performs the function required of it: that the attention step catches attention, that the need step points out a serious problem, and so on.

A SAMPLE OUTLINE FOR A PERSUASIVE SPEECH

An abbreviated outline[14] for a persuasive speech arguing that students be given greater voice in the management of their college might, for example, take this form:

---

[14]In an outline for a full-length speech, each of the steps may contain two or more major points or ideas (I, II, III, etc.) and also a number of subordinate or supporting points.

Citizens Without Votes

Attention step

I. "Taxation without representation" was the rallying cry of our Revolutionary forebears.
   A. It epitomized the plight of the voteless citizens of the American colonies.
   B. It stirred them to action against "the mother country."

Need step

I. Today as students at Old Ivy College, we are voteless citizens of our academic community.
   A. We have no voice in determining the fees that are assessed against us.
      1. Tuition is set by the Board of Trustees.
      2. Other charges are fixed by the Business Office.
   B. We have no voice in determining academic requirements.
      1. Degree programs are established by the Faculty.
      2. Grading policies are determined by the Dean.
   C. We have no voice in the government of our residence halls.
      1. Rooms and roommates are assigned arbitrarily by the Director of Dormitories.
      2. Policies affecting visiting privileges and study periods are set by the hall counselors.

Satisfaction step

I. This state of affairs must end.
   A. We students should be given a voice in determining the fees we are charged.
      1. We should be allowed to make recommendations to the Board of Trustees.
      2. We should have student representatives who are allowed to meet regularly with officials in the Business Office.
   B. We students should be given a voice in determining the establishment of academic policies.
      1. We should have a voting representative on the Committee on Curriculum.
      2. We should be consulted whenever a change in grading policies is contemplated.
   C. We should be granted complete control of our residence halls.
      1. Democratically elected dormitory *councils* should assign rooms and roommates.

2. All residents should vote on policies affecting visiting privileges and study periods.
II. Fair and just policies of a similar nature already have been successfully instituted at many other colleges.
   A. At Mountain Top College, representatives of the Student Senate sit on all faculty committees.
   B. At Seaside College, students have complete control of their residence halls.
III. In all cases where students have been given such authority, they have proved responsible.
   A. They have discharged their duties faithfully and fairly.
   B. They have acted conscientiously and with consistently good judgment.

Visualization step

I. The proposed reforms would bring two important benefits to Old Ivy.
   A. They would provide important new inputs and insights into solving the many serious problems our college faces.
   B. They would heal the misunderstandings and breaches now developing between students and faculty/administration.

Action step

I. Begin action here and now to secure adequate student representation in college affairs.
   A. You owe it to yourself as a student.
   B. You owe it to the college community of which you are a member.
II. Raise your voices loud and strong in a modern-day variation of that old revolutionary war cry: "No relaxation until we get representation!"

USING THE MOTIVATED SEQUENCE IN A SPEECH OPPOSING A POLICY

As you have seen, a speech urging the adoption of a policy should (1) hold the attention of the audience; (2) show that there is a need for some action; (3) present a solution that will satisfy the need; (4) visualize the advantages of behaving as the speaker proposes; and (5) request the action or approval indicated.

The speech which opposes a policy ("The administration should not forbid freshmen to drive cars on campus") also must begin by capturing and sustaining listeners' attention. Beyond this point, however, such a speech must *negate* or at least strongly *counteract* the contentions which claim a need, propose a solution to that need, and/or visualize the advantages supposedly emanating therefrom. In other words, when you are speaking to *oppose* a policy, you set out to prove that:

(a) There is *no* need for a change; things are perfectly all right as they are.

(b) The proposed policy does *not* provide a practicable solution to the alleged problem; it would not remove the evil or deficiency.

(c) Instead of bringing benefits or advantages, the proposed policy would actually introduce *new and worse evils:* it would be costly, unfair, dangerous to our liberties, difficult to administer, etc.

Sometimes all three of these contentions will be used in a speech urging the rejection of a proposed course of action. At other times, not all of them will apply; and the speech will be planned accordingly. If, however, any one contention can be proved beyond reasonable doubt, a discriminating listener will reject a proposal, since obviously no one wants to adopt a policy that is unneeded or impracticable or one that may introduce new problems and evils. Proof beyond reasonable doubt on all three contentions constitutes the strongest possible case against a recommended change.

A SAMPLE OUTLINE OF A SPEECH OPPOSING A POLICY

Here is part of an outline of a speech in which a proposed action is opposed on the ground that it is unneeded, impracticable, and undesirable. In order to make the major contentions stand out more clearly, the attention step and detailed supporting material have been omitted:

THE PROPOSED PARKING RAMP

Not needed

I. The parking ramp which the mayor proposes be built in the central business district of our city is not needed.

A. The three parking lots now existing in this area are never filled.

B. With gasoline scarce and expensive, more people are leaving their cars at home and riding the bus downtown.

Impracticable   II. Even if the parking ramp were needed, its construction at this time would be impracticable.
    A. Building materials and construction costs are at an all-time high.
    B. The revenue generated by the ramp in the form of parking fees would be far less than the mayor estimates.

Undesirable   III. Finally, even if such a ramp were both needed and practicable, its construction would not be desirable.
    A. The ramp would be an "eyesore," visible from many parts of the city.
    B. A number of long-established businesses now standing on the spot proposed for the ramp would have to move to less desirable locations.

USING THE MOTIVATED SEQUENCE IN A SPEECH ADVANCING A CLAIM OF FACT

How should persuasive speeches on factual claims be organized and developed? Here, as in policy speeches, the motivated sequence furnishes the basic pattern, needing only to be adapted to meet the special requirements imposed by the subject matter; thus:

1. *Getting attention:* Secure the attention and interest of the audience.

2. *Showing the need:* State clearly the point to be established and show your listeners why it is important. Do this by pointing out (a) why the matter at hand concerns them personally or (b) why it concerns the community, state, nation, or world of which they are a part.

3. *Satisfying the need:* (a) If they are not already obvious, set forth the criteria upon which a proper judgment rests. (b) Advance the exact point to be proved and offer evidence and argument to support your claim.

4. *Visualizing the results:* Picture the advantages of accepting your recommendation or point of view, or the disadvantages of rejecting it.

5. *Requesting action or approval:* Appeal for the acceptance of your contention and, when appropriate, for a determination to adopt your view or to follow your advice.

A SAMPLE OUTLINE OF A SPEECH ON A CLAIM OF FACT

The five steps of the motivated sequence, adapted as suggested above, are illustrated in the following outline:

SAFE AT HOME

Attention step
    I. Everyone has heard the expression "safe at home."
   II. But is your home really a safe place to live?

Need step
    I. This is a question of importance to each of us.
      A. Our own well-being is at stake.
      B. The well-being of our families is at stake.

Satisfaction step
    I. In answering the question of home safety, we must consider two *additional* questions.
      A. How many accidents occur in the home?
      B. How serious are these accidents?
   II. In neither case are the facts encouraging.
      A. Statistics gathered by the National Safety Council show that, in the year 1971, accidents in the home were responsible for 4,200,000 disabling injuries.
        1. Of these, 110,000 resulted in some form of permanent disability.
        2. The cost of such accidents — including lost wages, medical expenses, and insurance payments — was estimated at more than $2 billion.
      B. In the same year, home accidents were the cause of 27,500 deaths.
        1. Falls were the cause of 10,000 deaths.
        2. Burns, suffocation, and poisons were other leading causes.

Visualization step
    I. Unless we are aware of these dangers and guard against them, we, too, may be numbered among the victims of home accidents.
      A. We may be "laid up" for long periods of time.
      B. Our children and loved ones may be killed or permanently injured.

Action step
    I. Take steps to avoid such tragedies today.
      A. Put firm railings and good lights on all staircases.
      B. Keep matches and combustible materials out of the reach of children.
      C. Dispose of all plastic bags as soon as they are emptied.

D. Keep all poisonous substances under lock and key.

II. Remember, your home will be a safe place only if you yourself make it so.

USING THE MOTIVATED SEQUENCE IN A SPEECH ADVANCING A CLAIM OF VALUE

When speaking on a claim of value with a view to persuading your listeners that they should agree with your judgment of a person, practice, institution, or theory, you may adapt the basic pattern of motivated sequence as follows:

1. *Getting attention:* Capture the attention and interest of the audience.
2. *Showing the need:* Make clear that a judgment concerning the worth of the person, practice, or institution is needed. Do this by showing *(a)* why a judgment is important to your listeners personally, or *(b)* why it is important to the community, state, nation, or world of which they are a part.
3. *Satisfying the need: (a)* Set forth the criteria upon which an intelligent judgment may be based. *(b)* Advance what you believe to be the correct judgment and show how it meets the criteria.
4. *Visualizing the results:* Picture the advantages that will accrue from agreeing with the judgment you advance or the evils that will result from failing to endorse it.
5. *Requesting action or approval:* Appeal for the acceptance of the proposed judgment and for a determination to retain it.

A SAMPLE OUTLINE OF A SPEECH ON A CLAIM OF VALUE

Each of the five steps in the basic pattern of the motivated sequence, adapted as suggested above, is present in the following speech outline:

THE VALUES OF INTERCOLLEGIATE DEBATE

Attention step

I. In recent years intercollegiate debate has come under strong attack from many quarters.
   A. Philosophers and social scientists have charged that debate is a poor way to get at the truth of a disputable matter.
   B. Educators have charged that debate develops bad habits of contentiousness and dogmatism rather than of objectivity.

Need step (Evaluation necessary)	I. How we evaluate debate is important to each of us for at least two reasons: 　A. As students we are concerned because we help support the debate program on this campus through our activity fee. 　B. As citizens we are concerned because the method of decision-making employed in an intercollegiate debate is essentially the same as that employed in the courtroom and in the legislative assembly.
Satisfaction step (Criteria)	I. Like any extracurricular activity, debate can be evaluated according to two important criteria: 　A. Does it develop abilities and traits of mind which will aid the student in his or her course work? 　B. Does it develop abilities and traits of mind which will be of value in later life?
(Evaluation provided)	II. The experience of many years has shown that debate is valuable. 　A. Debate helps the student do better work in his or her courses. 　　1. It teaches the student to study a subject thoroughly and systematically. 　　2. It teaches the student to analyze complex ideas quickly and logically. 　　3. It teaches the student to speak and write clearly and convincingly. 　B. Training in debate is of value in later life. 　　1. It establishes habits of courtesy and fair play. 　　2. It instills self-confidence and poise.
Visualization step	I. Picture the serious students of debate in the classroom and in their post-college careers. 　A. As students, they will know how to study, analyze, and present material. 　B. As business or professional people, they will be better able to meet arguments and to express their views in a fair and effective manner.
Action or approval step	I. Remember these facts whenever you hear the value of intercollegiate debate questioned. 　A. The contribution debate training makes to business or professional success has been affirmed by many prominent men and women who were debaters in college. 　B. We should encourage and support this worthwhile activity in every way we can.

A speech that is intended to show that an institution or practice has no value (for instance, a speech which argues that debate training is useless or undesirable) may be developed according to a similar pattern. But in the satisfaction step, instead of showing that the practice or institution in question meets the criteria you outlined, show that it fails to meet them. Then, in the visualizaton step, picture for your listeners the uselessness of the institution or the ways in which it is actually harmful.

PROBLEMS FOR FURTHER STUDY

1. One key problem facing any speaker attempting to persuade or to actuate listeners is that of finding "common ground"—discovering criteria or standards which are acceptable to the audience and which justify the value, policy, or action proposed. Compare the usefulness of a knowledge of "values" and "motives" in solving this problem. In making the comparison, consider the following: (a) Is the treatment of *values* in Chapter 3 of use to you as you search out "common ground"? (b) Or do you prefer to analyze audiences less philosophically and more psychologically, using the *motives* described in this chapter as common touchstones? (c) Do you really think that it makes a difference whether you approach questions of criteria/standards/common-ground philosophically rather than psychologically, or vice versa? Defend your positions on these questions.

2. In a politically/economically active country such as ours, persuasive discourse plays a vital role in many human transactions: the politician wants your vote; the shopkeeper wants your money; the "good cause" wants your time and energy. (a) Examine closely the texts of several political speeches, advertisements for goods and services, and brochures describing social organizations or clubs. (b) Category by category (politics, advertisements, organizational brochures), list the *motives* appealed to in each type of persuasive discourse. (c) Upon critical inspection, do you find any common *patterns* in these motive appeals? Do politics, business, and social services each appeal to certain motives more often than others? Do these three types of persuasion appeal principally to one or two levels in Maslow's prepotent hierarchy; and, if so, what do these facts lead you to conclude about each type of persuasion?

3. With several other members of your class, attend a meeting at which one or more speeches to persuade are presented (a political or campus rally, a meeting of the student senate or city council, or a public hearing).

After the event, prepare and present to the class a joint report which includes the following: the nature and purpose of the gathering; the initial attitude of the audience; the type of claim the speaker(s) advanced; the methods used to develop and support it (them); the extent to which the speaker(s) made adjustments to the listeners' attitudes, beliefs, and value-orientations; and the probable effect the speech(es) had in influencing the audience to accept the claim(s). Write a joint report and present it to the class.

4. Assume that you are going to *(a)* sell a set of encyclopedias to a stranger; *(b)* persuade an instructor to raise a grade; and *(c)* convince a dormitory, fraternity, or sorority corridor to elect you to the dorm or house council. In each instance, which of the following methods do you think is more likely to ensure persuasion: impressing your listeners with a motive for believing what you want them to believe, or showing them the logic of your proposal by presenting well-supported information and well-reasoned arguments? Discuss and defend your choice in each instance.

5. What motive appeals would you employ if you were attempting to induce an audience of college students to take the following actions: *(a)* contribute to the campus charity drive, *(b)* enlist in the army, *(c)* study harder, *(d)* give up their automobiles, *(e)* have an annual physical examination, *(f)* learn to speak Russian, *(g)* drop out of college?

ORAL ACTIVITIES AND SPEAKING ASSIGNMENTS

1. Participate in a class discussion on the ethics of persuasion. Among other questions, consider: What methods and appeals may legitimately be used in effecting persuasion? What methods and appeals should always be avoided? What methods and appeals appear to be sometimes legitimate, sometimes unethical? Are there any circumstances in which a person not only has the right, but also the obligation, to undertake persuasion by any means at his or her disposal? (Andersen's and Diggs' work, as designated in the "Suggestions for Further Reading," will be useful here.)

2. Choose a subject for a six-minute persuasive speech. Build your speech on the pattern provided by the motivated sequence. Show a strong need directly related to the interests and desires of your listeners. Demonstrate through reasoning and examples how your proposal will satisfy this need. Use the positive, negative, or contrasting method to build the visualization step. Workable topics might include the following:

Conquering urban blight.
A fair deal for the farmer.
Redefining our concept of "the aged."

Teaching children to read.
Religion and life.
Reforming the undergraduate curriculum.
Improving our mental-treatment centers.
Protecting the consumer.
Meeting the increased cost of public education.
Revamping intercollegiate athletic programs.
Raising the level of television programs.

3. Present a five-minute speech, the purpose of which is to persuade members of your speech class to take a recommended action. Show that a problem or situation needing remedy *actually exists*. Show your listeners why *they* (and not someone else) should be concerned, and why you think a specific action on their part will be a concrete, influential move toward a remedy. Use carefully reasoned arguments, strong motivation, and vivid and compelling language. On a future "check-up" day, see how many members of the audience actually have taken the recommended action. For example, you may urge an audience to *sign a petition* proposing that:

Graduating seniors should be excused from final examinations.
Students should be able to designate how their "activities fees" are spent.
Campus food services should be improved.
Advertising sound trucks should be prohibited on the campus.
The college should establish a cooperative bookstore (or grocery, or gasoline station).

(Be sure to have the petition available.)

Or, you may ask the other members of your class to *write letters to their congressmen* urging that:

The congressional seniority system for committee chairmanships should be abolished.
Your senator or representative should hold regular office hours on campus.
All election campaigns should be financed publicly.
Your congressional delegation ought to vote for Bill X.
Political candidates should be allowed to purchase only five-minute blocks of paid television time.

(Be sure to tell them who their congressmen are and where they can be reached.)

Or you may request that they *attend a meeting, a hearing, or an activity*. For instance, ask them to:

Go to a public hearing on pollution control for your city.
Attend a campus religious-revival meeting.
Join a newly organized student theatrical group.
Watch a campus debate tournament.
Give blood through the local Red Cross chapter.
Volunteer for work at a local psychological-crisis center.
Attend a meeting to organize a student-community center.
Picket a speaker representing a cause you oppose.

(Be sure to tell them when and where!)

SUGGESTIONS FOR FURTHER READING

John Ward, *A System of Oratory* (1759), Lectures IV through IX. A tight summary of the classical view of finding "common ground" when attempting persuasion.

Kenneth E. Andersen, *Persuasion: Theory and Practice* (Boston: Allyn & Bacon, Inc., 1971). One of the newer persuasion textbooks which integrates traditional theory and current experimental research, and which presents a useful treatment of ethics, demagoguery, and social action.

Gary Lynn Cronkhite, "Logic, Emotion, and the Paradigm of Persuasion," *Quarterly Journal of Speech* L (February 1964): 13–18. An interesting attempt to dispel the common notion that "logic" and "emotion" are separate realms in the mind.

B. J. Diggs, "Persuasion and Ethics," *Quarterly Journal of Speech* L (December 1964): 359–373. Reprinted in Douglas Ehninger, ed., *Contemporary Rhetoric; A Reader's Coursebook* (Glenview, Ill.: Scott, Foresman and Company, 1972), pp. 139–152. A provocative discussion of what certain kinds of persuasion can do to a listener in various situations.

Marvin Karlins and Herbert I. Abelson, *Persuasion: How Opinions and Attitudes Are Changed,* 2nd ed. (New York: Springer Publishing Co., Inc., 1970). A useful index to our current knowledge of persuasion, arranged in propositions documented with research findings.

Daniel Katz, ed., *Public Opinion Quarterly* XXIV (Summer 1960). An entire issue devoted to models for attitude-change.

Herbert W. Simons, "Persuasion in Social Conflicts: A Critique of Prevailing Conceptions and a Framework for Future Research," *Speech Monographs* XXXIX (November 1972): 227–247. An attack upon the "Establishment" bias in much of our analysis of persuasion, with suggestions for an alternative framework.

Chapter 12

Speaking for special occasions

Sᴘᴇᴇᴄʜᴇꜱ ᴛᴏ ɪɴꜰᴏʀᴍ ᴀɴᴅ ᴛᴏ ᴘᴇʀꜱᴜᴀᴅᴇ, as we have seen in Chapters 10 and 11, are the two kinds of oral communications you most often will be called on to make. Many occasions, however, require special types of speeches. You may have to introduce a visiting speaker or welcome a distinguished guest. You may be asked to announce awards, to pay a tribute to a person or a group, or to present a good-will speech on behalf of your business or profession. In this chapter we shall consider briefly these special types of speeches, as well as some of the duties of a chairperson in planning and conducting a meeting.

SPEECHES OF INTRODUCTION

Speeches of introduction are usually given by the chairperson. Sometimes, however, they are presented by another person who is especially well acquainted with the featured speaker.

Purpose: Creating a desire to hear the speaker

If you are invited to give a speech of introduction, remember that your main object is to create in the listeners a desire to hear the speaker you are introducing. Everything else should be subordinate to this aim. Do not bore the audience with a long recital of the speaker's biography or with a series of anecdotes about your acquaintanceship with him or her. Above all, do not air your own views on the subject of the speaker's message. You are only the speaker's advance agent; your job is to "sell" that person to the audience. Therefore, you must try (1) to arouse curiosity about the speaker and the subject in the minds of the listeners so that it will be easy to capture their attention, and (2) to motivate the audience to like and respect the speaker so they will tend to respond favorably to the forthcoming information or proposal.

Formulating the content

Usually the better known and more respected a speaker is, the shorter your introduction can be; the less well known he or she is, the more you will need to arouse interest in the speaker's subject and to build up his or her prestige. When presenting a speech of introduction, observe these principles:

Be brief. To say too much is often worse than to say nothing at all. For example, if you were to introduce the President, you might simply say, "Ladies and gentlemen, the President of the United States." The prestige of the person you introduce will not always be great enough for you to be so brief, but it is always better to say too little than to speak too long.

Do not talk about yourself. You may be tempted to express your own views on the subject or to recount anecdotes about your own experiences as a speaker. Avoid such references to yourself because they call attention to you rather than to the speaker.

Tell about the speaker. If, for instance, the guest speaker happens to be a man, you might typically answer such questions as: Who is he? What is his position in business or government? What experiences has he had that qualify him to speak on this subject? If the speaker happens to be a woman, tell who she is and what she knows or what she has done. Highlight her experience and expertise. In no case, however, should you praise the person's ability as a speaker. *Let the individual demonstrate that.*

Emphasize the importance of the speaker's subject. Point out to the audience the importance of the subject the speaker is about to discuss. In introducing an airline executive, you might say: "Nearly all of us from time to time travel by air or have friends or loved ones who do. Therefore, it is important for us to understand what the airlines are doing to ensure the safety and comfort of their passengers. . . ."

Stress the appropriateness of the subject or of the speaker. If a community is contemplating a program of urban renewal and redevelopment, a speech on the principles of city planning is especially timely. If your organization or firm is marking an anniversary, the founder — appropriately — should be one of the speakers. Reference to such pertinent information is obviously in order and serves to relate the speaker more closely to the audience.

Use humor if it suits the occasion. Nothing serves better to put an audience at ease and to create a friendly feeling than congenial laughter. Take care, however, that the humor is in good taste and does not come at the expense of someone else. In particular, do not risk offending the speaker whom you are introducing or detract from his or her prestige.

SPEECHES FOR COURTESY: WELCOMES, RESPONSES, ACCEPTANCES

Most speakers, at one time or another, will have occasion to give a speech for courtesy either on behalf of themselves or on behalf of an organization they represent.

Typical situations

Speeches for courtesy are given to fulfill one of three obligations:

Welcoming visitors. When a distinguished guest is present, someone — usually the presiding officer — should extend a public greeting.

Responding to a welcome or a greeting. An individual so welcomed must express appreciation.

Accepting awards. An individual who is presented an award for some special accomplishment is obligated to acknowledge this honor. Sometimes the award is made to an organization rather than to an individual, in which case someone is selected to respond for the group.

Purpose: Expressing sentiment and creating good feeling

The speech for courtesy has a double purpose. The speaker not only attempts to express a sentiment of gratitude or hospitality, but also to create an aura of good feeling in the audience. Usually the success of such a speech depends upon satisfying one's listeners that the appropriate thing has been said. Just as courtesies of private life put people at ease, so public acts of courtesy create good feeling in the recipient and the audience.

Formulating the content

The scope and content of a speech for courtesy should be guided by the following principles:

Indicate for whom you are speaking. When you are acting on behalf of a group, make clear that the greeting or acknowledgment comes from everyone and not from you alone.

Present complimentary facts about the person or persons to whom you are extending the courtesy. Review briefly the accomplishments or qualities of the person or group you are greeting or whose gift or welcome you are acknowledging.

Illustrate; do not argue. Present incidents and facts that make clear the importance of the occasion, but do not be contentious. Avoid areas of disagreement. Do not use a speech for courtesy as an opportunity to air your own views on controversial subjects or to advance your own policies. Rather, express concretely and vividly the thoughts which already are in the minds of your listeners.

SPEECHES OF TRIBUTE:
MEMORIALS, DEDICATIONS, FAREWELLS, PRESENTATIONS

A speaker may be called on to pay tribute to another person's qualities or achievements. Such occasions range from the awarding of a trophy after an athletic contest to a eulogy at a memorial service. Sometimes tributes are paid to an entire group or class of people — for example, teachers, soldiers, or mothers — rather than to an individual.

Typical situations

Memorial services. Services to pay public honor to the dead usually include a speech of tribute, or eulogy. Ceremonies of this kind may honor a famous person and be held years after that person's death — witness the many speeches on Lincoln. More often, however, they honor someone personally known to the audience and recently deceased. Eric Sevareid's "Eulogy for the Astronauts" (pages 165 – 167) is an excellent example of the latter circumstance.

Dedications. Buildings, monuments, parks, etc., frequently are constructed to honor a worthy cause or to commemorate a person or group of persons. At the dedication it is appropriate to say something about the purpose to be served and the person or persons commemorated.

Farewells. When a person retires or leaves a company to enter another field or when anyone generally admired leaves the community, public appreciation of his or her fellowship and accomplishments may be expressed in a speech befitting the circumstance.

Presentation of awards. Frequently, awards are presented to groups or to individuals for outstanding achievements or meritorious service. Their presentation calls for appropriate remarks.

Physical environment and social context have a profound and powerful effect in shaping a speaker's message. Nowhere is this principle more evident or more valid than in the special occasion, or "circumstantial" speech in which the nature, setting, and mood of the occasion determine clearly and completely all aspects of the message.

Clockwise from upper left: Louisiana State University Photo; Photo by University of Colorado Information Services; Rae Russel.

Purpose: Creating appreciation

A speech of tribute is designed to create in those who hear it a sense of appreciation for the traits or accomplishments of the person or group to whom tribute is paid. If you cause your audience to realize the essential worth or importance of the person or group, you will have succeeded. But you may go further than this. You may, by honoring a person, arouse deeper devotion to the cause he or she represents. Did this person give distinguished service to community or country? Then strive to enhance the audience's sense of patriotism and service. Was this individual a friend to young people? Then try to arouse the conviction that working to provide opportunities for the young deserves the audience's support. Create a desire in your listeners to emulate the person or persons honored. Make them want to develop the same virtues, to demonstrate a like devotion.

Formulating the content

Frequently, in a speech of tribute, a speaker attempts to itemize all of the accomplishments of a person or a group. Such a speech lacks impact because, in trying to cover everything, it emphasizes nothing. Try, instead, to be selective, to focus your remarks by observing the following rules:

Stress dominant traits. If you are paying tribute to a person, select a few aspects of his or her personality which are especially likable or praiseworthy, and relate incidents from the individual's life or work which illustrate these distinguishing qualities.

Mention only outstanding achievements. Pick out only a few of the person's or group's most notable accomplishments. Tell about them in detail to show how important they were. Let your speech say, "Here is what this person (or group) has done; see how such actions have contributed to the well-being of our community. . . ."

Give special emphasis to the influence of the person or group. Show the effect the person's behavior or the group's activities have had on others. Many times, the importance of people's lives can be demonstrated not so much in any traits or material accomplishments as in the influence they exercised on associates.

Admirable personal characteristics, achievements, and influence are not mutually exclusive. Most speeches of tribute probably will include references to all three. But in the interests of unity and of maximum impact upon the audience, you will be wise not to mention too many reflections on any one facet. Avoid complicated details and long enumerations. The few things you do tell, relate in an interesting way. Let each event you talk about become a story, living and personal. In this way, you can most readily lead your audience to admire the person or the group to whom the tribute is paid.

SPEECHES OF NOMINATION

Closely related to the speech of tribute is the speech to nominate. Here, your main *purpose* is to review the accomplishments of some person whom you admire. This review, however—instead of standing as an end in itself—is made to contribute to the principal goal of the speech: obtaining the listeners' endorsement of the person as a nominee for an elective office.

In a speech of nomination, your *manner of speaking* generally will be less formal and dignified than when you are giving a speech of tribute. It should, however, be businesslike and energetic. In general, the content of the speech will follow the pattern already described; but the illustrations and supporting materials should be chosen with the intent to show the nominee's qualifications for the office in question.

As you probably have observed, in political conventions the name of a proposed candidate often is withheld until the very end of the nominating speech in order to heighten the drama of the situation and to avoid premature demonstrations. This practice should not, however—except in very special circumstances—be used elsewhere. In most situations, before you come to the concluding phase of your speech, most of your listeners probably will guess whom you are talking about anyway. As a mere trick of rhetoric, the device is too obvious to be genuinely effective.

SPEECHES FOR GOOD WILL

Every speech seeks an affirmative response from the audience, but the type of speech now to be considered has as its principal aim the generating of good will.

Ostensibly, the objective of a good-will speech is to inform; actually, however, it seeks to enhance the listeners' appreciation of a particular institution, practice, or profession—to make them more favorably disposed toward it. By skillfully blending facts with indirect arguments and unobtrusive appeals, the speaker attempts to develop a positive attitude toward the subject. In short, the good-will speech is a mixed or hybrid type: it is an informative speech that has a persuasive dimension.

In recent years speeches of good will have played an increasingly important role in the public-relations programs of many business firms. More than eighteen hundred speeches of this kind were made in a single year by representatives of one large Chicago corporation. But business firms are not alone in this practice; schools, churches, and governmental agencies also employ good-will speeches as a means of winning approval and support.

Typical situations requiring speeches for good will

There are many situations in which good-will speeches are appropriate, but the three which follow may be considered typical:

Luncheon-club meetings. Gatherings of this kind, being semisocial in nature and having a "built-in" congenial atmosphere, offer excellent opportunities for presenting good-will talks. Members of such groups—prominent men or women from all walks of business or professional life—are interested in civic affairs and in the workings of other people's professions.

Educational programs. School authorities and leaders of clubs and religious organizations often arrange educational programs for their patrons and members. At such meetings, speakers are asked to talk about the businesses or professions in which they are engaged and to explain to the young people in the audience the opportunities offered and the training required in their respective fields. By use of illustrations and tactful references, a speaker may—while providing the desired information—also create good will for his company or group.

Special demonstration programs. Special programs are frequently presented by government agencies, university extension departments, and business organizations. For example, a wholesale food company may send a representative to a meeting of nutritionists to explain the various kinds of frozen fish that are available, and to demonstrate new ways of preparing or serving them. Although such a speech would be primarily informative, the speaker could win good will indirectly by showing that the particular business or organization desires to increase customer satisfaction with its products or services.

Purpose: Creating good will unobtrusively

Clearly, then, the *real* and the *apparent* aims of the good-will speech differ. Insofar as the audience is concerned, the purpose may appear to be primarily informative. From the speaker's point of view, however, the purpose also is persuasive. As we have noted, by presenting information, the speaker attempts in a subtle and unobtrusive way to gain support for the profession or organization he or she represents.

Formulating the content

In selecting materials for a good-will speech, keep these suggestions in mind:

Present novel and interesting facts about your subject. Make your listeners feel that you are giving them "inside information." Avoid talking about what they already know; concentrate on new developments and facts that are not generally known about your organization.

Show a definite relationship between your subject and the lives of the members of your audience. Make your listeners see the importance of your organization or profession to their safety, success, and happiness.

Offer some definite service. This may be in the form of an invitation to visit your office or shop, or even the simple offer to answer questions or to send brochures.

These suggestions may need to be modified to suit the subject and the occasion. But never lose sight of one fact: Indirectly, you must demonstrate to your listeners that your work or service is of value to them.

ACTING AS CHAIRPERSON[1]

Whether the occasion is a public lecture, a planned entertainment for a dinner meeting of a business or professional group, or a series of speeches at a conference, the success of any program is often largely

---

[1]For the chairperson called upon to conduct a meeting according to parliamentary rules, a concise summary in table form, "Parliamentary Motions," will be found on pp. 328–329. For more complete coverage of these matters, refer to John W. Gray and Richard G. Rea, *Parliamentary Procedure: A Programmed Introduction*, rev. ed. (1974); or *Robert's Rules of Order Newly Revised* (1970) — both published by Scott, Foresman and Company, Glenview, Ill.

determined by the effectiveness with which the chairperson or toast-master presides. A good chairperson does not say much and does not parade an exuberant or domineering personality. However, the audience senses the chairperson's unobtrusive control of the situation and appreciates the efficiency with which the meeting proceeds. Sincerity, energy, and decisiveness—these are the personal qualities which mark the behavior of an effective chairperson.

Commanding the situation

The first duty of a chairperson or toastmaster is to take charge, to command the situation, to be boss without being bossy. A person entrusted with this responsibility has three important obligations: *(a) Make the audience feel that all is going well.* People like to see that things are smoothly organized and running efficiently and to know that someone is in control. *(b) Keep the program moving.* If the chairperson is uncertain or hesitant, people become fidgety, and the meeting starts to drag. But if the chairperson is decisive and keeps things moving, the audience usually will be attentive and orderly. *(c) Discourage unwarranted opposition.* Persons occasionally come to a meeting for the purpose of creating trouble or arbitrarily opposing the plans to be presented. If, however, they see that the presiding officer is in command and if there are no unnecessary or awkward delays in the program, they may be discouraged from carrying out their intention.

Basic responsibilities of the chairperson

If, as chairperson, you are to command the situation, you must prepare yourself in advance of the meeting. Do not trust to the inspiration of the moment merely because you are not the principal speaker. Basically, proceed as follows:

1. Determine the purpose of the meeting. Is it merely to entertain or inform the audience, or are specific proposals or plans to be acted upon?

2. Acquaint yourself with the program. Know who is going to speak or sing or play; know the title of each speaker's talk and the name of each artist's selection; understand the function of each part of the program in advancing the purpose of the whole.

3. Make a time schedule. Determine how long the meeting or program should last; apportion the time among the various persons who are scheduled to appear; and before the meeting begins, tell all participants tactfully exactly how much time they will have at their disposal.

4. Carefully prepare your own remarks. You may have to modify them later, but you must always be ready with something.

5. Start and stop the meeting promptly. Be on time yourself, and make sure that the other program participants are, too; then keep things moving as nearly on schedule as possible.

Incidental duties of the chairperson

In addition to the general duties just described, the presiding officer frequently has three incidental responsibilities: *(a)* setting the keynote, *(b)* performing duties of courtesy, and *(c)* preserving order.

Setting the keynote. At the beginning of a program, it is sometimes difficult to get people settled down and ready to listen. If this is the case, your first duty, of course, is to establish order and to direct the attention of the audience to the platform. Then, with a few carefully chosen remarks, you may proceed to set the proper mood or atmosphere for the meeting.

If the occasion is to be one of fun and good humor, let your opening statement reflect this feeling. If, on the other hand, the occasion has a serious, businesslike purpose, speak quietly and to the point. Mention the aim or objective of the meeting and the organization under whose auspices it is being held. Refer to the background of events that led up to the gathering, and review any special rules or procedures that will prevail. Be careful, however, not to say too much and thereby "steal the thunder" of the speakers who are to follow you. Merely set the stage for them; do not occupy it yourself.

Nor does your duty of setting the proper mood end with your opening remarks. Each time you introduce a new speaker or make any comment at all, you should try to maintain and enhance the mood of the meeting. Do not inject facetious comments which will destroy the serious arguments of a preceding speaker; and in introducing the talk to follow, do not laboriously analyze the intended subject and thus mar the good humor which the next speaker may hope to create. Experience will make you better able to judge the kinds of remarks that are called for. But from the first, common sense combined with alertness to what is happening will provide a reasonably sure guide.

Performing duties of courtesy. As we indicated previously, a presiding officer is frequently expected to perform acts of courtesy for the group he or she represents. Such acts should never take the form of long and elaborate speeches. Often they may be incorporated in your opening remarks or in a brief comment at the close of the meeting. Above all, expressions of courtesy should be sincere. Do not try to exhibit the size of your vocabulary or the fertility of your imagination. Express a genuine welcome or an honest appreciation in simple language, mention one or two pertinent facts, and proceed with the program. Your attitude and the tone of your voice will express your feeling as fully as any words you can say.

Preserving order. If, as chairperson, you strike the appropriate note at the beginning of the meeting and keep the program running smoothly, you will seldom have trouble preserving order. Disorder is more often the result of restlessness than of bad intentions. Therefore, if you notice a disturbance in the audience, do not immediately bark at the offenders; instead, increase the tempo of the program and make your own remarks more lively. You will find in many cases that the commotion will cease.

On rare occasions, in your role as chairperson you may have to administer a reprimand to the entire audience or to someone in it. Do this only as a last resort; but if you are forced to such an extremity, do not be halfhearted about it. In no uncertain terms, let the persons know that they are disturbing the meeting by their actions; then, if they persist, have them ejected by the ushers or the police. It is much better to go through with this unpleasantness than to lose command of the situation entirely. After such an incident has occurred, however, do or say something which will quickly and forcibly call the attention of the audience back to the program, and make no further references to the disturbance.

PROBLEMS FOR FURTHER STUDY

1. Speeches of nomination often follow the motivated sequence. In the *attention step*, the speaker indicates his or her intention to place a name in nomination for a given office; in the *need step*, the qualifications needed by a person holding the office are examined; in the *satisfaction step*, the nominee's qualifications are shown to meet the needs indicated; in the *visualization step*, expected accomplishments of the nominee are projected; and, in the *action step*, the nominee's name is formally put into nomination, often with a call for endorsement. Examine one or more speeches of nomination—frequently found in collections of speeches, in summaries

of national party conventions, and in *The New York Times* — to see if you can discern the motivated sequence at work. Was it altered in any way? Why?

2. Keynote speeches at political conventions are another interesting genre of speechmaking. Read Edwin Miles' article, "The Keynote Speech at National Nominating Conventions" *(Quarterly Journal of Speech*, XLVI [1960]: 26–31). Then, from sources noted in Problem 1, find a more recent keynote speech, and determine if its characteristics are similar to those which Miles identified. Also consider such questions as these: Has keynote speaking changed markedly with nationwide television coverage? Has the lack of strong party unity in recent years affected such speeches? Why are keynote speeches generally delivered by young, rising politicians? As you see it, what is the full range of general and specific purposes served by the keynote speech?

3. Interview a faculty member who serves as chairperson of your campus lecture committee, or a faculty member who frequently introduces visiting lecturers or artists. Ask that person about his or her conception of a good speech of introduction, and about rules or principles which should be followed in introducing speakers.

4. This chapter argued that good-will speeches usually are informative speeches with underlying persuasive purposes. Describe various circumstances under which you think the informative elements should predominate in this type of speech, and then describe other circumstances in which the persuasive elements should be emphasized. In the second case, at what point would you say that the speech becomes openly persuasive in purpose? Or, if you prefer to work with advertisements, scan magazines to find so-called "public service" ads — ones which emphasize what a company is doing to help society with its problems or to promote social-cultural-aesthetic values. Ask yourself similar questions about these advertisements.

ORAL ACTIVITIES AND SPEAKING ASSIGNMENTS

1. Assume that you are to act as chairperson on one of the following occasions (or on some similar occasion):

A student-government awards banquet.
A special program for a meeting of an organization to which you belong.
A kickoff banquet for a schoolwide charity fund-raising program.
A student-faculty mass meeting called to protest a regulation issued by the dean's office.

In your role as chairperson, *(a)* plan a suitable program of speeches or entertainment; *(b)* allocate the amount of time to be devoted to each item on the program; *(c)* outline a suitable speech of introduction for the featured speaker or speakers; *(d)* prepare publicity releases for the local media; *(e)* arrange for press coverage; etc. Work out a complete plan—one that you might show to a steering committee or a faculty adviser. You may divide your responsibilities as chairperson into three phases: "Pre-Event Duties," "Duties at the Event," and "Post-Event Duties"; then comment upon the full range of activities necessary for a chairperson to handle these obligations successfully.

2. Your instructor will prepare a list of special-occasion, impromptu speech topics, such as: "Student X is a visitor from a neighboring school; introduce him/her to this class." "You are Student X; respond to this introduction." "Dedicate your speech-critique forms to the state historical archives." "You have just been named Outstanding Classroom Speaker for this term; accept the award." "You are a representative for a Speech-writers-for-Hire firm; sell your services to other members of the class." You will have between five and ten minutes in which to prepare, and then will give a speech on a topic assigned or drawn from the list. Be ready also to discuss the techniques you employed in putting the speech together.

3. Prepare for delivery in class a five-minute good-will speech on behalf of a campus organization (or some national organization, such as the Boy Scouts or the YWCA) to which you belong. Select "new" and/or little-known facts to present; pay particular attention to maintaining interest; keep your arguments and appeals indirect; and show tact and restraint in your speaking manner. Be prepared to answer questions after your speech is completed.

4. Prepare a five-minute speech paying tribute to:

A man or woman important in national or world history.

A group of volunteers who participated in a successful (or unsuccessful) charity drive.

Someone in your home community or college who, though never famous, contributed in a significant way to the success, well-being, or happiness of many others.

A group of scientists who have just completed an important project.

An outstanding athlete or team which has received state or national recognition.

Founders of an organization for civic betterment.

An especially talented student in your class.

SUGGESTIONS FOR FURTHER READING

Pericles, "Funeral Oration." Reprinted, among other places, in Carroll C. Arnold, Douglas Ehninger, and John C. Gerber, *The Speaker's Resource Book: An Anthology, Handbook, and Glossary* (Glenview: Scott, Foresman and Company, 1966), pp. 191–195. Perhaps the most famous special-occasion speech ever delivered, and still worthy of study.

Eugene E. White, *Practical Public Speaking*, 2nd ed. (New York: The Macmillan Company, 1964), Chapter XV, "Speeches of Special Types," pp. 343–368. A detailed introduction to special-occasion speeches.

Guy R. Lyle and Kevin Guinagh, *I Am Happy to Present: A Book of Introductions* (Bronx, N.Y.: The H. W. Wilson Company, 1953). A formulary approach to speeches of introduction, useful in triggering a wide variety of ideas.

Ronald J. Matlon and Irene R. Matlon, eds., *Table of Contents and Index of National and Regional Speech Communication Journals* (New York: Speech Communication Association, 1971), "Public Address," pp. 170–175. An index to scholarly articles analyzing situational speaking, including special-occasion addresses.

Chapter 13

Communicating with another person

Pᴇʀsᴏɴ-ᴛᴏ-ᴘᴇʀsᴏɴ sᴘᴇᴇᴄʜ ᴛʀᴀɴsᴀᴄᴛɪᴏɴs are, of course, the most common form of oral communication and are also among the most important.[1] Countless numbers of such encounters, ranging from chance street-corner meetings to carefully planned business interviews and diplomatic interchanges, take place every day. This is, moreover, the form of communication with which, by long habit, we are most familiar. It is the form we have used most frequently from the time when, as infants, we made our first efforts to engage the attention of others; and, regardless of our station and vocation as adults, it is doubtless the form we will continue to employ most often throughout our lifetime.

SOME GENERAL PRINCIPLES OF
INTERPERSONAL SPEECH COMMUNICATION

As a rule, a person-to-person speech transaction falls into three discernible steps or stages:[2]

1. An opening period of exploration or "fencing" in which the ice is broken, rapport built, and a working relationship established between the persons involved.

2. A period in which, through the processes of interaction and mutual stimulation, the subject matter of the transaction is explored or its business is conducted.

3. A stage in which the encounter is terminated and closed off.

---

[1]See, for example, Michael Argyle, *Social Interaction* (New York: Aldine-Atherton, Inc., 1969); W. G. Bennis et al., eds., *Interpersonal Dynamics* (Homewood, Ill.: Dorsey Press, 1964); Elihu Katz and Paul Lazarsfeld, *Personal Influence* (Glencoe, Ill.: The Free Press, 1955).

[2]Compare these steps with the "succession of stages of activity" described in C. David Mortensen, *Communication: The Study of Human Interaction* (New York: McGraw-Hill Book Company, 1972), pp. 258–266.

Establishing rapport

If two friends or associates who see each other several times a day come together to discuss a matter of common interest, they may turn to the topic at hand with few if any preliminaries. Usually, however, the parties to a social conversation or a business conference first take a few moments to feel each other out and to build the rapport and good feeling upon which a healthy relationship depends. Long experience, as confirmed by recent research, has isolated a number of factors that are important in this regard.[3] Useful guides for establishing rapport include the following:

Respect existing customs and conventions. In establishing rapport with another person—and especially with a stranger whose status or position is superior to your own—nothing is more important than adhering in a reasonable way to the conventions that normally govern behavior in interpersonal speaking situations. The degree of politeness or formality that should be preserved, how close to the other person you are expected to stand or sit, the degree of intimacy permissible in language and subject matter, whether you may touch your partner physically—all are, to a greater or lesser extent, determined by custom. To violate established procedures in these and similar respects is always to run the risk of alienating the person you are talking with, and hence of getting the relationship off to a strained or halting start.

Find a common bond of interest. If two persons find they have nothing in common, their relationship soon ends and each goes his own way.* On the other hand, if they discover that they both have a

---

[3]On establishing rapport and maintaining interaction in the interpersonal speech encounter, see among other works: David Berlo, *The Process of Communication* (New York: Holt, Rinehart & Winston, Inc., 1960), pp. 106–132; Michael Argyle, *The Psychology of Interpersonal Behavior* (Baltimore: Penguin Books, Inc., 1967), pp. 46–48; John W. Keltner, *Interpersonal Speech Communication* (Belmont, Calif.: Wadsworth Publishing Company, Inc., 1970), pp. 274–275 *et passim;* James C. McCroskey, Carl E. Larson, and Mark L. Knapp, *An Introduction to Interpersonal Communication* (Englewood Cliffs, N.J.: Prentice-Hall, Inc., 1971), pp. 37–53; R. Wayne Pace and Robert R. Boren, *The Human Transaction* (Glenview, Ill.: Scott, Foresman and Company, 1973), pp. 190–199, 309–316; Thomas Scheidel, *Speech Communication and Human Interaction* (Glenview, Ill.: Scott, Foresman and Company, 1972), pp. 238–263.

*Throughout this textbook, as you may have noted, the authors have tried consistently to exclude anything that might be interpreted as "sexism." In this chapter, however, where it has often been imperative to make reference singly to each individual in a two-person transaction, to use in every instance both masculine and feminine pronouns (he or she, him or her, his or hers, etc.) would have created a repetitive, involved, and distractive effect. Therefore, to avoid a cumbersome and awkward style, the authors have elected to use only the masculine form of the third-person singular pronoun.

lively interest in baseball or art or politics, or if they find that they have had similar experiences in military service or foreign travel, they are likely to enter into a long and animated conversation. Take a few minutes to search out the interests of the person you are talking with; and when you find a topic of mutual concern or hit upon a common set of convictions or values, use this as a basis for building a congenial relationship.

Show a genuine interest in the other person. Be interested in the ideas the other person is expressing, and indicate this by giving signs of positive reinforcement. Show by your facial expressions, nods of the head, alertness of bodily posture, and other evidences of attention and openness that you anticipate an interesting and enjoyable interchange.

Put the other person at ease. Whenever you have reason to believe that the other party to an interchange will be uncomfortable or apprehensive, begin by getting him to talk about himself or discuss some subject with which you know he is familiar. Let your own manner show openness and warmth rather than distance and reserve. Call the person by name. Come out from behind a desk or table to take a chair next to his. Indicate by word and manner that you have plenty of time to hear him out or to consider his problem. Offer him coffee or a cigarette, or arrange to conduct your business over lunch. Above all, be at ease yourself. Ease and relaxation are highly contagious: if you yourself appear relaxed, the other person also will tend to be less tense.

Build the other person's confidence in you. Along with doing all you can to put the other person at ease and show interest in what he is saying, build up his confidence in your discretion and good judgment. If you are conversing about a confidential matter, assure him that you will not reveal to others anything he may tell you on a private basis. Give him reason to believe that you will keep any promises you make or carry out any tasks you agree to perform. Do not appear excitable or seem in any way sly or devious. In two-person interaction, as in all other forms of speech communication, the ability to inspire trust is an important asset.

Be open-minded—don't prejudge the other person. Sometimes, on the basis of information that has come to us prior to the encounter, we have a tendency to pigeonhole or stereotype the individual we are talking with. We may have read or heard that he is a flaming liberal or an arch conservative, or been told that he is a nuisance or a bore. We may know that he recently lost two jobs and, therefore, mark him down as "hard to get along with." We may think that because he is a member of an ethnic minority, he has all of the characteristics which the popular imagination attributes to that group. Prior information about a person we are to talk with always is helpful, of course; and if the transaction is an important one, we obviously should try to learn as much about him as we can. We must not, however, make the serious mistake of closing our minds in advance and letting such prejudgments color our thinking during the course of the interchange.

Be natural—avoid pretense and artificiality. One of the best ways to build rapport with another person is simply to be *yourself.* Speak in a natural tone—without assuming "airs." Do not brag or exaggerate. Don't adopt a superior manner or pretend to be what you are not. Nothing causes one to lose face more readily than to have pretenses of this sort exposed.

Be subject- or problem-oriented. Sometimes people engage in interpersonal speech encounters not for the purpose of promoting sociality or exchanging ideas, but rather with the aim of confusing or belittling the other party. They view the transaction as an opportunity to conduct a personal vendetta, to degrade or embarrass their partner, to gratify their own egos, and to demonstrate their own superiority.

Not only are such tactics to be decried on moral grounds, but they also are to be avoided for quite practical reasons. No matter how subtle the techniques employed, sooner or later it nearly always becomes evident to the other individual that your real aim is to attack him. As a result, he "puts up his guard" against you, thus destroying once and for all any possibilities of a harmonious and beneficial relationship.

Ask "open" questions. A simple but effective way to break down another person's initial reserve and establish a productive relationship is to ask "open" rather than "closed" questions. A closed question is one that invites or compels a simple "yes" or "no" response. An open question, on the other hand, asks the respondent to supply information or to express and support an opinion. Instead of asking, "Did you by any chance read the editorial in this morning's paper?" ask "What did you think of the editorial in this morning's paper?" or "How well do the ideas in this morning's editorial agree with your own reactions to the election?" An open question not only requires the quiet or reluctant individual to begin talking, but it also may call forth ideas which will serve as springboards to an interesting conversational exchange.

Try to be an interesting and worthwhile person. A final technique for building rapport in a person-to-person speaking situation is to make as certain as you can that you yourself are an interesting and worthwhile person to talk with. Express original and stimulating ideas, view old facts in a fresh light, link the trite and commonplace with the novel, inject an occasional bit of humor into your remarks. In short, be well informed, alert, and intellectually alive.

SITUATION

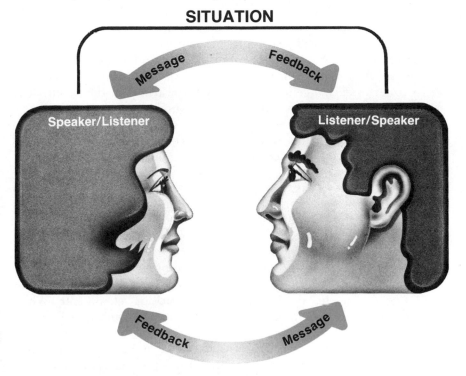

Figure 1. Communicating with Another Person

Maintaining interaction

Good interpersonal communication depends not only on the removal of barriers and the establishment of an initial rapport, but also on a lively exchange of ideas throughout the course of the speech encounter. If one person dominates the conversation or intimidates the other, interaction is impaired, and the speech experience becomes both less satisfying and less productive than it might otherwise be. To generate continuing and productive interaction in a person-to-person speech transaction, observe the following guidelines:

Give timely signs of reassurance. A productive interaction between two people is more likely to be achieved when each of the two feels that he is receiving a fair and sympathetic hearing. Avoid, even in the heat of argument, doing or saying anything that threatens your partner's ego or leads him to believe that you are impatient with him. When you agree with what he is saying, indicate this by your facial expression or a nod of the head. When you disagree, focus your rebuttal on the substance of his remarks rather than on his character or competence. Signs of reassurance often will draw out a shy individual and encourage him to express insights that he might otherwise refrain from advancing.

Share the channel. For the most part, we talk with other individuals in order to exchange ideas or enjoy the warmth of their company. Neither of these objectives can be attained, however, if both persons in the interchange are not given easy access to the communication channel. Do not dominate the conversation to the point that the other person is shut out or merely becomes a sounding board against which your own convictions are tested.

Adapt to the conversation as it develops. Ordinarily, you come to a two-person conversation not knowing exactly what the other person plans to say or how he will react to your ideas. For this reason, person-to-person speech encounters tend to take many unexpected turns and twists. Some persons, seemingly blind to developments, plow ahead minute after minute with comments or arguments they have prepared in advance. As a result, their remarks are often irrelevant and contribute little to advancing the interaction or enriching its contents. When speaking with another individual, be flexible in your approach. Of course, if the conversation is to be an especially important one, settle in your own mind on the points you wish to make and even on a tentative order in which you might present them. But once the interchange has begun, be ready to adjust your plans to the situation *as it develops*. In this way, you will be able to keep the "ball" of conversation passing back and forth, and you will be sure that what you say bears on the point under consideration.

Negotiate differences. Healthy interpersonal relationships cannot be built on a foundation of submerged disagreements or smoldering resentments. When differences arise, instead of pretending they do not exist, bring them into the open and face them frankly. Often a difference can be settled readily and amicably if the issues are laid out and examined. Even if it cannot, it is still better to know where the other person stands and to agree to differ rather than to let buried misunderstandings or disagreements impair the future progress of the conversation.

Be a good listener. In order to speak to the point and carry the conversation toward a satisfying conclusion, you must listen carefully to what the other individual is saying.[4] Do not assume that when he speaks you can relax your attention or spend the time preparing a remark of your own. Concentrate on the ideas he is expressing, evaluate their substance and worth, and relate them to the matter under consideration. Then frame your own response accordingly. Two persons, no matter how profound each may be in his own right, cannot carry on a productive interchange unless each listens attentively to the other.

Balance the desire to control with the willingness to be controlled. Good person-to-person communication is a cooperative enterprise in which the participants are more interested in maintaining a healthy and continuing relationship than in enhancing their own egos or asserting their own superiority. This does not mean that you must give in on every point or violate your convictions simply for the sake of being agreeable. It does, however, mean a willingness to share the direction the conversation takes and the conclusion it reaches. It is useless for two persons to try to exchange ideas or beliefs if one of them insists on dominating every aspect of the discussion.

Search out the other person's "hidden agenda." In many instances, there will be a difference between your partner's actions and his intentions, between what he says or does and what he thinks, between what appear to be and what actually are his motives. When you suspect this to be the case, take time to dig beneath surface appearances and try to find out what his real feelings and intentions are. When he supplies detailed information on a point at issue, is his real aim to share useful knowledge or to display his brilliance? When he concedes a point, is it because he really agrees or because he is merely trying to be congenial? Is he engaging in social conversation not for its own sake, but as a way of softening you up for a "sales pitch"? Fair and objective answers to such questions are important if you are to assess accurately the progress and outcome of a speech encounter.

Reduce your own defensiveness. It is natural for all of us to protect our own ego and to resent unjustified attacks on it. Self-protectiveness is not, however, to be confused with the excessive sensitivity or defensiveness which leads an individual to interpret every comment as a slur or personal put-down. When talking with another person, get your

---

[4]Review the principles of good listening presented in Chapter 2, pp. 20–33.

mind off yourself. Don't "carry a chip on your shoulder." If you set out to look for slights and deprecations every time you converse with someone else, you will almost certainly find them. Productive interaction in person-to-person speech communication depends in large part upon keeping an objective attitude not only toward the subject and the person you are discussing it with, but also toward yourself.

Respect and trust the other person. Any person who is worth talking with is deserving of trust and respect. Much of what we have just said about building rapport and maintaining interaction comes down to this simple rule: *Understand, respect, and trust your partner; treat him as you wish him to treat you.* Respect his right so speak up in behalf of what he believes. Respect his feelings and sensibilities. Assume him to be a person of integrity and good will. Sometimes, of course, your assumptions will be proved wrong. To start with suspicion and distrust, however, is to condemn the relationship to failure without giving it a fair chance.

Terminating the transaction

The third stage in a person-to-person speech encounter is its termination or conclusion. Here, too, certain principles and guidelines should be observed; namely:

Know when to terminate the conversation. Even the most interesting interchange between two people can become tiresome if continued for too long. Many persons who are fascinating conversationalists in every other respect never seem to know when to stop talking—when to break off the interaction, or to rise, thank their hostess, and depart. Develop a sense of *timing.* Sense when the business of an interpersonal interchange has been completed or when your partner begins to tire, and excuse yourself at this point. By continuing longer you may lose all you have gained in the way of understanding, persuading, or building and maintaining good will.

Observe the appropriate conventions. Observing the appropriate customs and conventions is important not only when opening a conversation, but also when closing it. You are expected, of course, to thank your host or hostess at the end of a social event or to thank the individual who has granted you a business or professional interview. Likewise, when breaking off a conversation, tell the other person you have enjoyed talking with him. To ignore these and similar conventions is to display poor manners and run the risk of undoing any progress you may have made or benefit you may have achieved earlier.

Person-to-person speech transactions include everything from intimate whispers to formal, structured interviews. They are unique because, in every instance, they involve only two people, each of whom is the focus of attention of the other, and each of whom is responsible for giving and responding to feedback.

Summarize the progress and outcomes. If the interchange had for its purpose the reaching of an agreement or settling upon a course of action, generally you should take a few moments at its close to summarize the points on which you have reached agreement or to review the unresolved differences. This helps to ensure that both of you understand matters in the same way; and if action is required, both of you will know exactly what to do in carrying it out.

Arrange for the next encounter. If two persons who meet to solve a problem or review a situation are unable to conclude their business at a single encounter, they should not separate before agreeing as to when and where they will meet again. They should also determine in general how they will proceed at their next encounter. This will help not only to make the subsequent meeting more efficient, but will also enable each one to plan his contributions in a more purposeful manner.

INTERVIEWS

The term *interview* is commonly used to refer to that type of speech communication in which two persons *prearrange* an encounter and in which at least one of the two has a serious, preconceived purpose and seeks to achieve that purpose by eliciting appropriate verbal responses from the other.[5] Because at least one of the two individuals (and, often, both) has this serious, preconceived purpose, interviews differ from random, unstructured "social conversations" where, as a rule, congeniality and enjoyment are the primary ends.

Interviews serve a variety of purposes and are widely used in such activities as selling, counseling, problem solving, polling of public opinion, providing medical diagnosis, and giving psychiatric therapy. Here, however, we shall be concerned with only two of the most important and basic types: (1) *the information-seeking interview and* (2) *the job-seeking interview.*

THE INFORMATION-SEEKING INTERVIEW

A well-managed information-seeking interview requires careful planning and purposive analysis of the nature and extent of the data desired, and normally involves seven separate but related tasks:

---

[5] Adapted from Robert S. Goyer, W. Charles Redding, and John T. Rickey, *Interviewing Principles and Techniques* (Dubuque, Iowa: Wm. C. Brown Company, Publishers, 1968), p. 6.

1. Selecting the informant.
2. Obtaining the informant's cooperation.
3. Learning about the informant.
4. Developing a plan or procedure.
5. Formulating specific questions and tactics.
6. Conducting the interview.
7. Interpreting and evaluating the results.[6]

Selecting the informant

Although selecting the informant—the person from whom information is to be sought—may appear to be a simple matter, this is not always the case. If your subject is a controversial one and you intend to interview only one informant, try to choose someone who will approach the subject with reasonable objectivity and be able to give you all relevant points of view. If you plan to gather the necessary information from a large number of individuals, select them at random or choose those most likely to represent all prevailing shades of opinion. In every instance, pick your informant or informants with care. The data you gather will be no more reliable than the persons with whom you talk.

Obtaining the informant's cooperation

If you wish to interview a busy or important individual, usually you will obtain better results if you get in touch with him in advance. Write or telephone for an appointment, telling him your purpose and explaining why you think he can supply you with the desired information. Promise to keep his identity confidential if he wants you to do so; and if you would like to tape all or a part of the conversation, be sure to get his permission. Promise also that, if he prefers, you will let him check over any written materials in which you quote him directly. If the person or persons you wish to interview are employed by someone higher up or are subject to the authority of another person, be sure to take the steps necessary to obtain that individual's permission before proceeding.

Learning about the informant

Between the time you obtain permission to conduct an interview and the time the interview actually takes place, find out as much as you can

---

[6]Compare these steps with those found in Raymond L. Gorden, *Interviewing Strategy, Techniques, and Tactics* (Homewood, Ill.: Dorsey Press, 1969), pp. 42–48.

about the person you will be talking with. What is his current position? What positions has he previously held? What books or articles has he written? Has he been interviewed on this same subject or similar ones before? What opinions has he expressed? Information of this kind will help you frame more pertinent questions and will also help you interpret and evaluate the responses you receive.

Developing a plan or procedure

An interview, like any other important speech transaction, requires planning and preparation. To enter upon it unprepared will in most instances waste the time of your informant and greatly reduce the profit you derive.

Clarifying and focusing your purpose. Before you make detailed plans for an interview, get clearly in mind the precise purpose you wish to achieve. *What is it that you want to know?* Do you wish to learn more about the early history and development of the subject? About its economic or social aspects? About its moral and ethical implications? Are you interested in digging out new facts or do you want interpretation of facts you already know? Only when a definite and focused purpose is clear in your own mind can you hope to elicit from your informant those facts and judgments which will be of maximum use to you.

Choosing the format of the interview. With your specific purpose clarified and information about your informant carefully gathered, you are ready to choose the format you will follow in conducting the interview itself.[7] Although many variations are possible, the formats from which you may select are basically these: (1) the structured interview, (2) the nonstructured interview, and (3) the guided interview.

In the *structured interview,* each of the questions you wish to ask and the exact sequence in which you will ask them are determined in advance. Usually, the questions are written out word for word, and you read them to the informant, noting his responses in spaces provided for this purpose.

The *nonstructured interview,* though also carefully planned and aimed at achieving a specific purpose, is more flexible, allowing you to word your questions as you go along and to determine the most productive order in which to ask them.

---

[7] In this connection, see Stephen A. Richardson, Barbara Snell Dohrenwend, and David Klein, *Interviewing: Its Forms and Functions* (New York: Basic Books, Inc., Publishers, 1965), pp. 32–55.

The *guided interview* strikes a balance between the structured and the nonstructured formats. Although most or all of your questions may be worded and arranged in a preferred sequence, you are free to depart from your plan in order to follow up on interesting points, or to skip matters you had planned to bring up but on which your informant is reluctant to talk.

Choose the interview format by considering its suitability to the purpose you wish to achieve, the subject you are investigating, and the qualifications of the informant. The format preferred by the informant (if that information can be ascertained) should, of course, weigh heavily in the choice of the procedure to be followed. In any case, however, always have a definite format in mind before you begin an interview and stay with that arrangement until you have good reason to abandon it.

Formulating specific questions and tactics. Regardless of the format you select, you will find it important to settle on the principal questions you wish to raise and to determine at least tentatively the order in which they might best be introduced. See to it that your questions are clear, specific, and to the point, and that the majority of them are of the "open" rather than the "closed" variety. Plan to begin the interview with questions likely to arouse the interest of the informant and stimulate him to start talking freely. Save for last the questions that probe into difficult or sensitive matters. Finally, think over your plan again to make certain that any question which logically grows out of a previous answer or which assumes a certain set of facts will not be asked until the proper groundwork has been laid.[8]

Conducting the interview

In conducting the interview itself, bear in mind the following "do's" and "don't's":[9]

Be on time. When a busy person does you the courtesy of agreeing to an interview, the least you can do is to appear at the appointed time.

---

[8]For further discussions of the question-answer process in the interview situation, see Robert D. Brooks, *Speech Communication* (Dubuque, Iowa: Wm. C. Brown Company, Publishers, 1971), pp. 129–134; W. V. D. Bingham, B. V. Moore, and J. W. Gustad, *How to Interview* (New York: Harper & Row, Publishers, 1959), p. 74; and Stephen A. Richardson, Barbara Snell Dohrenwend, and David Klein, *Interviewing: Its Forms and Functions* (New York: Basic Books, Inc., Publishers, 1965), pp. 138–217.

[9]Compare the advice given here with that found in John W. Keltner, *Interpersonal Speech Communication* (Belmont, Calif.: Wadsworth Publishing Company, Inc., 1970), pp. 276–280.

Remember that in supplying information you desire, he is helping *you;* you are not helping him.

Restate your purpose. Even though you already have told the informant your purpose in a prior letter or phone call, take a minute or two at the outset to remind him and also to make clear why you think he can be of help. This will strengthen the focus of the interview and direct the informant's attention to the areas you are most interested in.

Observe not only "what" the informant says, but also "how" he says it. The vocal tone or inflection with which the informant makes a response may be highly revealing of his attitude on a given point—whether he regards it as important or unimportant, desirable or undesirable, etc. Changes in his facial expression and bodily posture provide similar cues. These kinds of *feedback* are basic to all successful communicative interaction and must be taken into careful account when you are trying to interpret an informant's comments and draw correct conclusions about him and the answers he is giving to your questions.

Move the interview ahead at a lively pace. Don't rush the informant, but don't let the conversation drag or die. When one question has been answered to your satisfaction, move on to the next one without a long and awkward pause or undue shuffling of notes and papers. Preserve a businesslike manner at all times, avoiding side issues or wandering into matters totally unrelated to the topic you are exploring.

Respect your informant's time. When you have concluded the last of the questions you wish to ask, terminate the interview and depart. To prolong the interaction unduly is to run the needless risk of sinking into trivial matters or retreading ground already covered.

Terminate the interview with thanks. Don't forget to thank your informant as you depart. Also assure him once again that you will not reveal anything he has told you in confidence and that, if he desires, you will give him an opportunity to approve of any passages in which you quote him directly.

Make a record of what transpired. Either during the course of the interview or immediately thereafter, when everything the informant said is still fresh in your mind, make a record of his remarks. You will be surprised at how much you may forget after only a short time.

Don't request an interview until you are already well informed on the subject. The more you know about it, the more intelligent and provocative your questions will be and the better you will be able to evaluate your informant's responses. As a rule, an interview should not be scheduled until you are well along with your other research into the topic. It should never be used as a way of avoiding the thorough study of printed sources or the gathering of information by firsthand observation.

Don't parade your own knowledge of the subject. Your purpose in requesting an interview is to get information from the respondent, not to give it. Demonstrate your knowledge of the subject by asking intelligent questions, but do not use the encounter as an excuse for "showing off" your own brilliance.

Don't reveal your doubts or disagreements in point of view. If your informant says something with which you disagree or which you believe to be wrong, keep your feelings to yourself. Do not frown, shake your head, or look skeptical. Above all, do not argue with him about the matter. Remember that your purpose is to get your informant's view of the subject — not to expound or defend your own.

Interpreting and evaluating the results

The final step in an information-seeking interview consists of *interpreting* and *evaluating* what your informant has told you. To make the necessary interpretations and evaluations you may have to draw inferences and conclusions from data he has supplied. Compare his opinions with those expressed by other persons. Think back over the conversation to spot subtle evidences of bias or partisanship which went undetected during the interview itself. Sometimes you will need to decide how certain statements of fact are to be classified or categorized. In any event, do not consider your task complete until you have reviewed in your own mind all the informant has said and determined its meaning and worth as you understand them.

THE JOB-SEEKING INTERVIEW

How well you acquit yourself in an interview with a prospective employer will, as a rule, be the key to success when you are applying for a job of any kind. Indeed, if the job under consideration is really important to you, in few situations in life will your speaking skills be more important or your success as a communicator more readily evident.[10]

---

[10]See, for example, Harry Walker Hepner, *Psychology Applied to Life and Work,* 4th ed. (Englewood Cliffs, N.J.: Prentice-Hall, Inc., 1966), pp. 239–257, 301–321; Robert S. Goyer, W. Charles Redding, and John T. Rickey, *Interviewing Principles and Techniques* (Dubuque, Iowa: Wm. C. Brown Company, Publishers, 1968); Roger M. Bellows, *Employment Psychology: The Interview* (New York: Holt, Rinehart & Winston, Inc., 1954); and Walter Van Dyke Bingham and Bruce Victor Moore, *How to Interview,* 3rd rev. ed. (New York: Harper & Row, Publishers, 1941).

Communicative purposes of the job-seeking interview

On relatively rare occasions, an employer will have determined in advance that a particular person is well qualified to fill a position, and will use the interview to try to persuade that person to accept an offer. More commonly, however, the direction is reversed; and the applicant tries to induce the employer to hire him. From this, however, we must not conclude that in the job-seeking interview the applicant's purpose is simply to persuade. Usually, both the interviewer and the applicant also want *to inform* and *to be informed* and to have an opportunity *to know and appraise* each other. For this reason, a job-seeking interview typically goes through five steps or phases: (1) *initiation,* (2) *investigation,* (3) *negotiation,* (4) *actuation,* and (5) *termination.* (We call your particular attention at this time to the sample job-seeking interview on pages 381–387, which is analyzed according to these steps.)

Process phases of the job-seeking interview

Initiation. In the first phase of the interview, the participants meet, exchange greetings, introduce themselves, and perform the expected courtesies. They try to "break the ice," to reduce the necessarily formal atmosphere somewhat, to "personalize" it, to put each other at ease, and to get the interview off to a good start.

Investigation. As the interviewer and the applicant endeavor to sustain and advance the interaction, they move into an *investigative* phase. They begin to "feel each other out," to determine what the other is like. They attempt to find out what interests the other, how quickly or strongly he reacts to certain stimulus-statements. They ask and answer questions—tentatively at first, and then with increasing confidence and openness. They try to discover topics that may be pursued "safely" and profitably, to detect promising lines of inquiry on which the other is likely to converse freely. The applicant begins to sense what the interviewer is after and tries to provide appropriate responses.

Negotiation. If both interviewer and applicant feel that the employment goal is possible and mutually attractive, the process next moves into the *negotiative* phase. When the job is an unusually important one or the employment conditions and remunerations are more than ordinarily complex, this phase may be lengthy and detailed. Usually, however, the interviewer describes the exact nature of the job and explains and interprets—within broad outlines at least—the employer's policies, procedures, pay schedules, and fringe benefits. The applicant, for his part, gives some indication to the interviewer that he has an interest in the job as outlined (but not yet offered), or that he really is not interested, or that he might be interested subject to certain conditions. As yet, however, the interviewer has not made an actual job-offer, nor has the applicant made a definite commitment one way or the other.

Actuation. Clearly now the interaction stands at the climactic moment. A decision must be *made*, and it must be *actuated*. To hire or not to hire, to accept or not to accept—this is the crux. Customarily, the interviewer makes the move. If he doesn't, however, and if the investigative phase is clearly at an end, the applicant may decide to venture a carefully phrased question, something like: "I've been wondering . . . if it turns out that you're interested in my possibilities for the job, when would you want me to start work?"

Frequently, in actual practice, a flat offer and acceptance do not materialize in an interview of this kind. Typically, the outcome may take one of three turns: (1) *outright employment or rejection,* (2) *referral to another person* for a second or follow-up interview, or (3) *deferral or postponement* of a final offer or acceptance until a designated future date.

Quite often, for example, after a tentative offer has been extended and the applicant has tentatively indicated his satisfaction with it, the interviewer may say, in substance: "I like very much what I have seen and heard so far. But if we agree you're to have the job and if you agree to take it, you'll be working closely with the manager of Department X, Ms. Soandso. I'd like you to meet and talk with her before we make a final decision."

Or, again, he may say, "A number of other applicants are interested in this job, and I've promised to talk with them, too. I think, therefore, we'll have to defer making a final choice until Friday of next week." Regardless, however, of whether the decision at *this* time is acceptance, referral, deferral, or rejection, the actuative stage of the interview is finished, and the process now moves into its concluding phase.

Termination. In the terminating phase of the interaction, the pair observe the conventional courtesies of thanking each other, the applicant for the opportunity and consideration given by the interviewer, the interviewer for the interest, information, and time given by the applicant. If the ultimate decision has been referred to another person, there should be a clear understanding as to the time and place for the next interview, with whom it will be, etc. If the decision has been deferred, there should be an expressed understanding as to when it is likely to be forthcoming, where, and from what source.

Although this terminating phase is typically brief and may sometimes appear to be anticlimactic, do not undervalue its importance. The effects of an interview, like the effects of other speech communications, have a way of lasting far beyond the moment of their immediate conclusion. If the interaction can be made to end on an air of friendliness, good will, and mutual respect, there is always a chance that there may be future openings for which the applicant may be considered or for which he may wish to re-apply.

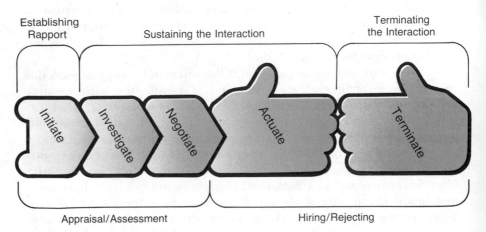

Figure 2. Process Phases of the Job-Seeking Interview

The applicant

To this point, we have been describing the job-seeking interview in general terms, as a process of progressive interaction between the person seeking and the person offering employment. Let us now look at the process specifically from the point of view of the applicant. What questions should you ask yourself when preparing for a job-seeking interview? How should you conduct yourself as the interview proceeds? Against what criteria or standards should you measure your performance and estimate your probable success?

Questions the applicant should ask himself or herself. In a study reported by Harry Walker Hepner in his *Psychology Applied to Life and Work,* one hundred college students and graduates who had applied for positions were asked to list what worried them most before, during, and after their employment interviews.[11] The concerns reported centered, for the most part, on such factors as *lack of experience, truth-telling, self-presentation, salary, reasons for applying, job details, nervousness,* and *judging the probable success of the interview and its results.* To allay such concerns and to ready yourself for participating in a job-seeking interview, try to evolve acceptable answers to the following questions:

1. How can I best determine the approach to take with this interviewer?
2. How can I "sell" myself — my qualifications and capabilities?
3. Should I admit that I have no work experience?
4. How do I answer, "What can you *do?*"
5. Without any experience, how can I convince a prospective employer of what I can do?
6. How can I answer, "Why did you choose this type of work?"
7. Should I talk freely and frankly about what I consider my abilities?
8. How can I best emphasize my scholastic achievements — since, at this time, that's really all I have?
9. How can I overcome the nervousness I'm almost sure I'll have before and during the interview?
10. What can I, as probably the younger and "lesser" party to the interview, do to help create a friendly, informal atmosphere?
11. While being interviewed, should I ask questions about the job until I thoroughly understand all that is involved?
12. Or should I wait until I get the job and am able to see for myself what's required of me?
13. Am I able to do, actually, what this job requires?
14. Will I find the work rewarding in other than a financial sense?
15. Will I fit in? Will I like the people I will be working with?
16. Am I sure — or making sure now — that I am aware of the difficulties and disadvantages of the job and am ready to cope with them?
17. How can I tell whether I'm making a good impression on the interviewer and giving him the "right" answers?
18. How can I tell that I'm getting accurate answers to the questions *I* am asking?
19. Should I try while being interviewed to determine what the job offers in terms of employee advancement and its probable rapidity?
20. What is the best way to answer, "What salary do you expect?"
21. How am I to know that I'm not asking too much or too little?
22. Or should I say, "Well, from my study of the pay rates in this field, the *range* for this type of job appears to be somewhere between

---

[11]Harry Walker Hepner, *Psychology Applied to Life and Work,* 4th ed. (Englewood Cliffs, N.J.: Prentice-Hall, Inc., 1966), pp. 247–248.

$_____ and $_____. How well does that align with what you as an employer have in mind?"
23. During the interaction, should I attempt to introduce the names of persons who would recommend me?
24. At what point in the interview do I ask the interviewer, "Do I get the job?"
25. How can I judge the success of the interview?[12]

If you think carefully about questions such as these, you not only will give a better account of yourself during the course of the interview, but also can better decide whether to accept the position if offered.

Some useful guidelines for the applicant. In general, your behavior before and during the job-seeking interview should be guided by the principles of productive interpersonal interaction described in the opening pages of this chapter. In addition, you should try to observe the following specific recommendations:

1. If you have not previously supplied a personal data sheet or filled out a job-application form, *bring a summary of your training and experience to the interview itself* so the prospective employer may study and use it for reference. Do not, however, make this resume or summary too long and detailed. Organize the information clearly and stress the points which bear directly on the job for which you are applying. Do not forget to include the names of three or four persons to whom he can write or telephone for recommendations.

2. If appropriate to the job-seeking circumstances, *also bring to the interview a sample of your work:* a drawing or design you have made, a report you have prepared, an article, term paper, or story you have written—something you have created. Leave these materials with the interviewer if he wishes to study them further.

3. In the initiatory and also in the early part of the investigative phase at least, *let the interviewer take the initiative, set the general tone and direction of the interaction, and draw you out in his own way.* He may be deciding not only whether to hire you, but also considering the department to which you might best be assigned, how well you compare with other employees in the same age bracket, etc. For many good reasons unknown to

---

[12]The questions here presented are derived in part from Hepner, but the list has been modified and expanded on the basis of the authors' own observations.

you, he may lead the discussion into fields that seem to you remote from the business at hand and even prefer to do much of the talking himself.[13] Later, the balance of the interaction will undoubtedly shift and "equalize" in ways that will give you an opportunity to voice your questions and concerns.

4. Show a knowledge of the business or institution the employer represents. Be able to discuss its past history, its present condition, and its future prospects. Understand the philosophy by which it is guided and the policies to which it adheres.

5. Focus on what you can do for the employer, not what he can do for you. Inquire about working conditions, fringe benefits, vacations, and the like, but make it clear that you are more interested in doing a good job and in meriting the confidence he may place in you.

6. Don't oversell yourself by asserting that you are sure you can "do anything" the employer asks, or can solve any problem that arises. *Be confident, but modest.* In no way suggest that the job is beneath your abilities or that you are interested in it only because you can find nothing better.

7. Use good speech and correct grammar. *Be courteous.* Say "yes, sir" or "yes, ma'am." Look directly at the interviewer as you talk. Be poised and alert.

8. In those portions of the interview where the subject and context indicate that you should lead the conversation, tell the interviewer about yourself and point out those aspects of your training and experience that particularly qualify you for the job opening. Then *ask intelligent questions about the nature of the work, company policy and procedures, and opportunities for advancement.*[14] Many experienced interviewers believe they can tell more about a person by the questions he asks than from any other single source of information.

9. Do not become so interested in getting the job that you lose sight of your own best interests. During the course of the conversation, elicit from the interviewer the information and—to the greatest extent possible—the commitments you desire. Remember that any employment interview not only provides

---

[13]Francis E. Drake, *Manual for Employment Interviewing,* Research Report No. 9 (New York: American Management Association, n.d.), pp. 12–14.

[14]Walter Van Dyke Bingham and Bruce Victor Moore, *How to Interview,* 3rd rev. ed. (New York: Harper & Row, Publishers, 1941), p. 83.

the employer with a chance to size you up, but it is also an opportunity for you to size up him and the institution he represents.

Profile of an effective applicant. In line with what has been said about the nature of the employment interview and the concerns and objectives of the job seeker, you should be able now to construct a picture-profile of an ideal applicant.[15] Measure yourself against the criteria it includes. In proportion as you are able to satisfy them, your chances of success in a job search should be greatly increased.

You know the kind of work you want and can perform. You know *why* you want the job—what your short-range and long-range *goals* are. You cannot hope to "sell" yourself and your qualifications unless you know what you have to offer.

You are well informed. You have read books, papers, and trade or professional journals having to do with your vocation and career. You have studied your potential employer's organization, its scope, and history. You are familiar with his product or service, his vital interests, and at least a few of his problems.

You want to make a contribution to the organization you work for.

You know that ideas are a rare commodity, and so you have trained yourself to *think* and *analyze* as well as to *do.*

You are proud of your abilities and capabilities and eager to talk about them if invited to do so, but you are modest. You do not boast, overestimate yourself, or promise obviously impossible results.

You conceive of the interview as a transactional process, and you are alert and well prepared to cooperate with the interviewer in moving it forward in positive, productive directions.

You are fully aware that the effective applicant must be able not only to give intelligent and knowledgeable answers, but must also ask sensible, information-gathering questions—about the job, company potential and policies, growth opportunities, pay scales, employee-evaluation frequency, fringe benefits, etc.

---

[15]For an analysis of negative traits in an applicant and their effect on the success of the job-seeking interview, see Charles S. Goetzinger, "An Analysis of Irritating Factors in Initial Employment Interviews of Male College Graduates" (Ph.D. diss., Purdue University, 1959). Reported in William D. Brooks, *Speech Communication* (Dubuque, Iowa: Wm. C. Brown Company, Publishers, 1971), p. 139.

You have determined in advance of the interview some of the questions you will ask, and you have also planned two or three useful approaches you will take when and as opportunities arise.

You tell the truth about your background and qualifications even if your answers are disadvantageous to you and your cause.

You give careful attention to the clarity and intelligibility of your speech and language because effective communication so largely depends upon these qualities.

You use good judgment about such matters as your personal appearance and appropriateness of dress, bodily cleanliness, neatness, and the conventional courtesies because most people—including employers—are strongly influenced by first impressions.

You know what the "going" wage and salary ranges are for the kind of work you will be doing. While you recognize that, at least until you have proved your worth, the employer is entitled to start you "low," you also recognize that you are entitled to have your performance and contribution reevaluated on a regular basis and to receive deserved remuneration accordingly.

You are open, sincere, honest, and friendly, conducting yourself always as you would in any polite and businesslike conversation.

PROBLEMS FOR FURTHER STUDY

1. In your Personal Speech Journal, keep a log of all person-to-person speech transactions in which you take part during an entire day. For each encounter, note especially the following factors: (*a*) the relationship between you and the other person as that relationship is structured by the societal position or power held by each of you; (*b*) your communicative goals and the goals of the other person; and (*c*) the extent to which you feel these goals were accomplished.

2. Observe an information-seeking interview. (A televised interview or "talk show" may prove a fruitful source.) Describe and evaluate the overall performance of the interviewer, indicating as much as you can about his or her skill in handling the "do's" and "don't's" suggested on pages 295–297.

3. Inconspicuously observe one or more person-to-person exchanges at a party, in the student union, in a restaurant, or in some similar place.

Analyze the encounters in terms of: *(a)* the apparent purposes of each person; *(b)* the opening, maintenance, and terminating tactics used by each; and *(c)* the degree to which each person apparently follows the advice given in this chapter. Finally, evaluate this chapter's advice on communicating with another person: Is it adequate? Is it realistic? Do "real-world" encounters—especially the ones you deem "successful"—follow the patterns suggested, or would you want to "correct" the textbook?

4. Choose a public personality whom you would like to interview, employing a *structured* format. Prepare a list of questions suitable for this individual, situation, and purpose. Your questions should reveal *(a)* your exact purpose in conducting the interview and *(b)* the adequacy of your preliminary research with reference to the basic subject and the qualifications of the informant to provide helpful information regarding it.

ORAL ACTIVITIES AND SPEAKING ASSIGNMENTS

1. As a class, prepare a list of "fencing" techniques—that is, of remarks commonly used in opening an interaction with another person. Then probe the significances of this list by answering such questions as:
   a. What *topics* tend to be mentioned most frequently: recent events? physical surroundings? personalized references to the other person? reportive statements about your own internal states of mind?
   b. What *purposes* are revealed in your lists: desire to meet a person whom you don't know intimately? need to pass the time with another who just happens to be near you (as in an elevator)? hope that you can secure something from someone else?
   c. What kind of *interaction* will each of these types of remarks probably generate: a short, quick exchange? a one-sided conversation dominated by you or the other person? an earnest discussion demanding considerable time? a transaction inviting others to join you?

2. Set up an appointment for an information-seeking interview with an "expert," and use some portion of the opinions, facts, etc., you get from it in your next speech. (Deans, career specialists, sales and business personnel, political figures, etc.—all are normally accessible for interviews.) Follow this chapter's advice on information-seeking interviews, and—in either a class report or an entry in your journal—describe and evaluate your own abilities as an interviewer.

3. Pair off with another member of the class and engage in a job-seeking interview in which you demonstrate the principles and guidelines set forth in this chapter. With your partner, agree upon *(a)* the assignment of roles of interviewer and applicant, *(b)* a description of the specific job or position to be sought, *(c)* the nature of the company doing the hiring,

(d) the experiential and educational requirements for that job, and *(e)* the personal qualifications needed by the applicant.

Exchange no further information. Prepare *separately* for your in-class presentation which should simulate, insofar as possible, a "real-life" job-seeking interview. At the conclusion of demonstration interviews, the entire class should react to the participants' general effectiveness and ineffectiveness, and should suggest possible factors responsible for the results. (As part of your preparation for this activity, you may wish to study the sample job-seeking interview on pages 381–387.)

SUGGESTIONS FOR FURTHER READING

Castiglione, *The Book of the Courtier*. A delightful guide to dyadic communication in the Italian Renaissance, especially revealing in what it implies about a culture's effect upon communicative encounters with another person.

Eric Berne, *Games People Play: The Psychology of Human Relationships* (New York: Grove Press, Inc., 1964). A probe into the states of mind of people who avoid directness and honesty in their contacts with others, including a wide variety of "games" played.

Charles J. Stewart and William B. Cash, *Interviewing: Principles and Practices* (Dubuque, Iowa: Wm. C. Brown Company, Publishers, 1974). A textbook treating informational, persuasive, employment, appraisal, and counseling interviewing.

Erving Goffman, *Interaction Ritual: Essays on Face-to-Face Behavior* (Garden City, N.Y.: Doubleday & Company, Inc., 1967), "On Face-Work," pp. 5–46. A difficult-but-rewarding examination of interpersonal communicative maneuvering.

Karen Krupar, *Communication Games* (New York: The Free Press, 1973). A structured textbook illustrating important interpersonal communication principles through game simulations.

Irving J. Rein, *Rudy's Red Wagon: Communication Strategies in Contemporary Society* (Glenview, Ill.: Scott, Foresman and Company, 1972). A popularized, provocative treatment of various forms of interpersonal manipulation that are prevalent today.

William W. Wilmot and John R. Wenburg, *The Personal Communication Process* (New York: John Wiley & Sons, Inc., 1973), and their *Communication Involvement: Personal Perspectives* (New York: John Wiley & Sons, Inc., 1974). A textbook and reader expanding discussion of the "transactional approach" to communication treated in this chapter.

Cómmunicating in small groups

INCREASINGLY THE FUNCTIONS of government, business, industry, and education are carried on by small groups of people meeting as committees, boards, or councils. Politicians, legislators, corporate executives, teachers, ministers, social workers, hardhats, community-action leaders—indeed, persons from all walks of life utilize small group communication to explore subjects, identify problems, and initiate constructive courses of action. As a result, the need to become a skilled communicator in the small group situation is more important today than at any earlier period in history.

From your previous experience with communicating in groups— in the classroom and in social, religious, and campus organizations— you undoubtedly have discovered that merely having a number of people talk over a matter does not always produce the desired result. Sometimes an intelligent or experienced individual can grasp a situation or solve a problem more efficiently when working alone. On the other hand, a collective judgment is often superior to an individual one: a group is more likely than an individual to take into account all aspects of a question; a group decision is more democratic than an individual decision; and, since people tend to support decisions which they have helped frame, a group decision is more likely to produce permanent and satisfying results.[1]

The efficiency and productivity of group communication, as of any cooperative activity, can be increased if the participants plan for the session in advance and are familiar with methods of participation

---

[1] On the relationship between group consensus and subsequent behavior of the discussants, as well as on the group communication process in general, see especially Warren G. Bennis et al., *Interpersonal Dynamics: Essays and Readings in Human Interaction*, rev. ed. (Homewood, Ill.: Dorsey Press, 1968); Dorwin Cartwright and Alvin Zander, eds., *Group Dynamics: Research and Theory*, 2nd ed. (New York: Harper & Row, Publishers, 1960); Robert S. Cathcart and Larry A. Samovar, eds., *Small Group Communication* (Dubuque, Iowa: Wm. C. Brown Company, Publishers, 1970); Joseph Luft, *Group Processes: An Introduction to Group Dynamics* (Palo Alto, Calif.: National Press Books, 1970).

and leadership. The purpose of this chapter is to help you gain an understanding of the principles upon which successful discussion rests.

TYPES OF GROUP COMMUNICATION

The two most common types of group communication are (1) *learning discussions* and (2) *decision-making discussions.*

Learning discussions

In a learning discussion, the participants exchange information and ideas in order to increase their understanding of a subject. As a rule, this type of group communication is not very rigidly structured. A recognized expert may give a speech or lecture in order to introduce the subject, but the participants devote most of their time to an informal exchange of facts and ideas. Their purpose is to learn from one another.

A common type of learning discussion takes place in the college classroom. Another occurs when men and women in the same business or profession talk about their experiences, review recent developments, or consider publications of common interest. In addition, members of social clubs, religious organizations, and civic groups often conduct learning discussions on matters of mutual concern. Essentially, then, this type of group communication serves an information-enhancing or fact-finding function.

Decision-making discussions

In a decision-making discussion, the aim is to arrive at an agreement concerning a future policy or course of action. The president of an organization calls a meeting of the executive committee or board of directors so that the group may hear reports and determine policies. The business manager of a student dramatic organization gathers the group's officers to establish the budget for the next play or to work out a ticket-selling campaign. The rules committee of a women's self-government association meets to revise the regulations governing women students. In these instances and countless others, small group communication is used to make decisions and to evolve policies.

ESSENTIALS FOR EFFECTIVE COMMUNICATION IN GROUPS

Group communication, to be productive, places certain demands upon *(a)* the group as a whole, *(b)* the individual participant or discussant, and *(c)* the leader of the group. Each of these components should bring to the discussion process a number of essential qualities and should assume particular responsibilities for its success.

Essentials for the group as a whole

The first essential for profitable group communication is *order.* This does not imply great formality; indeed, formality is often undesirable. It does imply, however, that only one person talk at a time, that members be courteous, and that they keep their remarks relevant. A second essential is *cooperation.* If one person monopolizes the discussion, it usually will get nowhere. Participants must be willing to share the speaking time and to listen to views at variance with their own. A third essential, in group decision-making particularly, is a *willingness to compromise.* There are times, of course, when compromise is not desirable; but reasonable concessions hurt no one and sometimes are the only way of reaching an agreement. Finally, the group should have a *feeling of accomplishment.* Unless the members believe they are getting somewhere, their interest and enthusiasm will soon diminish. For this reason, a commonly understood objective should be set and the field for discussion appropriately limited. Moreover, the topic should be phrased as a question and made as specific and impartial as possible. "What of our youth?" for example, is too vague and would probably result in a rambling exchange of generalities; but "Why do teen-agers often rebel against parental authority?" is more specific and would give the group a definite problem to consider.

Essentials for the participant

For the participant in group communication the most important requirement is a *knowledge of the subject* being considered. If you know what you are talking about, you will be forgiven many faults. A second essential is an *acquaintance with the other members of the group.* The more you know about them, the better you will be able to judge the value of their remarks and to determine the role you must play in order to make the group process profitable. Equally important is *close attention to the discussion* as it progresses. Unless you listen to what is going on, you will forget what already has been said or lose track of the direction in which the thinking of the group seems to be moving. As a result, you may make foolish comments, require the restatement of points already settled, or misunderstand the positions taken by other participants.

Finally, you should make *meaningful contributions to the discussion*. If you keep quiet, you may learn a good deal; but you will not help anyone else understand the subject or solve the problem at hand. Develop the ability to present your ideas — when they are pertinent — clearly and tactfully.

Essentials for the leader

If a discussion is to prove fruitful, the leader of the group must be alert, quick-witted, and clear-thinking — able to perceive basic issues, to recognize significant ideas, to sense the direction an interchange is taking, to note common elements in diverse points of view, and to strip controversial matters of unnecessary complexity. Moreover, a good discussion leader must be capable of the *effective expression* needed to state the results of the group's analyses clearly and briefly, or to make an essential point stand out from the others.[2]

Another important quality of a discussion leader is *impartiality*. The leader must make sure that minority views are allowed expression and must phrase questions and comments fairly. In this way, a spirit of cooperation and conciliation will be promoted among participants who may differ from one another vigorously. Discussion groups are no different from other groups in preferring leaders who are fair. There is no place for a leader who takes sides in a personal argument or who openly favors some of the members at the expense of others. To help ensure that all may participate in a democratic, representative way — especially if the discussion is a formal, decision-making one — the leader should have a working knowledge of parliamentary procedure and the commonly employed motions. For a table of such motions, see pages 328–329.

Finally, a discussion leader should have an *encouraging or permissive attitude* toward the participants. There are times, especially at the beginning of a discussion, when people are hesitant to speak out. Provocative questions may stimulate them to participate, but even more helpful is a leader whose manner conveys confidence that the members of the group have important things to say about an important subject.

---

[2]We are aware of the distinction sometimes drawn between the "appointed" or "nominal" group leader and the so-called "real" or "emergent" leader — the person who, because of superior knowledge, prestige, or insight, is most influential in moving the discussion forward and determining the direction it will take. However, we still prefer the term *leader* rather than *chairperson* to describe the individual who presides, because it seems to reflect more accurately the duties he or she is expected to perform.

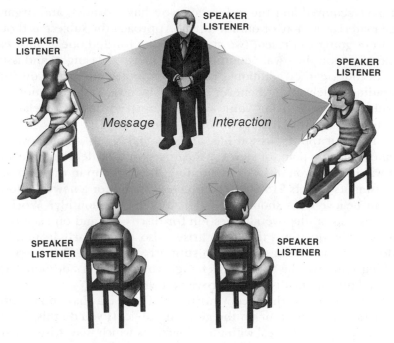

SPEAKER
LISTENER

SPEAKER
LISTENER

SPEAKER
LISTENER

Message   Interaction

SPEAKER
LISTENER

SPEAKER
LISTENER

Figure 1. Communicating in a Small Group

PREPARING FOR GROUP COMMUNICATION

General preparation

How should you prepare to participate in a discussion or to lead one? As we have already suggested, two fundamental steps are required: (1) you must investigate the subject or problem to be considered, and (2) you must analyze the group which is to consider it.

Investigation of the subject. Many persons believe that they do not need to prepare as carefully for a discussion as for a speech. In reality, just the opposite is true. For an interchange of ideas with a group, you cannot narrow the subject or determine the purpose for yourself; nor can you control the direction the deliberation will take. Because so many eventualities must be considered, preparing for group communication is, in many ways, a greater challenge than preparing for a speech.

Carefully think through each facet of the subject to be discussed. First, review what you already know about it. Go over the information you have acquired and the judgments you have formed, and organize these materials in note or outline form. Approach the subject as though you were going to present two speeches, one for and one against each phase of it; you then will be familiar with more of its angles and issues.

Second, gather additional material; supplement what you know by reading widely and, whenever possible, by observing conditions and consulting experts. Bring your knowledge up to date. Correlate this new information with the opinions you already hold.

Third, if the discussion has decision-making as its purpose, formulate a *tentative* point of view on the question. Decide what your position will be. Are you in favor of limiting membership in the club or of increasing its size? Is $150,000 too much to spend for a new clubhouse? Do you believe dues should be paid annually or monthly? Work out your position on the overall question for discussion and on each of the more specific questions that may arise. Also have clearly in mind the evidence and reasoning needed to support your views. But keep your thinking tentative; be willing to change your mind if additional facts disclosed during the discussion prove you wrong.

Finally, examine the effect your point of view may have on the other members of the group or on the general public. If you do this, you will be better prepared to deal with any objections which may arise. Possibly someone will oppose a solution you support on the ground that it would cause her to lose money or to retract a promise; forethought not only will prepare you for her opposition, but also may suggest another, more workable solution. If an audience will be present to hear the discussion and to participate in a question-and-answer period, or if radio and television audiences will hear you, do not forget to take into account their probable knowledge of and attitude toward the subject.

Analysis of the group. Even though you are thoroughly familiar with the subject matter to be discussed, you will be handicapped unless you understand the nature of the group and the objectives at which it aims. Have the members come together merely to investigate, or do they have power to make decisions? What resources are at their command? Of what larger unit is the group a part? If you are a member of the student council, for example, you should understand not only the functions of the council but also its relation to the policies and traditions of your college or university. As a part of your analysis, investigate also the individuals who compose the group. In this way you will come to know that Mr. X usually exaggerates or has an ax to grind and that his comments, therefore, must be taken with a grain of salt, but that Ms. W is thoughtful and well informed, and usually makes comments that bear serious consideration. In addition, you should understand something of the social structure of the group—who the natural leaders and followers are and in what relation the members stand to one another. Answer as well as you can the following questions: What is the official position of each member? What are each individual's personal traits? What knowledge does each one have of the questions that will be raised? What attitude will each one have toward the ideas or proposals you intend to introduce?

DEVELOPING THE DISCUSSION PLAN

When people are communicating in groups, there is a possibility that much time may be lost by needless repetition or by aimless wandering from point to point. A carefully developed discussion plan will guard against this danger.

Ideally, the entire group should cooperate in framing the plan the discussion is to follow; but if this is impossible, the leader must take the responsibility for formulating it. In the pages immediately following, we shall consider separate plans for learning discussions and decision-making discussions. Although the plans outlined can be used in most situations, at times modifications may be required because of peculiarities in the composition of the group or because in a decision-making discussion the problem already has received considerable attention, either by individuals or by the group in earlier meetings.

A plan for learning discussions

Sometimes a learning discussion concerns a book or parts of it, or is based upon a study outline or syllabus prepared by an authority in a given field. In such cases, the discussion generally should follow the organizational pattern used in this resource. The ideas in the book or outline, however, should be related to the experience of individuals in the group; and an effort should be made to give proper emphasis to the more important facts and principles. When the group finds that previously prepared outlines are out of date or incomplete, the leader and/or the other participants should modify them so as to bring the missing information or points of view into the group's considerations.

When learning discussions are not based upon a book or outline, the leader and/or the group must formulate their own plan. The first step in this process is to *phrase the subject for discussion as a question*. Usually the question is framed before the actual discussion begins. If not, the leader and the members of the group must work it out together. Ordinarily, it is phrased as a question of fact or of value. (See pages 239–241.) Questions of fact, such as "What are the essentials for effective discussion?" or "What is our community doing to combat the increasing crime rate?" seek an addition to or a clarification of knowledge within the group; questions of value, such as "Is civil disobedience ever justified as a form of social protest?" or "Is our Middle Eastern policy effective?" seek judgments, appraisals, or preferences. The following suggestions should help you develop a satisfactory discussion plan for both types of questions.

Introduction. The introduction consists of a statement of the discussion question by the leader, together with one or two examples showing its importance or its relation to individuals in the group.

Analysis. In this step the group explores the nature and meaning of the question and narrows the scope of the discussion to those phases which seem most important. These considerations are pertinent:

1. Into what major topical divisions may this question conveniently be divided? (See pages 137–140 for some suggestions.)
2. To which of these phases should the discussion be confined?
   a. Which phases are of the greatest interest and importance to the group?
   b. On which phases are the members of the group already so well informed that detailed discussion would be pointless?

At this point the leader summarizes for the group, listing in a logical sequence the particular aspects of the question that have been chosen for discussion. (Suggestions on pages 137–140 also apply here.)

Investigation. In the investigative phase of the discussion, the members focus on the topics they have chosen in the preceding step. Under *each topic*, they may consider the following questions:

1. What terms need definition? How should these terms be defined?
2. What factual material needs to be introduced as background for the discussion (historical, social, geographic, etc.)?
3. What personal experiences of members of the group might illuminate and clarify the discussion?
4. What basic principles or causal relationships can be inferred

from consideration of this information and these experiences?

5. Upon which facts or principles is there general agreement and upon which points is information still lacking or conflicting?

Final summary. At the close of the discussion, the leader briefly restates (1) the reasons which have been given for considering the question important and (2) the essential points which have been brought out under each of the main topics. His or her summary need not be exhaustive; its purpose is merely to review the more important points in a way that will cause them to be remembered and that will make clear their relationship to each other and to the general subject.

A plan for decision-making discussions

As we stated earlier, the principal function of a decision-making discussion is to consider a problem with the aim of reaching a consensus on what to do and how to do it. If, as in the case of an executive committee, the group meets regularly, the members may not know prior to the meeting what will be discussed. More frequently, however, the members know in advance the problem to be considered. At times, a serious difficulty or conflict of interests may be the very reason for calling the group together.

Decision-making discussions characteristically raise questions of policy. (See pages 238–239.) Examples of such questions are "What can be done to give students a more effective voice in the affairs of our college?" and "How can our company meet the competition from foreign imports?"[3] As you will see in the following suggested procedure, answering such questions also requires answering subsidiary questions of fact and of value.

The steps in the ensuing plan for decision-making discussions are adapted from John Dewey's analysis of how we think when we are confronted with a problem.[4] Although presented here in some detail, this

---

[3]Not all discussions of this kind deal with problems or policies over which the group has immediate control. For example, a decision-making group may discuss "Should we deemphasize intercollegiate athletics?" or "What can the government do to ensure a stable food supply at reasonable prices?" The systematic investigation of these subjects, however, requires substantially the same steps as for matters over which the group has direct control. The only difference is that instead of asking, "What shall we *do?*" the group, in effect, asks, "What shall we *recommend* to those in authority?" or "What *would* we do if we ourselves were in positions of authority?"

[4]See Chapter 7, "Analysis of Reflective Thinking," in *How We Think* by John Dewey (Boston: D. C. Heath & Company, 1933). Cf. pp. 242–244 of this textbook, where these steps are discussed in connection with the development of a speech to persuade.

plan is only one of several possible ways of deciding upon a course of action and, therefore, is intended to be suggestive rather than prescriptive. Any plan that is developed, however, probably should follow — in general — a problem-solution order. Moreover, steps in the plan always should be stated as a series of questions. (We call to your particular attention the sample problem-solving discussion on pages 387–394, which follows the general plan outlined below.)

Defining the problem. After introductory remarks by the leader touching on the general purpose of the discussion and its importance, the group should consider:

1. How can the problem for discussion be phrased as a question? (*Note:* Usually the question has been phrased before the discussion begins. If not, it should be phrased at this time.)
2. What terms need defining?
   a. What do the terms in the question mean?
   b. What other terms or concepts should be defined?

Analyzing the problem. This step involves evaluating the problem's scope and importance, discovering its causes, singling out the specific conditions that need correction, and setting up the basic requirements of an effective solution. The following sequence of questions is suggested for this step:

1. What evidence is there that an unsatisfactory situation exists?
   a. In what ways have members of the group been aware of the problem, how have they been affected by it, or how are they likely to be affected?
   b. What other persons or groups does the situation affect, and in what ways are they affected?
   c. Is the situation likely to improve itself, or will it become worse if nothing is done about it?
   d. Is the problem sufficiently serious to warrant discussion and action at this time? (If not, further discussion is pointless.)
2. What are the causes of this unsatisfactory situation?
   a. Are they primarily financial, political, social, or what?
   b. To what extent is the situation the result of misunderstandings or emotional conflicts between individuals or groups?
3. What specific aspects of the present situation must be corrected? What demands must be met, what desires satisfied?
   a. What evils does everyone in the group wish corrected?

b. What additional evils does a majority in the group wish corrected?

c. What desirable elements in the present situation must be retained?

4. In light of the answers to Questions 1, 2, and 3 above, by what criteria should any proposed plan or remedy be judged? (See pages 240–241.)

a. What must the plan do?

b. What must the plan avoid?

c. What restrictions of time, money, etc., must be considered?

5. In addition to the above criteria, what supplementary qualities of a plan are desirable, though not essential?

At this stage the leader summarizes the points agreed upon thus far. Particularly important is a clear statement of the agreements reached on Questions 4 and 5, since the requirements there set forth provide the standards against which proposed remedies are judged. Moreover, agreement regarding criteria tends to make further discussion more objective and to minimize disagreements based upon personal prejudices.

Suggesting solutions. In this step, every possible solution is presented. The group asks:

1. What are the various ways in which the difficulty could be solved? (If the group is meeting to discuss the merits of a previously proposed plan, it asks: What are the alternatives to the proposed plan?)

a. What is the exact nature of each proposed solution? What cost, actions, or changes does it entail or imply?

b. How may the various solutions best be grouped for initial consideration? It is helpful to list all solutions, preferably on a blackboard.

Evaluating the proposed solutions. When the discussants have presented all possible solutions which have occurred to them, they examine and compare these solutions in an attempt to agree on a mutually satisfactory plan. The following questions may be asked:

1. What elements are common to all the proposed solutions and are therefore probably desirable?

2. How do the solutions differ?

3. How do the various solutions meet the criteria set up in Ques-

tions 4 and 5 of the analysis step? (This question may be answered either by considering each plan or type of plan separately in the light of the criteria agreed upon, or by considering each criterion separately to determine which solution best satisfies it.)

4. Which solutions should be eliminated and which ones retained for further consideration?
5. Which solution or combination of solutions should finally be approved?
    a. Which objectionable features of the approved solution or solutions should be eliminated or modified?
    b. If a number of solutions are approved, how may the best features of all the approved solutions be combined in a single superior plan?

As soon as agreement is reached on these matters, the leader sums up the principal features of the accepted plan. In groups which have no authority to act, this statement normally concludes the discussion.

Deciding how to put the approved solution into operation. When a group has the power to put its solution into operation, the following additional questions are pertinent:

1. What persons or committees should be responsible for taking action?
2. When and where should the solution go into effect?
3. What official action, what appropriation of money, etc., is necessary? (*Note:* If several divergent methods of putting the solution into effect are suggested, the group may need to evaluate these methods briefly in order to decide on the most satisfactory one.)

When these matters have been determined, the leader briefly restates the action agreed upon to be sure it is clear and fully acceptable to the group.

Adapting the decision-making plan to the question

The discussion plan suggested above covers the process of decision making from an initial analysis of existing conditions to the implementing of the action chosen. This entire process, however, is not always required in a discussion. As Harrison S. Elliott points out in his book, *The Process of Group Thinking,* "A group may face a question in any one of five stages: (1) a baffling or confused situation; (2) a problem definitely defined; (3) alternatives specifically suggested; (4) a single definite proposal; (5) ways and means of carrying out a conclusion."[5] How much of the five-step decision-making process needs to be included in the discussion plan depends, then, upon the stage at which the question comes before the group. The participants can then limit their outline so as to pick up the discussion at that stage without needless backtracking and time-consuming reconsideration of points already settled. The leader should, of course, study the entire outline in order to make the necessary adaptation in the event that something presumably settled, turns out, actually, still to be in doubt or in dispute. A thorough understanding of the basic stages of the process, as explained on pages 317–320 and reviewed in Figure 2 below, can help you determine the most appropriate and efficient starting point for achieving productive outcomes.

Figure 2. A Five-Step Plan for a Decision-Making Discussion

For example, a discussion requiring only the final three steps of the process occurred some years ago in a large university. Three student organizations had made plans to produce musical comedies on the campus during the same week. Obviously, three such shows would conflict with one another, but none of the organizations wanted to give up its plan entirely. All thought that the best solution would be for the three groups to combine their efforts in a joint production; but they realized that the differences in membership requirements, financial policies, and skills required of the participants would make this difficult. Therefore, a preliminary meeting was held in which representatives of the student organizations and representatives of the faculty decided that a joint plan, to be acceptable, must provide for (1) skilled professional direction; (2) opportunity for all students, regardless of organization membership, to try out for roles or to work on the stage

---

[5]Harrison S. Elliott, *The Process of Group Thinking* (New York: Association Press, 1932), p. 89 ff.

crew; (3) equal representation of the three student groups on the managing board; and (4) provision for an adequate financial guarantee.

A second discussion then was scheduled. In preparation for it, the chairperson obtained from members of the joint committee several definite and detailed proposals. She had typewritten copies of these proposals (with the names of the authors omitted) placed before each member at the beginning of the meeting. In opening the discussion, the chairperson restated the four general requirements listed above and secured their confirmation by the group. From this point on, the discussion focused upon the typewritten proposals. The group found that the three plans had a number of common features; they ironed out the differences; they added some details and dropped others; they found a revised plan to be acceptable and adopted it; and they made provisions to put it into operation. Thus, beginning with the suggestion and evaluation of solutions, this second discussion followed almost exactly the procedure indicated in the preceding section of this chapter. The definition and analysis steps, however, were omitted, since these matters had already been settled before the discussion began. Similar abridgments of the five-step discussion plan can often be made, depending upon the stage at which the question comes before the group.

Adapting the discussion plan to the occasion

When circumstances indicate that a procedure other than those suggested here would lead to more rapid progress and more fruitful results, do not hesitate to devise a different type of discussion plan. In the beginning, however, you will be wise to follow rather closely the procedures described; later, when these procedures are firmly in mind, adaptations and modifications may be made as the need arises. Reliable guides for making the necessary adaptations are the good sense and experience of the leader and the group.

PARTICIPATING IN DISCUSSION

One of the principal differences between a public speech and a discussion is that in a speech one person does all the talking, whereas in a discussion everybody contributes. During the greater part of the time, however, a participant in group communication is a listener rather than a speaker. For this reason, you should know how to evaluate the ideas advanced by others, as well as how and when to advance your own.

Evaluating the contributions of others

In evaluating a speaker's remarks you should pay close attention to the evidence and reasoning upon which his or her judgments rest. The same rule applies in discussion. When a participant makes a seemingly important contribution, test it by asking yourself the following questions:

1. *Is the speaker expressing an authoritative opinion?* Is this participant qualified by training and experience to speak as an expert on the topic under consideration?
2. *Is the speaker's statement based on firsthand knowledge?* Has the participant actually observed the evidence or merely reported someone else's findings?
3. *Are the speaker's sources of information reliable?* What are the origins of the information being presented? Is there sufficient explanation of where and how it was obtained?
4. *Is the speaker's opinion unprejudiced, or is it influenced by personal interest?* Does this participant have a position to uphold or an ax to grind? Does this individual stand to profit personally from some decision the group may reach?
5. *Is the speaker stating his or her views frankly?* Is this participant revealing all the known data, or concealing items that are unfavorable to his or her cause?
6. *Are the facts or opinions presented by the speaker consistent with human experience?* Do they sound plausible? Could they reasonably be true?
7. *Are the facts or opinions presented by the speaker consistent with one another?* Are they consistent with the reports made by reputable authorities?
8. *What weight will other members of the group give to the speaker's opinion?* Is this participant's prestige so great that the group will agree with her in the face of conflicting evidence? Is he so little respected that he will not be believed unless someone else supports his opinion?

If, while comments are being offered, you ask questions of this kind, you can evaluate the discussants' ideas more easily and accurately. In addition, you will be better able to estimate the reaction of the group to any contributions you may make.[6]

---

[6]For a fuller discussion of the principles of good listening as they apply in all types of speech situations, review Chapter 2, pp. 20–33.

Making contributions

Although you cannot be a good discussant unless you are a good listener, neither can you be a good discussant if you fail to advance constructive ideas, useful information, and sound judgments. As we pointed out earlier, the best listeners in the world, if they *only* listen, contribute little toward understanding or solving the problem confronting the group. When and how, therefore, should you enter into the discussion? How should your contributions be phrased and presented?

There is no simple answer to the question "When should I talk and when should I keep quiet?" Usually, you should speak out when you are asked a direct question, when you have a worthwhile idea to offer, or when you can correct or clarify the remark of another person. More important than any specific rules or cautions, however, is the general reminder that discussion is *a cooperative process*. You should neither monopolize the conversation nor consistently remain silent. Speak when you believe you can be of definite help to the group, but also give the other discussants a full and fair opportunity to express their views. Usually, the most interesting and profitable discussions are those in which all members of the group participate more or less equally.

When you speak, then, keep in mind the cooperative nature of the discussion process. Advance your ideas tentatively and present the evidence and reasoning upon which they rest. Speak to the point, indicating clearly that you understand the particular issue under consideration. Show by your manner as well as your words that you are more interested in helping the group attain its objective than in impressing your ideas on the others; try to accept criticism and treat disagreement objectively; be tactful and courteous; keep your voice and manner calm. Holding fast to these guidelines in the heat of an animated discussion may not always be easy, but at least try to develop the habit of participating with these suggestions in mind.

LEADING THE DISCUSSION

A discussion leader, in addition to having all the skills and attributes of a good participant, should have other abilities as well. One who would lead a group toward a productive speech transaction of this kind should know how to get discussion started and keep it stimulated, how to prevent it from wandering, how to bring out the essential and pertinent facts, how to draw out silent members and keep overtalkative ones in check, how to resolve conflicts, and how to summarize and interpret group progress. No wonder good discussion leaders are rare![7]

Starting the discussion and evoking response

To get the discussion started, the leader may follow the suggestion made on page 318—briefly stating the question to be discussed and stressing its importance, especially as it relates to the participants. These introductory remarks should be made with vigor and earnestness, suggesting the vital nature of the subject. They should be expressed in concrete terms supported by specific instances, but they should not be so long that they seem to exhaust the subject. Moreover, they should lead into a series of provocative questions designed to draw members of the group into the discussion. If such questions fail to produce a response, the leader may call on certain individuals by name, asking them to relate their experiences or to express their opinions. Or the group leader may go to the chalkboard and start a list. Such a list could include various aspects of the subject or causes of the problem, terms needing definition, proposed courses of action—anything which calls for enumeration or classification. Curiously enough, people who hesitate to begin a discussion are often ready to add to a list.

Still another method of evoking response is to start by bringing out one or more extreme points of view on the question. The leader can state these views, or—better—can call on members of the group who hold them. Nothing spurs participants into active discussion so quickly as a statement with which they disagree. The danger of this method is, of course, that it may provoke a verbal battle which consumes too much time or stirs up personal animosity. Usually, the problem which brought the group together is sufficiently provocative to start the exchange; but if the discussion lags at the beginning or hits a "dead spot" later, the leader and/or other members of the group may find the foregoing methods helpful in energizing or renewing it.

Directing the discussion

The tendency of a group to stray from central issues can be greatly diminished if the leader outlines on a chalkboard the points that re-

---

[7]The problems of group leadership are discussed in detail in Michael Burgoon, Judee K. Heston, and James McCroskey, *Small Group Communication: A Functional Approach* (New York: Holt, Rinehart & Winston, Inc., 1974), Chapter 10, "Leadership in the Small Group," pp. 143–156.

quire consideration. When people see what needs to be taken up and in what order, they are likely to focus their attention on these matters. Unless a participant suggests that an important item has been omitted from the outline and asks that it be included, the leader can direct attention to the prearranged points, one after another, and thus keep the discussion progressing steadily. Using the outline on the chalkboard as a skeletal plan, many leaders like to fill in the details as they are introduced, thus providing the group with a visual record of its progress. If, in spite of this planning, the discussion takes an irrelevant turn—if a participant reverts to something already decided, jumps ahead to a point not yet in order, or introduces a seemingly extraneous idea—the leader usually needs only to draw attention to the matter currently before the group. Of course, common sense and fairness must be the constant guides for this kind of leadership. Sometimes the discussion strays because the fault is in the outline, and the participant who moves away from it may be making an important contribution.

Bringing out the facts

If the leader follows the preceding suggestions, the information needed to solve the problem or cover the subject usually will be brought out. If the participants are fair-minded and well informed and if the discussion plan includes all the necessary steps, no special effort beyond that already indicated will be required. Unfortunately, discussions do not always proceed perfectly, and the leader sometimes must make sure that important facts are not ignored and that opinions are not mistaken for factual evidence.

When something important apparently has been overlooked, the person directing the discussion may tactfully inquire, "Has anyone noticed that . . . ?" and proceed to add the missing fact. Or the leader may say, "Mr. Smith called my attention yesterday to the fact that . . . . Has anyone else noticed this to be true?" It is generally better, however, to ask a participant a specific question designed to bring out the needed information. Similarly, if there is a tendency to dwell on one point of view to the exclusion of an equally important one, the leader may call attention to the oversight by suggesting, "Perhaps we should ask Paul to express his ideas on this" or "I have heard this other point of view expressed, too . . . . What do you think of it, Barbara?"

Although a discussion leader should never directly accuse another member of the group of twisting facts or making unsupported statements, false declarations or doubtful assertions by a participant should not be allowed to pass unchallenged. Ideally, other members of the group should inquire into a speaker's data and claims; but if no one else does, the leader may handle the matter tactfully by asking for further details or for the evidence on which the statement is based. For example, the individual who is directing the discussion may say, "I wonder if you would tell us, Mike, what has led you to this conclusion?" or "Is that a statement of your own opinion, Mary, or have you observed it to be true in practice?" By skillful questioning, a good discussion leader can direct attention to all aspects of a question, see that the important facts are carefully considered, and put the group on guard against unsupported assertions. Whenever possible, however, the person charged with the group leadership should draw the necessary facts and ideas from the other participants, and should never dominate the discussion unduly.

Ensuring equal participation

At times, one or two persons in the group may begin to monopolize the conversation. Not infrequently such individuals have a great deal to contribute, but there is also a very strong possibility that they will repeat themselves or expand obvious points needlessly. When this occurs, the leader may avoid recognizing a talkative participant by not looking directly at him or her. Or the leader may call upon other individuals, by name if necessary, asking them questions which will move the discussion forward and away from the overworked point or the overtalkative person. In extreme cases, the leader may find it necessary to suggest in a tactful manner that if the discussion is to be profitable, all members must have an opportunity to participate; or the group or its leader may even have to invoke a limit on the number of times any one discussant can speak. If the time for the close of the discussion is drawing near, sometimes a statement of that fact will spur into action members who hitherto have remained silent. Remember that while the leader does not have the right to tell the group what to think, he or she does have the obligation to maintain an atmosphere in which all members can think most productively; and such an atmosphere will not be possible unless all feel that they have an equal chance to participate.

In larger and more formal situations, as we noted earlier, the leader will find it particularly advantageous to have a practicing knowledge of "Parliamentary Procedure for Handling Motions." These motions, as summarized in the chart on pages 328–329, can do much to imbue the proceedings with a general sense of fairness and stability.

PARLIAMENTARY PROCEDURE FOR HANDLING MOTIONS

Classification of motions	Types of motions and their purposes	Order of handling	Must be seconded	Can be discussed	Can be amended	Vote required [1]	Can be reconsidered
Main motion	(To present a proposal to the assembly)	Cannot be made while any other motion is pending	Yes	Yes	Yes	Majority	Yes
Subsidiary motions [2]	To postpone indefinitely (to kill a motion)	Has precedence over above motion	Yes	Yes	No	Majority	Affirmative vote only
	To amend (to modify a motion)	Has precedence over above motions	Yes	When motion is debatable	Yes	Majority	Yes
	To refer (a motion) to committee	Has precedence over above motions	Yes	Yes	Yes	Majority	Until committee takes up subject
	To postpone (discussion of a motion) to a certain time	Has precedence over above motions	Yes	Yes	Yes	Majority	Yes
	To limit discussion (of a motion)	Has precedence over above motions	Yes	No	Yes	Two-thirds	Yes
	Previous question (to take a vote on the pending motion)	Has precedence over above motions	Yes	No	No	Two-thirds	No
	To table (to lay a motion aside until later)	Has precedence over above motions	Yes	No	No	Majority.	No
Incidental motions [3]	To suspend the rules (to change the order of business temporarily)	Has precedence over a pending motion when its purpose relates to the motion	Yes	No	No	Two-thirds	No
	To close nominations [4]	[4]	Yes	No	Yes	Two-thirds	No
	To request leave to withdraw or modify a motion [5]	Has precedence over motion to which it pertains and other motions applied to it	No	No	No	Majority [5]	Negative vote only
	To rise to a point of order (to enforce the rules) [6]	Has precedence over pending motion out of which it arises	No	No	No	Chair decides [7]	No
	To appeal from the decision of the chair (to reverse chair's ruling) [6]	Is in order only when made immediately after chair announces ruling	Yes	When ruling was on debatable motion	No	Majority [1]	Yes
	To divide the question (to consider a motion by parts)	Has precedence over motion to which it pertains and motion to postpone indefinitely	[8]	No	Yes	Majority [8]	No

					Two-thirds	Negative vote only
Privileged motions	To object to consideration of a question	In order only when a main motion is first introduced	No	No	No	Chair decides	No
	To divide the assembly (to take a standing vote)	Has precedence after question has been put	No	No	No	No vote required	No
	To call for the orders of the day (to keep meeting to order of business) [6, 9]	Has precedence over above motions	No	No	No	No vote required	No
	To raise a question of privilege (to point out noise, etc.) [6]	Has precedence over above motions	No	No	No	Chair decides [7]	No
	To recess [10]	Has precedence over above motions	Yes	No [10]	Yes	Majority	No
	To adjourn [11]	Has precedence over above motions	Yes	No [11]	No [11]	Majority	No
	To fix the time to which to adjourn (to set next meeting time) [12]	Has precedence over above motions	Yes	No [12]	Yes	Majority	Yes
Unclassified motions	To take from the table (to bring up tabled motion for consideration)	Cannot be made while another motion is pending	Yes	No	No	Majority	No
	To reconsider (to reverse vote on previously decided motion) [13]	Can be made while another motion is pending [13]	Yes	When motion to be reconsidered is debatable	No	Majority	No
	To rescind (to repeal decision on a motion) [14]	Cannot be made while another motion is pending [14]	Yes	Yes	Yes	Majority or two-thirds [14]	Negative vote only

1. A tied vote is always lost except on an appeal from the decision of the chair. The vote is taken on the ruling, not the appeal, and a tie sustains the ruling.

2. Subsidiary motions are applied to a motion before the assembly for the purpose of disposing of it properly.

3. Incidental motions are incidental to the conduct of business. Most of them arise out of a pending motion and must be decided before the pending motion is decided.

4. The chair opens nominations with "Nominations are now in order." A member may move to close nominations, or the chair may declare nominations closed if there is no response to his/her inquiry, "Are there any further nominations?"

5. When the motion is before the assembly, the mover requests permission to withdraw or modify it, and if there is no objection from anyone, the chair announces that the motion is withdrawn or modified. If anyone objects, the chair puts the request to a vote.

6. A member may interrupt a speaker to rise to a point of order or of appeal, to call for orders of the day, or to raise a question of privilege.

7. Chair's ruling stands unless appealed and reversed.

8. If propositions or resolutions relate to independent subjects, they must be divided on the request of a single member. The request to divide the question may be made when another member has the floor. If they relate to the same subject but each part can stand alone, they may be divided only on a regular motion and vote.

9. The regular order of business may be changed by a motion to suspend the rules.

10. The motion to recess is not privileged if made at a time when no other motion is pending. When not privileged, it can be discussed. When privileged, it cannot be discussed, but can be amended as to length of recess.

11. The motion to adjourn is not privileged if qualified or if adoption would dissolve the assembly. When not privileged, it can be discussed and amended.

12. The motion to fix the time to which to adjourn is not privileged if no other motion is pending or if the assembly has scheduled another meeting on the same or following day. When not privileged, it can be discussed.

13. A motion to reconsider may be made only by one who voted on the prevailing side. It must be made during the meeting at which the vote to be reconsidered was taken, or on the succeeding day of the same session. If reconsideration is moved while another motion is pending, discussion on it is delayed until discussion is completed on the pending motion; then it has precedence over all new motions of equal rank.

14. It is impossible to rescind any action that has been taken as a result of a motion, but the unexecuted part may be rescinded. Adoption of the motion to rescind requires only a majority vote when notice is given at a previous meeting; it requires a two-thirds vote when no notice is given and the motion to rescind is voted on immediately.

Resolving conflict

One of the most difficult tasks of the leader in group decision-making is resolving conflict. Although discussion is a cooperative process, progress toward the understanding or solution of a problem can seldom be made unless alternative ideas are examined. If everyone immediately agreed with each new opinion as soon as it was advanced, there would be no point in arranging to discuss the matter. On the other hand, irrational or heated conflict, with the undesirable attitudes it engenders, stifles discussion and renders reflective choices and sound judgments difficult.

Because rational disagreement is essential, but emotional or personalized contention is harmful, the leader must walk a middle path. When there is danger that the conflict is becoming destructive, someone must take steps to curb it. In particular, the leader must be able to distinguish between disagreement based on honest differences in interpretation of facts and contentiousness based on irrational desires and prejudices. When the conflict centers in the interpretation of facts, the difference may be resolved by a careful retracing of the reasoning upon which the competing interpretations rest. When the conflict becomes irrational, especially if the interchange becomes overheated, the leader should urge participants to introduce only the facts and reasoning upon which a rational decision may be based. At times, the person directing the discussion may suggest that the group delay consideration of the disputed point until other, less controversial matters have been settled; or, when the circumstances seem to justify such action, the leader may even urge that the group adjourn and resume the discussion at a later date when all participants have had a chance to cool off.

Advice about the handling of conflict necessarily must be general and incomplete. It is impossible to foresee and provide against all of the situations in which destructive dispute may arise. Chiefly through experience, the leader increasingly learns how to deal with certain kinds of cases; through imagination and resourcefulness, he or she invents conflict-resolving techniques as the need arises. But always, the leader must be alert to the possibility of harmful contention, watchful for its emergence, and ready to curb it before it gets out of hand.

Summarizing progress periodically

Throughout, the leader should note the points upon which most members of the group agree and should restate these points in brief sum-

Small group communication may be formal, structured, and preplanned; or it may be informal, unstructured, and spontaneous. Whatever the circumstances, this form of interaction involves a cooperative and relatively systematic process in which persons exchange and evaluate ideas and information in order to understand a subject or solve a problem or arrive at a decision.

Top to bottom: Michael D. Sullivan; Eastern Michigan University Photo; Rae Russel.

maries at appropriate times during the course of the discussion. This directs attention to matters not yet covered or which remain to be settled. These ongoing summaries also instill a sense of accomplishment and motivate the group to proceed toward a conclusion.

In addition to making internal summaries, at the close of the discussion the leader should make a final summary, reviewing the ground covered and—in a decision-making discussion—emphasizing the points of agreement without overlooking any important minority view. If some matters remain unsettled, these should be noted, especially if there is to be a later meeting. The tone of this final summary should be objective, but should give full weight to the progress or accomplishments of the group.

PUBLIC DISCUSSIONS

On many occasions, when group consideration of a matter is desirable or urgent, the number of persons is so large that small group procedures are impractical. In these situations, if communication is to have maximum meaning and value, modifications of the methods and plans just described are clearly called for. These modifications produce discussion which may be described as audience-oriented or public discussion. The two most common types of public discussion are: (1) *the panel discussion, and* (2) *the symposium.*

Panel discussions

When a group is too large to engage in an informal learning or decision-making discussion, or when its members are not sufficiently informed to communicate profitably in a group, four or five individuals—usually seated on a platform—may discuss the question for the benefit of the larger group. The individuals in this small group, or "panel," are chosen either because they can supply the facts needed for intelligent discussion or because they represent views held by segments of the larger group and can, therefore, act as their spokespersons. The members of the panel carry on an exchange of ideas and viewpoints among themselves, asking questions of one another and agreeing or disagreeing as if they were in a learning or decision-making situation. In a public discussion of this type, however, they speak *for* the audience and not merely *before* it.

Symposiums

In a symposium several people—usually three to five—give short speeches, each presenting a different point of view or each treating a different facet of the subject. The symposium is a form of public discussion that is common at large conventions or conferences, where a number of experts are invited to speak on specific aspects of a problem.

Both the symposium and the panel discussion may be followed by an *open forum* in which the participants answer questions asked by members of the audience. Various combinations and modifications of the panel and symposium are used, but the essential characteristic of both is that most of the talking is done by a small group of experts or spokespersons while the larger group listens.

A plan for public discussions

For a panel discussion before an audience, the plan may follow lines similar to those presented earlier for learning and decision-making groups. If the purpose is to inform only, the learning plan may be used; if the purpose is to consider a problem or to discuss a course of action, the decision-making plan is more suitable. Any plan that is followed, however, should provide for utilizing the specialized information of the individual panel members. Although the participants should not limit their remarks to their special field of knowledge, they should at least be given first opportunity to discuss matters relating to that field. Unless this is done, the very purpose of selecting a panel to discuss the question for an audience is likely to be defeated.

If the discussion is a symposium, the plan normally provides for dividing the topic and assigning a different phase of it to each of the discussants. The number of speakers often determines the divisions of the subject. For example, one speaker may describe the problem, and each of the other speakers may then suggest and evaluate a different type of solution; or each speaker may discuss a different aspect of the question, one concentrating on the political aspect, another on the economic aspect, etc. After the speakers present their prepared remarks, the discussion may be opened for questions from the audience.

Broadcasts of public discussions

Of the various types of group-communication formats, the panel discussion probably is the one most frequently broadcast. Local radio stations present students, civic leaders, and others in panel shows each week; radio and television networks give time to the analyses of current events by government officials or news commentators. Symposiums, although more formal than panel discussions, also are adaptable to broadcasting because speeches can be precisely timed. Speakers who hold different points of view present their opinions concisely and without interruption, after which they may engage in an informal exchange of ideas.[8]

Special preparation for public discussions

Whether the discussion is to be held before an audience or is to be broadcast, a preliminary warm-up period or even a practice session may prove helpful. Such a session breaks the ice and often stimulates a more animated and vigorous exchange of ideas. Moreover, a session of this kind enables the leader to explain any special details of procedure. Sometimes practice discussions are recorded so that the participants may analyze their remarks and improve their presentation. Discussants, however, should never write out their remarks and read them from a script because this tends to rob them of their spontaneity and liveliness. Care also must be taken not to continue preliminary sessions until the participants become stale. Repeated rehearsals in which the same things are said in the same way result in a presentation that sounds cut-and-dried. Either limit the length and number of practice periods, or see that new material or fresh points of view are brought in at each session.

PROBLEMS FOR FURTHER STUDY

1. Compare and contrast *small group discussion,* as defined in this chapter, with other types of interchanges—social conversations, interviews, arguments or debates, etc. Consider such communication variables as *(a)* opportunities for interaction, *(b)* opportunities to gain information about other persons participating in the interchange, *(c)* opportunities to control the emotional and physical environment in which communication takes place, and *(d)* opportunities to reach mutually satisfying communicative outcomes. You may find it helpful to examine the summary chart, "Basic Forms of Speech Communication: Some Qualities and Interrelationships," page 355.

---

[8]For advice on the manner of speaking best adapted to radio and television see Chapter 15, pp. 338–354.

2. Remembering that a good question for discussion should be stated briefly, clearly, and objectively, frame a question on each of the following subjects suitable *(a)* for a study group and *(b)* for a decision-making group:

The college grading system.	College curriculum decisions.
Governmental support of the arts.	The future of the automobile.
Public political lobbies.	Intercollegiate athletics.

3. Read the sample discussion reprinted on pages 387–394. What methods did the leader use to get it started, keep it on track, and terminate it? How did the leader (and others) handle conflict? How did the leader encourage participation by all of the members of the group?

4. Compare and contrast the processes of preparing for a discussion and for a speech: Does each demand certain skills the other does not? If so, what are these skills?

5. Watch one of the weekly television shows on which persons from government, business, or the professions are questioned by a panel of newspaper reporters ("Meet the Press," "Face the Nation," "Issues and Answers," etc.). To what extent do the formats and procedures used on these shows adhere to the principles of public group discussion outlined in this chapter? Do you think that departures from suggested formats make them more or less effective for considering current problems?

6. Assume that, as a part of a mythical National Student Week, you have been asked to arrange on your campus a panel discussion or symposium to which all students and faculty members will be invited. *(a)* Select a subject you think would be of interest to such an audience. *(b)* Assuming you have a moderate budget to allow you to invite at least two "outside" persons of prominence, indicate whom you would ask to participate. *(c)* When and where would you hold the meeting? *(d)* How long would it last? *(e)* Which public-discussion format would you employ?

ORAL ACTIVITIES AND SPEAKING ASSIGNMENTS

1. The class will be divided into groups of three to five persons, and each group will be asked to build an agenda on a topic suggested by the instructor. Take ten or fifteen minutes to build the agenda, and then reassemble as a whole class. Each group will then present its agenda so that all class members can compare and contrast the various approaches to agenda building. Formulate answers to the following questions: How were the agenda different? Why were they different? Does the exercise indicate to you ways in which the agenda reflects a group's biases or concerns? Can you see why agenda building is more than a formality?

2. With another member of the class, attend a symposium, panel discussion, learning group, or an activity of a decision-making group: meeting of a board of regents, city council meeting, school-sponsored symposium, school-sponsored training workshop, college faculty meeting, student government meeting, TV symposium, multi-person interview, etc. One of you should concentrate upon the *exchange of ideas*—propositions advanced, kinds of evidence marshaled in support of positions, interdependent suggestions for conclusions and/or solutions; the other observer should concentrate upon the *socio-emotional climate* created in the discussion—the extent and intensity of feelings expressed, the methods by which emotional support for others was evidenced, the extent and kind of interpersonal conflict that became apparent, ways in which personalized conflict was handled, etc. Then, together, prepare a short oral report on your findings—and their implications—for the rest of the class.

3. Meet with four or five classmates. Select a nominal leader; choose a question; agree upon a format; gather information in accordance with a discussion plan; then present a discussion for the class as a whole. Other members of the class, as designated by the instructor, will criticize and evaluate the discussion after it is concluded and offer suggestions for improvement. If possible, the discussion should be audiotaped or videotaped for your subsequent personal analysis. Here are some subjects:

How effective is our freshman-orientation program?
How are American cities solving their traffic problems?
What makes a novel/play/film great?
What are the social and ethical implications of organ-transplant surgery?
How can we reconcile the demands of both the ecological and the energy crises in this country?
How well are American colleges and universities preparing students for life?
What can be done about America's child-abuse problem?
Is protest dead on the campuses of American colleges?
How should the basic speech communication course be taught?
Is it possible to put into law reasonable controls over pornography?
What has the United Nations accomplished?
Can individual citizens ever make their collective voices heard in Washington?

4. Your instructor will provide you with a list of twelve to fourteen statements of fact/opinion and belief/value. You and your classmates first will examine each statement and check it with an "agree" or "disagree." Then you will gather in small groups of four or five persons and compare your

checkmarks. If all of you agree or all of you disagree with the statement, pass over it; but, if some of you agree and some of you disagree, talk about it; try to resolve your differences so that *all* of you either agree or disagree. Do this for all of the statements. After a specified period of discussion, gather again as a class and report on your attempts at resolution-of-differences: What kinds of pressure did each of you experience? Did you (or others) yield? Did some of you yield more often than others? Why? What disagreements were resolved semantically (i.e., by checking how each member of your group was using a particular word)? Which ones were resolved through factual support? Which ones were resolved by forcing other persons to question their attitudes and values? In general, does the exercise reveal anything important about group processes and decision-making?

SUGGESTIONS FOR FURTHER READING

William M. Sattler, "Socratic Dialectic and Modern Group Discussion," *Quarterly Journal of Speech* XXIX (April 1943): 152–157. The classic article describing relationships between the ancient world and the twentieth-century conceptions of discussion.

Wayne Brockriede, "Arguers as Lovers," *Philosophy and Rhetoric V* (Winter 1972): 1–11. A metaphorical discussion of communication participants as rapists, seducers, and lovers.

Michael Burgoon, Judee K. Heston, and James McCroskey, *Small Group Communication: A Functional Approach* (New York: Holt, Rinehart & Winston, Inc., 1974). A small, basic textbook integrating various social-psychological perspectives with discussion techniques.

Irving L. Janis, *Victims of Groupthink: A Psychological Study of Foreign-Policy Decisions and Fiascoes* (Boston: Houghton Mifflin Company, 1972). A provocative exploration of the stultifying, negative aspects of group communication.

John D. May, *American Problems: What Should Be Done? Debates from "The Advocates"* (Palo Alto, Calif.: National Press Books, 1973). A reprinting of twelve public-television programs, illustrating one of the public-discussion formats.

Joseph E. McGrath and Irwin Altman, *Small Group Research: A Synthesis and Critique of the Field* (New York: Holt, Rinehart & Winston, Inc., 1966). A readable series of abstracts of social-scientific studies of group processes and decision-making.

Chapter 15

Communicating on radio and television

A KNOWLEDGE OF BROADCASTING TECHNIQUES and skill in their use can be valuable assets for most people in today's world of electronic communication. Any man or woman in business, a profession, or a position of community leadership may be called upon to speak over the local radio or television station. The aim of this chapter, therefore, is to point out the most important differences between face-to-face speaking and speaking over the air to an unseen audience, and to suggest briefly how the principles and procedures previously presented may be adapted to the broadcasting situation.[1] You will observe that, although important differences do exist, many of the same fundamental principles apply; and, more often than not, what is good speaking before a visible audience also is good speaking over the air.

THE RADIO AND TELEVISION AUDIENCE

The radio and television audience is sometimes called "universal" because anyone who has a receiving set within the power range of the station may be listening. The audience is likely to be composed of persons of both sexes and of all ages, creeds, occupations, interests, and degrees of intelligence. Only the hour of the broadcast, the location of the station, and the special nature of the program are limiting factors. Surveys have shown that women listeners and viewers predominate during the morning and early afternoon hours when husbands are at work and children at school. Children give their attention mainly in the late afternoon and early evening and on Saturdays; men listen or watch during the evenings and on Sundays. At mealtime the audience for a public speech is likely to be varied; but it may be small, since most people prefer information about news events, markets, and weather at this

---

[1] In this chapter, the term "broadcast" will be used inclusively to mean both "telecast" and "radiocast."

time. Insofar as location is concerned, a metropolitan station tends to draw a larger urban audience; and a station in a smaller city, a larger rural audience. However, the more powerful stations and the networks reach every kind of community. Some stations cater to certain types of listeners and viewers, and some program series are specifically designed for certain groups. College stations, for example, direct many programs to students and faculty.

An important characteristic of radio and television audiences is that the listener or viewer is usually alone or in a small, intimate group. Although the audience as a whole may be large, the persons comprising it are not gathered in a mass, but are scattered about in living rooms, offices, automobiles, and the like. While each individual no doubt is aware that others are watching or listening to the same program, he or she is primarily attuned to the immediate surroundings and expects the speaker to talk in a conversational manner suited to that environment.

Two further factors need to be remembered: (1) listeners or viewers can easily turn off a broadcast at any time, and (2) they are likely to have many distractions. People hesitate to make themselves conspicuous by leaving an audience while a speaker is talking directly to them in person, but they feel no hesitation about tuning out a radio or television program. In addition, anyone trying to pay attention to a broadcast is likely to be surrounded by distracting noises — the baby's crying, the clatter of dishes, a conversation at the other end of the room, or the roar of traffic. To compete with these distractions, the material to be communicated must have a high degree of interest value.

TYPES OF BROADCASTS

Nearly all broadcast speaking falls into one of three broad types or categories: (1) interviews, (2) informal discussions, and (3) speeches or lectures.[2]

Broadcast interviews

Of the three types of broadcasts mentioned, perhaps the most common is the interview. Public officials and persons prominent in business,

---

[2]We are excluding from consideration here and throughout the chapter news reporting or commentary and entertainment broadcasts.

education, or the arts are constantly in demand as guest participants in radio or television interviews and "talk shows." But even the proverbial "man in the street" may be asked to comment on local or national affairs.

When speaking over the air, whether in the role of interviewer or interviewee, you should in general adhere to the principles of good interviewing as outlined in Chapter 13. In addition, however, you must bear in mind certain considerations peculiar to the broadcast situation. Important among these are the following: *(a)* Keep questions and answers as brief as is consistent with a fair statement of the ideas being expressed. *(b)* Avoid technical terms and highly specialized topics or lines of inquiry; or, if you must engage in them, try to explain in simple language exactly what you are talking about. Remember that your listeners will, for the most part, lack the background necessary to understand technical words and concepts. *(c)* If you are the interviewer, keep your eye on the clock and move the conversation along rapidly enough so that you will be able to cover all important aspects of the subject under consideration and thus give the listeners a full and rounded view. *(d)* As an interviewee, speak — as a rule — to the interviewer rather than the camera. *(e)* Avoid simple yes-or-no answers in favor of brief explanations of your position; and even though the interviewer may at times "needle" or goad you, never appear agitated or angry. *(f)* Above all, prepare for the interview as carefully as you would for a speech; and, if possible, find out in advance the topics the interviewer intends to cover. In this way, you will avoid being surprised by questions you had not anticipated and may eliminate what might otherwise be embarrassing hesitations or periods of silence.

Broadcast discussions

Broadcast discussions, although like non-broadcast discussions in most respects, have three characteristics which render them unique. First, they are carried on not so much for the benefit of the participants as for that of the listening or viewing audience; second, the discussion usually is focused on a theme or problem of general interest to which the participants are expected to contribute information and insights from their specialized backgrounds of knowledge or experience; and third, the discussion must be tailored to the strict time limit which broadcasting schedules impose.

Within these limits, however, when participating in a broadcast discussion either as a leader or as a participant, proceed in essentially the same way as you would if the discussion were not being broadcast. Speak when you can contribute a worthwhile idea or a useful piece of information; keep your comments brief and to the point; avoid emotionalized conflict; and help move the discussion toward a satisfying conclusion.

Often a warm-up period or even a complete practice session is useful when preparing a discussion for broadcast. As a result of such a session, the ice is broken and the participants are more likely to join in a vigorous give-and-take before the "live" microphones or television cameras. In addition, the participants have an opportunity to learn each other's views, and the leader can gauge the temper of the group and decide how best to draw out a wide variety of opinions. To re-emphasize a point we made in the preceding chapter, take care, of course, not to extend such sessions until the participants become stale or the discussion itself begins to lose spontaneity.

Broadcast speeches and lectures

When broadcasting a speech or lecture, three things are of the utmost importance: (1) your talk must fit exactly within the time limit prescribed; (2) your appeals must reach as many different kinds of people as possible; and (3) the structure of your speech must be simple and easy to follow.

1. Fit your talk to the exact time limit. Most stations operate on a schedule that is adhered to with only thirty seconds' leeway; if a program runs overtime, it is cut off. Moreover, programs start on schedule; therefore, allow yourself plenty of time to get to the studio and to catch your breath before you begin speaking. Remember, too, that your speech will comprise only a *part* of the program. If you are given a fifteen-minute "spot," you will not have a full fifteen minutes available because announcements and introductory remarks will consume part of that time. Find out how many minutes actually are yours and what kinds of signals will be given to indicate how the time is going. Without realizing it, many people talk faster in a studio than elsewhere and therefore tend to finish ahead of schedule. Prepare for this eventuality by having an additional illustration or story which you can insert near the end of your speech if you see that you are getting through too early. Prepare also to cut a paragraph or two, should this become necessary. "Back-time" your speech by noting on the manuscript or Teleprompter copy at what point you have one or two minutes of material remaining. If, near the end of the broadcast, the clock shows that you have too much or too little time, adjust your remarks accordingly.

2. **Make your appeals as universal as possible.** Remember that all kinds of people may be listening or watching. Relate your appeals to their everyday experiences and try to interest as many of them as you can.

Use lively, concrete material. Avoid abstract theorizing; listeners will tune you out unless you make your speech come alive with stories, illustrations, and comparisons.

Employ as many factors of attention as possible. In choosing ideas, give special emphasis to *the vital* — use materials related to the impelling needs and desires of many people; to *activity* and *reality* — use materials characterized by movement and concreteness; and to *suspense* — arouse curiosity or expectation that some valuable information will be presented later. (Review the factors of attention, pages 206–211.)

Give your speech a sense of continuous movement and development. A radio or television talk must never bog down or ramble. Keep your listeners aware that you are getting somewhere, that you have an objective and are moving steadily toward it.

3. **Make your speech easy to follow.** In addition to these extra incentives to paying attention, listeners who are not present in the room with you often need special aids to understanding.

Use simple (but not childish) wording and sentence structure. Avoid technical terms where common ones will do; but if you must use technical terms, explain them. Also avoid flowery, over-elegant language and long, complex sentences. Do not, however, talk down to the audience.

Use simple speech organization. Intricate patterns of organization and lengthy chains of reasoning have no place in a broadcast talk. Rarely is there time to make complex arguments clear; and because you cannot see your listeners, you cannot tell whether they understand. A few main points, clearly related and simply supported, should furnish the basic structure of your speech.

Make your transitions clear. When you pass from one idea to another, indicate this fact by a sentence or two or by a distinct change of rate or pitch. In a television broadcast, you can indicate transitions by movement or a gesture; but over the radio, your voice and language must do this work. Do not allow your transitions to become stereotyped; vary them and keep them informal. Do not overwork such phrases as "In the first place" and "Second"; they seem too stilted. You might say instead, "It's too costly, for one thing," "There's no need to labor that point," or "But let's look at something else for a minute."

THE MANNER OF SPEAKING FOR RADIO

When speaking for radio transmission, remember that your listeners cannot see you and, therefore, that you cannot give them visual cues by means of gestures, facial expression, and bodily movement. Nor will you be able to employ visual aids in explaining or proving an idea. All meaning must be conveyed by *the voice alone:* attention must be captured and held, thoughts made clear, and action impelled through the use of rate, inflection, and vocal force.

Using the microphone

Many different types of microphones are available for radio and television use. Some pick up sounds equally well from all directions; others pick up sounds made directly in front of them, but do not pick up as well those made beside, above, or behind them. Ask the announcer or the technician in the studio how far from the microphone you should stand or sit, and from what angle you should speak into it. Ask also about the volume level at which you should talk.

The loudness of the sound picked up by most microphones varies inversely in approximate geometric ratio to the distance of the microphone from the source of the sound. To illustrate, if you speak with the same degree of force, a sound picked up at a distance of one foot will be four times louder than a sound picked up at a distance of two feet. Therefore, to avoid vocal fading or increasing the volume of the voice too much, always remain approximately the same distance from the microphone. Especially when you have an actual audience as well as a microphone in front of you, do not move about too freely. Hand, lapel, and chest microphones have been developed in order to give the speaker more mobility; but you still may produce an uneven volume if you turn your head too often or move about too much. In the studio, the temptation to move is not so great; if you are seated or standing comfortably, you are likely to remain in that position. However, if you are reading your material from a manuscript, be careful not to bob your head because this movement may cause the volume to fluctuate markedly.

Although the fundamental principles of speech communication apply to speaking on radio and television, certain distinguishing characteristics make this communicative form unique: the audience is very large but usually unseen; the use of sophisticated broadcasting equipment requires specialized knowledge; and the time limits are fixed and inflexible.

Clockwise from upper left: Vilms/ JEROBOAM, INC.; Bob Lawrence/University of New Mexico; Elaine F. Keenan, NEST, S.F.

Most radio equipment is extremely sensitive; and for this reason sudden increases in volume will produce "blasting," an effect similar to that created by hitting the keyboard of a piano with a clenched fist—a crash of sound rather than a clear tone. The engineer in the control room can, within reason, modulate the volume of your voice, building it up or toning it down; but he or she cannot anticipate every sudden change. Therefore, keep your vocal force reasonably even.

Amateurs commonly make two mistakes which result in sounds that are intensified by the sensitivity of broadcasting equipment. *The first is rattling or rustling papers close to the microphone.* Any sound in the studio is amplified over the air; therefore, at its worst, paper rustling may sound like the rapid firing of a gun, the flapping of an awning in an angry wind, or the crushing of an orange crate into kindling. At the very least, it will make your listeners aware that you are reading your remarks, and thus destroy the illusion of direct communication. If you use a manuscript, choose soft paper, unclip it before you approach the microphone, and lay each sheet aside quietly when you have finished reading it. You will, moreover, create less noise by resting your manuscript on the table or speaker's stand rather than holding it in your hand. (A note of caution: *Check the pages of your manuscript before the broadcast to make sure they are in the correct order.* No pause seems as long as that which occurs when you turn to page three and find page four.) *The second mistake is tapping the microphone or table.* This, too, may be only a slight noise in the studio but a loud one over the air. Avoid drumming on the table or thumping it for emphasis. Let your gestures be noiseless.

Because broadcasting equipment amplifies sound and because radio listeners focus their attention entirely upon your voice, the distinctness of your speech and the accuracy of your pronunciation are especially important. Errors and crudities that might pass unnoticed on the platform will be very noticeable over the air. Do not, however, talk so carefully that your speech sounds artificial. To speak over-precisely is almost as bad as to speak indistinctly, for it calls attention to the utterance rather than to the thought. Try to avoid both extremes.

Another point to consider is that the quality of a speaker's voice often is changed in transmission. In general, high-pitched voices are less pleasant over the radio, whereas those of moderately low pitch are sometimes improved in the process of broadcasting. The best way to check the effect of transmission on your voice is to have *an audition* or to make *a tape recording* of the broadcast so you can listen to yourself.

The fact that you can talk conversationally before the microphone and do not have to increase vocal force in order to project to a live audience should improve the quality of your voice because most people have better vocal quality when they speak in a quiet and relaxed manner. Keep the resonating passages open, however. The silence of the studio and the lack of direct audience response may cause you to forget you are communicating and allow your voice to become flat and colorless. In articulation, pay particular attention to two kinds of sounds: the plosives —*p* and *b*—and the sibilants—*s, z,* and *sh.* When amplified electronically, a plosive sound, which is produced by the sudden release of air from the lips, may strike the listener's ear as a kind of miniature explosion. Because of the high frequency at which sibilant sounds are produced, they tend to become a whistling or hissing noise if they are given too much emphasis. If you have trouble with sibilants, use sparingly words in which these sounds occur in stressed positions, or—better—learn to subdue your production of them.

Compensating for the lack of visual cues

The visual cues a speaker gives a face-to-face audience add emphasis, convey additional meaning, help hold attention, and fill in gaps left by pauses. When, as in radio speech, the burden is thrown entirely on the voice, variety of vocal expression is more than a valuable asset; it is essential. Refer to Chapter 5 and study again the sections on rate and pitch; practice the exercises given there to develop vocal flexibility. As we have already warned, however, avoid sudden changes in vocal force.

When broadcasting by radio, you should speak at a fairly rapid rate. This does not mean that you have to rush, but it does mean that you cannot allow your speech to drag. Long pauses are especially to be avoided. In a face-to-face speaking situation, you sometimes can emphasize a point by standing silent, holding your listeners' attention by your facial expression and the apparent tension of your body; but all of this is lost to the radio listener who sees nothing and "hears" only silence. In radio speaking, therefore, pauses must be used sparingly and must be of shorter duration. On the platform you may pause to search for the exact word to express a thought; you are thinking it out with your listeners, and they are seeing you do it. On the air, such pauses may suggest that as a speaker you are ill-at-ease and unprepared.

Because groping for words is a major sin in radio broadcasting, most people write out their speeches word for word and read them from manuscript. This procedure not only ensures their knowing what to say next but also makes it certain that they will finish on time. There is one disadvantage, however. As a rule, people cannot write with the informality of oral style; and even when they can, they have difficulty reading aloud in a conversational manner. But this disadvantage can be overcome with practice. Experts almost unanimously advise using a manuscript for a radio speech and learning to read from it naturally.

When preparing for a broadcast speech, then, practice reading your manuscript aloud. Do not read it for the first time as you stand before the microphone and address your audience. Master or alter difficult sound combinations in advance. Become so familiar with your material that you can ad-lib if you happen to lose your place or misplace a page. Above all, practice reading with a mental image of your listeners before you; make your reading sound like talk. Do not stress unimportant words, such as *the, of,* and *to.* Avoid both a monotone and an artificial inflection.

THE MANNER OF SPEAKING FOR TELEVISION

Unlike radio broadcasting, telecasting permits your audience to see you while you speak. Therefore, your appearance, facial expression, and movement can help convey your thought just as they do when you are speaking to an audience face to face. In fact, the way the television camera picks up your image, especially in close-ups, makes your appearance and movement even more important than when you address audiences in person.

Although you need not depend on your voice alone when speaking on television, neither can you talk exactly as you would if you were speaking directly to an audience immediately in front of you. Instead, your voice and movements must conform to limitations imposed by the microphone and camera.

Generally, you will find that the suggestions we have given for using the microphone and avoiding distracting noises are pertinent to television as well as to radio broadcasts. In addition to observing these directions, however, you also must adapt to the distractions of the heat and brilliance of the television studio's dazzling lights, to the movement of the cameras on their booms or dollies, and to the restriction of your movement within the area upon which the lights and cameras are focused. And, throughout, this adaptation must seem natural. Avoid equally a stunned or disconcerted appearance and a tendency to "play to the gallery."

The technical aspects of television are changing rapidly, and facilities at different stations vary considerably. Hence, each time you broadcast you probably will need special advice from the directors and technicians in order to adapt your presentation to prevailing conditions. For this reason, the following discussion omits detailed instructions and includes only suggestions which are fairly universal in their application.

Adapting vocal delivery for television

While many of the vocal requirements of radio broadcasting apply equally to television, important differences should be noted. Since, when speaking on television, you are seen as well as heard, you can talk more slowly and can pause longer for transitions or emphasis. When a program is broadcast over both radio and television, however, pauses should not be too long nor the rate of speaking too slow.

In telecasts, be careful also to maintain a quiet, conversational manner. Especially in intimate studio surroundings, remember that you are conversing with your listeners as a guest in their homes. Vocal variety and emphasis are needed; but a tone that is too excited, an excessively rapid rate, or an over-assertive inflection may be offensive.

Adapting movement and appearance to the television camera

The adjustment of the television camera's lens and its distance from the speaker determine how much of his or her body will be shown. Moreover, the camera's position determines the angle from which the speaker is viewed. Usually, to provide variety, camera angles and distances are changed during the broadcast. Often more than one camera is used, the broadcast pickup shifting from one to another so that the picture changes from a distant view to a close-up or from a front to an angle shot; or the camera is moved so that the angle shifts gradually. If an audience is present, the camera may go from speaker to audience and back again. The director will instruct you ahead of time where you are to stand or sit, and how far you may safely move without getting beyond the focal depth or angle of the camera or outside of the lighted area. If you intend to use visual aids, such as maps and models, be sure they are placed where the camera can include them.

The effect which televising has upon colors, textures, and patterns requires special attention to makeup and clothing. The bright lights cause the normal reddish color of the lips to fade out and the usual shadows around the eyes and nose to disappear, so that the face appears flattened. Hence, makeup is necessary to ensure that facial color and contour will look natural. Makeup also must be used to reduce glare (perspiring skin or a bald head may gleam unless toned down with dull grease paint or panchromatic powder) and to obscure blemishes or stubble (a man's shaven face may appear dirty and unkempt unless basic makeup is applied). Finally, clothes must be chosen so as to give life to the image, but clothing having high degrees of contrast should be avoided.

Adapting movement and appearance to the type of broadcast

Some broadcast discussions and speeches originate in a studio without an audience present; others originate before a live audience gathered in the studio or meeting in an auditorium or assembly hall. In television, the difference between these two types of speaking situations is particularly important. If the audience is present, you will be expected to talk to your listeners, not to the camera. Your posture, movements, and gestures must be adapted to the people immediately before you.

The studio telecast without an audience present is more intimate. Here, as we have said, you must think of yourself as talking to your listeners in their living rooms. If you are giving a formal speech, you may stand while speaking, especially if you have something to point out or to demonstrate. More often, however, you will be seated at a desk or in a large, comfortable chair. In either case, your movements should be suited to easy, animated conversation. Stand or sit in a relaxed manner. Change your position from time to time, and use your hands to emphasize and clarify your statements. Now and then, lean forward slightly to emphasize important ideas. Your gestures, however, should be restrained; move the hand and forearm in a relatively small arc and avoid declamatory mannerisms. Remember, too, that televising often tends to make physical movements seem more rapid than they really are. Look at the camera, but do not stare at it continuously. Above all, do not rely heavily on a manuscript or notes. If you must read all or part of your remarks, you may be able to arrange for the use of a Teleprompter. This device puts a copy of your speech, in large type, on or near the camera. Thus, even though you are reading, you can maintain fairly good eye contact with the viewers.

Using visual aids on television

When you want to illustrate or exemplify your ideas on television, visual aids can be especially helpful. These aids may take numerous forms, and there are—in general—two ways in which they may be used: (1) they may be placed near the speaker and used as they would be in a face-to-face speaking situation—that is, with both the "visual" and the speaker in view; or (2) they may be used by themselves, with nothing else appearing on the television screen.

In the first case, the primary consideration should be the *size* of the aid that is being employed. In preparing it, consider how long a camera shot will have to be in order to include both the speaker and the visual aid in the picture that you want the viewer to see. Make sure also that all diagrams, drawings, and lettering are large enough to be seen easily.

When the visual aid alone is to appear on the screen, the primary consideration is *shape*. The television screen is three units high and four units wide. This ratio, therefore, must be followed when you are preparing the aid. This is not to suggest that visuals of different shapes always must be avoided; but if they are used, they should be placed on a non-distracting background that is sized in accordance with the three-by-four ratio. Most stations also have facilities to use common 35mm slides. Keep in mind, however, that the edges of these slides—especially the tops and bottoms—will not always appear on the screen that the viewer will see.

Whether the visuals you plan to use are to be shown alone or together with you as a speaker, by all means check well in advance with the station's manager and engineers to make certain that those materials are of a type which can be easily used in the studio from which the broadcast will originate. In any event, avoid the use of pure black-and-white objects or drawings because they do not photograph well.

PROBLEMS FOR FURTHER STUDY

1. Marshall McLuhan considers radio a "cool" medium and television a "hot" medium because to him radio is more involving, more "participatory," in that the listener psychologically must supply more data. (See the

writings of McLuhan recommended in "Suggestions for Further Reading.") Informally test the foregoing generalization by listening to speakers over both media. (Educational television and national public radio offer speeches daily.) As you conduct this testing, consider the following questions: *(a)* In monitoring your own reactions to speakers over each medium, do you feel you have to "work harder" to capture the radio message? Why? How? *(b)* Do you find yourself trying to imagine what the radio speaker looks like and is doing? Why? *(c)* Do you think the mannerisms of so-called "unprofessionals" on television get in the way of clear and effective communication? Would such speakers probably get themselves and their messages "across" better over radio? (To find out, try closing your eyes and listening to some of the speeches.) *(d)* What do your answers to these questions tell you about McLuhan's generalization?

2. On three or four consecutive days, listen to a select number of popular television newscasters and attempt to determine those aspects of vocal and physical delivery upon which their effectiveness rests. Are the same factors of effectiveness present for all of them? If not, how do they differ? To what extent do you find it possible to recommend a single standard or ideal style which all television newscasters should follow?

3. Compare the television newscasters studied in Problem 2 with television weather forecasters and sportscasters. What differences do you see in oral and physical presentation? Why? Why do you think that in our contemporary culture people tend to view news commentators in seemingly different frames or with different psychological sets than they use for weathermen and sports reporters?

4. Compare one of the television newscasters studied in Problem 2 with a well-known radio newscaster. How do the communicative techniques of the radio speaker differ from those used by the television newscaster? If the two were to exchange media, would either or both of them lose some of their effectiveness?

5. Select a speech to inform or persuade — preferably one which you presented to the class earlier this term. Using it as a basis and observing the rules of good television speaking described in this chapter, adapt the contents of that speech to a manuscript suitable for a ten-minute television presentation.

6. Interview the manager or program director of a local radio or television station to get his or her ideas concerning the nature of an effective broadcast speech. Ask the manager or director to explain some of the special rules and restrictions which a radio or television speaker must observe in regard to libel and the ethical responsibility of public utterance. Write a report on the results of this interview.

ORAL ACTIVITIES AND SPEAKING ASSIGNMENTS

1. Participate in a class discussion on the topic "Male Dominance of Radio and Television News." The broadcast industry—with some notable exceptions—has assumed for years that this country really *wants* its news and sports from men. The industry allows women to offer the weather and special features, and to handle occasional reportorial assignments; but few make it to the "anchorman's desk," and those who do seldom have dramatically high listener/viewer ratings. Why? Why does this culture seemingly demand lower-pitched and, generally, stronger voices for news and sports commentators? To what can we attribute this? Merely a "that's-the-way-it's-always-been-done" attitude? Something in the way we treat news? Lack of perceptive and imaginative recruitment policies? Outright prejudice?

2. Prepare and present from manuscript a ten-minute informative or persuasive speech especially adapted for radio. In choosing and developing a subject and in wording and delivering your speech, observe insofar as possible the various recommendations set forth in this chapter, and check the timing. If possible, deliver the speech in an actual radio studio. If such equipment is not available, *improvise* a radio setting with an aural tape recorder: Set up the recorder in an empty room with only an "engineer" available to start and stop it, deliver the speech to the microphone, and then play the recording back to the class and/or instructor.

3. Prepare and present—from notes, cue cards, or a Teleprompter—a five-minute television speech to inform or persuade, following advice on subject-matter, eye contact, and bodily movement offered in this chapter. If possible, deliver the speech to a videotape recorder. If none is available, present the talk to any large, inanimate object, meanwhile making sure the rest of the class is generally out of your central line of vision.

SUGGESTIONS FOR FURTHER READING

Sydney W. Head, *Broadcasting in America: A Survey of Television and Radio,* 2nd ed. (New York: Houghton Mifflin Company, 1972). A widely respected overview of the broadcasting industry, including the physical, economic, social, and legal bases of these electronic media of communication.

Marshall McLuhan, *Understanding Media: The Extensions of Man* (New York: McGraw-Hill Book Company, 1964), especially Chapter 2, "Media Hot and Cold"; and Chapters 30–31, "Radio: The Tribal Drum" and "Television: The Timid Giant," pp. 22–32, 297–307, 308–337. Fascinating, provocative introductions to McLuhan's analyses of mass media.

Wilbur Schramm, *Men, Messages, and Media* (New York: Harper & Row, Publishers, 1973). The latest theoretical-analytical formulations of the mass communication process from one of the field's stellar scholar-philosophers.

Wilbur Schramm and D. F. Roberts, *The Process and Effects of Mass Communication,* rev. ed. (Urbana, Ill.: University of Illinois Press, 1971). Perhaps the most complete and up-to-date review of mass communication research, and an excellent introduction to questions of ethics and effectiveness.

R. M. W. Travers, et al., *Research and Theory Related to Audio-visual Information Transmission* (Salt Lake City: Bureau of Educational Research, University of Utah, 1966). A superior introduction to what we know about audiovisual media and learning.

Edgar E. Willis, *Writing Television and Radio Programs* (New York: Holt, Rinehart & Winston, Inc., 1967), especially Chapter 12, "Documentaries, News, and Features." A useful introduction for radio-television speakers.

Now that you have completed your study of the fifteen chapters of this book, you almost certainly have a broader understanding of what goes on in the speech communication process: the essential elements, their interdependence and interrelationships, and their interaction. You should also have a deeper awareness of the types of situations and contexts in which oral interchanges ordinarily take place; specifically, the forms of person-to-person, small group, public, and mass/electronic communication. Some of the pertinent and inherent variables are singled out in the accompanying chart, "Basic Forms of Speech Communication: Some Qualities and Interrelationships." To review what you have been studying in this regard, we suggest that you examine it critically and analyze it in terms of your own experiences and observations. Ask yourself whether you would have chosen these particular variables and described the interrelationships in exactly the same way. Very probably you will discover that certain key variables which you deem important have been omitted or that you would have evaluated the relationships somewhat differently. Quite likely, you will want to redevelop, reorganize, and—perhaps—expand the chart to better fit your *own* concepts and analyses.

BASIC FORMS OF SPEECH COMMUNICATION:
Some Qualities and Interrelationships

CHARACTERIZING VARIABLES	INTERPERSONAL	SMALL GROUP	PUBLIC	MASS/ELECTRONIC
Number of Persons	2	3 to 12	Few to thousands	Potentially unlimited
Degree of Intimacy	High	Relatively high	Relatively low	Generally low
Degree of Formality	Usually minimal	Usually low	Conversational but restrained	Varies widely
Time Limits	Usually flexible	Usually flexible	Usually fixed	Nearly always fixed
Need for Prestructuring of Message	Minimal to medium	Minimal to medium	Usually necessary	Nearly always necessary
Role of Nonverbal Factors in Projection of Message	High	High	High	High
Alternation of Speaker-Listener Roles	Frequent	Frequent	Rare or nonexistent	Nonexistent
Opportunities for Perceiving Listener Feedback	Maximal	High	Somewhat limited	Nonexistent
Opportunities for Adjusting to Listener Feedback	Maximal	High	Somewhat limited	Nonexistent
Opportunities to Assess Fulfillment of Communicator Purpose	Numerous	Numerous	Limited and delayed	Possible but delayed
Opportunities for Mutual Exploration of Ideas	Many	Many	Few if any	None

Appendix

A SPEECH TO INFORM

The student speech which follows was prepared to fulfill an assignment in a beginning public-speaking course at the University of Iowa. Members of the class were instructed to present a three-minute informative talk on a subject of interest to themselves and their classmates, and to organize their material in a clear, easy-to-follow fashion. In accordance with this directive, Mr. Dennis Ragan chose an old and familiar topic, but treated it in a novel way. Throughout, his ideas are expressed clearly and economically.

Backaches*
Dennis Owen Ragan

Introduction
Rhetorical question to catch attention

Does your back ever hurt? If it does, don't feel you are alone. The majority of the people in the world suffer from backaches of one kind or another, either chronically or occasionally./1

Body
Description of primary and secondary causes to set up basic plan of speech

Backache sufferers give many reasons for their aches and pains. They may say that they are due to improper lifting and carrying, nervous tension, overexertion, lack of exercise, or any one of a host of others. These are all valid causes, but they are secondary in nature. The primary cause of the two main types of backaches man suffers from is the fact that he walks upright on two feet./2

Begins distinguishing the first of two principal causes
Explanation and description — with specific instances and data

The first common type of back trouble man suffers from is the slipped disc and its associated vertebral and spinal nerve pain./3

Since man walks upright, all his weight is directed downward onto his feet, with the spine acting as a supporting rod for his back. This condition heavily compresses the vertebrae and the cartilaginous pads or discs between them. A sudden wrong move or a fall can cause a disc to slip out of position. This results in the vertebrae rubbing together or pinching the spinal nerves which lie within the vertebrae. Those of you who have slipped a disc know the immense pain this causes./4

The other common type of back trouble is strain of the muscles of the back./5

Uses detailed contrast (quadraped versus biped) to establish second principal cause

In an animal that walks on four feet, the line of gravity (by this term I mean an imaginary line drawn through the animal perpendicular to the ground in such a way that equal amounts of the animal's weight lie both in front of and behind the line) lies just behind the animal's shoulders. The animal's organs hang suspended in and supported by the rib cage. The four feet support the weight (especially the front legs, since this is where most of the weight is), with no strain placed on the back muscles./6

*Reproduced by permission of Mr. Dennis Owen Ragan.

Man's line of gravity lies about two inches in front of his spine. Thus, most of his viscera and body weight are in front of his spine, causing him to be front-heavy, with a tendency to fall forward. Since he does walk upright, his rib cage cannot support his organs. They have a tendency to drop forward and down. In order to prevent either of these conditions from happening, the stomach muscles must pull the viscera up and back toward the spine for support and balance./7

Rounds out main idea of speech by relating primary causes to secondary ones

The secondary causes I mentioned earlier now come into play. If for any reason the stomach muscles are weak and cannot do their job, the back muscles have to take over. They must hold the viscera up and maintain balance as well as keep the spine stiff and the body erect, which is their normal function. The muscles of the back were not designed for this extra load, and severe back-muscle strain can result./8

Conclusion
Restates central theme with a vivid and semi-humorous touch

The biological sciences teach us that evolution has so specialized man that he stands at the head of the animal kingdom. As far as his back is concerned, he might be better off to be standing at the head of the animal kingdom on four feet instead of two./9 □

SPEECHES TO PERSUADE AND TO ACTUATE

Persuasive speeches advancing claims of policy are often set in a problem-solution framework, which forms the core (need and satisfaction steps) of the motivated sequence. Professor Waldo W. Braden, Chairman of the Department of Speech at Louisiana State University, uses a problem-solution sequence effectively in the following keynote-type speech, "Has TV Made the Public Speaker Obsolete?" More specifically, he seems to be asking, "Is there not a grave danger that the image-making techniques imposed by television may consign to oblivion the full and genuine communication between the politico and the people at the very time when the democratic process stands in dire need of it?"

Following an attention-getting introduction, Professor Braden carefully forecasts the stages in which he will develop the "problem" section of his address: first, "a little theoretical background" on the implications of freedom of speech; next, a look at political campaigning in pre-television days; and, finally a review of contemporary campaign practices in terms of radio and television. In the development of these successive stages, the speaker sets up five possible solutions—all of which he promptly rejects (by his use of the "this-or-nothing" technique) in favor of a solution he really prefers: a search after an informed and interested public. Especially note how Speaker Braden justifies his proposed solution both logically and psychologically: logically *by his development of the problem,* psychologically *by taking into careful consideration the predispositions and motives of the listeners.*

Has TV Made the Public Speaker Obsolete?*
Waldo W. Braden

I was somewhat surprised when I was invited to speak at this luncheon today because, as you know, I am not a broadcaster or a teacher of radio and television or a member of the Council for Better Broadcasts. Perhaps the explanation of my invitation is that I go to football games with the local arrangements chairman, Clinton Bradford. I am the former teacher of your gracious president, Martha Kennedy, and I directed the doctoral dissertation of Mrs. Kennedy's husband./1

I have one little claim that permits me to attend this meeting. In 1969, John Pennybacker and I assembled for Random House the little book entitled *Broadcasting and the Public Interest.* On the team, John upheld the Industry, and I argued for the Consumer. During our eighteen months of collaboration, we frequently engaged in vigorous and sometimes stormy debate. I must admit that I sometimes baited my young colleague by repeating Ferry's statement to the effect that mass communication delights in "the shoddy, the tasteless, the mind dulling, the useless." But at those moments when the Devil egged me on, I always stirred John to give most eloquent rebuttals. Of course, I overstated my case. I do hope that today I will not be repossessed; but if I am, perhaps you will need to call an exorcist to rid me of my evil thoughts. I assure you that I am an avid and enthusiastic viewer of television. I thoroughly enjoy football games, Ironsides, and all kinds of entertainment./2

Many of [us] . . . like millions of [other] Americans, think ourselves lucky to live in a television age in which the average home set operates as much as seven hours per day and the average male watcher like myself may devote as much as 3,000 days or nine years of his life to viewing football games and other excitement on the magic tube. Recently a select list of prominent Americans from many fields was asked to rate eighteen powerful institutions according to their influence; they placed television at the top, above the White House, the Supreme Court, and the newspapers. But it is my belief, as I shall attempt to make clear, that the gains and benefits of television have also brought some question-

---

*"Has TV Made the Public Speaker Obsolete?" by Waldo W. Braden, from *Vital Speeches of the Day*, Volume XXXX (June 1, 1974), pp. 500–503. Reprinted by permission of Vital Speeches of the Day.

able results, particularly in the political forum. Some have suggested that without our knowing it television controls our lives even in a political sense and has made the world into a global village. Many of our attitudes and feelings are shaped by television./3

What I am saying was recently confirmed by a published interview with Alistair Cooke, chief U.S. correspondent for *The Guardian*, one of England's most distinguished newspapers. . . . When asked "What effect is television having on American society and the generation formed by this new experience?" he replied: "We are all getting more information now than we can cope with. I think that's the reason for the sort of low-key hysteria—Thoreau's 'quiet desperation'—that a lot of us live in. The images overwhelm our ability to make judgments or handle our government and our lives because we are so continuously aware of the disruption that's going on everywhere."/4

Let me tell you the route I intend to follow in this speech which I probably should have entitled, "The First Amendment, Public Decision Making, and Television." . . . First, I intend to sketch a little theoretical background involving the implications of the First Amendment to the Constitution. Second, I intend to do a flashback and discuss how the political speaker faced the voters in pre-television days. Third, I shall consider how and why television has altered the role of the speaker and politician./5

Let me start with a little background. Why did the Founders think it was necessary to include a Bill of Rights in the Constitution? Why did they lead off that Bill of Rights with the First Amendment which reads in part "Congress shall make no law . . . abridging the freedom of speech, or of the press; or of the rights of the people peaceably to assemble, and to petition the government for a redress of grievances." That declaration did not suddenly appear in the Constitution of the United States. Our English forebears had long experience with denial of their rights and had due cause to hold such freedom precious and important./6

Why did a statement concerning freedom of speech and press lead off the Bill of Rights? Why was the First Amendment given priority over the next seven amendments which protected property rights?/7

In my opinion Madison and others recognized that the free exchange of ideas, the give-and-take of debate, the posing of questions for office-seekers to answer was at the very heart of the democratic process or a government controlled by the citizens. It has frequently been said that "ours is a government by talk," which is another way to say oral decision making. If free government is to operate, the citizen must have free access to many kinds of opinions and arguments, varied points of view—that is, if the voter is to choose intelligently among the alternatives. Judge Learned Hand said, "Right conclusions are more likely to be gathered out of a multitude of tongues than through any kind of authoritative selection."/8

We operate on the premise that the collective opinions arrived at openly and without fear are likely to give us the most satisfactory decisions. They may not always be the *best* or the *right* ones, but from the point of view of the majority they are the least objectionable./9

Today I am talking about the role of public debate. How does the campaigner—the discusser, the debater, the interviewer—fit into this picture? Oral communicators, with the reporters, keep the citizenry informed, healthy, and capable of making reasonable and desirable judgments./10

Now let me turn to my flashback and discuss the speaker's role in pre-television days. In the old days, the politician—the policy maker, the leader—had to go directly to the voters. He might go by riverboat, or in rugged country he might walk or go by horseback, or in later times by train. Moving about among the voters was within the reach of any aspiring politician who was vigorous and eager. He did not need a big bankroll; he needed energy and courage. The office-seeker made extensive speaking tours, sometimes even travelling with his opponent and on a given day sharing the platform, or as they said, "dividing time." A good example of this confrontation was the Lincoln and Douglas campaign of 1858. They carried their canvass into the nine congressional districts in Illinois; after speaking in the first two, they agreed to seven public engagements from Freeport, Illinois, to Little Egypt and back again. They made long speeches, asked each other searching and difficult questions, and employed shrewd and sometimes tricky strategies. What these two frontier lawyers did was not unusual, for it happened all over the place in Louisiana, Indiana, Tennessee, Ohio, and even Texas./11

What did these face-to-face encounters contribute to the voter? Of course, the voter could hear the candidate and observe him under pressure. He could note how the candidate handled hostile questions and damaging arguments. The brave and vocal listener might actually get into the act by putting a question to a speaker or by sneaking in a little refutation. At least he met the office-seeker face to face, shook hands with him, rubbed shoulders with fellow party members, challenged the opposition, and even engaged in a little physical violence when arguments seemed inadequate./12

At these hustings an officer-seeker could not hide behind a ghost-writer or avoid the queries of his fellow citizens. In full view, a speaker had to adjust his arguments to local conditions, had to cope with the unexpected, the unforeseen, and the embarrassing. There was no way to edit or cover up a faulty pronouncement or change a bad impression. An answer given to significant questions—like the one Lincoln addressed to Douglas at Freeport—stood. And Douglas' answer cost him the presidency in 1860./13

I am not saying that these face-to-face forays were free of nonsense and theatrical displays and did not sometimes mislead or pander to baser motives. At times, rationality lost out to flag raisings, parades, fireworks, and barbecues. Yes, these were the Log Cabin campaigns; the Davy Crocketts with coonskin caps and the ignorant Zach Taylors and some politicians got by with front-porch campaigns, letting their surrogates speak for them. But there is one significant difference. In the face-to-face encounters, the listener actually participated. He might get drunk, do silly things, but he was involved. He was there! He did not sprawl at home in his easy chair with a can of beer in hand and view a *show* carefully written, edited, rehearsed and planned in some far-off New York office by a sleek public relations man. When he made a fool of himself, he had only himself to blame./14

Now let us turn to the present. Let us consider how television has altered the role of the speaker and politician./15

The consumer—the voter—the average citizen no longer has an opportunity to judge a speaker by old means and in the old ways, and many persons who have significant ideas or who aspire to represent us will never be able to gain a hearing with significant numbers of voters. The would-be politician—in a hurry to move up the ladder—will not take time to go to Dry Prong or Waterproof to speak to the citizens because it is too slow and he knows that he won't be able to pull the voters away from Gunsmoke or Ironsides. More likely, he will employ a public relations firm, buy time on the local radio or, still better, on the local television. Newton N. Minow and his colleagues, in their new book *Presidential Television,* observe:

> Television's most significant political characteristic probably is its ability to present an image of a politician—providing an indication of his character and personality. An aspiring political leader today is likely to rise faster and further if he "comes across" well on television. . . . It is not unusual for politicians at all levels to hire television advisers, speech therapists, makeup artists, or other professionals to put on the leader's television image./16

What puts television and, to a lesser extent, radio beyond the reach of many persons who might make great contributions? Let me mention three inherent factors: (1) It is expensive; (2) it is technically complex to operate; and (3) it lends itself to manipulation out of the view of listeners./17

With this audience, I need not dwell long on these three characteristics./18

First, TV is so expensive that it is beyond the reach of many who might seek office or contribute to our political life. In 1970, during an off-presidential election, candidates spent $158 million on political broadcasts. In that campaign the three candidates for the governorship of New York spent more than $2 million on television and radio broadcasts. Nelson Rockefeller reportedly used $6 million dollars and utilized a staff of 370 full-time employees. A one half-minute spot announcement on the leading Baton Rouge TV stations costs as much as $150 to $300 at prime time and $50 for poorest time (probably at 1:30 in the morning). To present a fifteen-minute speech on the leading channel in Baton Rouge at 7:30 P.M. cost as much as $300 to $500. To broadcast a half-hour speech over Louisiana TV networks might cost $25,000 or $30,000. It is estimated that a half-hour program broadcast simultaneously on three national networks at prime time would cost $250,000 or one million dollars for four such shows./19

Minow and his colleagues write:

> Robert Bendiner, in the *New York Times,* notes that "to get elected to high public office today, a candidate must either be a man in the top tax brackets himself or, more serious, a man unhealthily dependent on those who are and have axes to grind." Certainly the high cost of campaign advertising can allow a heavily financed candidate to dominate the most important means of communication, adding credence to the cynics' view that politics is but a rich man's game./20

My second point is that television is beyond the reach of many persons because it is technically complex to operate. The Great Debates of 1960 between John F. Kennedy and Richard M. Nixon dramatically illustrated this statement. As the debates progressed, it became evident that program format, camera position, lens openings, temperature of the studio, lighting, makeup, dress, and the positions of the debaters were most important. In fact, much to his dismay, Richard Nixon soon discovered that a free form of debate involved many uncontrolled elements which could be embarrassing. In 1968, he took no chances. He assembled a large staff of experts — writers, producers, directors, cameramen, coaches, and makeup men — to make sure that he presented an attractive image to the viewing public. In 1972, he took even fewer risks — expressing himself as little as possible before the cameras. Both Nixon and McGovern found the thirty- and sixty-second short spot announcements to their liking. What can a political candidate tell of significance in a half minute?/21

My third reservation about television is that it lends itself to manipulation out of view of the listener. The most dramatic demonstration we have had of editing in recent years was the CBS special, "The Selling of the Pentagon." In the name of producing an interesting show, the producer and his helpers lifted material out of context, rearranged interviews, and actually included some footage that had been filmed on another subject at another time./22

When you view a speaker—or the product, as they say in the Industry—what do you actually know about what you are seeing? Is he reading what someone else has written? How much has he rehearsed? Has the film been edited? By that I mean, have embarrassing or awkward portions been deleted? Is the camera actually revealing the real man or what the director or public relations man wants you to see? Are you seeing the real personality or an image created by some clever advertising man?/23

Is it any wonder that we live in an age characterized by what the Quaker philosopher Elton Trueblood calls "deep sickness"? Let me quote Alistair Cooke again. When he was asked, "Are Americans becoming more cynical as they view television and the extravagant promises it proclaims?" he answered, "Yes . . . this is an open society, and whether you like it or not, it does encourage cynicism. It makes demands on the maturity and judgment of the individual that are more severe than any he ever had to meet when he had only the press to ponder."/24

Many of you have perhaps wondered why I entitled my speech "Has TV Made the Speaker Obsolete?" Quite obviously, in a TV age only those with great resources or great power can gain access to effective use of this powerful means of communication./25

Minow and his colleagues argue that: "The drafters of the American Constitution strove diligently to prevent the power of the President from becoming a monopoly, but our inability to manage television has allowed the medium to be converted into an electronic throne." They argue convincingly that through the prestige of his office the President has an unfair advantage over all of his competitors. However, this analysis does not go far enough. Not only has the President made television into "an electronic throne," but also anyone with adequate financial support can buy time. Because it is expensive, technical, and capable of being manipulated, television is a tool at the disposal of the rich, the Establishment, the labor union, the pressure group—in fact, any faction that has great resources. It is not a medium generally at the disposal of the man, the minority group, the have-nots, the intellectuals, and at times even the opposition party with financial problems./26

At the present time, we have a tussle going on between the President and the TV industry. The President has the clout to command free time, and the networks dare not deny him his national audience. But let us change the characters in the drama. Suppose it were a struggle matching big television versus a man of limited resources or perhaps a minority leader or the leader of an unpopular group. Then how would scenes be played? Remember when poor, misguided Agnew dared to make a speech about the networks in Des Moines, Iowa? As a result, day after day on news programs, on talk shows, in television editorials, the whole thrust of the TV industry was turned on the Vice President. Now suppose Agnew had been a little American. The manipulation of television has changed the balance so that the First Amendment no longer works the way it was intended to./27

What has television done to the speaker or office-seeker?

On the positive side, if he has the resources or power, it provides him a great audience—that is, if he can put on a good show./28

On the negative side, if he is a little American, he can't even get into the game. But if he does sell himself to a bankroll, it may make out of him an image, an actor, and often a puppet of those who pay the bills./29

It is likely to cause him to put his message in broad, sweeping generalizations designed to offend no group, but to soothe a significant percentage of the viewers. Remember, ratings or the percentage of the market are more important than ideas or sound advice./30

What about the consumer? It is possible that we may elect a profile, a voice, a smile, an image who may be ignorant, immoral, and unwise./31

The time has come for me to resolve the difficulties that I have gotten myself into in this speech./32

At this moment there are several things that I could do./33

First, I could stop. Many of you would no doubt think that wise. But that would be the coward's way out, and cowards die many deaths, but the valiant die but once./34

Second, I could advocate the abolition of the First Amendment. Although I would not find support for that proposition here, there are persons in this country that would favor that drastic course of action./35

Third, I could advocate the return to the "Good Ole Days," and some of you probably have concluded that that is what I would like. But the "Good Ole Days" never really existed. Besides, who wants to wear a coonskin cap!/36

Fourth, I could advocate the elimination of speaking. You know that I would never favor that./37

Fifth, I could advocate the abolition of the networks. But I do not see how I could give up Ironsides, Lawrence Welk, Lucy, and Matt Dillon—even if I do have to see them six times on reruns./38

No, there must be a better solution to the problem that I have presented to you today./39

We must have an alert citizenry trained to evaluate what they see on television and [who] have the courage to demand that what is "cheap and shoddy" be taken off the air and to demand that the industry use the air waves fairly. When licenses are renewed, they must attend the hearings and speak./40

We must have a strong Federal Communication Commission which will resist pressure from all directions. It must not be under the control of President Nixon or NBC or Walter Cronkite. [The] FCC must not be a slave of any pressure group or business group. /41

I would hope that the Federal Communication Commission will always make its first concern the protection of the consumer. I am hopeful that more persons like Nicholas Johnson will be appointed to the Commission./42

I commend the Council for Better Broadcasts because its program starts educating viewers and citizens at the right time and in the right way. The persons who participate in your surveys and programs will be the influential citizens of tomorrow, and it may be that a member of your group will sometime have an opportunity to serve on the Federal Communication Commission or some other federal communication agency./43

One further word. The confrontation between speaker and voters must not be replaced. It must not be replaced if the First Amendment is to be meaningful. We must force the advocate to face the voters in a variety of situations giving them ample opportunity to express themselves in questions and rebuttal./44

The First Amendment was intended more for the protection of the consumer than it was the communicator. Newspapers and television talk about their rights under the Constitution. But, I think, even more important are the rights that the consumer has to full and complete information, access to all points of view, and opportunity to make up his mind without coercion or force and without being lulled into inactivity by a public relations man./45

It is highly appropriate that I remind you of two planks of the preamble of the Constitution of your organization. They read:

> . . . Recognizes that the Public Interest in the area of TV must be defined and protected by the public itself;
> . . . Recognizes that, since all broadcasting is done in the public domain, listeners and viewers have rights, privileges, and duties./46

In this scientific age, we are fond of describing our problems with statistics — statistics obtained from sampling procedures, from governmental census figures, from comparisons of last year with this year, and so on. Many human beings, however, at least pretend not to understand or like "mere numbers." Often, for those people, pertinent and vivid examples — specific instances and/or illustrations — have more rhetorical power than numerical data.

In the claim-of-policy speech which follows, Patricia Warren, a student at the University of Akron, when participating in the 1971 Interstate Oratorical Association Contest, chose to rely principally upon instances and illustrations for support as she worked through two aspects of an educational problem and proposed three solutions for it. Some illustrations, including her opening one, were conjured out of her imagination; others, such as the one from Cleveland, she had experienced personally. One was humorous; most were very serious. With this variety, Ms. Warren was able to communicate meanings to her listeners both connotatively and denotatively. The resulting speech is simple, clear, and effective.

Bring Forth the Children*
Patricia Warren

Attention step

Illustration

And Allen had of course arrived — as the law required — escorted by one (or both) parent (parents) not as the law required, but as the officer suggested. He had no personal belongings with him, not that they were forbidden — he just didn't have any. He had a coat; he had part of a coat (the rips and tears secured with safety pins and high hopes). And his shoes were worn through and stuffed with cardboard — not that it would matter in there. Even looking at the building frightened him; the bars, the screened-in windows, and locked doors, the people inside he had never seen (but had heard of) who were strict and cold, generous only in the distribution of punishment and the resurrection of easily forgotten rules. The door opened. He went in. And Allen began his first day at school./1

Analogy

In 1965, World Refugee Year, Yul Brynner wrote a book. It concerned the miserable, inhumane conditions of people trapped behind psychological fears and yards of barbed wire. He called it *Bring Forth the Children,* because there were so many children, so many young lives being squandered and futures going to waste. The North American parallel to the European refugee children are the children right here, not in reformatories, not in detention homes, but in a huge segment of supposedly sacred American institutions — in the inner-city schools./2

Need step

The experience of little Allen Myers is not unusual. It is far too common. John Goodlad, dean of the UCLA College of Educa-

---

*Reprinted from *Winning Orations,* 1971, by special arrangement with the Interstate Oratorical Association, Duane L. Aschenbrenner, Executive Secretary, University of Nebraska at Omaha.

tion, concluded that the schools are "anything but the palaces of an affluent society." On the contrary, he writes, "They look more like the artifacts of a society that did not really care about its schools, a society that expressed its disregard by creating schools less suited to human habitation than its prisons." Goodlad's statement was not limited to inner-city schools alone, but rather, its

relevance is heightened there. While statistics and reports show that the already poor condition of inner-city schools is continually growing worse, percentages indicate that the majority of students in the U.S. presently attend these schools. Each year, over 360,000 black students alone go into the adult world unequipped to obtain or hold jobs. It is therefore logical to conclude that the present school system does not reduce the urban crisis, but rather directly contributes to it./3

In more benevolent rhetoric, inner-city schools do not respond to the unique demands of inner-city school children. There are two major defects that show this inadequacy to be inherent in the system./4

The first problem is the physical environment. Is a school an institute of education, or a junior-American public prison? I re-

cently visited Addison Junior High in Cleveland, Ohio. Discipline, not learning, is the emphasis there, so much so that rigid disciplinary action is almost a self-fulfilling prophecy. Teachers go into the schools armed to the teeth against preconceived ideas of misbehavior that are 10% hearsay and 90% imagination. Not that discipline is unnecessary—when a twelve-year-old boy brings a loaded weapon to the school cafeteria, something is needed, and fast. But fair discipline occurs only after the fact, not in premonition of some future disturbance./5

The question that arises now is why do so many children misbehave so much? Lack of interest in school work may be one reason, home upbringing another. But there is a third, all-encom-

passing reason: a lack of basic human behavioral needs. These needs were defined by Dr. Matthew DuMont, Chief Psychiatrist for the Kerner Commission on Civil Disorder. Three of them apply here. They are the needs for stimulation, for self-esteem, and for environmental mastery./6

Let's take a closer look at that twelve-year-old with the gun. Chances are he isn't doing very well in school. He comes from a large family, or at least a family more concerned with survival as a whole than with him as an individual, so he doesn't get much attention. He is poor. School is dull. At school, however, he soon discovers that it can be fun if he does what he wants to do rather than what the teacher says. Aside from that, disobeying makes him the center of attention, and thus he feels important. It gives him a sense of power to be able to halt a lesson or change a routine by knocking over chairs, running around the room, bringing a loaded weapon to school. Stimulation, Self-Esteem, Environmental Mastery. The kid isn't delinquent. He's desperate. The climate for such deficiencies is present in all inner-city school children who have been deprived of their basic human behavioral needs—just one of the situations that makes the problems of teaching them unique./7

Second sub-area
Couple this deprivation to a second area of defect. In this area, there are three factors vital to the education of all school children: advanced techniques, highly qualified personnel, and a curriculum with direct relevance to their background. In the inner-city schools all three factors are virtually non-existent./8

First, because of a lack of sufficient funds, the modern technological advancements that we are so proud of—televisions, tape recorders, teaching machines, pencils, paper—are least available where most needed./9

The same holds true for qualified personnel. Least available where most needed. The problem here stems basically from the education of the educator. Take a look at teacher-training pro-
Specific instance
grams. For example, in the University of Akron, College of Education, required courses include subjects like "Problems in Education" that show why upper-middle-class white Anglo-Saxon protestant Johnny can't read, rather than why fourteen-year-old Cynthia, undernourished, unmarried, and pregnant, doesn't give a damn about modern math. There are more relevant courses, like Music Appreciation and Handicrafts, so that children on ADC and other poverty programs can sing "My Country 'Tis of Thee" and make art projects out of the same stuff they go home and eat off the walls. We expect our teachers to be well trained and highly qualified in their role as educators. But how can this be when we teach them in one culture and expect them to teach those of another?/10

Humorous anecdote
This culture gap can also be applied to [the] school curriculum. In an inner-city parochial school, an old Catholic nun—in all the pomp and circumstance of theological education—spent the entire semester grinding her definition of God into the minds of her third-grade class. "God is a Supreme Being," she said over and over, "God is a Supreme Being." One day she decided to test the results of her efforts. "Tommy," she said, "tell us who God is." And Tommy stood up and very proudly announced, "God is a Green Bean."/11

Explanation
What went wrong? Very simply this. The nun, in her overt desire to teach, forgot the basic need for children, as well as adults, to relate what they hear to what they know. Classroom texts and materials that place inner-city children in extra-environmental situations force them to relate to a culture they cannot adapt to; therefore, it means nothing to them. In Tommy's case, he had no conception of what "Supreme Being" actually meant, so he related it to his own life as best he could. The result was a green bean./12

A ghetto child doesn't care what two and two equals, unless knowing that the answer is four will put food in his stomach. He doesn't care that Dick and Jane and Spot visit Grandpa on the farm, or that the Union has fifty states or that plants go through photosynthesis. Dick and Jane on the farm don't even parallel Bill and May in the street—and what's a farm, anyhow?/13

*Illustration used
as summary of
problem*

A few months ago, two ghetto students visited the University of Akron. They went to a good restaurant and ordered hamburgers because they couldn't read the menu. One of them ordered french fries and sat looking at them for ten minutes because he couldn't figure out how to eat them with a fork. The boys were fifteen and sixteen years old. Pseudo-sociologists would call them "culturally deprived"—but they weren't deprived. They were

*Contrast by
means of specific
instances*

from a different culture altogether—a culture that doesn't need menus or three different forks for one meal, any more than it needs knowledge of photosynthesis, any more than white middle-class students need the Chinese alphabet. To teach inner-city children, courses must be adapted to the standards of inner-city culture. And the public school system has thus far failed to recognize that these standards and its standards are not quite the same./14

*Satisfaction
step*

So how do you do it—do you bring forth the children? It would be absurd to assert that one could isolate and treat the problems of the inner-city school separately from other related problems such as the race relations and the urban crisis itself. However, it is possible to assert that, combined with effective social action in related problem areas, certain specific changes can produce meaningful results./15

First solution

A first step would be to issue federal and state appropriations to rebuild and improve schools, to furnish modern technical equipment and free meals. But no physical change will yield re-

Second solution

sults unless there is a concern for a second step. Relevant teacher-training programs, classroom textbooks and materials must be redesigned with an awareness of inner-city culture. I am not suggesting that we perpetuate the cultural inadequacies of the inner-city school, but it is impossible to achieve meaningful, productive behavior in an affluent society unless you relate to and move forward from the students' own frame of reference./16

Third solution

Third, the schools must take on new and increased responsibilities to the students. The disciplinary philosophy of *in loco parentis* must be revised, and the purpose of dealing specifically with the needs of the students established as a standard goal./17

*Visualization
step*

An illustration of some of these points in action occurs every morning in the Cleveland schools when teachers in the inner-city sit down to breakfast with their children. The act may seem trivial, but the relevance is not. Even something as simple as eating breakfast together has its merit. It brings people closer. Two cultures acting as one./18

Action step (or conclusion)   We cannot ignore the crisis in the inner-city school, if for no other reason than the poet's observation that the child is the father of the man./19

We must "Bring forth the children."/20

An Equal Rights Amendment has been introduced in Congress at every session since 1923; political parties have endorsed it since 1940; and periodic hearings in both legislative houses have kept it near the floor. Yet it did not receive an official endorsement in Congress until August 10, 1970, when the House of Representatives passed it by a vote of 350 to 15. That vote signaled the ERA's significant presence on the American constitutional scene. The impressive margin by which the amendment passed reflected the impact of the women's liberation movement on the country as a whole; but just as importantly, it reflected the impact of an especially effective rhetorical campaign waged in the House of Representatives by Congresswomen Martha W. Griffiths of Michigan, Edith Green of Oregon, and Shirley Chisholm of New York. After numerous hearings and protracted delays, the House moved the Equal Rights Amendment out of its Committee on the Judiciary and onto the floor, where it was vigorously opposed and vigorously defended. Eventually, as the final vote drew near, Representative Chisholm rose to refute the case of the opposition.

The situation, of course, did not really call for a fully documented speech supporting a policy because many such speeches had already been given. Indeed, the heat of Congressional debate often tends to diffuse essential ideas and — in the process of airing all of the ramifications of a major question of policy — to separate its key elements almost completely. Rather, the situation demanded a relatively short, clearly organized speech which would pull together in a relatively objective and dispassionate manner all of the strings of arguments which had become scattered and disassociated as a result of the prolonged debate. A veteran of civil and women's rights' struggles, Representative Chisholm — given her general popularity and reputation, her skills, and her silence to this point on this day — was perhaps the ideal speaker for the task at hand.

Notice particularly the crispness of her speech and the tightness of her plan: the need is set out clearly, succinctly; each of the objections (especially those of Representative Emanuel Celler) is taken, one at a time, in a clear and orderly manner; the illustrations are simply cited in most cases and are piled one on top of another to build an imposing edifice of factual argument; and the conclusion then raises the audience's awareness out of the minutiae of legal-economic effects to a broader sociological generalization, thus bringing the "law" and the "people" together in a climactic inducement to action.

In Support of the Equal Rights Amendment*
Shirley Chisholm

*Generalized
need*

*Constitutional
remedy is needed*

Mr. Speaker, House Joint Resolution 264, before us today, which provides for equality under the law for both men and women, represents one of the most clear-cut opportunities we are likely to have to declare our faith in the principles that shaped our Constitution. It provides a legal basis for attack on the most subtle, most pervasive, and most institutionalized form of prejudice that exists. Discrimination against women, solely on the basis of their sex, is so widespread that it seems to many persons normal, natural, and right. Legal expression of prejudice on the grounds of religious or political belief has become a minor problem in our society. Prejudice on the basis of race is, at least, under systematic attack. There is reason for optimism that it will start to die with the present older generation. It is time we act to assure full equality of opportunity to those citizens who, although in a majority, suffer the restrictions that are more commonly imposed on minorities, to women./1

*Answer to the
"real-solution"
argument of
Celler (analogy)*

The argument that this amendment will not solve the problem of sex discrimination is not relevant. If the argument were used against a civil rights bill — as it has been used in the past — the prejudice that lies behind it would be embarrassing. Of course, laws will not eliminate prejudice from the hearts of human beings. But that is no reason to allow prejudice to continue to be enshrined in our laws — to perpetuate injustice through inaction./2

*Positive legal
effects*

*Series of
specific
instances*

The amendment is necessary to clarify countless ambiguities and inconsistencies in our legal system. For instance, the Constitution guarantees due process of law, in the fifth and fourteenth amendments. But the applicability of due process to sex distinctions is not clear: Women are excluded from some State colleges and universities. In some States, restrictions are placed on a married woman who engages in an independent business. Women may not be chosen for some juries. Women even receive heavier criminal penalties than men who commit the same crime./3

What would the legal effects of the equal rights amendment really be? The equal rights amendment would govern only the relationship between the State and its citizens — not relationships between private citizens./4

The amendment would be largely self-executing, that is, any Federal or State laws in conflict would be ineffective one year after date of ratification without further action by the Congress or State legislatures./5

---

*Originally printed in the *Congressional Record*, 91st Congress, 2nd Session, Volume 116, Part 21, pp. 28028-28029, August 10, 1970.

Refutation of the "confusion" argument

Opponents of the amendment claim its ratification would throw the law into a state of confusion and would result in much litigation to establish its meaning. This objection overlooks the influence of legislative history in determining intent and the recent activities of many groups preparing for legislative changes in this direction./6

State labor laws applying only to women, such as those limiting hours of work and weights to be lifted, would become inoperative unless the legislature amended them to apply to men. As of early 1970 most States would have some laws that would be affected. However, changes are being made so rapidly as a result of the Title VII of the Civil Rights Act of 1964, it is likely that by the time the equal rights amendment would become effective, no conflicting State laws would remain./7

Refutation of "usefulness" argument

In any event, there has for years been great controversy as to the usefulness to women of these State labor laws. There has never been any doubt that they worked a hardship on women who need or want to work overtime and on women who need or want better paying jobs, and there has been no persuasive evidence as to how many women benefit from the archaic policy of the laws. After the Delaware hours law was repealed in 1966, there were no complaints from women to any of the State agencies that might have been approached./8

Jury service laws not making women equally liable for jury service would have to be revised./9

Extended examples of legal applicability

The selective service law would have to include women, but women would not be required to serve in the Armed Forces where they are not fitted any more than men are required to serve. Military service, while a great responsibility, is not without benefits, particularly for young men with limited education or training. Since October 1966, 246,000 young men who did not meet the normal mental or physical requirements have been given opportunities for training and correcting physical problems. This opportunity is not open to their sisters. Only girls who have completed high school and meet high standards on the educational test can volunteer. Ratification of the amendment would not permit application of higher standards to women./10

Survivorship benefits would be available to husbands of female workers on the same basis as to wives of male workers. The Social Security Act and the civil service and military service retirement acts are in conflict./11

Public schools and universities could not be limited to one sex and could not apply different admission standards to men and women. Laws requiring longer prison sentences for women than men would be invalid, and equal opportunities for rehabilitation and vocational training would have to be provided in public correctional institutions./12

Different ages of majority based on sex would have to be

harmonized./13

Federal, State, and other governmental bodies would be obligated to follow nondiscriminatory practices in all aspects of employment, including public school teachers and State university and college faculties./14

Positive economic effects

What would be the economic effects of the equal rights amendment? Direct economic effects would be minor. If any labor laws applying only to women still remained, their amendment or repeal would provide opportunity for women in better-paying jobs in manufacturing. More opportunities in public vocational and graduate schools for women would also tend to open up opportunities in better jobs for women./15

Indirect effects could be much greater. The focusing of public attention on the gross legal, economic, and social discrimination against women by hearings and debates in the Federal and State legislatures would result in changes in attitude of parents, educators, and employers that would bring about substantial economic changes in the long run./16

Present discriminations unfair to both sexes

Sex prejudice cuts both ways. Men are oppressed by the requirements of the Selective Service Act, by enforced legal guardianship of minors, and by alimony laws. Each sex, I believe, should be liable when necessary to serve and defend this country./17

Each has a responsibility for the support of children./18

There are objections raised to wiping out laws protecting women workers. No one would condone exploitation. But what does sex have to do with it? Working conditions and hours that are harmful to women are harmful to men; wages that are unfair for women are unfair for men. Laws setting employment limitations on the basis of sex are irrational, and the proof of this is their inconsistency from State to State. The physical characteristics of men and women are not fixed, but cover two wide spans that have a great deal of overlap. It is obvious, I think, that a robust woman could be more fit for physical labor than a weak man. The choice of occupation would be determined by individual capabilities, and the rewards for equal work should be equal./19

Internal summary of legal and economic arguments

This is what it comes down to: artificial distinctions between persons must be wiped out of the law. Legal discrimination between the sexes is, in almost every instance, founded on outmoded views of society and the prescientific beliefs about psychology and physiology. It is time to sweep away these relics of the past and set future generations free of them./20

Inadequacies of existent laws

Federal agencies and institutions responsible for the enforcement of equal opportunity laws need the authority of a Constitutional amendment. The 1964 Civil Rights Act and the 1963 Equal Pay Act are not enough; they are limited in their coverage—for instance, one excludes teachers, and the other leaves out administrative and professional women. The Equal Employment Opportunity Commission has not proven to be an adequate device, with its powers limited to investigation, conciliation, and recommendation to the Justice Department. In its cases involving sexual discrimination, it has failed in more than one-half. The Justice Department has been even less effective. It has intervened in only one case involving discrimination on the basis of sex, and this was on a procedural point. In a second case, in which both sexual and racial discrimination were alleged, the racial bias charge was given far greater weight./21

Summation of the need for a new law

The "time is now" argument

Evidence of discrimination on the basis of sex should hardly have to be cited here. It is in the Labor Department's employment and salary figures for anyone who is still in doubt. Its elimination will involve so many changes in our State and Federal laws that, without the authority and impetus of this proposed amendment, it will perhaps take another 194 years. We cannot be parties to continuing a delay. The time is clearly now to put this House on record for the fullest expression of that equality of opportunity which our Founding Fathers professed./22

They professed it, but they did not assure it to their daughters, as they tried to do for their sons./23

The "we must start somewhere" argument

The Constitution they wrote was designed to protect the rights of white male citizens. As there were no black Founding Fathers, there were no founding mothers—a great pity, on both counts. It is not too late to complete the work they left undone. Today, here, we should start to do so./24

Conclusion of appeal for action

In closing I would like to make one point. Social and psychological effects will be initially more important than legal or economic results. As Leo Kanowitz has pointed out:

Quotation for an additional, broader inducement to action

Rules of law that treat of the sexes per se inevitably produce far-reaching effects upon social, psychological, and economic aspects of male-female relations beyond the limited confines of legislative chambers and courtrooms. As long as organized legal systems, at once the most respected and most feared of social institutions, continue to differentiate sharply, in treatment or in words, between men and women on the basis of irrelevant and artificially created distinctions, the likelihood of men and women coming to regard one another primarily as fellow human beings and only secondarily as representatives of another sex will continue to be remote. When men and women are prevented from recognizing one another's essential humanity by sexual prejudices, nourished by legal as well as social institutions, society as a whole remains less than it could otherwise become.†/25

---

†For an examination of this speech in its specific and larger contexts, see Hamida and Haig Bosmajian, eds., *The Great Argument: The Rights of Women* (Reading, Mass.: Addison-Wesley Publishing Company, Inc., 1972), esp. pp. 199–255.

The following speech, delivered to a joint session of Congress on December 8, 1941, was President Franklin Delano Roosevelt's message requesting a declaration of war against Japan. Prior to that date, the United States had been negotiating around the clock with that nation to keep the peace; and, seemingly, all was going well. Then suddenly, on Sunday morning, December 7, the Japanese launched a massive, surprise attack on Pearl Harbor, Hawaii, sinking eight American battleships and other smaller craft and leveling planes and airfields.

Our nation was numbed; Congress was indignant, and the President moved quickly. The joint session was held in the House chamber; the galleries were overflowing, and the speech was broadcast worldwide.

Notice that this message contains only a short attention step (because the surprise attack created all of the necessary attention), a longer need step (because everyone was wondering what was happening in the Pacific), a quick satisfaction step (for, of course, wartime strategies could not be discussed publicly), an "heroic" satisfaction step (because the nation needed to be steeled for war), and — finally — a concise, sharply drawn action step (because there could be no question in the minds of this audience that immediate and significant action must be taken). Note especially Roosevelt's careful structuring of the need step. Because it relied principally upon detailed information, it generally followed the statement/illustration/reinforcement/pointing pattern suggested in Chapter 10.

For a Declaration of War Against Japan*
Franklin Delano Roosevelt

Attention step

TO THE CONGRESS OF THE UNITED STATES: Yesterday, December 7, 1941 — a date which will live in infamy — the United States of America was suddenly and deliberately attacked by naval and air forces of the Empire of Japan./1

Need step

Background orientation

The United States was at peace with that nation and, at the solicitation of Japan, was still in conversation with its government and its Emperor, looking toward the maintenance of peace in the Pacific. Indeed, one hour after Japanese air squadrons had commenced bombing in Oahu, the Japanese Ambassador to the United States and his colleague delivered to the Secretary of State a formal reply to a recent American message. While this reply stated that it seemed useless to continue the existing diplomatic negotiations, it contained no threat or hint of war or armed attack./2

Statement of the problem

It will be recorded that the distance of Hawaii from Japan makes it obvious that the attack was deliberately planned many days or even weeks ago. During the intervening time the Japanese

*Originally printed in the *Congressional Record*, 77th Congress, 1st Session, Volume 87, Part 9, pp. 9504–9505, December 8, 1941.

government had deliberately sought to deceive the United States by false statements and expressions of hope for continued peace./3

Illustration

The attack yesterday on the Hawaiian Islands has caused severe damage to American naval and military forces. Very many American lives have been lost. In addition, American ships have been reported torpedoed on the high seas between San Francisco and Honolulu./4

Specific instances

Yesterday the Japanese government also launched an attack against Malaya./5

Last night Japanese forces attacked Hong Kong./6

Last night Japanese forces attacked Guam./7

Last night Japanese forces attacked the Philippine Islands./8

Last night the Japanese attacked Wake Island./9

This morning the Japanese attacked Midway Island./10

Reinforcing summary

Japan has, therefore, undertaken a surprise offensive extending throughout the Pacific area. The facts of yesterday speak for themselves. The people of the United States have already formed their opinions and well understand the implications to the very life and safety of our nation./11

Satisfaction step

As Commander-in-Chief of the Army and Navy I have directed that all measures be taken for our defense./12

Visualization step

Appeal to power and pride

Always will we remember the character of the onslaught against us./13

No matter how long it may take us to overcome this premeditated invasion, the American people in their righteous might will win through to absolute victory./14

Appeal to patriotism

I believe I interpret the will of the Congress and of the people when I assert that we will not only defend ourselves to the uttermost but will make very certain that this form of treachery shall never endanger us again./15

Overcoming fear

Hostilities exist. There is no blinking at the fact that our people, our territory, and our interests are in grave danger./16

Reverence for strength, nation, and God

With confidence in our armed forces—with the unbounded determination of our people—we will gain the inevitable triumph—so help us God./17

Action step

I ask that the Congress declare that since the unprovoked and dastardly attack by Japan on Sunday, December 7, a state of war has existed between the United States and the Japanese Empire.†/18

---

†For a fuller analysis of this speech, see Hermann G. Stelzner, "'War Message,' December 8, 1941: An Approach to Language," *Speech Monographs* XXXIII (November 1966): 419–437. Also reprinted in Robert L. Scott and Bernard L. Brock, *Methods of Rhetorical Criticism; A Twentieth Century Perspective* (New York: Harper & Row, Publishers, 1972), pp. 289–312.

A SPEECH OF ACCEPTANCE

As anyone who has watched a Motion Picture Academy Award ceremony can testify, speeches of acceptance often are stumbling, halting affairs with a profusion of thanks and embarrassment. Actually, however, the formality and dignity of the occasion invite exceptional — even great — discourse. While accepting an award or gift, a speaker can, for instance, strive to inspire others to the pinnacle he or she has reached. William Faulkner (1897 – 1962), renowned novelist and critic of the human race, endeavored to provide that type of inspiration when, on December 10, 1950, he accepted the Nobel Prize for Literature. The public might well have expected a "poor" speech (he had no reputation as a lecturer) filled with the kind of pessimism so characteristic of his novels. Instead, he greeted his listeners with a positive and stirring challenge to improve mankind.

Notice that Mr. Faulkner quickly pinpoints a particular audience — "the young men or women writing today" — to whom he directs much of his speech. Then, through a series of antitheses, he articulates the attitudes that are appropriate and useful to the artist, after which he concludes his remarks with a moving visualization step aimed at crystalizing the duties and obligations of writers for all time. Study this speech with your thoughts trained especially on Chapter 8, "Wording the Speech," and Chapter 14, "Speaking for Special Occasions."

On Accepting the Nobel Prize for Literature*
William Faulkner

I feel that this award was not made to me as a man, but to my work — a life's work in the agony and sweat of the human spirit, not for glory and least of all for profit, but to create out of the materials of the human spirit something which did not exist before. So this award is only mine in trust. It will not be difficult to find a dedication for the money part of it commensurate with the purpose and significance of its origin. But I would like to do the same with the acclaim too, by using this moment as a pinnacle from which I might be listened to by the young men and women already dedicated to the same anguish and travail, among whom is already that one who will some day stand here where I am standing./1

Our tragedy today is a general and universal physical fear so long sustained by now that we can even bear it. There are no longer problems of the spirit. There is only the question: When will I be blown up? Because of this, the young man or woman writing today has forgotten the problems of the human heart in conflict with itself which alone can make good writing because only that is worth writing about, worth the agony and the sweat./2

He must learn them again. He must teach himself that the basest of all things is to be afraid; and, teaching himself that, forget it forever, leaving no room in his workshop for anything but the old verities and truths of the heart, the old universal truths lacking which any story is ephemeral and doomed — love and honor and pity and pride and compassion and sacrifice. Until he does so, he labors under a curse. He writes not of love but of lust, of defeats in which nobody loses anything of value, of victories without hope and, worst of all,

*"On Accepting the Nobel Prize for Literature" by William Faulkner. Reprinted from *The Faulkner Reader*. Copyright 1954 by William Faulkner. Random House, Inc.

without pity or compassion. His griefs grieve on no universal bones, leaving no scars. He writes not of the heart but of the glands./3

Until he relearns these things, he will write as though he stood among and watched the end of man. I decline to accept the end of man. It is easy enough to say that man is immortal simply because he will endure: that when the last ding-dong of doom has clanged and faded from the last worthless rock hanging tideless in the last red and dying evening, that even then there will still be one more sound: that of his puny inexhaustible voice, still talking. I refuse to accept this. I believe that man will not merely endure: he will prevail. He is immortal, not because he alone among creatures has an inexhaustible voice, but because he has a soul, a spirit capable of compassion and sacrifice and endurance. The poet's, the writer's, duty is to write about these things. It is his privilege to help man endure by lifting his heart, by reminding him of the courage and sacrifice which have been the glory of his past. The poet's voice need not merely be the record of man, it can be one of the props, the pillars to help him endure and prevail./4

A SPEECH OF DEDICATION

The following remarks were made by Mr. Harold Haydon at the unveiling of "Nuclear Energy," a bronze sculpture created by Henry Moore and placed on the campus of the University of Chicago to commemorate the achievement of Enrico Fermi and his associates in releasing the first self-sustaining nuclear chain reaction at Stagg Field on December 2, 1942. The unveiling took place during the commemoration of the twenty-fifth anniversary of that event. Mr. Haydon is Associate Professor of Art at the University, Director of the Midway Studios, and art critic for the Chicago Sun-Times.

By combining specific references to the artist and his work with more general observations concerning the function of art and man's hopes and fears in a nuclear age, Mr. Haydon produced a dignified and thoughtful address, well suited to the demands of the occasion.

The Testimony of Sculpture*
Harold Haydon

Since very ancient times men have set up a marker, or designated some stone or tree, to hold the memory of a deed or happening far longer than any man's lifetime. Some of these memorial objects have lived longer than man's collective memory, so that we now ponder the meaning of a monument, or wonder whether some great stone is a record of human action, or whether instead it is only a natural object./1

There is something that makes us want a solid presence, a substantial form, to be the tangible touchstone of the mind, designed and made to endure as witness or record, as if we mistrusted that seemingly frail yet amazingly tough skein of words and symbols that serves memory and which, despite being mere ink blots and punch-holes, nonetheless succeeds in preserving the long human tradition, firmer than any stone, tougher than any metal./2

We still choose stone or metal to be our tangible reminders, and for these solid, enduring forms we turn to the men who are carvers

*"The Testimony of Sculpture," by Harold Haydon. Reprinted from the *University of Chicago Magazine*, January, 1968. Copyright © 1968, The University of Chicago.

of stone and moulders of metal, for it is they who have given lasting form to our myths through the centuries./3

One of these men is here today, a great one, and he has given his skill and the sure touch of his mind and eye to create for this nation, this city, and this university a marker that may stand here for centuries, even for a millennium, as a mute yet eloquent testament to a turning point in time when man took charge of a new material world hitherto beyond his capability./4

As this bronze monument remembers an event and commemorates an achievement, it has something unique to say about the spiritual meaning of the achievement, for it is the special power of art to convey feeling and still profound emotion, to touch us in ways that are beyond the reach of reason./5

Nuclear energy, for which the sculpture is named, is a magnet for conflicting emotions, some of which inevitably will attach to the bronze form; it will harbor or repel emotion according to the states of mind of those who view the sculpture. In its brooding presence some will feel the joy and sorrow of recollection, some may dread the uncertain future, and yet others will thrill to the thought of magnificent achievements that lie ahead. The test of the sculpture's greatness as a human document, the test of any work of art, will be its capacity to evoke a response and the quality of that response./6

One thing most certain is that this sculpture by Henry Moore is not an inert object. It is a live thing, and somewhat strange like every excellent beauty, to be known to us only in time and never completely. Its whole meaning can be known only to the ever-receding future, as each succeeding generation reinterprets according to its own vision and experience./7

By being here in a public place the sculpture "Nuclear Energy" becomes a part of Chicago, and the sculptor an honored citizen, known not just to artists and collectors of art, but to everyone who pauses here in the presence of the monument, because the artist is inextricably part of what he has created, immortal through his art./8

With this happy conjunction today of art and science, of great artist and great occasion, we may hope to reach across the generations, across the centuries, speaking through enduring sculpture of our time, our hopes, and fears, perhaps more eloquently than we know. Some works of art have meaning for all mankind and so defy time, persisting through all hazards; the monument to the atomic age should be one of these./9

AN EMPLOYMENT INTERVIEW

Often, for both the interviewer and the applicant, the job-seeking interview is a potentially frustrating communicative interchange. Indeed, some interviews take on characteristics of a melodramatic legal interrogation, replete with verbal parries, thrusts, dodges, maneuvers, and counter-maneuvers — in short, a communicative combat. Frequently, the feeling that the interviewer and the interviewee have opposing, or at least competing, purposes makes the employment interview an extremely complex affair, creating tensions where there could most beneficially be a joint effort toward relaxing them and in general creating an uncomfortable atmosphere more appropriate to "strategic one-up-manship" and expedient game-playing.

Job-interviews, however, need be neither frustrating nor nightmarish. Rather, they can — and should — be permeated from the outset by a determination and a willingness to seek mutually advantageous goals. Such an interview provides golden opportunities for employer and applicant to talk person-to-person about common problems and interests. As Harry Walker

Hepner emphasizes in his excellent Psychology Applied to Life and Work, *the job-seeker is not asking a favor, nor is the prospective employer granting a privilege. Each one has something worthwhile to offer, and each one has certain needs which may or may not prove of mutual advantage. The job-seeking interview can be a uniquely valuable instrument to help explore these matters calmly and intelligently in a climate of amiability and mutual respect.*

The good interviewer strives to put an applicant at ease and probes carefully and courteously, a step at a time. The good interviewer is likewise a good listener, continuing throughout to give off impressions of sympathy, understanding, and interest in the applicant as a person. *The good applicant, by the same token, is convinced (as we pointed out in Chapter 13, pages 302 – 305) that straightforwardness and directness are the best policies, and presents himself or herself openly, listening carefully but also asking informed, clear, and insightful questions. If both persons, then, carry forward their purposes in a climate of forthrightness and sensitivity, the job-seeking interview can be a highly satisfying and successful communication* transaction *in the true sense of that term.*

The transcript of the job interview reprinted below illustrates, we think, a maximally successful interchange. You will note that it is process-oriented, having five discernible stages — the initiative, the investigative, the negotiative, the actuative, and the terminative phases — and thus indicating that both the interviewer and the applicant knew what they were seeking and how to go about seeking it. Both appear to know the kinds of information they need, and both seem to emerge from the transaction pleased and sufficiently informed.

A Job-Seeking Interview: A Transcript*

NAME OF EMPLOYING COMPANY: *Wilson-Petty Paper Products*
INTERVIEWER: *Mr. Richard Scott*
JOB APPLICANT: *Ms. Jane Farwell*
TYPE OF POSITION AVAILABLE: *Customer Service Representative (CSR)*

1. The initiative phase

(As Ms. Farwell enters Mr. Scott's office, he rises and takes the initiative in observing the amenities.)

SCOTT: How do you do, Miss Farwell? Please come in.

JANE: *(Pleasantly; correcting him.)* Ms. Not "Miss." *(Smiles agreeably.)* But just call me Jane.

(Wanting to put the interaction on a positive, informal plane.) I hope I haven't kept you waiting.

SCOTT: Not at all . . . Jane. *(Also smiles.)* I appreciate your coming in on such a rainy day.

JANE: I was lucky enough to get a ride, so there was no problem.

SCOTT: Good. *(Indicating a chair.)* Won't you sit down? I'm Dick Scott.

JANE: *(Seating herself.)* Thank you.

*This transcript — reprinted here in somewhat modified form — is taken from Alan Monroe and Douglas Ehninger, *Principles and Types of Speech Communication,* 7th ed. (Glenview, Ill.: Scott, Foresman and Company, 1974), pp. 76–86.

(Scott picks up Jane's written application from his desktop and studies it for a few moments as he reseats himself.)

2. The investigative phase

SCOTT: *(Asking an "ice-breaker" question.)* Well . . . how do you feel—now that you're out of school?

JANE: Well, I have mixed feelings about it. *(Seriously, conscientiously.)* I really enjoyed school, and I'm almost sorry it's over. But at the same time, I'm really looking forward to starting a career.

SCOTT: I know exactly how you feel. I felt the same way myself when I graduated. *(Scanning job application papers.)* I see that you went to State University at Brookville. *(Encouraging the applicant to talk about herself.)* What made you decide to go there?

JANE: Well, when I started college, I really didn't know what I wanted to do or be, and State had a wide range of fields of study. Plus, it was far enough away from home for me to be independent, but not so far as to be inconvenient. *(Suggesting that money, economy are important considerations.)* Plus—the state universities are considerably less expensive than private colleges.

SCOTT: Yes, I guess the financial aspect is pretty important to us all. *(Continuing to draw the applicant out.)* Tell me . . . are you living away from home now?

JANE: No, I just can't afford to live by myself until after I've worked a while. So I'll be staying at home for the next few months at least—living with my parents.

SCOTT: What about your father . . . what does he do?

JANE: He manages the furniture division of Smith and Blake Department Store—near our home.

SCOTT: How about your mother? Does she work, or is she a housewife?

JANE: *(Somewhat sharply, in spite of herself.)* *Any* woman who is "a housewife" *works*, Mr. Scott.

SCOTT: *(With a small, apologetic laugh.)* You're right, Jane. What I meant was—does your mother work *outside* the home?

JANE: *(Reflecting a positive attitude toward the working-woman role.)* My mother has worked part time as a teacher's aide since I started to school. She has always enjoyed working.

SCOTT: *(Returning to the open-ended type of question.)* Tell me, what made you decide to come here to Wilson-Petty Products for a job?

JANE: Well, I saw your ad in the Sunday paper, saying that you have several positions open for college graduates. *(Showing a familiarity with the company.)* And since I've been familiar with Wilson-Petty products and have used them for some time, I felt that this might be an ideal place to start a career. Plus, it's easy to get here from Kingston, where I live.

SCOTT: Do you have a car, Jane?

JANE: No, I'll have to rely on public transportation or a car pool until I can save enough to buy a car. If I decide I really want and need one, that is. Ecology, you know.

SCOTT: I see. *(Thoughtfully; trying to measure how serious she is about a career.)* Jane, at the moment you're living with your parents . . . and I gather that you want a working career. I've been wondering . . . do you have any plans for marriage in the near future?

JANE: *(Cautiously resisting what she feels may be a personal intrusion.)* N-n-no . . . not at the moment. Of course, you realize *(with an emphasis she hopes Scott won't miss), personal* plans like that can change, though.

SCOTT: I understand. But, well—there is no one special person you're planning to marry at this time?

JANE: No, not at present.

SCOTT: *(Trying a touch of humor to ease the pressure.)* Incidentally, we have a lot of eligible bachelors here. *(Laughs, then resumes in a more serious tone.)* A moment ago you said that you liked Wilson-Petty products. Why?

JANE: Oh, I guess I think your things reflect good taste, mostly. *(Welcoming an opportunity to show her familiarity with the company's products.)* I always try to use your stationery—when I can afford stationery, that is. I like nice writing paper and notecards and things like that. And yours just always stand out on the store shelves.

SCOTT: That's very nice of you to say that. We've always felt that way, of course. *("Selling" her on the company.)* We've been very fortunate in having a lot of really good people working for us—both women and men. *(Starting a new tack.)* Tell me, Jane . . . outside of working, what are your plans for the near future?

JANE: I really don't know. But I've thought

about that a lot. I think someday I might want to go back to school and get an advanced degree of some kind—depending on where my interests take me in the near future. And I may want to get married in the next few years—I don't know. I'd like to get involved in community activities: maybe do volunteer work of some kind when I can. But I really can't be too definite right now. I've got to get a job first.

SCOTT: I can understand that. *(Indicating the application papers again.)* I see here that you got your degree in psychology. What made you decide on that as a major?

JANE: Well, the study of people's *behavior*—the workings of their minds—has always fascinated me.

SCOTT: I have to agree with you there. What subject did you do best in at school?

JANE: Psychology, naturally. That's another reason I wanted to study it—I was good at it. I had a B average in Psych.

SCOTT: I see. *(Wanting to know something about how the applicant gets along with other people.)* When you were at State University, where did you live?

JANE: In a dorm my first two years. Then I moved into an apartment and shared it with several other girls.

SCOTT: Why did you decide to move out of the dorm?

JANE: Mostly, I think, because I wanted to be more "on my own." *(Seizing the chance to let the interviewer know she can handle responsibility and that she wants "personal freedom," too.)* The dorms are really a kind of artificial housing arrangement—everything is done for you, and you don't really learn much about living in a real world. In an apartment you have to be responsible for meals, cleaning, paying the bills—you just learn more about life that way. Plus, there's more personal freedom if you live in an apartment.

SCOTT: *(Turning a page of the application forms.)* I notice that you were involved in several extracurricular activities on the campus. *(Looking for leadership qualities.)* What did you do for the Student Senate?

JANE: Well, the Student Senate was really like a student council, and I was my dorm representative during my sophomore year, and an off-campus representative in my junior year. I was too busy in my senior year to continue with the Senate.

SCOTT: Did you like that kind of work?

JANE: Oh, yes. *(Again emphasizing her personal interest in other people.)* I've always liked politics and community work, and this was a kind of combination of the two. We handled student grievances, and tried to make life on the campus a bit better for everyone. The Senate was a good introduction to the real workings of politics—on a very modest scale, of course.

SCOTT: I notice also that you were treasurer of the campus Psychology Society. *(Probing her experience and skill in handling money.)* Just what did *that* involve?

JANE: The treasurer keeps the books—financial records.

SCOTT: Financial records?

JANE: Yes, but there really wasn't that much to it. We weren't trying to make a profit or anything. I just kept track of dues and any money we made from fund-raising activities. And I paid out money for social events and the occasional guest speakers we had. That sort of thing.

SCOTT: *(Jocularly.)* Did you end up in the black or the red?

JANE: *(Laughingly.)* Oh, we just barely stayed in the black, but that's all we wanted.

SCOTT: *(Again probing for leadership qualities.)* I see that you were also chairman of the lecture committee for the Student Union. What did that entail?

JANE: Well, the Student Union at State sponsors once-a-month lectures by well-known or controversial people from all fields. The lecture committee "screened through" all the suggestions from the students, the faculty, and the community. Then—in essence—we decided upon the speaker. A faculty advisory committee did the final selecting from a list we would give them.

SCOTT: That sounds like a lot of responsibility.

JANE: It really wasn't a personal, individual responsibility. *(Demonstrating that she's a "team worker"—can work well with others.)* The group—the committee—worked together to find speakers. There was a lot of work for each committee member, I will admit that. But it was very interesting, and I enjoyed it immensely.

SCOTT: Interesting in what way in particular, Jane? *(Wanting to fit her qualifications to a specific job.)* Tell me a little more about it.

JANE: Well, for example . . . there were a great many requests for lectures by psychics or experts in the field of ESP. I always felt that this was quite a commentary—that we all want to be told about the future, the unknown. *(Revealing herself in a position of leadership and responsibility.)* Then, one of my jobs as chairman was to contact the person who was selected to give the lecture and make final arrangements for his appearance on campus, agree on an exact topic, and so forth. I always enjoyed the personal contact with these well-known people.

SCOTT: That would be pretty satisfying, I can well imagine. *(Wanting to know about the applicant's specific office skills.)* In contacting these various people, I suppose you had to do a lot of telephoning and corresponding. Do you know how to type?

JANE: Just for my own personal use. *(Trying to avoid being "stuck" in the typist niche.)* Not very fast, but adequately for my own purposes.

SCOTT: Do you know how to operate any office machines—a calculator, an adding machine, perhaps even a computer?

JANE: *(With a laugh.)* Well, I make a great Xerox, but that's about it.

(Scott laughs also. She has succeeded in using humor to cover up possible inadequacies . . . and in diverting the line of questioning. He refers to the application and resumes more seriously as he begins to explore her previous job experience.)

SCOTT: I see here that you worked for the last three summers at the Dalton Warehousing Company. How did you get the job?

JANE: The first year, a friend who worked there told me about an opening. *(Letting him know that she's capable of landing and holding onto a job.)* I applied for a job and got it. And each summer after that, they asked me to come back.

SCOTT: Did you like the Dalton job?

JANE: Well, it was pretty routine. *(And she wants more than a "routine" job.)* Mostly folding and stapling. Just processing orders. But I liked the people I worked with. And I was grateful for the job experience—and the money, of course. But I wouldn't want to make it my life's work.

SCOTT: *(Sounding her out as to the possible*

"competition.") I've been wondering, Jane . . . have you had a number of job interviews since you graduated? Talked with other companies?

JANE: No, I honestly haven't. I did go back to Dalton's, sort of out of loyalty. But they really didn't have any positions for a college graduate. *(Letting him know that she's being selective.)* Not the type of job I'm looking for. However, I do have a few leads now, and I plan to pursue them until I find just the right position for me.

SCOTT: Do you know what you're looking for?

(The interviewer is saying, in effect: "You define the job. If we have it, we may—just may—try to negotiate.")

JANE: Yes. I've always wanted a job where I work with *people*—where I can help people solve their problems, where I can maybe make someone's day just a little better. That's another reason why I chose psychology as a major. I felt that if I had a little more information about how and why people act as they do, I would know better how I could help them. *(Narrowing down the possibilities.)* I don't mean I want to be a counselor, or anything like that. But I do want a job where I'm dealing with people, and where I can help them.

SCOTT: *(Thoughtfully.)* I can see, all right, in a *general* way, how your psychology background could help in a job like that. *(Pinning her down to the nitty-gritty of what she actually has in mind.)* But—well, I'm not sure I see all of the specifics. Can you pin them down for me a bit?

JANE: Oh, I just think I would be able to understand people more because of my psych. I mean, I would be able to recognize—oh, say—stress situations, and be able to adjust my own behavior when I thought the situation required it.

SCOTT: I see.

(The applicant now wants to take the initiative and direct the course of the interaction.)

JANE: May I ask a question here?

SCOTT: Certainly. Go right ahead.

JANE: Well, exactly what positions are open here at Wilson-Petty's—positions that I qualify for?

(Having completed the investigative phase of the interview and having a fairly clear picture of the applicant's background, training, and

abilities, the interviewer is ready to begin fitting her into a specific job-situation.)

3. The negotiative phase

SCOTT: That's a very good question—one that I was about to bring up. As you mentioned, in our advertisement we indicated that we had several positions open for college graduates. A few of these jobs are for specialized or technical people. For accounting or design majors, for example. But we do have some openings in our Customer Service Department. And—certainly as a beginning at least—I believe you might find that working in customer service is very close to what you have in mind. Especially with your background in psychology.

JANE: *(Wanting to make sure of the meaning of the term.)* Just what is "customer service"?

SCOTT: What is *your* idea of a customer-service job? What do you think it might involve?

JANE: Well, from the job title, I'd guess it involves working with customers in some way or other.

SCOTT: You're pretty close. *(Explaining the specific nature and scope of the job.)* In some companies, it is referred to as *inside sales*. As you probably know, we have sales representatives who call on stationery and paper-specialty departments of large retail stores. The Customer Service Representatives—or CSR's, as they are often called—work as adjuncts to the sales force. There are plenty of chances for responsibility and growth in the job. *(Suggesting the possibilities, selling—but not over-selling—the opportunities.)* The CSR handles any problems that may arise in ordering, shipping, or billing. The CSR's also handle the sales for any smaller stores which don't do enough volume to justify having a sales representative call on them. And CSR's also prepare and send out sales promotions to stores—either on their own, or in conjunction with a sales representative.

JANE: What kind of opportunities for advancement are there in Customer Service?

SCOTT: Many. *(Trying to make the job sound appealing.)* There are opportunities aplenty—depending partially on you, of course. Just where do you want to *be*—what would you like to be *doing*—five years from now?

JANE: Well, as yet I don't really know that much about business. *(Not afraid to reveal her ambition to succeed.)* But I think I'd like someday to be some sort of manager or supervisor—someone who not only still works with people on the job, but also supervises people under her. I never want to get away from direct contact with people. I don't want to be any ivory-tower executive or anything like that—but, well, I would like to move up the corporate ladder, so to speak.

SCOTT: Then I think you'll find Customer Service a good position to start from. Several of our CSR's have become sales representatives, and sales managers can go on to become managers in our district and regional offices. And, of course, many go into management of some kind here and in the home office. Or, for those CSR's who prefer not to go out into the field into direct sales, there are many opportunities *inside*—either moving up within Customer Service or moving out into other departments: advertising, market research, or others. A job in sales or Customer Service is one of the best training grounds for advancement here at Wilson-Petty's.

JANE: I must say that sounds quite encouraging. Very appealing, really.

SCOTT: A CSR works hard. Let me emphasize that. But the long-range rewards can be good.

(The applicant wants to stress again that the salary, as well as the job, is important to her.)

JANE: Can you—well, can you tell me something about the more immediate rewards?

SCOTT: *(Genially.)* You mean salary and benefits, I take it.

JANE: Yes—for the person you decide to hire. Money isn't the first consideration, by any means. But—well, it's important.

SCOTT: I quite agree. Actually, at the moment, I'm afraid I won't be able to tell you exactly what the salary is for a CSR. That's decided by our Mr. Bedloe, head of the Customer Service Department, and is based on the applicant's experience, college background, and other factors. *(Wanting her to know that salary will not be a problem.)* I can say, however, that our salary ranges are competitive.

JANE: I can understand that.

SCOTT: As for benefits, we have life, medical, and major medical insurance, paid vacations, and sick time. *(Picks up brochure from desk, rises, and hands it to Jane.)* Maybe you'd like to look this over. It spells out our company's employment policies, working conditions, fringe benefits, and all the rest.

JANE: *(Taking the brochure.)* Thank you very much.

SCOTT: If you find that you do have any questions after you've read that brochure, just ask.

JANE: *(With evident enthusiasm.)* I surely will because—well, because this CSR job sounds as if it could be just what I want—working with people—a chance to work my way up. *(Expressing confidence in her ability to handle the job.)* I think I could really bring a lot to that job. And get a lot from it, too.

(Something close to a "meeting of the minds" has begun to form, and the interviewer is ready to take the decisive step toward doing something about it: actuation.)

4. The actuative phase

SCOTT: You know, Jane *(smiles, also evidences enthusiasm)* . . . I quite agree. And I'm glad you feel that way. I don't have *all* the say-so on who's hired and who isn't, but—well, let's just say I have some *influence. (Laughs, and Jane joins in.)* In my opinion, you could do Wilson-Petty a lot of good—and yourself, too. I've liked what you've said and the way you've said it. Spunk—but good sense with it. So if you

have the time now, I think you should talk with Mr. Bedloe.

(Since the applicant will be working with someone else, the interviewer makes clear exactly who that person is and assures the applicant a "referral" interview will be arranged promptly.)

JANE: *(Very pleased; rises.)* Oh, I've got the time, Mr. Scott—all the time in the world.

SCOTT: Fine. Fine. *(Crossing toward door to outer office.)* You might just take a chair out here in my outer office and look over that brochure while you're waiting. *(Opening the door for her.)* I'll put a call through to Mr. Bedloe and see if I can arrange for you to speak with him right away.

5. The terminative phase

JANE: *(Walking toward door.)* That would be great. *(Observing the concluding amenities.)* Thank you, Mr. Scott. Thank you *very* much.

SCOTT: *(Likewise concerned with the conventional courtesies.)* And I thank *you*. After you've had a chat with Bedloe, I'll want to talk with you again—more specifically—Miss Farwell. *(Catching himself.)* Er—uh—I—mean—Ms. . . . Ms. . . . *(having trouble pronouncing it)* . . . how do you *say* that, anyway?

JANE: *(Turns in doorway.)* I think it will be easier, Mr. Scott, if you just call me Jane.

(She laughs; he joins in, and they thus bring the interaction to a momentary close on a light, informal note. She goes out and closes the door.)

A PROBLEM-SOLVING DISCUSSION

The public discussion which follows provides a good example of a problem-solving group at work. It was conducted as part of an annual contest in which colleges and universities across the country submit twenty-five-minute audiotapes of undergraduate students participating in a consideration of a previously announced question. Judges listen to and evaluate these tapescripts in terms of the following criteria: (1) solid content and perceptive analysis of the question, (2) use of public panel-discussion techniques, and (3) interest-value to a reasonably intelligent adult audience. The panelists in this discussion, students at Kent State University, coached by Dr. Linda Irwin Moore and under the general direction of Dr. Carl M. Moore, were declared the winners of the 1974 competition, held in con-

junction with the Central States Speech Association Convention in Milwaukee, on April 5, 1974.

If you read the tapescript carefully, you will discover a well-ordered, exploration-and-solution process. The participants adequately oriented their unseen audience to the problem, narrowed the subject in accordance with the prescribed time limits, then approached it systematically, and completed each stage of the problem-solving process before moving on to the next (after the manner suggested in Chapter 14). You will notice that each of the panelists had carried out extensive research on the topic and was prepared to substantiate each point with statistics, examples, details, and the other forms of support. Note particularly the attention paid to definitions, to typical examples, and to generalizations; examine the blending of illustrative, statistical, and testimonial evidence. Note also how the leader opens the discussion, calls for each stage, summarizes agreed-upon conclusions, and pushes the group more deeply into the problem when she thinks they need more proof for positions taken. Observe, too, how the panelists interact, calling each other by name, controlling carefully their disagreements (to keep the group from drifting off into useless bickering), and supporting each other when desirable.

As you read through this discussion, bear in mind two things: (1) The panelists had to keep within a strict time limit; and, therefore, some stages — particularly the evaluation and summary — had to be treated briefly. (2) This transcription attempts to reproduce the audiotape faithfully; only vocalized pauses, a few "false starts," and the like have been cut. What you are encountering here is "oral," not "written," grammar and syntax at work; do not expect "proper" sentences or polished expression.

How Can the Government Best Protect the American Consumer?*

PANELISTS: *Judy Andino (moderator), Gary Pandora, Karen Brown, Jerry Pursley*

Introduction and background

JUDY: "Consumption is the sole end and purpose of all production. And the interest of the producer ought to be attended to so far as it may be necessary for promoting that of the consumer. The maxim is so perfectly self-evident that it would be absurd to attempt to prove it. But in the mercantile system the interest of the consumer is almost constantly sacrificed to that of the producer." Adam Smith noted this paradox of ethics in his book, *The Wealth of Nations*, and it is this issue — consumer

protection — that we will consider today in answering the question, "How can the government best protect the American consumer?" I'm Judy Andino, a senior, and I will act as moderator this evening. Joining in the discussion are these panel members: Gary Pandora, a junior; Karen Brown, a senior; Jerry Pursley, a senior./1

In considering the topic-question, this panel has agreed on some definitions of terms. "Consumer" is defined as any person who buys and uses food, clothing, and other services.

*Permission to transcribe and edit this discussion was granted by Professor Carl M. Moore as agent for Kent State University. The authors and the publisher wish to thank also the students' coach, Dr. Linda Irwin Moore, and the audio engineer, Martin Gallagher, for their work.

"Government" is defined as "the federal government." Because of the limited time span provided to treat the stated topic-question, we have imposed a limit on the aspect of governmental consumer protection we shall be discussing this evening. Coupled with the time limitation involved, however, is our concern for emphasis on a universal consumptive product, and thus we chose food. But then, perhaps our audience would be interested in hearing our specific rationale for selecting food./2

JERRY: One of the reasons for choosing the food industry is because it is the single largest industry in the United States; it's a $125 billion-a-year industry, and that makes it over six times as large as General Motors, America's largest industrial corporation./3

KAREN: I think, in addition, Jerry, that there is something that Judy hinted at, and that's the idea that food is such a basic commodity; regardless of what else the consumer may or may not have, he has to have food./4

Stage One
Defining the problem

JUDY: Well, food is definitely important to the average American consumer, but that leaves me with the question, "What are the problems with food?"/5

JERRY: Well, we saw basically three problems with food—that of food *prices*, food *shortages*, and food *quality*. And we came here tonight prepared to discuss all three of those; but due to limitations of time, I suggest that we limit our analysis to that of *food quality*./6

GARY: I would agree, Jerry. I believe that the quantity of food and food prices are certainly of vital importance to the consumer; but, essentially based on that, we're talking about the quality of food. And, if we haven't got good quality of food, then we're going to be in a lot of trouble./7

KAREN: I think we can all agree, then, that because of the time and the importance of food quality, we may as well just limit ourselves to that./8

JUDY: All right, then, if we are going to do that—to limit ourselves to quality alone—what do we mean by the term "quality," and what problems does the American consumer meet in food quality?/9

GARY: It's very difficult to give a specific definition of quality food or nutritional food. Generally, what is accepted is the recommended daily allowance, or the RDA. Now, this was established by the Food Nutrition Board of the National Research Council and the National Academy of Sciences. And the problem with the RDA is that, first of all, many nutritionists around the country say that it is too low; standards are not sufficient for what people need. And, second, the RDA is based on healthy people—healthy people being those who currently meet the standards of this low RDA. The problem, again, is that many people in this country do not meet even those low standards./10

JERRY: What you're saying, Gary, is pointed up in two surveys conducted by the Department of Agriculture, one in 1955, and the other in 1965. The Department of Agriculture found in their surveys that half of the people surveyed in 1955 had appallingly inadequate diets; and then in 1965, just ten years later, they found that had increased to two-thirds of those surveyed. And those people were deficient in protein, calcium, vitamins A and C, and all the other nutrients considered, except iron. I think it's important to point out that in the survey, they didn't survey the poor people, the people from the ghetto. This was a survey conducted in *urban* America, in the small urban areas and in rural areas./11

KAREN: Well, it seems to me, Jerry—and Gary, too—what both of you are getting at is that we have a problem as far as nutrients go in our specific diets, but that there are so many people involved that I don't think that we could ever hope to examine all their diets, or regulate their diets, or whatever. So maybe we ought to take a look instead at the quality of food that is available to the American consumer—food that he can choose to put into his diet if he wants to./12

Stage Two
Analyzing the problem

JUDY: If you are suggesting, then, that there is a declining value in food that comes to the consumer, I'd like to have some evidence. I'd like to know what are some specific examples./13

JERRY: Well, I'd like to point out that the trend that I mentioned was noted by the Department of Agriculture, and has been verified by the American Medical Association and the National Academy of Science. They have gone on record to indicate their concern about the diminished nutritive content of American foodstuffs, and they point out that problems in current methods used in food production, processing, storage, and the distribution of American foods are some of the primary problems in this area./14

KAREN: I think it's really interesting, Jerry, that they mention processing and refinement as a problem with food, because there are a couple of examples I noticed when we were doing our research. And one of them deals with a very basic food commodity, and that's *bread.* During the processing of bread—the refinement or roller milling or whatever term you want to use—bread loses about 98% of its manganese value, about 80% of its iron value, about 80% of thiamine nutrients that are available to it, and about 75% of the niacin. The list goes on down through the rest of the nutrients that could be gotten by the consumer through bread./15

JERRY: Well, I hate to sound discouraging, but I wonder how many of you had your breakfast this morning? When you had your breakfast, how many of you had breakfast cereals?/16

KAREN: I did./17

JUDY: Me, too./18

JERRY: Well, I have some sad news for you, then./19

ALL: Oh?/20

JERRY: A Georgia University study revealed that cereal *boxes,* if taken with milk and raisins, are as nutritious as all but the most sophisticated cereals. So probably you would have been better off eating the boxes./21

KAREN: Oh?/22

JERRY: Yet, the Food and Drug Administration has avoided the development of a standard on the cereals simply for that reason. They don't want to give breakfast cereals the respectability of being called a food./23

KAREN: Jerry, when I pulled out my cereal this morning, my Rice Krispies, on the box there is a label on the side that lists the kinds of vitamins and nutrients that are in that specific cereal. Is that label false?/24

JERRY: The listing on the cereal boxes is accurate, but it's accurate when the cereal is eaten *with milk and sugar./25*

GARY: Jerry, I might take issue with that because refined white sugar retains not one milligram of vitamins or minerals. I think in discussing refined flour or cereals or breads, it has been illustrated historically on at least two occasions that unrefined breads or cereals actually improved health. These occurred in World War I and in World War II. During that period in England and in Denmark, both of those countries did not refine their cereals or their breadstuffs. As a result, health improved. Also, I might add that when we talk of breadstuffs, this can be expanded to cereals as well as macaronies, spaghetti, noodles, crackers, cookies, pastries, cakes, cake mixes, on and on and on./26

JUDY: Everyone has some of those./27

KAREN: I think there's something else that everyone has some of. These all have been dealing with grains and things. But we mentioned before—Jerry did at the outset—about refining and processing having an effect on the nutritive value of food. On this we can look at one other processing agent, and that's *canning.* And that again, like Gary said, encompasses an awful lot of separate commodities. In those commodities there's the same kind of nutritive change that occurs in everything else we've been giving examples of. For example, in the processing of canned carrots, they lose about 65% of their potassium content; green beans lose about 60% of their potassium content; and tomatoes lose about 51%. And that same kind of list goes on through the rest of the vegetables and the rest of the vitamins. But I think that we ought to make one more thing clear in relation to this. In the book *Consumer, Beware* (1971), by Beatrice Hunter, she makes the statement that not only do these nutritive values come out during the canning process, but there are also chemical changes that may actually be harmful to the consumer. For example, in the canning of carrots, their sodium content is increased 45,000%; and that creates a vast danger to the consumer healthwise, in relation to hardening of the arteries and various other heart diseases./28

JUDY: OK. You seem to have labeled some of the potential dangers in the refining process, but this leaves me in an awful bind, an awful quandary. As an average American consumer, I think the refining process and the methods used in supplying food to the consumer are fantastic. I get the kind of foods that I want. Are we indicting the entire process as being a hazard to the American consumer?/29

JERRY: Not at all, Judy. I think we have to understand that in a country this size, with the population we have, that food has to be refined to a certain degree. It has to be processed. It's a practical matter. In order to get food to that many people, certain refinements are necessary. But what we want to point out is that there should at least be an awareness by the consumer that there is a nutritive loss in certain types of refinement, in processing—that the consumer should be aware of this nutritive loss./30

JUDY: Then that would be the crux of the matter—the lack of knowledge?/31

JERRY: Right./32

JUDY: All right. This I could conceive as definitely a problem. You've shown me with specific evidence of such basic foodstuffs as bread and breakfast cereals and sugar, and even canned foods, that the consumer does have a very definite lack of knowledge about the refining processes and what he is getting from it. But what about some real *harm*? Is there any real harm incurred through food quality?/33

GARY: I think that one of the important considerations as far as food quality is concerned is the *additives* that are put into food. There are many, many additives that go into our food—some for cosmetic purposes and others to add to the nutritional value and to help retard spoilage and such. In fact, we have over 2500 additives added to our food. And of those, less than half have been tested by the FDA./34

JERRY: I think it's important to realize that according to Marine and Von Allen, in *Food Pollution and Violation to Our Inner Ecology,* the average American annually eats three pounds of these food additives, many of which cause genetic mutations, give us cancer, or simply make us sick. And so there are real problems with these additives in food./35

KAREN: Well, I think if we're going to indict additives, up to now we've been talking kind of generally as to how many there are and what they may or may not do. I think it's important that we take a look at some of the ones that may actually be coming to the consumer—

that he may be ingesting into his system. And I think a good example is FD & C Citrus Red #2. It was reported in *Consumer Reports,* May of 1973. This particular additive is used as a coloring in the skin of oranges, the skin of potatoes to make them appear fresher, and in all candied yams to make them appear fresher. And this particular drug, through feeding tests, showed growth retardation and cancerous bladder changes in male rats and degenerative changes in female rats. And, ironically enough, it has been banned by the World Health Organization and by the Canadian Government. And yet, in the United States it's still used, and the FDA has made no attempt to warn the American public of just what the dangers may be./36

GARY: Karen, unfortunately, that is not the only example we can cite. One example I found was monosodium glutamate. In May, 1969, a test by Washington University revealed that MSG or monosodium glutamate had caused brain damage in two- to ten-day-old mice. Now, this was revealed to the FDA in May of 1969, but it was over five months before they took it out of baby foods./37

JUDY: But this is specifically the Food and Drug Administration's jurisdiction, their problem. Ah—I mean, don't they *test?* Don't they *inform* the consumer?/38

JERRY: Judy, unfortunately, most of the time they don't test. Most of the time they have to rely on the information provided by the industry in evaluating their own product. They don't have the resources, unfortunately; and, as a result, the American consumer is consuming additives that have some question as to their safety./39

KAREN: I think, Jerry, not only are there questions about a lot of this, but the Food and Drug Administration is, in many cases, not even raising those particular questions. There is what they call a provisional list, and additives will be allowed to be put into food for consumption by the American consumer while they're being tested or until tests occur. One particular additive, FD Red #2—it's not the same one I mentioned before; it's a different title—was kept on the market for ten years, even though other countries had banned it, because the FDA had not begun to run its tests yet./40

JERRY: I found there are a lot of people

really concerned about this. One that I found specifically is Dr. James Crow, in *Medical World News* of 1968. He stated that potentially irrevocable genetic damage might be done without immediate warning by some of the more than 10,000 natural and synthetic chemical agents now produced commercially, or by the million or more additional agents that may have been isolated or synthesized by man. Fewer than 200 of these suspected mutagens have been systematically assayed. And according to Victor Cohen, in the *Washington Post*, we may already be experiencing some of the effects of these potential mutagens in the increased rate in birth defects in this country./41

GARY: I think it's important that we realize in discussing additives that perhaps there are individual additives that are harmful. There may, of course, also be additives that are not harmful. But we have to realize that we really don't know what a *combination* of these individual additives can produce. And there's another danger right there./42

JERRY: Yeah, I agree with that, Gary. The problem I think that we have is with the FDA, and a lot of times not only with the provisional list and with the additives that they've okayed for use in this country, but *enforcement* is a real problem. Unfortunately, the FDA has to depend on voluntary compliance by industry. And, in the MSG case, for example, it took them five months to get it off the market after there was a lot of static about it. Dan Gerber, of Gerber Baby Foods, stated to his shareholders that the testing, in his opinion, by the FDA—or by Washington University, I'm sorry—was incomplete, and he felt that MSG should be left on the market until it was proven dangerous. Thus, he wanted to reverse the law; and instead of proving something safe before it was put on the market, he wanted to make sure it was proven dangerous before it could be taken off./43

JUDY: You're speaking of "safe" and "dangerous." What I've gleaned so far is that there are basically two types of additives. There are those that enhance the nutritional value and preserve the product, and these benefit the consumer. Then, there are those cosmetic additives, it seems to me, those that are for the producer's benefit./44

JERRY: That's correct, Judy./45

JUDY: Which one does the consumer get more of?/46

JERRY: Definitely the additives that are for cosmetic purposes; about 80% of them are for cosmetic purposes. For example, according to Marine and Von Allen, in the book *Food Pollution*, they noted that the Food Protection Committee lists 1622 additives currently in use. Of those, 1077 were used for flavoring; and as far as bulk is concerned, the vast majority of the additives we consume are for nothing but coloring./47

JUDY: But doesn't the FDA provide information on this? Don't they obey the Labeling Act?/48

JERRY: Well, no, they don't. Again they have to rely on, or at least they have been relying on, voluntary compliance. The Nader group, when they studied the FDA, found that in 1969 alone the FDA recommended 5052 label changes, but not one was adopted./49

KAREN: I would like to add just one more thing to that, Jerry, that would help to answer Judy's question; and that's the idea that the Fair Packaging and Labeling Act, which so many think protects us, doesn't really do that because there's no portion of that act which requires manufacturers to list how many or what type of additives are in a particular food product. In fact, in many cases the Food and Drug Administration treats those additives as trade secrets of the manufacturers./50

GARY: Jerry, you mentioned these so-called cosmetic additives or additives added simply to increase or enhance the appeal of food or taste of it. I think a very common example of this is brown dye, called caramel coloring. This is added to enriched white, refined bread; and when this caramel coloring is added, it gives it the appearance of being whole-grain bread, 100% whole wheat bread, when in fact it is the regular white enriched bread just colored brown./51

JUDY: OK, then, with all of this in mind, again the underlying problem seems to be a lack of consumer knowledge./52

KAREN, JERRY, GARY: Yes./53

JUDY: Then, to me, obviously the food-quality problem manifests itself as a kind of a two-headed monster for the American consumer. In two ways he's ignorant—ignorant of the refining process and what it does to the food he is getting; and additionally, he's ignorant of potential harm-inducing elements added to food in the guise of, say, cosmetic additives for taste and coloring. Will you agree with me that this seems to be the essence of the problem we've been discussing?/54

KAREN, JERRY, GARY: Yes! Definitely! Very definitely!/55

Stage Three
Suggesting solutions

JUDY: If, then, this is a problem that cries for a solution, what would be any criteria we would have to consider in proposing a solution?/56

KAREN: Well, I think the most obvious criterion would be that we have to deal with the *cause;* and because we define government as federal government, we should have some sort of federal agency that would get at the cause./57

JERRY: Judy, I think another criterion that we should keep in mind is that we don't want to diminish the *selectivity* of the American consumer. We don't want to take away his choices at the supermarket./58

GARY: Going beyond what you're saying, Jerry, we have to remember that the consumer has eaten these processed foods for a long period of time. Now, if we're going to tell him that there are problems with these foods, that the consumer can in fact be eating food that is harmful to him, we're attacking some pretty deep-rooted *attitudes, values,* and *beliefs.* And we're going to have to consider that in our solution./59

JUDY: That seems to me the biggest problem we've got to face, and one that's going to be crucial to any of the solutions we may come up with—that, as well as the other two very pertinent criteria we have set up. What would be a feasible solution that would somehow include all of these?/60

JERRY: I think one solution comes to mind right away. We mentioned that 80% of the additives in our food are in there for commercial reasons; they aren't in there for the good of the consumer at all. I think that all of these should be eliminated from foods./61

KAREN: Well, I think, Jerry, in order to do that, we're going to have to deal with the government agency that I mentioned before. And that probably would be the Food and Drug Administration, because we said that they

don't have standardization in their testing, and they don't have subpoena power to get information; they rely on voluntary compliance. So, it seems to me that in order to deal with that problem, we probably ought to *strengthen the Food and Drug Administration* so that it can do what it's supposed to be doing for the consumer./62

JUDY: Now, you're bargaining for quite a job there, because strengthening or reducing any bureaucracy is going to be a paramount problem. Why not just eliminate the FDA and start maybe somewhere else?/63

KAREN: Why, I think it's fairly obvious that right now the Food and Drug Administration is all we have to work with; and as you mentioned before, we live in a bureaucracy. To start a completely new agency would probably be much more difficult than to simply strengthen an agency that has already made itself felt somewhat in our American society./64

GARY: Judy, I think another thing that would have to be considered as a possible solution would be dealing with the consumer himself, dealing on the consumer level—that is, providing some type of information, some type of education-enlightenment, a realization that there is a problem with his food. Before any real change can be brought about, I think we have to *convince the consumer* that he does have a problem with his food. I would suggest that this could be done by utilizing the various consumer-information agencies from the federal, state, and down to the local level—getting them to supply information to the consumer and explain to him what the problem is and where it lies. I think also that using the FDA and the Department of Health, Education, and Welfare, public-service announcements could be made on national, state, and local media to try to inform the consumer./65

Stage Four
Evaluating the proposed solutions

JERRY: Gary, I think what you say makes a lot of sense. In the past we've seen problems with cyclamates, monosodium glutamate, and many other issues. The American consumer, when he's informed that there are dangers, has put the pressure on the politicians and the agencies that were supposed to protect him. So, I think consumer activity would be effective./66

JUDY: In other words, persuasion is preferred, but panic is more productive./67

KAREN (as all laugh): Right./68

JUDY: OK, but I see a kind of weakness in all of this. It seems to be realistic, but it also seems to be *restrictive* to me as a consumer./69

JERRY: Yes, I think in a sense it would be restrictive. The FDA may restrict the amount of poison you could eat each day./70

JERRY (amid more laughter): Then, they also may restrict you to eating steaks that are fresh, not just look fresh, but *are* fresh. It may diminish your selectivity a little bit, but I don't think you'd really complain about that./71

GARY: Well, Jerry, I may take issue with this, in that you suggest that we eliminate all the cosmetic additives. Perhaps they do not serve any purpose as nutritive value, but I think we may have to keep in mind that the consumer has to be prepared — that when we eliminate all cosmetic additives, that means his margarine will be white instead of yellow, that his oranges may not necessarily be oranges' color, or that perhaps certain foods that he's used to seeing will be colored somewhat differently./72

KAREN: I think that there is one more thing that can answer part of your question — about restrictions of the consumer — and it deals with something we haven't mentioned yet. That's the idea of the refining processes and the canning processes that we sort of indicted at the beginning of this discussion. I think what we should remember is that in this particular area, again, we're dealing with *informing* the consumer. There's no way that we can get rid of the refining process, because it services the consumer. So, what we should do is inform the consumer as to what the potential dangers are and where he could possibly get more nutritive value for the food he is eating./73

Stage Five
Choosing the preferred solution†

JUDY: All right, then, if we were to state one general theme of our entire discussion tonight, it would be that the problem for the consumer, in food quality, is his lack of knowledge of just what he is getting. It seems he doesn't know what he's getting — rather, what he *isn't* getting as a result of processing — and what he's getting with additives. And our solutions suggest that *information*, whether from the FDA or from the consumer groups, would be the foundation for a resolution to the problem — one that's realistic, not prohibitive, and perhaps even beneficial; for it would mean removing harmful additives. *Enlightenment* here seems to be the critical element. And I hope it would make a difference to the average consumer, say, someone like Mrs. Starkey, a homemaker, who was once before congressional hearings on color additives. It was in 1960, and at that time she had made a statement: "The shopper, really informed and looking for a plain food, with nothing added and nothing taken away, is like Diogenes with the lantern, unable to find an honest man." But if solutions such as those brought forth here tonight were implemented, her task might still be a difficult one; but with knowledge as her lantern, her path would be well lighted./74

---

†You will note that in Chapter 14 (p. 320), the fifth stage of the problem-solving discussion plan was "Deciding how to put the approved solution into operation." However, because of the nature of this group and the circumstances of the discussion, the final stage here is the choice of the preferred solution.

Index

Articulation, 83, 84–86
  exercises for, 99–100
  for radio, 346–347
Articulatory mechanism, photos of, 85
Association,
  of ideas, 205
  from loaded words, 174–175
  meaning derived from, 175–176
Attention,
  at beginning of speech, 183–184
  of broadcast audience, 343, 344
  defined, 206–207
  of discussion participant, 311
  evaluation of strategies for, 28
  factors of, 207–211
  gaining, 183–190, 205–211
  through gestures, 69
  in interpersonal communication, 285
  through personal reference or
    greeting,187, 217
  in speech of introduction, 267
  in speech to inform, 205–211, 212
  in speech to persuade, 244
  through startling statement, 187
  through vocal force, 90
Attention step, 244, 249
  examples of, 246, 368, 377
  outline using, 255
  skeletal plan using, 253
  in speech advancing claim of fact, 258
  in speech advancing claim of value, 260
  in speech opposing a policy, 256–257
Attitudes and beliefs of audience, 10, 14,
    29
  adapting motive appeals to, 234
  analysis of, 43, 47–52
  emotional basis of, 24
  fixed, 47–48
  influencing, 40, 195–196, 227
  prior attitudes, 50
  toward speaker, 49
  toward speech purpose, 26, 50–52
  toward subject, 37–38, 49–50, 314
  values involved in, 48–49
Attitudes of speaker, 6–7
  evaluation of, 29
  in good-will speeches, 274
  voice affected by, 81

Audience, 4, 9–10
  adapting motive appeals to, 234
  adapting physical behavior to, 73, 76
  adapting specific purpose to, 42
  analysis of, 42–55
  appeal to senses of, 168
  attitudes and beliefs of, 10, 14, 47–52
  capturing and holding attention of,
    183–190, 205–211
  contact with, 66–67
  discussion before, 314, 332–334
  interaction with speaker, 13–14
  listening, 21–30
  photos, 44–45
  radio, 339–340, 341, 343
  reactions of, 3, 12, 38–41, 82, 187
  social composition of, 43–47
  speaker's attitude toward, 6–7
  television, 339–340, 341, 343, 348, 350
  variables, 214
  See also *Attention; Attitudes and beliefs of
    audience*
Auditory imagery, 170
Authority,
  evaluating, 323
  tests of, 120
Awards,
  acceptance of, 269, 379–380
  presentation of, 270
Axiom, reasoning from, 236

B

"Backaches," 358
Back-timing a broadcast speech, 342–343
Balance of cognitions, 242
Barker, Larry I., 22n
"Barrel-Organ, The," 96
Barriers to communication, 68
Bauer, Gail, 190
Beebe, Steven A., 66n
Beginning a speech, 183–190, 197–198,
    212
  See also *Introduction of speeches*
Behavior of speaker, 49
Beliefs of audience. See *Attitudes and beliefs
    of audience*
Belongingness needs, 229

illustration, 321
Projection step. See *Visualization step*
Pronunciation, 83, 85–86
  exercises for, 100–103
  for radio, 346
Proof. See *Ethical proof; Supporting material; Reasoning*
Proximity as attention factor, 208
Psychological-social needs, 228–229
  as bases for speech to persuade, 242, 244
Psychology Applied to Life and Work, 300, 382
Public communication,
  model, 58
Public discussion, 332–334
  example of, 387–394
Public speaking. See *Speeches; Preparation; Practicing*
Purpose of a speech,
  for courtesy, 269
  to entertain, 38–39, 109
  general, 5, 38–41
  for good will, 275
  to inform, 38, 39–40, 204, 214–215
  of introduction, 267
  of nomination, 273
  to persuade, 38, 40–41, 227–261
  specific, 41–42
  of tribute, 272
Pursley, Jerry, 388–394

Q

Quality of voice, 82
  in broadcasting, 346–347
  exercises for improving, 94–96
Quantity of sound, 84
Questions,
  by discussion leader, 312, 319–320, 325
  interviewer's formulation of, 295
  by job applicant, 303, 305, 382
  for job applicant, 300–302
  open vs. closed, 286
  rhetorical, 187
  as subject for discussion, 312, 316, 318, 325
  See also *Problems*

Quotations,
  used to begin a speech, 188
  used to end a speech, 194–195

R

Radio,
  audience for, 339–340
  discussion for, 333–334
  manner of speaking for, 344–348
  manuscript use for, 36, 344, 346, 348
  transitions in speech for, 343
Ragan, Dennis Owen, 358
"Rainy Day, The," 95
Ramification used in need step, 250
Rapport in interpersonal speaking, 283, 284–287, 290
Rate of speaking, 84, 88–89, 93
  exercises for improving, 102
  for radio, 344, 347
  for television, 349
Raw data, 39
Read, Herbert, 177
Read speech, 36
  for radio, 346, 347–348
  for television, 350
Readers' Guide to Periodical Literature, 56
Reality,
  as attention factor, 208, 210, 343
  in visualization, 252
Reasoning, 235–237
  from axiom, 236
  from causal relationships, 236–237
  evaluation of, 28
  from example, 235
  forms of, 235–237
Reassurance in interpersonal speaking, 287–288
Receiver orientation, 43
Redding, W. Charles, 292
Reference, to begin a speech,
  personal, 185–187
  to practical experience, 250
  to subject or occasion, 184–185
Relaxation,
  exercises for throat, 94
  and gestures, 73

5 6 7 8 9 10 –GBC– 80 79 78

CHECKLIST AND INDEX FOR EVALUATION
AND IMPROVEMENT OF STUDENT SPEECHES

This chart may be used by instructors and students in evaluating speech outlines and plans as well as in reacting to speech materials as delivered. It lists many of the factors that contribute to effective communication, with references to relevant pages of the text. By using plus (+) or minus (−) signs or a rating scale of his or her own choosing, the instructor may evaluate both a student's outline and the effectiveness with which the speech itself is presented. Students may use the Checklist when preparing oral or written assignments or reviewing for examinations. The references to specific pages make it possible to find relevant textual materials quickly and easily.

AN. / Factors in audience analysis

1 Specific audience indicated (42-43, 46-47, 54)
2 Analysis of audience complete (42-55)
3 Primary interests and fixed attitudes of audience indicated and correctly stated (47-49, 55)
4 Attitude of audience toward speaker and subject correctly analyzed (49-55)
5 Occasion correctly analyzed (52-53, 54)
6 Subject appropriate (36-38)
7 Subject sufficiently narrow (37-38)
8 General purpose appropriate (38-41)
9 Specific purpose clear and possible to attain (41-42)

CONT. / Factors in content

10 Major ideas adequately proved or developed by:
  A Good use of explanation (111-112)
  B Good use of comparison/contrast (112-113)
  C Good use of illustration (113-115)
  D Good use of specific instances (115-116)
  E Good use of statistics (116-118)
  F Good use of testimony (119-120)
  G Good use of restatement (120-122)
  H Good use of nonverbal supporting materials — visual aids (122, 124)

11 Sound reasoning (235-237)
12 Types of claims clearly distinguished (238-241)
13 Good use of motive appeals (228-234)
  A Appeals strong (228-232)
  B Appeals adapted to subject and audience (233-234)
  C Appeals tactful (234)
14 Good use of factors of attention (207-211)

ORG. / Factors in organization and development

15 Major ideas properly established (142-144)
16 Clear sequence of ideas (137-142)
17 Major ideas concisely stated (142)
18 Major ideas of parallel importance (143-144)
19 Organization adapted to specific purpose (41-42)
20 Beginning (attention step) satisfactory (183-190, 249)
  A Aroused interest in subject (184-190, 207-211)
  B Suited to subject and purpose of speech (197-198)
21 Need step satisfactory (250)
  A Clearly developed (250, 255, 258, 259, 260, 261)
  B Ideas adequately supported (250)

414

(Continued on facing page)